Neža Kogovšek Šalamon

Erased

Citizenship, Residence Rights and the Constitution in Slovenia

PL ACADEMIC RESEARCH

Bibliographic Information published by the Deutsche Nationalbibliothek
The Deutsche Nationalbibliothek lists this publication in the Deutsche Nationalbibliografie; detailed bibliographic data is available in the internet at http://dnb.d-nb.de.

Library of Congress Cataloging-in-Publication Data
Names: Kogovšek Šalamon, Neža, 1978-, author.
Title: Erased : citizenship, residence rights and the constitution in Slovenia / Neža Kogovšek Šalamon.
Description: Frankfurt am Main : Peter Lang GmbH Internationaler Verlag der Wissenschaften, [2016] | Includes index.
Identifiers: LCCN 2016017772 | ISBN 9783631671689
Subjects: LCSH: Expatriation—Slovenia. | Citizenship—Slovenia. | Constitutional law—Slovenia. | Slovenia—Politics and government—1990-
Classification: LCC KKS6244.5 .S35 2016 | DDC 342.497308/3—dc23
LC record available at https://lccn.loc.gov/2016017772

ISBN 978-3-631-67168-9 (Print)
E-ISBN 978-3-653-06556-5 (E-Book)
DOI 10.3726/978-3-653-06556-5

PL Academic Research is an Imprint of Peter Lang GmbH.

Peter Lang – Frankfurt am Main · Bern · Bruxelles · New York · Oxford · Warszawa · Wien

This publication has been peer reviewed.

www.peterlang.com

Table of Contents

Acknowledgments

Twelve years ago, when I returned to Slovenia from my LL.M. course at the University of Notre Dame (USA) and a six-month internship at the New York-based Human Rights Watch, where I focused on issues of international justice, war crimes, and crimes against humanity, I was susceptible for getting engaged in difficult human rights challenges. At the time, Slovenian society was struggling to take responsibility for a mass violation of human rights that occurred in 1992, soon after the secession of Slovenia from the former Yugoslavia. The issue was known as "the erasure". I soon started working at the Peace Institute, a private independent research institution based in Slovenia, which was at the time already deeply involved in researching the erasure as well as its consequences, and in advocating for redress. Becoming part of the team, I started developing projects aimed at both further research and providing legal advice to the "erased" people. In this process I cooperated not only with a number of exceptional lawyers, activists, and academics who worked together to push for change in society, but also with the erased individuals themselves, who showed immense energy and fought relentlessly for their rights. During this process, when I started to pursue an academic career, I decided to write my dissertation on this topic. This was the first PhD thesis on the "erasure" written and defended at the Law School of the University of Ljubljana. After earning my PhD in 2011, I continued with my work in this field and this book is a result of this undertaking. There are many people and organisations who were involved in this process and whom I would like to thank: members of the project team gathered at or around the Peace Institute Lev Kreft, Sara Pistotnik, Katarina Vučko, Maja Ladić, Lana Zdravković, Veronika Bajt, Brankica Petković, Jovana Mihajlovič Trbovc, Jasminka Dedić, Uršula Lipovec Čebron, Jelka Zorn, Imma Tuccillo Castaldo; Blaž Kovač and Nataša Posel from Amnesty International Slovenia; Matevž Krivic, former Constitutional Court judge and legal representative of the Association of the Erased Residents of Slovenia; Niko Jurkas and Silva Stanković from this same association; Irfan Beširević, late Aleksandar Todorović and Mirjana Učakar from the Civil Initiative of Erased Activists; attorneys Andrea Saccucci, Anton Giulio Lana, Alice Sironi and Giulia Borgna who represented the erased people before the European Court of Human Rights; my academic mentor Professor Bojan Bugarič; professors Vlasta Jalušič, Ciril Ribičič and Vladimir Simič who were members of my doctoral commission; Open Society Foundations for supporting projects in the field of the erasure and believing that change is possible; Open Society

Justice Initiative, Equal Rights Trust and United Nations High Commissioner for Refugees for submitting their third party interventions in the *Kurić and Others v. Slovenia* case; Pasos – Policy Association for an Open Society for the Think-Tank Achievement Award 2012 which recognised the importance of our work; and PILNet for the 2012 European Award for Partnership in the Public Interest bestowed to Andrea Saccucci, Anton Giulio Lana and the Peace Institute for our cooperation in litigating the *Kurić* case. I am particularly grateful to Boštjan M. Zupančič, Judge at the European Court of Human Rights, who kindly wrote a preface to the this book, and Ágnes Bezeczky, the language and copy editor of this volume who made this complex material understandable for international readers. As always, any errors or oversights are mine alone.

The Author

Preface

The book you hold in your hands was instrumental in the process by which the European Court of Human Rights decided the question of possible violations concerning the "erasure" of individuals, non-citizens and residents in Slovenia, from the Slovenian residence register.

Legal and political background

Certain members of the Slovenian Government of the time, who had an insidious and stealthy *modus operandi,* were directly responsible for this "erasure", which was carried out secretly in most, if not all, of the "administrative units" [*upravne enote*] of the Republic of Slovenia. Who, apart from the prime minister, the minister of the interior and the state secretary in the ministry of the interior, was also responsible is still not known. Criminal trials against these individuals have not been initiated despite the fact that I, among others, have in my concurring opinion of the judgment of the European Court of Human rights (*infra*) entreated the authorities and subsequent governments to do so. The criminal liability of the conniving members of subsequent governments is similarly still not clear.

The story in short is as follows.

In the decades before the disintegration of the federal state of Yugoslavia, Slovenia was the most developed of the "federal republics", as they were called. Obviously, there were no borders between these quasi-states; there was among them a free flow of goods and also of workers. The economy in Slovenia called for more workers than it was able to supply. Persons from other "republics" were invited to the country. There, for many years, often decades, these nominal citizens of other "republics" established themselves with what in law would be called *animus manendi*, the intention to stay. Their children were born in this new cultural and economic environment and thus in many cases the problems that this book is about concerned two or even three consecutive generations.

Upon the disintegration of Yugoslavia, or more precisely upon the separation of the Republic of Slovenia from the federal state, the status of these people came into question. Ethnically, they were not Slovenians. Many spoke Serbo-Croatian or even Albanian and the local population continued to perceive them as foreigners. Thus, immediately after Slovenia seceded, the nationality status of these "foreigners" came into question. They had been duly listed in all the respective status registers, not only of residence but also employment, taxes, social security, etc. They were most often issued Slovenian identity cards and passports, etc., although this happened, naturally, in the context of the larger federal Yugoslav state. Upon the disintegration of Yugoslavia, some of those who wanted to register their Slovenian permanent residency and/or citizenship came to the counters of the said administrative units. They submitted their identity cards, passports and other requested documents. The officials in these units then proceeded with the perforation of these documents and made them null and void. Unbeknownst to the public at large and to the aggrieved persons in question, they were subsequently "erased" – hence the term – from the residence register with all the ensuing legal consequences.

Thereafter, the "erased" were not only deprived of their chance to become citizens of the Republic of Slovenia, they were also deprived of their legitimate residence permits. In turn, this implied the loss of social security benefits, the possibility of employment, retirement benefits, etc.

As I pointed out in my concurring opinion in the case of *Kurić and Others v. Slovenia* (Application No. 26828/06), delivered on 26 June 2012, *infra*, there were at the time at least 25 671 such wronged individuals and their respective families. I maintained that this had been a clerical attempt at "ethnic cleansing", which is perhaps a debatable designation strictly in terms of international law, but which certainly did describe the essence, legal or otherwise, of what had been going on.

How did this attempt come about?

In order to comprehend this, one has to keep in mind the principal political motivation for the secession of Slovenia, a process which catalysed the disintegration of the federal state of Yugoslavia. One of the political protagonists of that time, the late Jože Pučnik, had made it publicly known what he thought the policy towards the segment of the populace from other "Yugoslav republics" ought to be:[1]

> Don't be misled by illusions, because this is not a national but a social issue […] Personally, I oppose automatically taking over of the state of affairs as it was on the day of the referendum. If the Republic of Slovenia wants to ensure a firm social structure, we will have to introduce some kind of criteria when granting citizenship. Don't let us be apparently democratic and create problems that we will not be able to solve later. We must be aware of what it is possible to solve in Slovenia viewed from the social perspective – the national aspect of this issue is in fact of secondary importance. We are setting up a community that must ensure for itself, from the very beginning, the living circumstances, and we must be ready to eliminate the heritage of the Yugoslav federation, perhaps in an

1 Speech of Jože Pučnik in Ljutomer, Delo daily, 17 December 1990, p. 2.

> unwanted way as the need may be [...] It is necessary to calculate – demographically as well – what consequences could follow in five or ten years, along with the demands for cultural autonomy. Personally, I will endeavour, using all the influence I possess within the Social Democratic Party, to spare Slovenia the problems such as those that were seen in Knin. We do not want to see Knin in Slovenia and today we have an opportunity to solve these issues in a humane, socially responsible and legal manner. We should not allow rotten compromises or rally-driven democracy that could create troubles for us, such as those encountered by England, France and Germany and other countries that existed during the colonial period. Slovenia, in my opinion, should not allow itself to be burdened by these additional problems.

There can be no doubt that his statement was particularly nationalistic. The quote, however, was not an isolated occurrence. It had a legitimizing political impact on significant figures of the secession such as Lojze Peterle (Prime Minister at the time, now a European MP!) and Igor Bavčar (Minister of Interior at the time), the latter being a direct perpetrator of the "erasure", an accomplice before and during and after the fact, together with late Slavko Debelak, the state secretary at the Ministry of the Interior at the time.

Many of the leading politicians and intellectuals of that time adhered to the idea that the main purpose of Slovenia's secession was to preserve a pure Slovenian ethnic identity, whatever this actually meant. This is plainly obvious from Pučnik's separationist ideological statement, which, as we have said, was an inspiration to other important right wing protagonists advocating the secession of Slovenia. Yugoslavia was, for them, something undesirable, mostly from the point of view of pure ethnic identity; they felt that the "Slovenian nation" was being overwhelmed by the "southern brothers", as they were then derisively called.

The "erased" came to Slovenia mostly from Bosnia and Herzegovina, from Kosovo, but also from Serbia, Croatia and other parts of former Yugoslavia. They came as "guest workers" because Slovenia needed them much the same way that Germany and other Western European countries imported their workforce from abroad. In fact, the term "guest worker" comes from the German "*Gastarbeiter*".

The Social Context of Immigration

In many respects, this was an emblematic immigration situation in which the newcomers only slowly adapt to the new cultural environment.

In the United States, for example, which has extensive historical experience with immigration, it is said that it takes four generations for immigrants to assimilate into the American culture. The incoming group is not reckoned as the first generation; the first generation is the one already born in the United States. If we know nothing more, we already understand that immigration is a painful process and that the actual integration into the new cultural community occurs only during the change of subsequent generations. One basic requirement in this respect is the ability to speak the native language.

Indeed, in this respect there certainly were some problems with the workforce from other former republics of Yugoslavia. They mostly did not make the effort to learn the Slovenian language. After all, Yugoslavia was a living federal entity and many of the newcomers perceived Serbo-Croatian as the *lingua franca* of Yugoslavia, making it quite unnecessary to learn Slovenian. Obviously, this aroused antipathy on the part of Slovenians. The prevailing perception, in legal terms, was that they did not have the requisite *animus manendi*, the intent to stay in the country.

Another offshoot of this mentality, as I mentioned in my concurring opinion to the above case, was the assumption of much of Slovenia's population, which was not informed of how these people were underhandedly deprived of their resident status, that the "erased" did not actually want to acquire Slovenian citizenship. They allegedly had a "Yugoslav" mentality which led them to maintain that Serbian or even Yugoslav citizenship was more prestigious, better and more legitimate. Meanwhile, the great majority of Slovenians had never really accepted their "Yugoslav" identity. In other words, this was an ongoing cultural conflict.

To what extent this was actually true remains an open question, but the fact is that the public perceived the former guest workers to adhere to this "Yugoslav" attitude. Indeed, this probably made it easier for the Government at the time to produce the misapprehension that these people did not wish to register as Slovenian residents, let alone as citizens. Much antipathy among ordinary people to the judgment of the European Court of Human Rights also derived from these possibly false assumptions.

The Larger Question of Migrants

In some respects, the situation at the time of the "erasure" from the register of nationality may be compared to the migration crisis which is currently upon Germany and the rest of Europe.

First of all, it is no accident that East European countries, including former East Germany, are not at all in the mood to permit immigration from northern Africa. The residual values, as Raymond Williams[2] would have called them, were quite different in Eastern Europe than in Western Europe. These countries were

2 See the excellent article by Raymond Williams entitled Base and Superstructure in Marxist Cultural Theory, New Left Review I (1973) 82.

to a large degree isolated for decades not only from the West; they were, under the totalitarian regimes, for the same reason practically secluded from much of Eastern Europe, too. Much like in Slovenia, they developed a mentality centred on the desire to maintain their ethnic identity, since obviously under totalitarianism they were under constant threat coming mostly from the Soviet Union. Latvia is typical example of this outlook. It was subject to mass immigration by Russians during the Soviet era, who still represent about forty per cent of Latvian population. These Russians are deprived of Latvian citizenship; they are only entitled to permanent residence permits. We suspect that here, too, the political impetus behind the similarly discriminatory treatment of foreigners is very much the same as in Slovenia, the defence of ethnic identity.

Moreover, the current East European opposition to accepting the people fleeing from the embattled areas in North Africa derives from parallel socio-psychological characteristics. Williams's "residual values", in other words, hold sway over all East European ethnic groups and for similar historical reasons. Sad be it to say, the Slovenian overreaction, to put it mildly, is not an exception.

For example, in Latvia the authorities require Russian permanent residents (without Latvian passports) to take a language test that these people cannot possibly pass. So far, nobody has made a legal issue of the situation of Latvian Russians – no case has come before the European Court of Human Rights in Strasbourg – but in all fairness one must still maintain that the situation of Russians in Latvia is similar to that of the "erased" members of other ethnic groups in Slovenia. As I wrote many years ago in the case of *Ždanoka v. Latvia*:

> This has to do with the demographic *fact* that thirty per cent of the existing Latvian population speaks Russian. Presumably, this puts in jeopardy the pro-autonomy rule of the autochthonous majority in whose name the separation of Latvia (and the other two Baltic States) from the Soviet Union was carried out in the first place. [...] The large Russian-speaking minority in Latvia is a demographic by-product of the long-term illegal occupation by the Soviet Union. Does the historical fact that the occupation *was* illegal – and it is probably not an accident that the majority opinion emphasises the early illegality of the Molotov-Ribbentrop pact – imply that the residence of the Russian-speaking population in Latvia is itself illegal?[3]

3 *See* my dissenting opinion in the ECHR case of *Ždanoka v. Latvia*, application number *58278/00*, 2006.

Sociological Aspect

Sociologically, this whole cluster of assimilation problems has come to the fore in the current crisis, where various national groups in Eastern Europe, but also in the West, are reacting aggressively and with a great deal of prejudice against potential North African and Middle Eastern immigrants. Given the great cultural difference, which was minimal in the former Yugoslavia, between the native cultures in Europe and the North African and Middle Eastern immigrants, there are obviously going to be great problems in attempting to integrate and assimilate them. One aspect of this cluster of problems is as follows.

The power of a particular culture, European, American or otherwise, may be measured by the amount of positive identification this culture receives from the members of other cultures. To put it simply, those immigrating to the United States positively identify with "America" and they wish to hasten their own assimilation, sometimes to the point of burning all the bridges behind them. This testifies to the attractiveness of American culture and makes it much easier for the assimilation processes to begin and to continue, as a new generation of immigrants succeeds the previous generation that came to the United States. Slovenia, for example, was by far the most developed federal republic. Even today, people in the countries to the south tend to look up to Slovenia for its economic success after independence.

In this light, one would be inclined to speculate that the prospect of positive identification it received from the southern immigrants was not so minimal as to prevent assimilation.

Moreover, the second and the third generation of Southern immigrants born in Slovenia are not only doing well, they are contributing to the country's growth both economically and culturally.

Broader Considerations

Here I would like to introduce another *constatation*. Every nation, as long as it is isolated and closed to the negative and positive, mostly negative, feedback from outside of its territory and culture, tends to become culturally, politically, scientifically, etc. – self-referential. This is famously true of France and its *exception française.* The French, too, are not too eager to learn foreign languages, as they are somehow convinced that their own culture is superior. This has an impoverishing effect on French society, which is thus more likely to develop exacerbated idiosyncratic characteristics. The French situation, in this context, may be exceptional in that it makes it obvious that at least economic performance of the French Republic lags behind other European Union countries. The French are little able to learn from the positive experiences of other nations in the cultural, medical, scientific, etc. domains. This has obvious untoward consequences. The foreigner in France finds it easy to discern the drawbacks that such a national self-referential attitude has.

But this is true of all nations, big or small. The Americans, the British, the Scandinavians, the Italians, the Spanish, for obvious reasons the Germans to a lesser extent, and all the nations of Eastern Europe, are to some extent culturally self-referential. Inasmuch as they are locked in upon themselves, and especially if this happens behind the so-called language barrier, the consequences are perceptibly dysfunctional. Every nation, to put it bluntly, that is in this sense self-referential, is to some extent irrational. The two recent European World Wars, by no means an exception, are enough proof of this unhappy phenomenon.

This aggravates the culturally dysfunctional characteristics, as we said, since they do not receive corrective negative feedback from the outside world. The said language barrier represents a serious obstruction. Behind the walls of "national identity" protected by the national language that nobody outside this small world understands, all kinds of cracked ideas gain ground. Collective hysteria can spread, such as that which we currently witness vis-à-vis the immigrants in different national entities in Eastern Europe.

In systems theory it is taken for granted that robust systems and subsystems tend to be open to the outside world. Inversely, systems and subsystems that are weak tend to protect themselves like a shell closing in on itself if it feels itself to be in danger.

Given this premise, it is logical to assume that Eastern European nations are in this respect evidently "weak" and are constantly on the defensive as a result. Western countries in Europe have this problem much less, but even in France, which calls itself *"un pays d'accueil"*, there is a strong backlash gaining power in the right-wing political parties. It is based on the same self-justifying seclusionary attitude stemming from the current political and above all economic problems. It is hence not surprising that Germany, which doesn't have these problems to the same degree due to the pressures exerted upon it after WWII, is much more accommodating towards the current inflow of refugees from North Africa and Middle East. But even in Germany and especially in the territory of the former East Germany, we are as of late witnessing a significant regression.

The "Erased" in Slovenia: The Legal Facet of the Problem

Initially, let us reproduce the national judge's concurring opinion in the case of *Kurić et. al v. Slovenia* as cited above *in toto*.

The Separate Concurring Opinion

Especially in the international jurisdiction, this case raises very serious moral dilemmas. Some of these questions, as we shall see, were blocked from arising within the much narrower scope of the national jurisdiction. However, the historical spirit of the Convention, stemming from the similar *sequelae* of the Second World War, both enables the larger perspective and – necessitate nature – requires it! Indeed, in this and in other important cases this specificity of the broader perspective and especially of the enhanced objectivity due to the distance from the isolated national theatre seems to be the historically maturing purpose of our own international jurisdiction.

The number of persons allegedly affected since 1992 by this officially authorised legalistic attempt at ethnic cleansing, as Judge Vučinić rightly calls it, stands at 25,671. Following the new 1999 Citizenship Act – ultimately in conformity with the first judgment of the Constitutional Court – at least 6,621 of the aggrieved have apparently so far demonstrated their legal interest and have in fact regularised their residence or citizenship status. Up until 31 January 2012 the administrative units of the Ministry of the Interior had registered 229 applications for permanent residence as well as 101 applications for ex tunc regularisation. They had issued 59 permanent residence permits; 83 applications were rejected, whereas 87 applications were still pending. They had rendered 52 special and ex officio positive decisions, as well as 74 decisions upon a special application; of these, 10 applications were rejected administratively, whereas 17 were still pending. Against these decisions an administrative appeal was possible; up until 31 January 2012 there were 29 administrative appeals to the Ministry of the Interior. Presumably, after that recourse to a judicial decision is possible. Apparently, about half of the original 25,671 affected persons either no longer live in the Republic of Slovenia or have not so far manifested their legal interest in regularising their residence status. As for indemnification of the victims, the domestic law, as per the decision of the Constitutional Court, posted a five-year deadline ending in March 2004. Given the legislative disregard of the judgment of the Constitutional Court until 1999 and the obvious continuity of the violation, this closing date ought not to be applicable.

On the other hand, I hasten to add, one cannot be certain in how many of these cases the victims, that is, those entitled to standing (*legitimatio activa*) in potential future cases, have themselves indeed neglected to apply for their citizenship in due time. Also, the twenty-year postponement in legally resolving this question – on a case-by-case basis! – in the domestic legal system was to some extent due to the contrived and disingenuous impression, maintained in the misled Slovenian public, to the effect that at least some of the aggrieved had brought the problem upon themselves; allegedly their procrastination was due to their own nationalist (Serbian, Croatian etc.) ambivalence as to their *animus manendi* concerning their continued residence in the then newly established Republic of Slovenia. This was before, during and after the Balkan wars twenty years ago. One must therefore keep in mind that – at the time – it was far from obvious for many of those concerned, in the context of their own wishful thinking, that the megalomaniac myths of Greater Serbia or greater whatever in the Balkans were unfounded. The real, and not merely legal, victims of these primitive tribal wars – fraught with the narcissism of small differences and with the consequent unspeakable atrocities that followed in Croatia, Serbia and Bosnia and Herzegovina – are now counted in the hundreds of thousands of those killed, tortured, raped, and so on. Moreover, the perfidious instigation of certain continental European foreign intelligence services interested in the disintegration of Yugoslavia, which triggered the rest of the insane activation of the chauvinist and revanchist collective unconscious, has been duly publicised, especially in the American press, and is now an established historical fact. This unfortunate process caused the surfacing of figures now known to be psychopaths, who were personally responsible for all manner of inhuman callousness. The latter was simply unimaginable in Yugoslavia before this tsunami of cruelty actually started to roll over the country. The historian A.J.P. Taylor, for example, considered Josip Broz Tito to be the last of the Habsburgs, capable of keeping together a tolerant multinational community; A.J.P. Taylor did not live to see it disintegrate. On the other hand, from the corroborated retrospective view of twenty years, the disintegration of Yugoslavia was and continues to be an unmitigated disaster. In this historical reassessment, the French would say: *"A quoi tout cela a-t-il servi?"* No reasonable person can reasonably answer this question except by saying, as Erich Fromm would have, that this was a *folie à millions.* We do not wish to draw parallels here with the disintegration of the ex-Soviet empire and its consequences; suffice it to say, because this is a matter of international law, that Woodrow Wilson, before launching, under the influence of Tomáš Garrigue Masaryk, his famous catchphrase concerning the self-determination of nations – had been explicitly and repeatedly forewarned about the possible consequences. The consequences are now here; that is to say, the particularisation and balkanisation of national entities has in fact materialised. This will hopefully be compensated for, as I emphasised at the time in an article in El País, by universalisation in the context of the European Union. Nationalist squabbles would be in the Hegelian sense transcended and would, including border disputes, become largely inapposite within the context of the European Union. The European free movement of people, for example, makes what is at stake in this case simply sans objet. What has come apart on one level is, with the tragic historical delay, slowly coming together on a higher level. It is also increasingly clear that the keeping together, in the manner of A.J.P. Taylor, of this, in other words, the European entity, will require much political wisdom. Still, the historical delay has caused this case and many other still more appalling consequences. Some of them have ascended to international jurisdictions, most of them have not.

Because the ethnic cleansing attempt in the case before the Grand Chamber was done through misconstruction of the Slovenian Citizenship Act and its premeditated legal lacunae, the specificity of the case lies in its minutely recorded legalistic features. This is why we have a precise historical record of the number of the aggrieved, the number of those who were not provided for by the domestic system, in the manner of Article 41 of the Convention, and so on. The above-mentioned two-faced legalistic legacy of the communist system reminds us of the case of *Streletz, Kessler and Krenz v. Germany* ([GC], nos. 34044/96, 35532/97 and 44801/98, ECHR 2001-II); there, too, the façade of schizophrenic legality had been maintained, in East Germany, as seemingly intact.

Behind the façade the impunity had continued unimpeded. In the case before us we had an intentional lacuna in the law, which was then filled in by the semi-official but unpublished *dépêches* issued by the then Minister of the Interior and his Secretary of State. They were explicitly approved by the then Prime Minister and his Government. In terms of criminal law we may therefore speak of *dolus directus* in the first case and at least of *dolus eventualis* in the latter case. Meanwhile, the public had been misled to believe, as I said, that the thousands affected by this were simply negligent in failing to apply for their Slovenian citizenship. Fortunately, owing to the legalistic nature of the abuse, all these actions, correspondence and so on, as pointed out above, were recorded and are on file; the Grand Chamber had the opportunity to see the relevant correspondence and the *dépêches* and to take them into account. It remains to be seen whether the domestic criminal legal system will, vis-à-vis the protagonists, react accordingly; if not the issue will again come to Strasbourg under the procedural limbs of Articles 3 and 8, among others. Similarly, when it comes to compensating the 25,671 allegedly aggrieved persons, the judicial branch of the domestic legal system would, as in the judicial delay cases (see *Lukenda v. Slovenia*, No. 23032/02, ECHR 2005-X), be well advised to process all of the situations fairly and on a case-by-case basis.

In fairness to the national legal system, we must consider the honourable and courageous stance – faced with the continuity of this appalling situation – taken twice by the Constitutional Court in Slovenia. This proves all over again that the national defence of constitutional rights is the best antechamber for our own protection of human rights. The relevant judgments of the Constitutional Court in Ljubljana were snubbed by both the executive and the legislative branches at the time. The price will now be paid by the Slovenian taxpayer. As per recent information, the rest of the judicial branch, owing to its characteristic post-communist legal formalism, has likewise failed to compensate the aggrieved for the continuing violations such as we have established in the cases before us.

This case also proves that legal mills do grind slowly – but unremittingly. Precisely because of international jurisdiction, at least here, justice will have been done. Moreover, while justice as such cannot be defined, injustice is easily recognisable. The broader question is, therefore, why it was not recognised in the domestic legal system. Indeed, in post-communist legal systems there seems to be an irreconcilable mutual exclusion between mechanical legal formalism on the one hand and the simple sense of justice on the other. Often enough, we encounter this irreconcilability – *summum ius, summa iniuria!* – in other cases, including Western ones, except that in this colossal instance the Constitutional Court had identified the injustice. It was the malevolent political will that impeded the rule of law and blocked the proper judicial remedy.

The Implications of the Judgment of the European Court of Human Rights

From my own point of view, juridically, I have little to add. The edited version of the judgment is reproduced in the Annex of the book amply enough for lawyers and jurists to examine the nuances of this case.

It remains to be said that this judgment, as we have pointed out above, must nevertheless be placed in the broader European, and especially East European, context. Slovenia was chastised by the European Court of Human Rights, and rightfully so. Meanwhile, however, similar problems do arise in other East European countries and in different modalities also in their Western counterparts, even though they have never reached Strasbourg and its Convention machinery. Prejudices, national or otherwise, are an unhappy legacy even in modern Europe.

Although it is therefore fair to say that there are many problems deriving from European prejudices, the European Court of Human Rights is not in position to deal with most of them. This is due to the truth of proverbial legal adage, which stipulates that "there is no judge where there is no plaintiff". If these potential cases have never been brought before the Court in Strasbourg, it certainly does not mean that such problems did not, or do not, actually exist. They simply have not been prosecuted in front of the international jurisdiction.

Turkey, for example, has been condemned many a time in the European Court of Human Rights. To a large degree this is to be ascribed to the vigilance of Turkish human rights lawyers who have, to the best of my knowledge, prosecuted most of the cases in which human rights have been violated one way or the other. The number of Turkish cases in the European Court of Human Rights is therefore not only an indication of the number of human rights violations. It is also an indication of the willingness and capacity of Turkish lawyers to present them to the European jurisdiction.

Mutatis mutandis, this goes for most national situations in Europe. The number of suicides in French prisons is alarmingly high. Still, practically none of these cases ever reaches us in Strasbourg. How is this possible?

On the one hand, every case from a national jurisdiction must "exhaust domestic remedies" before it goes to Strasbourg. It may take years for the case to climb the legal hierarchy in national jurisdictions. The delay, as in this case, may therefore be considerable. In legal theory it is well known that the legal system and the law in general are very much in delay vis-à-vis actual social processes. In philosophy of law this is considered in the abstract, but in this particular case the delay is obvious *in concreto* and *in cameo.*

Another possible reason, in the optimistic view of the matter, is that the national courts and especially the constitutional courts, if individual constitutional complaint is available, may mandate adequate remedies in order to resolve the controversy in the domestic legal system. In fact, this is exactly what happened in the case at hand.

The Valiant Role of the Slovenian Constitutional Court

The Constitutional Court of Slovenia, as I also mentioned in my concurring opinion, has valiantly attempted to resolve the situation of the "erased". If things were to go their normal way, the issue would have been resolved domestically. However, the executive branch of the later Slovenian government was noncompliant; it did not want to abide by the judgment of the Constitutional Court. In itself, this obduracy was an assault on due process and the rule of law. Thereafter, in the absence of a domestic solution to the problem, Slovenia was subject to censure from Strasbourg and the price to pay was considerably higher than it would have been in Slovenia.

Nevertheless, I would like to reiterate that there may have been many analogous deprivations of the rights of foreigners in other countries—we mentioned Latvia because we know of it—that have never been pursued as far as the international jurisdiction in Strasbourg. This does not mean that everything is fine and that such deprivations of human rights do not exist.

This is important not because we would like to relativise the responsibility in this case of Slovenia, which had been proven beyond reasonable doubt. No, but if only Slovenia were to be stigmatized because of what has happened in conjunction with the "erased", this would not be acceptable because we may expect that similar nationalistic excesses are present in other countries in Eastern Europe.

Strategic Litigation

Instances of such maltreatment do also occur in Western Europe, if not to the same extent. I remember the Grand Chamber case against the Czech Republic,[4] in which the country was condemned for offering a discriminatory mode of education to Roma children. There, I did not agree with the outcome, but it is true that the Czech Republic was condemned for the discriminatory education of

4 ECHR, Case of *D.H. and Others v. The Czech Republic* (Application No. 57325/00), Strasbourg , 13 November 2007.

Roma children – when other countries, France among them, had not been offering any education whatsoever to Roma children.

This case was an obvious example of so-called "strategic litigation". This is often true even before the Court in Strasbourg, i.e., certain cases are advanced in order to further the acceptance of a precedent that might be useful in some future litigation in this Court but also, due to the binding nature of the Court's judgments, in all national jurisdictions, domestically.

Such was not the intent of litigation in the case this book is all about. Nevertheless, this precedent ought to be binding in all analogical European situations and perhaps especially so, as we have pointed out, in Eastern Europe. The question is therefore what the legal consequences were of having adopted this precedential judgment. This is an empirical question to be answered by academic writers.

In the end, let me commend the author of this book not only for her personal scholarly achievement. Not only will it, as we have pointed out, elucidate the background of the case of the "erased" before the European Court of Human Rights. It ought to serve as a *aide-mémoire* of other potentially similar problems arising in other European countries under the Court's jurisdiction. The issue is increasingly topical because of the influx of immigrants fleeing the wars and domestic "wars of everybody against everybody" in Syria, in Iraq, in Libya, in Tunisia, in Afghanistan, etc. The thorough analysis in this book is a ground-breaking contribution to the understanding, legal and otherwise, of these increasingly challenging social processes.

Conclusion

In conclusion, we reiterate the important moral dimension of this case.

The European Court of Human Rights is not only an international jurisdiction; it is relatively free from the domestic entanglements that inevitably determine much of the legal decision-making of, for example, the constitutional courts. This has to do with impartiality and objectivity as the European Court is far removed from domestic intricacies contaminating the outcomes. Since I was a judge of the Slovenian Constitutional Court for five years, I am aware of these local tangles.

Inversely, the European Court of Human Rights is like Wordsworth's *"cloud that floats on high o'er vales and hills"*, so much it is removed from the domestic intricacies providing for extrinsic rather than intrinsic evidence for the decision-making in particular constitutional cases. In this respect, this case was not only a fortunate development for human rights but also a proof of the possibility to extricate the situation from the domestic vicious circles and resolve it equitably on the international level.

I hope those studying this excellent work will be able to discern the lessons that other jurisdictions, too, may learn from the case of *Kurić et al. v Slovenia.*

Boštjan M. Zupančič, LL.M., S.J.D. (Harv.)
Professor of Law

Judge of the European Court of Human Rights

Introduction

Irfan was brought to Slovenia by his parents when he was one year old. His parents moved to Slovenia from Bosnia and Herzegovina in 1969 when both republics were still part of the same state – the Yugoslav federation. All members of the family had Yugoslav citizenship, as well as the local citizenship of Bosnia and Herzegovina. When they moved to Slovenia they did not need to change their citizenship, they just registered their permanent address in Slovenia and were – as citizens of the federal state – entitled to the same rights as those with the local citizenship of Slovenia. Irfan grew up in Slovenia: he went to school, found a job, got married and raised two children. In 1990, when he was 22 years old, he was in a car accident that forced him to be in and out of hospital for a time. In the meantime the country he lived in fell apart: on 25 June 1991 Slovenia declared its independence from Yugoslavia. He went to the local government office to file a citizenship application within the time limit set by the authorities, but the state official refused to take his application, as some documents were missing.

He continued to focus on his recovery and had started to look for a new job when he received an invitation to report to the local government office concerning his citizenship. There the clerk asked him if he had an identity card. When he presented his identity card the clerk took it, punched it to invalidate it and returned it to him saying: "From now on, you are erased". This came as a shock: it was 1992 and his identity card issued in April 1991 should have been valid until 2001. The clerk instructed him to go to the office for foreigners and regulate his status.

At the foreigners' office the officials, surprised that he spoke perfect Slovenian, told him to go to the Bosnian embassy to get a Bosnian passport. There was no Bosnian embassy in Slovenia at the time, the nearest one was in Italy. But he could not go there because he had no valid documents – they had been invalidated by the clerk at the local administration. This is where Irfan's saga really started. The erasure affected every aspect of his life. He lived in Slovenia without papers for ten years, from 1992 to 2002, when he finally obtained Slovenian citizenship on the basis of one of two laws passed by the Slovenian parliament to address the problem of large numbers of undocumented people stranded in Slovenian territory. During this period he separated from his wife and became homeless. His health chronically deteriorated because he had no health insurance and could not see a doctor. Since he was considered a foreigner, he was not even entitled to assistance from the Red Cross or Caritas. Once he was detained in the aliens' centre for having no documents. He wanted to resolve his status but was caught in a legal limbo created by the Slovenian authorities. He would have had more rights had he registered as a refugee from Bosnia.

Irfan belongs to a group of people who were subjected to an unlawful state measure known as "the erasure". The erasure was an act by which the Slovenian authorities unlawfully deprived more than 25000 people of their legal status and concomitant rights. It affected every sphere of people's lives, such as their freedom and personal safety, their personal and family life, access to health services, employment opportunities, social security and access to education. The authorities tried to justify it with the Aliens Act, but constitutional review declared the act unconstitutional and the erasure unlawful.

The injustices that the erased persons suffered remained unaddressed for many years. The absolute necessity of redressing the wrongs was confirmed by the pilot judgment delivered by the Grand Chamber of the European Court of Human Rights (ECHR) in the *Kurić and others v. Slovenia* case (2012). In the judgment, the court stated that the erasure and long delays in redressing the wrongs violated the Convention's prohibition of discrimination (Article 14), as well as the erased people's rights to private and family life (Article 8) and to effective remedy (Article 13). In recognition of these violations, the ECHR awarded six of the ten applicants 20000 EUR per person with respect to non-pecuniary damages, and invited the government of the Republic of Slovenia to sign, within three months, an agreement with the applicants on their compensation for pecuniary damages. Furthermore, the ECHR obliged the government to draw up an ad hoc domestic compensation scheme within one year, with a view to redressing the wrongs suffered by all erased persons. Since the friendly settlement was not agreed upon, the Court issued another judgment in 2014 awarding the applicants compensation of 37000 to 70000 EUR for pecuniary damages, depending on the individual circumstances of each applicant.

The ruling was a great shock for the Slovenian public and its political elites, given that for years many were convinced that it was possible to avoid redressing these wrongs by ignoring the Constitutional Court rulings, abusing the institution of the referendum, and propagating political populism. While these mechanisms can indeed be employed to achieve certain goals within the realm of domestic politics, they proved ineffective in an international judicial context. From the moment the judgment was delivered, the Slovenian government was obliged to report on the implementation of the ECHR ruling to the Committee of Ministers of the Council of Europe, which supervises the execution of the ECHR judgments. If Slovenia fails to observe the judgment and draw up an appropriate compensation scheme, the erased people can lodge compensation claims directly with the ECHR.

The ruling is a unique, almost cinematic epilogue to the two decades-long saga that began in 1991 when Slovenia gained independence. This book is devoted to this saga. It looks primarily into the legal aspects of the erasure, but also touches upon some of its key political and social aspects. In this context, the term "erasure" has two meanings. In the narrow sense of the word, it denotes the act itself by which the administrative authorities removed the records of thousands of people from the register of permanent residents. In a broader sense of the word, the term "erasure" refers to how the authorities interpreted the Aliens Act to deprive the erased individuals of their legal status and the rights deriving from this status. The book examines the erasure in both its narrow and broader sense. When I use the term "erasure", I usually refer to its broader meaning, i.e. the deprivation of legal status, except when I explicitly state that I am referring to it in the narrow sense, i.e. the act of erasure from the records itself.

The term used to denote the persons affected by this measure is "erased persons/people". This category includes all persons who were citizens of the Socialist Federal Republic of Yugoslavia (SFRY) until 25 June 1991, and citizens of one of its republics, and who had their permanent residence registered in Slovenia on the day of the referendum in Slovenia (23 December 1990) and on the day when Slovenia became an independent country (25 June 1991) but did not obtain Slovenian citizenship. A person who fell into this category was erased from the register of permanent residents and was considered to be living in Slovenia without legal status from the erasure onwards.

The book consists of five parts. Part I is dedicated to explaining the origins of Slovenian citizenship, which are important for understanding the background of the erasure. Part II is dedicated to the erasure itself, presenting how exactly it was carried out and what kind of consequences it had. Part III explores the possible political and societal motivations and conditions that made the erasure possible. Part IV analyses the ways in which the Slovenian Constitutional Court dealt with the erasure and the role of this Court in remedying the problem, while Part V describes the process of the implementation of the Constitutional Court rulings, a process so full of obstacles and delays that the case ended up before the ECHR. Finally, Part VI contains a comparative perspective and shows how the erasure was different from other exclusion policies in the field of citizenship and legal status in other successor states of the former Yugoslavia, the Czech and Slovak republics and in the Baltics.

The primary goal of this book is to present the issue of erasure to the international public, to raise awareness about harsh consequences that the deprivation of legal status has on people. Hence, the book aims to prevent such practices from happening in the future. The book deals with the erasure from the perspective of constitutional law, placing the constitution and its core human rights provisions at the centre of the argument. The book also calls for attention to those rare moments when newly built states are defining their citizenry. Regarding those moments, the book strives to demonstrate that, when granting citizenship during the independence process, the authorities need to respect the state's international obligations towards the population living in its territories. Last but not least, this book also aims to contribute to explaining the circumstances that led to the erasure, which continue to be relevant for the future measures aimed at redressing the wrongs.

In writing this book, I used various methodological approaches. The basic starting point for my research was the erasure in the wider sense of the term. Using different research questions, I placed the erasure in various legal or legally relevant contexts that over the past two decades proved to be important within the legal doctrine. While I presumed the innocence of those responsible for the erasure prior to examining the evidence, I also subscribe to the premise that human rights are inalienable and that they belong to each individual without discrimination. Therefore, I cannot in good conscience uncritically present "both sides of the story", as the evidence clearly shows that there really is only one side. This is an engaged work arising from my advocacy for human rights and aims to contribute to the improvement of legal culture in society.

Part I: The Legal Framework of Citizenship

> *In front of the Law there is a doorkeeper. A man from the countryside comes up to the door and asks for entry. But the doorkeeper says he can't let him in to the Law right now. The man thinks about this, and then he asks if he'll be able to go in later on. "That's possible", says the doorkeeper, "but not now".*
>
> *Franz Kafka, The Trial*

1. The Legal Acts of the SFRY and the Socialist Republic of Slovenia on Citizenship and Residence

To understand how and why names were erased from the register of permanent residents, some familiarity with the legal history of citizenship in Slovenia is required. The relevant historical period began when the territory of present-day Slovenia came under the jurisdiction of the Austro-Hungarian Common Civil Code in 1811, and continued until the National Assembly of Slovenia passed its independence-related legislation, including the Citizenship of the Republic of Slovenia Act, in 1991. This law, which I analyse in detail, established the citizenship of the Republic of Slovenia, which it based on the principle of continuity with citizenship of the Socialist Republic of Slovenia (hereafter: SR Slovenia). The key question is thus who was considered a citizen of SR Slovenia in 1991.

Slovenian citizenship was therefore primarily determined in the period between 1945 and 1991, when the country was one of the six socialist republics of the Yugoslav federation and the legislation of individual republics on citizenship and alien statuses was written according to the federal Yugoslav legislative framework. Earlier legal acts and the numerous peace treaties signed by various warring parties throughout this long period also had an effect on the acquisition of Slovenian citizenship when the country gained independence.

1.1 From 1811 to 1918: The Common Civil Code and *Heimatrecht*

In the territory of present-day Slovenia, the beginnings of the institution of citizenship were laid in 1811 with the introduction of the Common Civil Code (CCC), which was in force until the breakup of Austria-Hungary in 1918. The law did not apply to the region of Prekmurje, which belonged to the Hungarian part of the Monarchy, where citizenship was regulated by the Hungarian law on citizenship adopted in 1879. The CCC, in which citizenship was regulated by

Articles 28 – 32,[5] established a connection between a person's citizenship and his/her civil rights. Citizenship was tied to the homeland right or *Heimatrecht*, which literally meant the right to have a homeland, and implied the right of an individual to live undisturbed and to receive alms-house care in his/her municipality.[6] *Heimatrecht*, as a form of local citizenship, was regulated similarly in both the Austrian and the Hungarian part of the Monarchy; the registers were maintained on the municipal level. The notion of *Heimatrecht* implied a lasting link between the citizen and his/her municipality.[7] Every citizen had to have *Heimatrecht* in one of the municipalities, but it was not possible to have *Heimatrecht* in more than one municipality. The loss of citizenship entailed the loss of *Heimatrecht*; and *Heimatrecht* in one municipality was lost upon acquiring *Heimatrecht* in another.[8]

1.2 From 1918 to 1945: The Kingdom of Serbs, Croats, and Slovenes

After the end of WWI (1914–1918), on 1 December 1918, most of the Slovenian territory joined Croatia, Bosnia-Herzegovina, Serbia, and Montenegro to form the Kingdom of Serbs, Croats, and Slovenes (Kingdom of SCS), later renamed the Kingdom of Yugoslavia.[9]

During the years that followed, the issue of citizenship was primarily determined by two peace treaties: the Treaty of St. Germaine between the Entente powers (of the United Kingdom, France, and Russia) and Austria, which came into force in 1920, and the Treaty of Trianon between the Entente and Hungary, which came into force in 1921. In accordance with the *jus domicilii* principle (citizenship by place of residence), both treaties stipulated that all persons who resided outside the borders of the newly formed states of Austria and Hungary would receive the citizenship of one of the successor states established on former Austro-Hungarian territory. Accordingly, on the day the treaties came into force, the people who lived in the region of Slovenia became citizens of the Kingdom of Serbs, Croats, and Slovenes.

---

5 Jovanović, Državljanstvo socijalističke federativne republike Jugoslavije, 1977, p. 7.

6 Stariha, "Z nobenim delom se ne pečajo, le z lažnivo beračijo!", in: Zgodovina za vse 14 (2007) 1, p. 41.

7 Jovanović, Državljanstvo socijalističke federativne republike Jugoslavije, 1977, p. 15.

8 Kač, Krisch, Pregled predpisov o državljanstvu, in: Dnevi javnega prava, 1999, p. 608 and 609.

9 It was preceded by the state of the Slovenes, Croats, and Serbs that lasted only two months.

In addition, the Treaty of St. Germain allowed affected persons to opt for the citizenship either of the successor state in which they had residence or the state in which the majority of the ethnicity to which they belonged lived. In this sense, the Treaty of St. Germain ended the previous legal tradition according to which citizenship was tied to the person's residence rather than their ethnic affiliation or language.

In the regions of Primorska and part of Notranjska, which became part of Italy through the Treaty of Rapallo signed on 12 November 1920 between the Kingdom of Serbs, Croats, and Slovenes and Italy, not every individual with a permanent residence (*pertinenza*) acquired citizenship automatically. However, some specific groups were allowed to opt for Italian citizenship within one year.[10] On the other hand, ethnic Italians who found themselves in the Kingdom of SCS after the border changed saw their citizenship regulated by a 1920 executive decree of the Provincial Government of Slovenia.[11] Two further details are relevant in this context. First, the Kingdom of SCS passed the Law on Citizenship in 1928.[12] This was the first complete law passed after the establishment of the state,[13] and it based the notion of citizenship on the principles of single citizenship and *jus sanguine a patre* (This principle, which espoused patrilineal citizenship even when a person was born in Slovenia to a Slovenian mother, had an influence on the erasure; such persons were erased unless they applied to become citizens of the Republic of Slovenia). Second, Austro-Hungarian legal provisions on *Heimatrecht* were replaced with provisions on residents' affiliation to a municipality during the early 1930s.[14]

---

10 These included residents of Italian ethnicity who were not born in these regions, or acquired residency there after 24 May 1915, or had resided there in the past. Medved, From Civic to Ethnic Community?, in: Citizenship Policies in the New Europe, 2007, p. 213 ff.

11 Uredba o pridobitvi in izgubi državljanstva Kraljevine SHS z opcijo in prošnjo [*Decree on the acquisition and loss of citizenship of the Kingdom of SCS through an application*], Official Gazette of the Regional Administration for Slovenia, Kingdom SCS, No. 147/1920 in 122/1921. For more on the treaties and options they provided, see Jovanović, Državljanstvo socijalističke federativne republike Jugoslavije, 1977, p. 10–14.

12 Zakon o državljanstvu (Law on Citizenship), Official Gazette of Kingdom SCS, No. 254/1928.

13 Jovanović, Državljanstvo socijalističke federativne republike Jugoslavije, 1977, p. 17.

14 Medved, From Civic to Ethnic Community?, in: Citizenship Policies in the New Europe, 2007, p. 214.

1.3 From 1945 to 1974: Centralised Yugoslavia and the Primacy of Yugoslav Citizenship

The first Yugoslav law on citizenship was passed on 28 August 1945, soon after the end of WWII and before it was clear how the new, liberated Yugoslavia which grew out of the pre-war Kingdom of Yugoslavia would be organised.[15] Article 1 of the law stipulated that Yugoslav citizenship be composed of federal citizenship and citizenship of an individual republic. Furthermore, dual citizenship was prohibited. The law defined Yugoslav citizens as those individuals who were citizens under the 1928 Law on Citizenship (Article 35) on the day that the law came into force, along with those who had residence in one of the municipalities in the regions that became part of Yugoslavia by way of one of the international treaties. Since wartime destruction made it difficult to prove pre-war citizenship,[16] an additional provision granted citizenship to the individuals who belonged to one of the Yugoslav ethnicities and lived in the territory of Yugoslavia without the right to reside there, unless they decided to move or opted for their previous citizenship under Article 25. In 1948, an ex post facto provision was added, rendering ineligible for citizenship all individuals of German origin who were abroad when the law was passed, who had Yugoslav citizenship and residency in one of the municipalities on 6 April 1941 (when the attack on Yugoslavia began with the bombing of Belgrade), and who were "disloyal" to Yugoslav national interests before and during WWII.[17] Loyalty was defined as the key condition for obtaining citizenship, which is similar to the rationale underlying various proposals to resolve the status of the erased people (For example, the proposed amendment to the Constitutional Act, analysed in detail in Part V of this book, proposed "joining the territorial defence unit on the request of the Presidency" as one of the conditions for reacquiring a permanent residence permit in Slovenia; this was considered a test of loyalty to Slovenia). In 1993, the Constitutional Court of the Republic of Slovenia debated whether this retroactive revocation of some persons' Yugoslav citizenship was constitutional. It ultimately decided that the clause was not in contradiction with the general legal principles recognised at that time by "civilised" nations that were "victims of the national-socialist

15 Zakon o državljanstvu Demokratične federativne Jugoslavije, Official Gazette Of Democratic Federal Yugoslavia, No. 64/1945; amended Official Gazette of the Federal People's Republic of Yugoslavia, No. 54/1946, 90/1946, 104/1947, 88/1948, 105/1948.

16 Ragazzi, Štiks, EUDO Citizenship Observatory, Country Report: Croatia, 2010, p. 2.

17 Zakon o spremembah zakona o državljanstvu Demokratične federativne Jugoslavije, Official Gazette of the Federal People's Republic of Yugoslavia, No. 105/1948.

totalitarian regime".[18] However, as is evident from the Constitutional Court's Ruling No. U-II-1/04, loyalty is now no longer recognised as a self-evident justification for depriving a person of his/her rights.

In 1945, a Law on the revocation of citizenship for army officers and sub-officers of the former Yugoslav army who refused to return to the country, the members of military units that served the occupying forces and fled abroad, and persons who fled abroad after the liberation was adopted.[19] This law clearly shows that the members of military units and intelligence departments traditionally ran a higher risk than other persons of being refused citizenship or having their existing citizenship revoked (A similar pattern of citizenship legislation in certain Baltic countries shows that this was also true elsewhere).

In 1947, the Paris Peace Treaty between the Allies (the United States, the United Kingdom, France, and the Soviet Union) and Italy came into force. According to this treaty, persons who had their permanent residence in the territory of Yugoslavia on 10 June 1940 lost their Italian citizenship. In accordance with the obligation stipulated by the Treaty of Paris, Yugoslavia adopted a special regulation on citizenship[20] regarding persons of Italian origin in 1947. They were offered the option of obtaining Italian citizenship, and if they accepted it, they had to move to Italy within one year if so requested by Yugoslavia. In that same year, persons whose citizenship was not covered by the Treaty of Paris—for example, immigrants from the Littoral region who were members of one of the Yugoslav ethnicities[21]—were offered the option of obtaining Yugoslav citizenship.

The Paris Peace Treaty also established the neutral city-state called the Free Territory of Trieste (FTT) that existed for seven years until 1954. The circumstances surrounding the establishment of the FTT are not irrelevant to the erasure. The FTT was divided into Zones A and B. Zone A came under the military administration of the British allied forces, while Zone B was under the control of the Yugoslav Army. Zone A was annexed to Italy by the London Memorandum

18 Constitutional Court of the Republic of Slovenia, Ruling No. U-I-23/93.

19 Zakon o odvzemu državljanstva oficirjem in podoficirjem bivše jugoslovanske vojske, ki se nočejo vrniti v domovino, pripadnikom vojaških formacij, ki so služili okupatorju in pobegnili v inozemstvo, ter osebam, ki so pobegnile v inozemstvo po osvoboditvi, Official Gazette of the Federal People's Republic of Yugoslavia, No. 64/1945, Official Gazette of the Federal People's Republic of Yugoslavia, No. 86/1946 and 22/1968.

20 Official Gazette of the Federal People's Republic of Yugoslavia, No. 104/1947.

21 Medved, From Civic to Ethnic Community?, in: Citizenship Policies in the New Europe, 2007, p. 215. For more on the impact of the Paris Peace Treaty, see Jovanović, Državljanstvo socijalističke federativne republike Jugoslavije, 1977, p. 27.

and Zone B to Yugoslavia. The London Memorandum did not cover the issue of citizenship; that was regulated by the first of the three Treaties of Ossimo, also called the Agreement between the Socialist Federal Republic of Yugoslavia and Italy. The first paragraph of Article 3 stipulated that each party to the Agreement would regulate the citizenship of people who held Italian citizenship and had their permanent address within the Free Territory of Trieste on 10 June 1940, and enable the migration of minorities (i.e. the migration of the Italian minority from the Yugoslav territory to Italy, and the other way around).[22] In order to implement this provision, the Federal People's Republic of Yugoslavia adopted the Law on the Validity of Regulations[23] in 1954. Article 3 of this law granted Yugoslav federal citizenship to permanent residents in the former Zone B, while later laws on citizenship adopted in 1964 and 1976 enabled these people to retain their Yugoslav citizenship.[24] If such a person had not regulated his/her citizenship of the Slovenian republic by 25 June 1991, when Slovenia gained its independence, they found themselves among the group of people who were erased from the register of permanent residents.[25]

With its first Law on Citizenship in 1945, Yugoslavia introduced a combined citizenship system that involved two levels: federal and republic. Viewed from the perspective of both public and private international law, Yugoslav federal citizenship was one's primary citizenship. Every Yugoslav citizen also held citizenship

---

22 *Ibid.*

23 Zakon o veljavi ustave, zakonov in drugih zveznih pravnih predpisov na ozemlju, na katero se je z mednarodnim sporazumom razširila civilna uprava Federativne ljudske republike Jugoslavije, Official Gazette of the Federal People's Republic of Yugoslavia, No. 45/1954.

24 The Supreme Court of the Republic of Slovenia, Ruling No. U 2824/2005.

25 When researching the erasure I indeed did not come across any person who was erased for this reason. However, I know of the case of D.L., who found out that he did not have Slovenian republic citizenship by chance. Shortly before the six-month period for submitting applications for citizenship began, this person, who was born in the Free Territory of Trieste, intended to buy a property. To meet the legal requirements, he had to submit an SFRY citizenship certificate. When he requested this certificate in the Republic of Slovenia, he learned that he was not entered into the register of births of the Republic of Slovenia. He obtained the citizenship of SR Slovenia at the time and later, when it became an independent country, he automatically obtained Slovenian citizenship. If he had not done so, he would have expected, as a person born in Slovenia, to obtain citizenship automatically, and he would not have applied for it. In that case, he would have been erased.

of one of the Yugoslav republics, which was not affected by migration from one republic to another.[26]

The introduction of federal legislation regulating citizenship was followed in 1950 by the local Slovenian Law on Citizenship.[27] Article 1 of this law stipulated that only persons who held citizenship of the Yugoslav federation could also be citizens of Slovenia.

In 1964, a new Law on Yugoslav Citizenship was adopted.[28] Article 2 of this law stipulated that only Yugoslav citizens could hold citizenship of any of its republics and that the loss of Yugoslav citizenship entailed the loss of one's citizenship of a republic; federal citizenship had taken primacy over republic citizenship. Furthermore, the law eliminated the possibility of revoking one's citizenship due to absence from the country, introduced less demanding requirements for the naturalisation of emigrants, and eliminated the loyalty oath.[29] In 1965, the local Slovenian version of the federal law was adopted.[30] It based the acquisition of citizenship on the *jus sanguinis* principle. Article 2 stipulated that a child could obtain citizenship of SR Slovenia if he or she was born within the territory of Slovenia and if both of the child's parents were citizens of SR Slovenia and lived there at the time of the child's birth. If the child was not born in Slovenia, or if one of the parents was not a citizen of Slovenia or did not live there at the time of the child's birth, the child could only obtain citizenship of the Slovenian republic with the consent of both parents.

A Yugoslav citizen could not hold citizenship of more than one republic. Article 7 of the 1965 Slovenian law on citizenship stipulated that a person who acquired citizenship of another Yugoslav republic lost his/her citizenship of the Slovenian republic. In order to ensure that this provision was respected and to minimise instances of conflicting citizenships, the citizenship laws of all the republics were harmonised to be in line with each other except for minor differences.[31] The relevant governmental bodies were obliged to record the change of

---

26 *Ibid*, p. 216.

27 Zakon o državljanstvu Ljudske republike Slovenije, Official Gazette of the People's Republic of Slovenia, No. 20/1950.

28 Zakon o jugoslovanskem državljanstvu, Official Gazette of the Socialist Federal Republic of Yugoslavia, No. 38/1964.

29 Medved, From Civic to Ethnic Community?, in: Citizenship Policies in the New Europe, 2007, p. 215.

30 Zakon o državljanstvu Socialistične republike Slovenije, Official Gazette of the Socialist Republic of Slovenia, No. 11/1965.

31 Ragazzi, Štiks, EUDO Citizenship Observatory, Country Report: Croatia, 2010, p. 4.

citizenship in both republics concerned. It was fairly simple to switch citizenship from one republic to another. Initially, to obtain citizenship of another Yugoslav republic, a person had to reside there for three years, but this was reduced to only one year as early as 1946. After the introduction of the Law on Yugoslav Citizenship in 1964, the only requirement was a written statement by the person who wanted to become a citizen of another republic. These rules reflected Yugoslavia's centralised administration and the fact that one's citizenship of a republic did not have much practical importance.[32] All Yugoslav citizens had equal rights and obligations, except for certain specific rights such as the right to vote. According to the Law on the Registry of Voters,[33] adopted in 1945, only the citizens of a given republic could vote in that republic. Having one's registered permanent residence in that republic did not suffice. Some of the republics later modified this rule so that registered permanent residents could also participate in elections for delegates to the republic's Assembly.[34]

1.4 From 1974 to 1991: Decentralisation and the Primacy of Citizenship of the Republics

The 1974 Constitution of the Socialist Federal Republic of Yugoslavia (SFRY)[35] established the federation of six Yugoslav republics, which entailed the decentralisation of the administration. The state structure was transformed from a mainly centralised federal state into a federation of voluntarily united nations, with individual federal units – the Republics – obtaining greater authority. This changed the meaning of both elements of Yugoslav citizenship: citizenship of a republic became the primary form of citizenship and federal Yugoslav citizenship became secondary (similarly to the current status of EU citizenship). The definition of citizenship was set forth in Article 249 of the SFRY Constitution. It retained the original basis of SFRY citizenship[36]: every citizen of an individual republic was also a citizen of the SFRY and the citizens of individual republics

32 Medved, From Civic to Ethnic Community?, in: Citizenship Policies in the New Europe, 2007, p. 216.

33 Zakon o volilnih imenikih, Official Gazette of the Democratic Federal Yugoslavia, No. 59/1945.

34 Ragazzi, Štiks, EUDO Citizenship Observatory, Country Report: Croatia, 2010, p. 3.

35 Ustava Socialistične federativne republike Jugoslavije, Official Gazette of the Socialist Federal Republic of Yugoslavia, No. 9/1974.

36 Article 249, para 1 of the Constitution of the Socialist Federal Republic of Yugoslavia.

had the same rights and obligations within the territory of another republic as that republic's citizens.[37]

The Constitution of SR Slovenia was adopted the same year.[38] It, too, stipulated the primacy of citizenship of the republic (Article 5 stipulated that every citizen of SR Slovenia was also a citizen of the Socialist Federal Republic of Yugoslavia) as well as the equal legal status of the citizens of other republics in Slovenia (Article 6).

The same concepts were preserved in the Law on Citizenship of the SFRY[39] and the Law on Citizenship of SR Slovenia, both of which were adopted in 1976.[40] The latter stipulated that the citizens of other republics could obtain citizenship of the Slovenian republic upon application, provided that they had their permanent residence registered in Slovenia. The citizenship of children born in Slovenia continued to be determined based on *jus sanguinis*.

In accordance with Article 281 of the SFRY Constitution, federal citizenship and the status and residence permits of foreign nationals in the SFRY fell under the authority of the Yugoslav federation, while, in accordance with Article 321 of the Constitution, SR Slovenia had the authority to regulate its own citizenship, as did the other republics of the SFRY within their respective territories. Article 348 of the Constitution of SR Slovenia stipulated that the regulation of citizenship and civil status was to be effected through laws and executive acts; the responsibility for doing so was evenly distributed between the Chamber of Communities and the Socio-political Chamber, both of which were part of the National Assembly of SR Slovenia.

After 1974, the basic principle observed in granting citizenship throughout the federation was the "right of blood", or *jus sanguinis*, according to which the child obtained the same citizenship as his/her parents. If the parents held citizenship of two different republics, the parents had to decide which republic the child would become a citizen of.[41] The principle of *jus sanguinis* was combined with

---

37 Article 249, para 2 of the Constitution of the Socialist Federal Republic of Yugoslavia. See also Dedić, Jalušič, Zorn, The Erased: Organized Innocence and the Politics of Exclusion, 2003, p. 45.

38 Ustava Socialistične republike Slovenije, Official Gazette of the Socialist Republic of Slovenia, No. 6/1974.

39 Zakon o državljanstvu SFRJ, Official Gazette of the Socialist Federal Republic of Yugoslavia, No. 58/1976.

40 Zakon o državljanstvu Socialistične republike Slovenije, Official Gazette of the Socialist Republic of Slovenia, No. 23/1976.

41 Jovanović, Državljanstvo socijalističke federativne republike Jugoslavije, 1977, p. 52.

other principles (*jus loci*, naturalisation, etc.). However, the part of the provision which stipulated that the parents were to choose the citizenship of the republic consensually was often disregarded in practice, that is, the administrative authority did not check if the parents had truly reached a consensus, or if one parent alone determined the child's citizenship. In many cases, the administrative body determined the child's citizenship at birth based on the *jus sanguinis a patre* principle, even though it was no longer applicable. The valid citizenship was the one recorded on the child's birth certificate.[42]

Given the principle upon which Yugoslav citizenship was based and given that all Yugoslav citizens enjoyed the same rights and obligations across the country regardless of which republic's citizenship they held, many (perhaps most) SFRY citizens did not devote much attention to this feature of their citizenship; many may not even have known which republic's citizenship they held. Most frequently, it was persons who were born in one republic and later moved with their parents to another[43] who were in confusion about their citizenship, or persons born to parents who held the citizenship of different republics. The extensive case law mentioned later in this book on the issue of citizenship post-Slovenian independence bears this out. Many defendants claimed that they ought to have been recorded as citizens of SR Slovenia, but were not for various reasons. The primacy of republic citizenship was therefore mainly theoretical. In practice, despite changes in the constitution and decentralisation in 1974, it did not have any real significance.

1.5 Republic Citizenship and the Register of Residents

The notion of holding the citizenship of a republic was often confused with that of registering one's permanent address and the unique personal number that each person obtained from the authorities at birth. The SFRY maintained separate records of permanent residents and citizens. The term "register for keeping records of permanent and temporary residents and foreigners" was introduced by the Decree on the obligation to register/de-register one's address in 1945;[44] local register records were based on this decree.[45] Another law relevant for our

42 *Cf.* The Supreme Court of the Republic of Slovenia, Ruling No. X Ips 451/2004.

43 *Ibid.* See also The Supreme Court of the Republic of Slovenia, Ruling No. U 774/946.

44 Uredba ministrstva za notranje zadeve o prijavni in odjavni dolžnosti prebivalstva, Official Gazette SNOS, No. 46/1945.

45 Tršinar, Centralni register prebivalstva, 1999, p. 15.

discussion is the 1950 Decree that introduced family records.[46] With these two Decrees, the obligation to register one's address – which originally applied only to specific places in Slovenia – was extended to the entire republic.[47] Furthermore, the Regulation on the register of permanent residents[48] introduced local registers in the form of individual dossiers/records, which were the earliest form of the register that was later used across the entire territory of Slovenia.

The federal law on recording all permanent and temporary addresses[49] was adopted in 1965, obliging municipal bodies to keep records of their residents. In the same year, SR Slovenia adopted the local version of this law, which defined the register of permanent residents as a civil status registry and determined its structure. All adults were obliged to register their current address with the local administrative office.

While records had been maintained locally prior to this law, Slovenia centralised its record-keeping in 1970 with the law introducing the central register of permanent residents.[50] The data in this register did not yet include the unique personal identification numbers later dubbed EMŠO. In 1974 this law was replaced with the Law on residence records and the population register,[51] which legally connected the local registers of residents with the central register; it also introduced a procedure for deleting fictitious address registrations, a register of temporary addresses and the obligation to keep the history of past entries.

---

46 Odredba o razširitvi obveznosti prijave stalnega prebivališča oziroma prijave spremembe stanovanja in z navodilom o prijavljanju prebivališča državljanov FLRJ v Ljudski republiki Sloveniji, Official Gazette of the People's Republic of Slovenia, No. 22/1950.

47 Uredba o prijavljanju prebivališča, Official Gazette of the Federal People's Republic of Yugoslavia, No. 56/1948 and 39/1950), Odredbo o spremembah in dopolnitvah odredbe o pri javah stalnega in začasnega prebivališča (Official Gazette of the Federal People's Republic of Yugoslavia, No. 62/1952) and Rule Book on the registration of permanent and temporary residence (Official Gazette of the Federal People's Republic of Yugoslavia, No. 9/1959).

48 Uredba o ustanovitvi in vodenju registra stalnega prebivalstva, Official Gazette of the People's Republic of Slovenia, No. 9/1953 and 49/1957.

49 Temeljni zakon o evidenci stalnega in začasnega prebivališča občanov, Official Gazette of the Socialist Federal Republic of Yugoslavia, No. 9/1965.

50 Zakon o uvedbi centralnega registra stalnega prebivalstva v SR Sloveniji, Official Gazette of the Socialist Republic of Slovenia, No. 40/1970.

51 Zakon o evidenci nastanitve občanov in o registru prebivalstva, Official Gazette of the Socialist Republic of Slovenia, No. 4/1974.

The next important development was the introduction of a unique personal identification number in 1976.[52] A federal law defined the structure of the number,[53] and set out the obligation to enter it into certain documents and to keep records of all unique personal identification numbers. However, it did not designate the body responsible for these obligations; that decision was left to the individual republics. In order to introduce the unique personal identification numbers, SR Slovenia adopted a law[54] which defined this number as an identifier to connect data in the official records on members of the public in the republic. Based on this law and the act by which it was implemented,[55] all of the permanent residents of the SR Slovenia (note the difference between residents and citizens!) received an identification number from the Statistical Office.[56]

This explains why permanent residents in Slovenia who did not have Slovenian Republic citizenship received the "Slovenian" personal identification number, regardless of which republic's citizenship they held. The term "Slovenian" here denotes the range of numbers assigned to Slovenia. These facts are relevant to the erasure, since many erased individuals erroneously thought that their "Slovenian" personal identification number was proof that they were not obliged to apply for Slovenian citizenship, thinking that they would not have received the Slovenian personal identification number unless they held Slovenian republic citizenship.

However, the above explanation shows that the unique identification number was not related to one's citizenship. It was assigned on the basis of one's permanent address, and it was only a number that made it possible to connect disparate pieces of data. Many erroneously interpreted the fact that they were assigned a "Slovenian" personal ID number as proof that they had held Slovenian republic citizenship, or as sufficient grounds for automatically obtaining the citizenship of SR Slovenia. This indicates that people were unaware of the difference between

52 Zakon o uvedbi matične številke občanov, Official Gazette of the Socialist Federal Republic of Yugoslavia, No. 58/1976.

53 The structure of the unique personal ID was precisely defined and harmonised by the Agreement on the distribution of register numbers for the unique personal ID of the population, Official Gazette of the Socialist Federal Republic of Yugoslavia, No. 13/1978.

54 Zakon o enotni matični številki občanov, Official Gazette of the Socialist Republic of Slovenia, No. 1/1980.

55 Pravilnik za izvajanje zakona o enotni matični številki občanov, Official Gazette of the Socialist Republic of Slovenia, No. 7/1980.

56 *See* Tršinar, Centralni register prebivalstva, 1999, p. 15–19.

the personal ID number assigned based on one's permanent address and the acquisition of republic citizenship. "The consequence of the new legal situation was that the [central population register] appeared to be the register of citizens, which was never the intention behind this register".[57]

All this leads to the conclusion that the government did not invest enough effort in educating people about the difference between the population register, the meaning of the personal ID number, and the role of citizenship of a republic. This had especially serious consequences for lower working class immigrants from other republics of the former Yugoslavia.[58]

Comparing the history of the population register's introduction and maintenance in Slovenia with that of other Yugoslav republics shows that, despite the laws that were passed for this purpose, the introduction of population registers did not gain ground as quickly in the other republics as it did in Slovenia. The history of registering immigrants from other republics in SR Slovenia shows that, in some republics, the unique ID number was assigned only to adult persons over 18 years of age, that a large part (around 30%) of the population was not assigned this number at all, and that people received duplicate ID numbers owing to the decentralisation of record-keeping.[59] The next section, in which I analyse

---

57 *Ibid.*, p. 38.

58 The central population register contains not only data on current residence but also on previous residences and changes as a result of moving (*Ibid.*, p. 96). Owing to this fact, any erased person can request proof of their past registration of permanent residence in Slovenia from any municipality which, in accordance with the Central Population Register Act (Official Gazette of the Republic of Slovenia, No. 1/1999), keeps the records for those living in the area under its authority and has access to the central population register. A record of one's previous registration of permanent residence showing that said registration was terminated on 26 February 1992 therefore places a person in the group of the erased people, and can serve as proof of this fact before any state body or a third party. The Central Population Register Act stipulates that if a person moves, the record includes his/her previous place of residence (only the place and the country, rather than full address), as well as future place of residence if he/she moves to another country (Tršinar, Centralni register prebivalstva, 1999, p. 96–97). In the case of the erased people who never moved from Slovenia, this resulted in false records stating that the new place of residence from the date of the erasure was some arbitrarily chosen place in one of Yugoslavia's successor states, usually a person's place of birth or the place where he/she had lived before moving to Slovenia. Since the entries in the register of residents is an official document, the entry of unverified or supposed data into such a register is unlawful.

59 Tršinar, Centralni register prebivalstva, 1999, p. 29.

the population registers and their shortcomings, will reveal that the unique ID number assignment functioned only in theory.

From 1983 to 1999 this area was regulated by a law which stipulated that data on the addresses of Slovenian citizens and other persons with permanent residence in Slovenia be compiled in the population register.[60] This law set out the obligation to register one's permanent address, to register every change of address within eight days of moving to a new place or otherwise changing one's address, and to have one's previous permanent address deleted in case of a change. The body responsible for keeping the central register was the Institute of Statistics, while individual municipalities maintained municipal population registers. Temporary addresses were entered into the register of temporary residences.[61]

1.6 Citizenship Records

From 1947, when the population registers were first introduced,[62] until the breakup of Yugoslavia in 1991, population registers existed only at the level of the republics. Records of citizenship were decentralised and they were the responsibility of individual republics. There was no centralised, federal registry of citizens[63] (only the act of granting/discontinuing citizenship was recorded on the federal level).[64] The Rule Book on the Implementation of the FPRY's Law on Citizenship[65] was adopted in 1946 based on the 1945 Law on Citizenship, and, two years later, the registry of citizens was accordingly introduced as the official record of citizens. According to the Rule Book, citizenship was recorded in the place (i.e. the municipality) where the person had permanent residence. The citizenship of newborn babies was entered into the citizenship registry that contained the records of the parent from whom the child obtained citizenship of the republic. In Slovenia, local Instructions on how to keep the registry of citizens

60 Zakon o evidenci nastanitve občanov in o registru prebivalstva, Official Gazette of the Socialist Republic of Slovenia, No. 6/1983.

61 Until 1999, the register of temporary residents had not been connected with the central population register. This shortcoming was eliminated through the Central Population Register Act. Tršinar, Centralni register prebivalstva, 1999, p. 19.

62 Jovanović, Državljanstvo socijalističke federativne republike Jugoslavije, 1977, p. 46.

63 Ragazzi, Štiks, EUDO Citizenship Observatory, Country Report: Croatia, 2010, p. 3. *See also* Jovanović, Državljanstvo socijalističke federativne republike Jugoslavije, 1977, p. 45.

64 Jovanović, Državljanstvo socijalističke federativne republike Jugoslavije, 1977, p. 46.

65 Pravilnik za izvajanje zakona o državljanstvu FLRJ, Official Gazette of the Federal People's Republic of Yugoslavia, No. 98/1946.

were adopted,[66] according to which entries contained a note on Slovenian Republic citizenship but not on the citizenship of other republics. The Instructions were in force until 1965, meaning that if a child was born before 1965 in Slovenia to parents who had permanent residency in Slovenia, and if one or both parents held citizenship in a republic other than Slovenia and the child thus obtained the citizenship of another republic, this information was not entered in the Slovenian population register.

Končina writes that the 1964 Constitution led to the promotion of "Yugoslavianism", so the citizenship of individual republics was no longer consistently recorded. Beginning in that year, the population registers contained records on all SFRY citizens, regardless of the republic in which they had citizenship. "Accordingly, from that time on the citizen registry was no longer the register of the citizens of individual republics, but of the citizens of all the republics who at the time of entry permanently resided in Slovenia".[67]

This meant that a child born in Slovenia who obtained Serbian republic citizenship based on the consensual choice of his or her parents was entered into the Slovenian register of citizens as a citizen of the Socialist Republic of Serbia. This fact proved to be key when Yugoslavia was dissolved, as the successor states based the *ex lege* terms of obtaining citizenship on continuity with citizenship of the republics. As I will present in detail below, these persons later became stateless, were deprived of their legal status in Slovenia, and the wider implications of the erasure further complicated their situation.[68]

Less than a decade after the concept of "Yugoslavianism" was introduced, Yugoslavia was decentralised and re-organised as a federation, which led to the gradual abandonment of the population registers. In 1976, citizenship began to be entered in the register of births, and in 1982 the population registers were discontinued entirely.[69]

---

66 Navodilo za vodstvo razvida državljanov Ljudske Republike Slovenije, Official Gazette of the People's Republic of Slovenia, No. 42/1947.

67 Končina, Zakon o državljanstvu Republike Slovenije s komentarjem, 1993, p. 110.

68 The law stipulated that the population registers in individual republics contain data on all Yugoslav citizens, since every citizen of Yugoslavia also held citizenship of one of its republics. Only the records on persons who acquired Yugoslav citizenship through one of it embassies abroad were not entered into these registers, unless they settled in Yugoslavia and registered their residence in one of the Yugoslav republics. (Ragazzi, Štiks, EUDO Citizenship Observatory, Country Report: Croatia, 2010, footnote 12).

69 The Law on the Fundamental Records in the Population Register (Official Gazette of the Socialist Federal Republic of Yugoslavia, No. 6/1973), adopted in 1973, defined

2. The Pre-constitutional Legislative Documents of the Socialist Republic of Slovenia

2.1 The Referendum and the Statement of Good Intentions

Preparations for Slovenia's independence began in 1989 with the adoption of constitutional amendments to the 1974 Constitution of SR Slovenia.[70] I will not be able to discuss all the details of this complex process; instead, I will concentrate on the documents, events, and the aspects of independence that were relevant to the issue of citizenship and the status of aliens, and consequently, to the erasure.

In 1990, several pre-constitutional acts were adopted which provided the legal foundation for the Constitution of the Republic of Slovenia. With a well-defined citizenry being one of the fundamental elements of a new state (according to international law, a state should possess a permanent population, a defined territory, a government, and a capacity to enter into relations with other states),[71] certain provisions in these acts related to the citizens of SR Slovenia, others to the citizens of other SFRY republics living in Slovenia.

The milestone in the preparations for independence was 6 December 1990, when the Referendum on the Sovereignty and Independence of the Republic of Slovenia Act was adopted.[72] Two other documents bear the same date: the Statement of Good Intentions[73] and the Agreement on the Joint Action at the

---

citizenship as an integral part of one's personal status and made it obligatory to enter this data into the register of births. The legal basis for the elimination of population registers was provided by the 1974 Constitution, which also transferred the responsibility for citizenship issues to the individual republics. In addition, the 1976 Law on the Citizenship of the SFRY no longer contained provisions on the responsibilities concerning citizenship issues, meaning that the authority over these issues was transferred to individual republics. The law on the Citizenship of SR Slovenia adopted in 1976 made it obligatory to enter one's citizenship into the register of births/civil register, not the population register. The population register was discontinued by 1982, so the records of persons born after 1982 were no longer entered (Končina, Zakon o državljanstvu Republike Slovenije s komentarjem, 1993, p. 110).

70 Ustavni amandmaji IX do XC k Ustavi Socialistične Republike Slovenije, Official Gazette of the Socialist Republic of Slovenia, No. 32/1989.

71 Türk, Temelji mednarodnega prava, 2007, pp. 86–89.

72 Zakon o plebiscitu o samostojnosti in neodvisnosti Republike Slovenije, Official Gazette of the Republic of Slovenia, No. 44/1990.

73 Izjava o dobrih namenih, Official Gazette of the Republic of Slovenia, No. 44/1990.

Referendum signed by the political parties represented in the National Assembly and various parliamentary groups.

The Law on the Referendum set the date of the referendum for 23 December 1990 and defined its subject and the electorate. Article 6 of this law stipulated that all persons who had general voting rights in Slovenia under the Law on the Elections to the National Assemblies[74] had the right to take part in the referendum, meaning all adults over 18 who had their permanent address registered in Slovenia. In other words, in addition to the citizens of SR Slovenia and the members of the Italian and Hungarian ethnic minorities, eligible voters also included the citizens of other SFRY republics who, on the day that the referendum took place, had their permanent address registered in Slovenia, including those who were subsequently erased. The question asked at the referendum was, "Do you agree that Slovenia should become a sovereign and independent country?" The turnout was 93.2%; around 95% voted in favour of sovereignty and independence, which translates into 88.5% of all voters.[75]

While this law regulated the technical implementation of the referendum, the Statement of Good Intentions was an effort by the Assembly of the Republic of Slovenia to establish the conceptual foundations of the new state, targeted at everyone possibly affected by the referendum. Judging by its contents, the main addressees were the Slovenian nation, the Italian and Hungarian ethnic minorities, and all other voters in Slovenia. These "other voters" consisted of all the adult citizens of other SFRY republics over the age of eighteen who had a permanent address in Slovenia. Furthermore, the message's intended audience included the international public, since Slovenia needed international recognition to become a full member of the international community. Given these target groups, the message was not unusual.

Paragraph 1 stated that, if the referendum's outcome was positive, Slovenia would become a "democratic and welfare state, as well as a state governed by the rule of law" and that it would "comply with contemporary beliefs, safeguard civil rights and liberties". The Statement then proceeded to say that the new country would guarantee "the members of all other ethnicities and nationalities the right to an overall cultural and linguistic development, and to all those who have their permanent residence in Slovenia the right to obtain Slovenian citizenship, if they so desire". Paragraph 2 pointed out that "the establishment of the independent

74 Zakon o volitvah v skupščine, Official Gazette of the Socialist Republic of Slovenia, No. 42/1989.

75 Od plebiscita do samostojnosti (From Referendum to Sovereignty), http://www.slovenija2001.gov.si/pot/kronologija (10 December 2010).

Slovenian state, based on the right to self-determination, is not directed against anyone either within Yugoslavia or beyond its frontiers", and Paragraph 3 stated that Slovenia "shall observe all the principles of international law and, in terms of legal succession, all provisions of international agreements signed by the Socialist Federal Republic of Yugoslavia". The next sections will discuss whether the good intentions of this statement were implemented in practice with regard to the erased people.

Another important document for the study of the erasure is the above-mentioned Agreement signed by all political parties, the club of the delegates of ethnic minorities, and the club of independent delegates. The Agreement acknowledged a joint commitment to "guarantee to the Italian and Hungarian ethnic minorities and the members of all other Yugoslav ethnicities who live in Slovenia that the outcome of the referendum will not affect their political status".[76] The objective of both the Statement of Good Intentions and the Agreement was to attract the greatest possible number of voters to vote in favour of Slovenia's independence. However, while the minority, linguistic, and cultural rights of the Italian and Hungarian ethnic minorities were later enshrined in the Constitution, the right of citizens of other Yugoslav republics to live in Slovenia was purposefully disregarded. Part II of this book will explain how this was possible.

2.2 The Basic Constitutional Charter and the Constitutional Act Enabling its Implementation

On 25 June 1991 the National Assembly of the Republic of Slovenia declared Slovenia a sovereign and independent state and adopted the Basic Constitutional Charter on the Independence and Sovereignty of the Republic of Slovenia (hereafter BCC)[77] and the Constitutional Act Implementing the Basic Constitutional Charter on the Independence and Sovereignty of the Republic of Slovenia (hereafter CAIBCC).[78] The preamble to the BCC listed the reasoning behind its enactment, which included the fact "that the SFRY no longer functions as a state ruled by law and that in it human rights are seriously violated". Article III of the same Charter stated that "the Republic of Slovenia guarantees the protection of human rights and fundamental freedoms to all persons living in the territory of

76 Ogradi, Izbrisani državljani SFRJ, 2003, p. 16. *See also* Savanović, Geografska interpretacija izbrisa, 2007, p. 25.

77 Temeljna ustavna listina o samostojnosti in neodvisnosti Republike Slovenije, Official Gazette of the Republic of Slovenia, No. 1/1991I.

78 *Ibid.*

the Republic of Slovenia, regardless of their nationality, without any discrimination, in accordance with the Constitution of the Republic of Slovenia and valid international agreements".[79]

For the erased people, this article is important primarily because its diction suggests that the protection of human rights and fundamental freedoms is guaranteed to all persons under the authority of the state (which indeed is the state's purpose), not just to citizens or persons with permanent or temporary residence in the country. Similarly, the BCC was the first legislative or constitutional document to mention respect for the principle of non-discrimination.

Article 13 of CAIBCC contained more specific definitions of the terms under which citizens of other SFRY republics with permanent residence in Slovenia could apply for citizenship. It stipulated that citizens of other republics who had permanent residence in Slovenia and actually lived there on the day of the referendum (23 December 1990) had rights and duties equal to those of citizens of the Republic of Slovenia until they obtained Slovenian citizenship under Article 40 of the Citizenship of the Republic of Slovenia Act, or until the deadline specified in Article 81 of the Aliens Act expired; the only right suspended during this period was the right to own real estate, except through inheritance.[80]

3. The Adoption of the Independence Legislation

3.1 Introduction

When Slovenia became a sovereign and independent state, it acquired the right to define who Slovenian citizens were and to determine the conditions under which Slovenian citizenship could be obtained.[81] However, the rights arising from sovereignty are restricted by binding international standards pertaining to citizenship. The international conventions that Slovenia was obliged to observe were the 1930 Hague Convention on Certain Questions Relating to the Conflict of

79 The first paragraph of Article/Section II of the Basic Constitutional Charter on the Independence and Sovereignty of the Republic of Slovenia.

80 The Citizenship of the Republic of Slovenia Act, the Aliens Act, the Passports of the Citizens of the Republic of Slovenia Act and the State Border Control Act constituted the so-called independence legislation; Official Gazette of the Republic of Slovenia, No. 1/1991I.

81 Article 1 of the Hague Convention on Certain Questions relating to the Conflict of Nationality Laws dating from 1930 states that every country is sovereign in deciding who its citizens are.

Nationality Laws,[82] the 1961 UN Convention on the Reduction of Statelessness,[83] and the 1978 Vienna Convention on Succession of States in respect of Treaties.[84] While these conventions contain general principles that ostensibly bind sovereign countries, they are not very helpful in practice because sovereign countries need only observe a few specific guidelines when determining who can become a citizen of the country.[85] Two other international documents concerning the issue of nationality—the European Convention on Nationality drafted by the Council of Europe in 1997,[86] and the Draft Articles on Nationality of Natural Persons in Relation to the Succession of States, drafted by the International Law Commission with the United Nations Organization in 2001[87]—were not binding on Slovenia at the time when it gained independence. As a matter of fact, the Draft Articles never became an internationally binding document, while the European Convention on Nationality has not been ratified by Slovenia to this day.

Other international documents that include provisions on nationality are the Universal Declaration of Human Rights, Article 15 of which states that every person has the right to a nationality[88] (though this provision is not formally binding), and the International Convention on the Elimination of All Forms of Racial Discrimination,[89] Article 5 (d.III) of which stipulates that signatory states are obliged to guarantee the right of nationality to every person without discrimination. While this obligation is explicit, on the operative level the Convention gives individual states the freedom to choose their own method of implementation.

82 The Hague Convention on Certain Questions relating to the Conflict of Nationality Laws, done on 12 April 1930 under the auspices of the League of Nations, entered into force 1 July 1937.

83 The United Nations Conventions on the Reduction of Statelessness, New York, 30 August 1961, entered into force 13 December 1975. United Nations, Treaty Series, vol. 989, 175.

84 Vienna Convention on Succession of States in respect of Treaties, Vienna, 23 August 1978, entered into force 6 November 1996. United Nations, Treaty Series, vol. 1946, 3.

85 Medved, From Civic to Ethnic Community?, in: Citizenship Policies in the New Europe, 2007, p. 217 and footnote 13.

86 European Convention on Nationality, done in Strasbourg under the auspices of the Council of Europe on 6 November 1997, entry into force 1 March 2000.

87 Draft Articles on Nationality of Natural Persons in Relation to the Succession of States, UN International Law Commission, Annex to General Assembly Resolution 55/153, 2001.

88 The UN Declaration of Human Rights, adopted on 10 December 1948.

89 The International Convention on the Elimination of All Forms of Racial Discrimination, adopted on 21 December 1965, entry into force 4 January 1969.

International law is more specific on the rights of children, with nationality coming very close to an actual claimable right.[90] It is explicitly recognised in the Convention on the Rights of the Child,[91] Article 7 paragraph 1, and the International Covenant on Civil and Political Rights,[92] Article 24, Para 3 that refers to the rights of the child verbatim.[93]

Since international conventions only contain general provisions, the decisions relating to citizenship are still largely left to sovereign states insofar as such decisions are not restricted by international laws on human rights. It should also be noted that international law does not recognise citizenship as a right (of a person living in the territory of a specific country to obtain citizenship of that country if he/she has no right to obtain citizenship of another country), but as a privilege (it is only explicitly referred to as a right in the American Convention on Human Rights).[94] Had it been defined by international law as an inalienable right, it would be possible to obtain it by way of a lawsuit against a given state.[95] Indeed, citizenship is tied to many rights and benefits, so protecting citizenship status from state-by-state arbitrariness would yield obvious benefits.

The main goal behind all of the provisions on nationality in the documents listed above is to prevent statelessness. The prevention of statelessness is therefore

90 Accetto, Širše implikacije problema državljanstva, in: Dnevi javnega prava, 1999, p. 597.

91 Convention on the Rights of the Child, adopted on 20 November 1989, entry into force 2 September 1990.

92 The International Covenant on Civil and Political Rights, adopted on 16 December 1966, entry into force 23 March 1976.

93 Based on Mesojedec Pervinšek, Učinek mednarodnega prava, in: Dnevi javnega prava, 1999, pp. 648–649.

94 The practice of the Constitutional Court indeed supports the position that the right to acquire citizenship under Article 13 of CAIBCC and under Article 40 of the Citizenship of the Republic of Slovenia Act is a constitutional right. The Constitutional Court's ruling No. Up-38/93 states that "since Article 13 of CAIBCC stipulates the acquisition of citizenship under identical terms as Article 20 of the Citizenship of the Republic of Slovenia Act, the right to obtain citizenship under these terms acquired constitutional character, or put differently, it was elevated to the level of right guaranteed by the regulation on the constitutional level". This position was criticised on the grounds that, by elevating the right to obtain citizenship to the level of the constitutional right, the Constitutional Court actually expanded the range of rights and freedoms that could be protected through a constitutional complaint. Kranjc, Ustavna pritožba kot institut varstva človekovih pravic, in: Temeljne pravice, 1997, pp. 400–401.

95 Accetto, Širše implikacije problema državljanstva, in: Dnevi javnega prava, 1999, p. 596–597.

one of the key international legal standards that is binding on states when determining state policy.[96]

3.2 Establishing the Citizenship of the Republic of Slovenia in 1991

Policy makers in Slovenia lacked historical precedent in both statehood and citizenship policies on which they could rely when defining who the citizens of Slovenia would be. This is a detail that distinguished Slovenia from other countries that gained independence during the early 1990s. For example, Estonia and Latvia "revived" their laws on nationality that had been in force before the countries were occupied by the Soviet Union, setting the conditions for the acquisition of citizenship *ex lege*, based on the principle of continuity with citizenship before occupation.[97] Yet other countries, such as Lithuania[98] and Kosovo,[99] opted for a "zero option" policy, granting citizenship to every person who actually lived within their territory on a specific day, e.g. the day when independence was declared, or when the law on citizenship was passed or came into force.

Historically, the "zero option" policy was seen as more acceptable in countries in which the proportion of the "constituent nation" (the ethnic group that formed a nation-state) to other nationalities was very high,[100] or in countries where the population consisted of several ethnic groups of comparable sizes

96 For a long time, one of the key principles was the prevention of dual citizenship. There was once a resistance towards dual citizenship because it allegedly weakens person's affiliation to a nation (since a person with dual citizenship belongs to two nations). However, dual citizenship rarely caused conflict in the relation of a state and an individual. Today an increasing number of countries, particularly those witnessing strong emigration trends, endorse dual citizenship, with a view to maintaining contacts with their emigrants, some of whom are financially successful individuals. At the same time, many immigrant countries have started to allow dual citizenship, because renouncing their previous citizenship deterred many immigrants from applying for citizenship in the country that they immigrated to (Accetto, Širše implikacije problema državljanstva, in: Dnevi javnega prava, 1999, p. 594).

97 Krūma, Checks and Balances in Latvian Nationality Policies, in: Citizenship Policies in the New Europe, 2007, p. 69, and Järve, Estonian Citizenship: Between Ethnic Preferences and Democratic Obligations, in: Citizenship Policies in the New Europe, 2007, pp. 45–48.

98 Krūma, Lithuanian Nationality, in: Citizenship Policies in the New Europe, 2007, pp. 90–91.

99 Krasniqi, EUDO Citizenship Observatory, Country Report: Kosovo, 2010, pp. 3–4.

100 Medved, From Civic to Ethnic Community?, in: Citizenship Policies in the New Europe, 2007, pp. 216–217.

(Bosnia-Herzegovina).[101] By contrast, the constituent nations whose native populations shared their country with other ethnic groups that accounted for a large part of the total population felt more "threatened".

Documentary sources confirm that policy makers in Slovenia were aware of the practice of granting citizenship based on the *jus domicilii* principle with an option, a practice that took root in Central and Eastern Europe during the 20th century.[102] This was an inclusive approach that took into account individual preferences by allowing a person to opt for another country's citizenship, while also minimising statelessness and multi-nationality. However, the principle also had an exclusive component – individuals who chose to exercise the option and took another country's citizenship were obliged to leave the country whose citizenship they renounced.[103] This is indicative of a low tolerance for the presence of foreign nationals in the country and of the desire to punish individuals who took another country's citizenship.

Policy makers in Slovenia chose to disregard the principle of *jus domicilii*. According to Mesojedec-Pervinšek, it "was ruled out" because of the "escalation of the political crisis".[104] However, this position was both legally and generally untenable, and it had terrible consequences. Due to this decision, the tensions between Yugoslavia's successor states prevailed over the protection of individual rights. Its consequences included the erasure of the records of children whose parents did not apply for their citizenship, or persons who did not apply for citizenship because they expected to obtain it automatically.[105] Had citizenship been granted according to the *jus domicilii* principle, their interests and rights would have been better protected.

In 1991 the bill on citizenship of the new independent state was drafted at the Ministry of the Interior. Once the government, which proposed the law, endorsed

---

101 Sarajlić, EUDO Citizenship Observatory, Country Report: Bosnia and Herzegovina, 2010, pp. 1–7.

102 Mesojedec Pervinšek, Predpisi o državljanih in tujcih, 1997, p. 10.

103 *Ibid.*

104 *Ibid.*

105 This issue has not yet been sufficiently researched. It is a fact that many erased people, and particularly those who were born in Slovenia, were convinced that they held Slovenian republican citizenship. Some claimed that they firmly believed that their parents had not agreed at the time of their birth that they should be assigned the citizenship of another republic, but left it to them to decide when they came of age which republican citizenship they wanted to take. To their surprise, they realised that their republican citizenship had already been determined, without such a choice being made by either their parents or themselves. Interview with Lev Kreft, 14 July 2011.

it, it was submitted to the National Assembly of SR Slovenia, where Igor Bavčar, the Secretary for Administrative Internal Affairs, advocated for it on behalf of the government. An analysis of the parliamentary debates leading up to the passage of the Citizenship of the Republic of Slovenia Act shows that there was a wide variety of opinions on how to define the terms for obtaining citizenship. While the delegates of the Socio-political Chamber and the left-wing parties advocated the equal treatment of all permanent residents in Slovenia regardless of their republic citizenship, the delegates of the right-wing parties assumed a restrictive and nationalist stance.[106] Neither group, however, devoted sufficient attention to the situation of citizens of the other SFRY republics who lived in Slovenia but did not have their permanent address registered there, which suggests their tacit consensus that this group be excluded from the right to acquire citizenship under the same terms as legally registered residents.[107]

The left-wing parties tabled many amendments to this bill in an effort to ensure the greatest possible level of protection for the citizens of other republics. Certain proposals were radical (for example, the proposal that all permanent residents should automatically obtain citizenship in addition to the right to opt for another citizenship). The most persuasive argument, which influenced policy makers and the majority in the National Assembly, was that Slovenia's citizenship policy would be crucial to its international recognition. Fearing that the international community would not recognise Slovenia, they found it necessary to show that the country was capable of establishing the fundamental underpinnings of sovereignty: determining its borders and defining its citizenry in a democratic and internationally acceptable manner.[108]

---

106 The most active delegates in the left-wing parties were Lev Kreft, Metka Mencin, Franco Juri, and Jaša Zlobec. During the period of pre-independence euphoria, this trans-party group was very alert to details in the fundamental laws that established the state. In addition, Jernej Rovšek, a deputy Human Rights Ombudsman who at the time was a lawyer with the legislative service in the National Assembly, played an important role. Rovšek drew attention to the restrictive elements in the proposed law on Slovenian citizenship. The majority in the National Assembly pursued an expressly nationalist course, arguing that ethnic homogeneity represented the only way for Slovenia to be sovereign. By contrast, left-wing parties endeavoured to achieve the highest international standards and to embed them in the law on citizenship. Interview with Lev Kreft, 14 July 2011.

107 Zorn, "We, the Ethno-Citizens of Ethno-Democracy", in: Journal for the Critique of Science, 35 (2007) 228, pp. 58–59. Also Interview with Lev Kreft, 14 July 2011.

108 Interview with Lev Kreft, 14 July 2011.

The bill on the Citizenship of the Republic of Slovenia was passed into law on 5 June 1991. It contained two sets of provisions: one defined the acquisition of Slovenian citizenship based on the birth and naturalisation principle, and the other contained transitional provisions including the terms for acquiring citizenship based on the continuity principle and through extraordinary naturalisation. Under Article 39 of the Citizenship of the Republic of Slovenia Act, all persons who held the citizenship of the Republic of Slovenia and of the SFRY on the day the law came into force became Slovenian citizens whether or not their republic citizenship was entered into the citizenship registry. In other words, this group did not have to apply for citizenship; they obtained it automatically based on the continuity with republic citizenship.[109] The fact that the principle of continuity was applied also meant that all regulations concerning citizenship in effect in the SFRY became part of Slovenian law.[110]

During the period 1990–1992, while the SFRY was in the process of breaking up, federal Yugoslav citizenship ceased to exist, while republic citizenships remained intact and indeed became the citizenship by which the international community recognised persons residing in the former Yugoslavia.[111] Since the registers of citizenship were not properly maintained in the SFRY, the Citizenship of the Republic of Slovenia Act included a provision (Article 43) which required the relevant administrative body to enter the citizenship of all persons who held Slovenian republic citizenship into the register of births where this had been omitted. This provision provided the legal basis for a fact-finding procedure by which the Ministry of the Interior researched persons' citizenship, saving those affected the effort of having to undertake this task themselves.[112] However, this only benefitted those citizens who already held Slovenian republic citizenship (and thus obtained the citizenship of the new state automatically). The law did not contain any provision obliging the Ministry to forward the data on the holders of other republic citizenships to the other successor states. Consequently, all persons whose citizenship had not been duly registered in the other SFRY republics became stateless (more on this below). The citizens of other SFRY republics who had their permanent address registered in Slovenia did not acquire

109 Mesojedec Pervinšek, Predpisi o državljanih in tujcih, 1997, p. 16.

110 *Ibid.*, p. 21.

111 Medved, From Civic to Ethnic Community?, in: Citizenship Policies in the New Europe, 2007, pp. 216–217.

112 Končina, Zakon o državljanstvu Republike Slovenije s komentarjem, 1993, p. 13. This provision proves the fact that records on republican citizenship were poorly maintained. Had they been properly maintained, the provision would be redundant.

citizenship automatically based on the *jus domicilii* principle; they had to apply for it. Slovenia determined the terms under which they could acquire citizenship unilaterally, meaning that, in contrast to the practice that gained ground after the First and the Second World Wars, no international agreement was signed. The terms were set out in Article 40 of the Citizenship of the Republic of Slovenia Act and they were more favourable than those of the naturalisation procedure. Citizens of another SFRY republic could acquire Slovenian citizenship if, on 23 December 1990, i.e. the day of the referendum on sovereignty and independence, they had their permanent address registered in Slovenia and actually lived in Slovenia. The application had to be submitted within 6 months of 25 June 1991, when the law came into force.[113]

Children who were citizens of another SFRY republic had to apply for Slovenian citizenship under the same conditions as those offered by the naturalisation procedure. This was regulated in Article 40, Para 2, which stated that a "child under 18 may acquire citizenship of the Republic of Slovenia under the provisions of Article 14 hereof", and Article 14 stated that a child under 18 could acquire citizenship if one of his/her parents acquired it. Article 40 did not include restrictive conditions such as a command of Slovenian, proof that the person had sufficient means of livelihood, or the renunciation of another country's citizenship, but their omission was not an obvious decision. At Session 19 of the Socio-political Chamber, the delegates voted to add knowledge of Slovenian as an additional condition (twenty-six delegates voted in favour of it, fourteen were against, and four abstained), but after the delegates from the Liberal Democracy Party and others left the session in protest and the arguments against it were reiterated, the vote was repeated, and the option was turned down.[114] The Chairman of the Social Democratic Party, Jože Pučnik, also advocated excluding people based on their ethnicity, albeit shrouded in the rhetoric of economics. On 16 November 1990, he said the following:

> Don't be misled by illusions, because this is not a national but a social issue [...] Personally, I oppose automatically taking over of the state of affairs as it was on the day of the referendum. If the Republic of Slovenia wants to ensure a firm social structure, we will have to introduce some kind of criteria when granting citizenship. Don't let us be apparently democratic and create problems that we will not be able to solve later. We must be aware of what it is possible to solve in Slovenia viewed from the social perspective – the national aspect of this issue is in fact of secondary importance. We are setting up a

---

113 Paragraph 1 of Article 40 of the Citizenship of the Republic of Slovenia Act.

114 Zorn, "We, the Ethno-Citizens of Ethno-Democracy", in: Journal for the Critique of Science, 35 (2007) 228, p. 59.

community that must ensure for itself, from the very beginning, the living circumstances, and we must be ready to eliminate the heritage of the Yugoslav federation, perhaps in an unwanted way as the need may be [...] It is necessary to calculate – demographically as well – what consequences could follow in five or ten years, along with the demands for cultural autonomy. Personally, I will endeavour, using all the influence I possess within the Social Democratic Party, to spare Slovenia the problems such as those that were seen in Knin. We do not want to see Knin in Slovenia and today we have an opportunity to solve these issues in a humane, socially responsible and legal manner. We should not allow rotten compromises or rally-driven democracy that could create troubles for us, such as those encountered by England, France and Germany and other countries that existed during the colonial period. Slovenia, in my opinion, should not allow itself to be burdened by these additional problems.[115]

Moreover, other proposals contained even stricter requirements aimed at excluding people who could potentially become a financial burden for the state. For example, the Social Democratic Party proposed that individuals applying for citizenship submit a medical report as proof that their state of health did not pose a financial threat for Slovenia, but it failed to garner support for this proposal.[116] Had these and certain other additional conditions been accepted, the implications of the erasure would have been even greater, since many more people would have been denied citizenship.[117]

The acquisition of citizenship under Article 40 was termed a "one-time extraordinary naturalisation"[118] and the conditions were much more favourable than those applicable to regular naturalisation.[119]

---

115 Pučnik: Slovenija ne more več čakati, nabralo se je preveč slabega (*Slovenia Cannot Wait Longer, Too Many Bad Things Already*). Delo daily, 17 December 1990, p. 2.

116 *Ibid.*, p. 26.

117 Mekina, B., A Monument to the Erased, in: Journal for the Critique of Science, 35 (2007) 228, p. 47.

118 The Constitutional Court of the Republic of Slovenia, Ruling Up200/ 0414, paragraph 8.

119 These include the renunciation of previous citizenship, ten years of actual residence in Slovenia, of these five years of continuous living in Slovenia preceding the application, accommodation, and a permanent source of income, a command of Slovenian, that "the person has not been sentenced to a prison sentence longer than one year in the country of which he/she is a citizen or in Slovenia for a criminal offence which is prosecuted by law provided that such an offence is punishable pursuant to the regulations of his/her country as well as pursuant to the regulations of the Republic of Slovenia", that "the person's residence permit in the Republic of Slovenia has not been annulled", and that "the person's naturalization poses no threat to the public order, security or defence of the State".

3.2.1 *The Condition of Citizenship of another SFRY Republic*

Citizens of other SFRY republics with permanent residence in the Republic of Slovenia who wanted to apply for citizenship under Article 40 had to submit their birth certificates as proof that they held the citizenship of another Yugoslav republic (Croatia, Bosnia-Herzegovina, Serbia, Montenegro, or Macedonia). This requirement was upheld by the Slovenian Supreme Court.[120] Persons who could not obtain their birth certificates for whatever reason, or persons who could not prove that they held citizenship of another SFRY republic, were denied Slovenian citizenship and were later erased.

This decision of the Supreme Court is open to criticism. The court could have required a less demanding procedure to show one's SFRY citizenship. With this requirement, the government imposed on individuals the burden of proving a fact that should have been obvious from official records, and more importantly, it adopted a course of legal formalism that disproportionately affected certain individuals.

3.2.2 *The Condition of a Registered Permanent Address on 23 December 1990*

A registered permanent address allegedly proved that one had genuine ties with Slovenia, demonstrating that the person in question exercised her/his economic, social, and certain political rights there. This means that citizenship was intended for people who lived in Slovenia for a longer period of time,[121] given that the applicant had to have a permanent address registered by 23 December 1990 at the latest. Put differently, the persons eligible to apply for citizenship were those who had the right to vote in the referendum on Slovenia's independence, and those who could have voted had they been over 18. It was also the real reason why this requirement was one of the conditions for acquiring citizenship; in harmony with the promise in the Statement of Good Intentions, the option of acquiring Slovenian citizenship was given only to persons who had the right to vote in the referendum. Their genuine connection with Slovenia was a less important factor.

The official state registry was the basis for verifying the registration of a permanent address.[122] Accordingly, persons who registered their permanent address in Slovenia after 23 December 1990, could not apply for citizenship under

---

120 The Supreme Court of the Republic of Slovenia, Ruling U 317/944.

121 Končina, Zakon o državljanstvu Republike Slovenije s komentarjem, 1993, p. 134.

122 Kutoš, Pregled sodne prakse Vrhovnega sodišča RS v zvezi s 40. členom Zakona o državljanstvu, in: Dnevi javnega prava, 1999, p. 633.

Article 40. Neither could the citizens of other SFRY republics who had a temporary address — or did not have it even though they lived in Slovenia, as the case may have been. If a person had a temporary address registered in Slovenia and was granted citizenship mistakenly, the administrative procedure to grant him/her citizenship was renewed[123] after the mistake was discovered and his/her citizenship was revoked.

The discussion above begs the question whether it was justifiable to make the registration of a permanent address a prerequisite for gaining citizenship and to thus give the distinction between permanent and temporary residents such importance. Registering a permanent address did not necessarily demonstrate that a person had genuine ties with Slovenia. It was merely a formality, and conversely, a failure to register a permanent address was not sufficient grounds to assume that the person lacked genuine ties with Slovenia.

There were many reasons why the citizens of other SFRY republics chose not to register a permanent address in Slovenia even if they had lived there for a longer period of time. Some were not aware of this possibility, while others did not devote sufficient attention to it. This lack of awareness can be explained by the fact that Slovenia was the only SFRY republic that kept records on immigration from, and emigration to, other republics,[124] which leads to the conclusion that even when it was part of Yugoslavia, Slovenia's migration policy was an exception compared to other Yugoslav republics. In addition, in certain cases it was not possible at all to register a permanent address, for example, if the person worked in Slovenia and lived in a dormitory, or was studying in Slovenia, or lived in a building that had no building permit.[125]

Additionally, a review of the case law explains why certain individuals only had a temporary address registered in Slovenia. For example, one applicant for citizenship argued that he had registered a permanent address in Slovenia in 1976, but in late 1989 he divorced, cancelled his permanent address, and registered a temporary address in a hostel where he lived for some time. After the referendum he moved into a house of his own and registered a permanent address again.[126] Another applicant explained that his permanent address was registered in Slovenia, but was then advised by the interior department to register a

---

123 *Ibid.*

124 Medved, From Civic to Ethnic Community?, in: Citizenship Policies in the New Europe, 2007, p. 239, footnote 19.

125 Ogradi, Izbrisani državljani SFRJ, 2003, p. 42.

126 Supreme Court of the Republic of Slovenia, Ruling No. U 25/1993.

temporary address, which he did.[127] Still another applicant stated that she rented an apartment for six years, but the owner refused to allow her to register her permanent address there, so she had no other option but to register a temporary address.[128] Nevertheless, the Supreme Court decided that for the purpose of acquiring citizenship under Article 40 was "legally irrelevant what reasons were behind the fact that permanent residence was not registered in official records on the date of the referendum".[129] It strains credulity to agree with such a reasoning, because this apparently neutral condition unjustifiably excluded certain individuals who should have acquired citizenship had the goal of genuine ties truly been pursued. As a consequence, a citizen of another republic who moved to Slovenia shortly before the referendum and registered a permanent address there on the day before the referendum, was considered eligible to acquire Slovenian citizenship, while someone who had lived in Slovenia for fifteen years or more could fail to qualify for it. If the government truly wanted to observe the principle of genuine ties with Slovenia, there was no need to adhere to the formalistic registered permanent address requirement.

3.2.3 The Condition of Actually Living in Slovenia

The 1991 Law on Citizenship stipulated that a person had to actually live in Slovenia to be eligible to obtain citizenship. However, the meaning of "actually living in Slovenia" was explained only later, through case law. It should be noted that the Statement of Good Intentions did not mention this requirement. It was added later (included in CAIBCC) and the argument was that the registration of permanent residence alone could not ensure the achievement of the legislator's intent — that is, to grant citizenship to persons who actually lived in Slovenia rather than those who just had their permanent address registered there.[130] This goal could not be inferred from the pre-independence documents. Indeed, it would have been preferable had this been the only requirement for obtaining citizenship, because people residing in Slovenia temporarily and people who did not have a registered temporary or permanent address but did actually live in Slovenia would have had access to citizenship under easier terms.

Actually living in Slovenia, similarly to having a registered permanent address, was supposed to demonstrate one's genuine ties to the country. This requirement

127 Supreme Court of the Republic of Slovenia, Ruling No. Up 891/92.

128 Supreme Court of the Republic of Slovenia, Ruling No. Up 230/92.

129 *Cf.* Supreme Court of the Republic of Slovenia, Ruling No. Up 296/1992.

130 Končina, Zakon o državljanstvu Republike Slovenije s komentarjem, 1993, p. 134.

was fulfilled if a person actually lived in Slovenia from 23 December 1990 (the date of the referendum) until the date when his/her citizenship certificate was issued,[131] rather than just having his/her permanent address formally registered there.[132]

Judging by the case law, the notion of "actually living in Slovenia" is an inadequately defined legal term. Its meaning is determined on a case-by-case basis by a decision-making body which also takes into account the legislature's intent behind enacting it.[133] The Constitutional Court's Ruling Up-77/94 dated 16 September 1997 states that it is not permissible to use such an inadequately defined legal term to establish whether or not an applicant meets the requirements for obtaining citizenship. The notion of inadequately defined legal term leaves some room for the administrative body to exercise judgment and make the most appropriate decision, while taking into account all the essential circumstances surrounding the case in question. What these essential circumstances are, and what the meaning of the inadequately defined legal term is, can be garnered from the wording of the provision, academic legal commentaries, or other laws that regulate some comparable area.[134] In accordance with Article 22 (equal protection of rights) and Article 14 (equality before the law) of the Slovenian Constitution, when employing the institute of discretionary decision and dealing with an inadequately defined legal term, the administrative body is obliged to be consistent in every comparable case which it decides. In other words, the reasoning behind its decisions should be consistent unless there is a justifiable reason to deviate from it.[135]

Certain criteria for fulfilling the condition of actually living in Slovenia were defined in the Decision of the Executive Council of the National Assembly.[136] It stated, among others, that the condition was fulfilled if a person was abroad for job-related reasons which were not in conflict with the interests of the Republic of Slovenia and if, before leaving the country, he/she had lived in Slovenia for at

131 Polič, Kdo "tukaj dejansko živi", in: Pravna praksa 12 (1993) 22, pp. 16–17.

132 Medved, From Civic to Ethnic Community?, in Citizenship Policies in the New Europe, 2007, p. 218.

133 Supreme Court of the Republic of Slovenia, Ruling No. U 473/92. Also Kutoš, Pregled sodne prakse Vrhovnega sodišča RS v zvezi s 40. členom Zakona o državljanstvu, in: Dnevi javnega prava, 1999, p. 633.

134 Constitutional Court of the Republic of Slovenia, Ruling No. Up-77/94, paragraph 7.

135 *Ibid.*, para. 10.

136 Executive Council of the National Assembly of the Republic of Slovenia, Decision No. 20701/ 914/ 68 dated 13 January 1992.

least one year, had attended school in Slovenia, had held regular employment in Slovenia, or was the owner of a property there.

The question that was raised within the case law was whether or not this requirement should be considered fulfilled if the applicant for citizenship was absent. In most cases, the Supreme Court adopted the explanation that it was not necessary for the applicant to be continuously physically present in Slovenia, since in addition to physical presence there were other indicators on the basis of which it was possible to conclude that a person performed all, or the majority, of his/her essential activities in Slovenia (e.g. work, residence, and fulfilling of obligations towards the state, such as paying taxes).[137] Furthermore, in the Supreme Court's view,[138] the requirement of actually living in Slovenia was met only when residence in Slovenia was legal, meaning that persons who cancelled their permanent address did not meet the requirement. The Court's rationale was that granting citizenship to persons who actually lived in Slovenia but did so illegally would contradict the legal order and the logical interpretation of Article 40 of the Citizenship of the Republic of Slovenia Act.[139]

In the view of the Supreme Court, the address at which a person resided was irrelevant to fulfilling the requirement of actually living in Slovenia. It was also not necessary for the person to live at the address registered as his/her permanent residence.[140] However, if the person was not physically present in a specific

---

137 Supreme Court of the Republic of Slovenia, Ruling No. U 473/92. See also Kutoš, Pregled sodne prakse Vrhovnega sodišča RS v zvezi s 40. členom Zakona o državljanstvu, in:Dnevi javnega prava, 1999, p. 637.

138 Supreme Court of the Republic of Slovenia, Ruling No. U 805/1993.

139 It should be noted, though, that in 2002, when the Amendment to the Citizenship of the Republic of Slovenia Act was adopted (Zakon o spremembah in dopolnitvah zakona o državljanstvu Republike Slovenije, Official Gazette of the Republic of Slovenia, No. 96/2002), the stance of the legislature was precisely the opposite, given that this law enabled the erased people who had actually and continuously lived in Slovenia since the date of the erasure, and who met certain other requirements, to acquire citizenship regardless of whether or not they resided in Slovenia lawfully. Similarly, the Act Regulating the Legal Status of Citizens of Former Yugoslavia Living in the Republic of Slovenia that was adopted somewhat later stipulated that permanent residence permit should be granted to persons who could prove that they actually lived in Slovenia, and this requirement was considered fulfilled even if the person lived in Slovenia unlawfully.

140 In this specific case, the appellant argued that the family house in which he lived was damaged so the children moved temporarily from Slovenia while he and his wife lived with the friends. The Supreme Court asked the administrative body to verify

place, whether he/she actually lived there depended on several factors, including the duration of his/her absence and the reasons for it,[141] as well as whether the absence was intentional.[142] In one of its rulings, the Constitutional Court stated that in such cases all evidence indicating that a longer absence was caused by circumstances beyond the applicant's control should be taken into account.[143]

In certain cases involving persons who left Slovenia and lived abroad, the Supreme Court ruled that the requirement of actually living in Slovenia was not fulfilled and that the applicant was not eligible to obtain citizenship. For example, one person was absent for seven months to attend school.[144] The Court based this ruling on the Regulation[145] of the criteria used by the administrative bodies and the judiciary to establish whether a person met the requirements for obtaining citizenship. According to Article 2 of this Regulation, a longer absence from Slovenia that could not be considered a tourist trip, as well as repeated longer absences indicating that the person returned to Slovenia only to circumvent the Regulation, were considered a termination of actually living in Slovenia. Paragraph 2 of the same article states that actually living in Slovenia was not to be considered terminated if the person had been sent to a foreign country by a Slovenian company to work, study, undergo medical treatment, or if the person was a crew member of a ship whose home harbour was in the Republic of Slovenia, because these reasons were beyond one's control.[146] This provision raises the question of why the above absences should be treated differently than, for example, the absence of a child who was sent abroad for schooling by parents (their decision being beyond the control of the child), or a self-initiated trip abroad for

---

the truthfulness of this statement, the reason for children's absence, and its duration. Supreme Court of the Republic of Slovenia, Ruling No. U 287/1992.

141 Supreme Court of the Republic of Slovenia, Ruling No. U 473/92.

142 Supreme Court of the Republic of Slovenia, Ruling No. U 1837/947. In this case, the appellant travelled to Bosnia-Herzegovina to spend there the Labour Day holiday. However, this coincided with the beginning of the war in Bosnia (late April) so he managed to return only in December 1992 with the help of the Red Cross.

143 Supreme Court of the Republic of Slovenia, Ruling No. Up 200/04-14.

144 Supreme Court of the Republic of Slovenia, Ruling No. U 781/93.

145 Uredba o merilih za ugotavljanje izpolnjevanja določenih pogojev za pridobitev državljanstva Republike Slovenije, Official Gazette of the Republic of Slovenia, No. 47/1994.

146 The provision in Article 2, Para 2 of the Regulation on the Criteria for Assessing the Fulfilment of Condition for the Gaining of Citizenship of the Republic of Slovenia by naturalisation was repeated several times in the bills that aimed to resolve the issue of erasure, for example, the proposals for the Constitutional Law in 2005 and 2007.

medical treatment if the person had good reasons to undertake it (for example, because the required medical treatment was not available in Slovenia).

The Supreme Court particularly stressed the argument of loyalty to the country. It adopted the viewpoint that, by stipulating the condition of actually living in Slovenia, the legislature expected applicants to truly meet this requirement at least during the period following the referendum, until they acquired citizenship. It was supposedly "the way" to express loyalty towards the country that they were applying to become citizens of during the "critical and uncertain" period immediately preceding and following Slovenia's independence.[147] The argument appears justified at first glance; since actually living in Slovenia was one of the requirements for obtaining citizenship, applicants should have been aware of it and should have taken into account the possibility that a longer period of study abroad could be taken as a termination of actually living in Slovenia, even if the decision to remain in Slovenia would require them to sacrifice their professional or personal preferences. However, the Supreme Court's stance overlooks one of the essential criteria relevant to determining whether a specific place is considered a domicile.

For a country to most accurately incorporate into its constituency those who have truly demonstrated their wish to join it, the definition of domicile involves two elements: the objective element, i.e. actually living in a specific place, and the subjective element, i.e. the intention of the person to live permanently in that specific place. If a person travels abroad for study or work without the intention of becoming a permanent resident of a foreign country, then the subjective condition is not fulfilled. In such a case, a person's domicile can only be the place from where he/she moved to another place to study or work. It also seems that in such cases the importance of loyalty was overstated, and that expectations regarding the expressions of loyalty were unrealistic. The individuals who studied or worked abroad probably did not give much thought to whether their absence from the country would be considered disloyal and prevent them from gaining citizenship. This suggests a discrepancy between the expectations of the government and people's awareness of what was expected from them to qualify for citizenship. If people accepted work abroad or went abroad to study, their move was not necessarily (or not at all) an expression of disloyalty, but rather of a desire to improve their lives or develop personally. Accordingly, it could be said that the

147 Supreme Court of the Republic of Slovenia, Rulings No. U 781/93 and U 562/93. See also Kutoš, Pregled sodne prakse Vrhovnega sodišča RS v zvezi s 40. členom Zakona o državljanstvu, in: Dnevi javnega prava, 1999, p. 638.

ruling of the Supreme Court effectively set out a hierarchy of values, with loyalty, which supposedly proceeded from one's physical presence in Slovenia, ranked higher than the desire to improve one's welfare. The requirement of actually living in Slovenia is indeed sensible when seen as representative of close ties with the country, but it should have been interpreted in its wider sense while taking into account the constitutional principle of proportionality.

Furthermore, long-term work abroad was also taken as the termination of actually living in Slovenia.[148] Even the ownership of property in Slovenia did not suffice if the person did not live there.[149] Similarly, persons who held seasonal jobs in Slovenia and returned to another republic for six months every year did not meet this requirement.[150] On the other hand, there were absences that were considered justified, such as the few-months-long absence of a person who went to Bosnia-Herzegovina to visit relatives in the summer of 1991 and was caught up in the war there. The Supreme Court determined that such circumstances were beyond the control of the person in question.[151] However, in such cases, general references to the war were not sufficient; the person was asked to submit proof that he/she could not return to Slovenia.[152]

Analysing the case law on denied applications for citizenship showed that the Supreme Court applied stricter criteria to citizens of other republics who were members of the Yugoslav People's Army (YPA). In processing the applications of non-YPA soldiers, the approach that gained currency was to take into account the period of a person's absence, the reasons for it, and the potential intention behind it. By contrast, in cases involving members of the YPA, their very departure along with their involvement with the YPA when it withdrew from Slovenia was considered a termination of living in Slovenia. The explanation was that army personnel were obliged to obey the YPA's orders and that their place of residence depended on these orders.[153] The practice of the Supreme Court was

---

148 For example, Supreme Court of the Republic of Slovenia, Ruling No. U 832/92.

149 Supreme Court of the Republic of Slovenia, Rulings No. U 1003/93-12 and U 204/94.

150 Supreme Court of the Republic of Slovenia, Ruling No. U 832/92-5. See also Kutoš, Pregled sodne prakse Vrhovnega sodišča RS v zvezi s 40. členom Zakona o državljanstvu, in: Dnevi javnega prava, 1999, pp. 63–636.

151 Supreme Court of the Republic of Slovenia, Ruling No. U 1837/94-7.

152 Supreme Court of the Republic of Slovenia, Ruling No. U 1489/93-4. See also Kutoš, Pregled sodne prakse Vrhovnega sodišča RS v zvezi s 40. členom Zakona o državljanstvu, in: Dnevi javnega prava, 1999, p. 638.

153 For example Supreme Court of the Republic of Slovenia, Rulings No. U 241/92 and U 753/92.

fully consistent with the view of the Executive Council of the Republic of Slovenia on the issue of whether the withdrawal from Slovenia and involvement with the YPA should be considered a justified, work-related absence. It issued a decision in June 1991 stating that the absence of active YPA members who declined the invitation of the Presidency of the Republic of Slovenia to join the territorial defence forces constituted the termination of one's residence in Slovenia.[154]

The Supreme Court observed the same rules even when YPA members and employees provided explicit reasons for living outside Slovenia for a period of time, such as the applicant who argued that he left Slovenia to be treated in the military hospital in Bosnia-Herzegovina, because the military hospital in Slovenia had closed down (the Supreme Court did not take a stance on his statement).[155] Another applicant stated that he submitted his resignation to the YPA within one month of moving away from Slovenia because he did not want to leave, and he supported his claim with a document proving that his employment with the YPA ended on 27 November 1991, but the Supreme Court did not take his statement into account. When the Constitutional Court judged this specific case, it ruled that "decisions on whether or not to grant citizenship under Article 40 of the Citizenship of the Republic of Slovenia Act based merely on the explanation that a person's departure from the Republic of Slovenia with the YPA and his/her continued employment with the YPA constituted the termination of actually living in the Republic of Slovenia, without establishing the decisive factors, is in contradiction with the provision guaranteeing equal protection of rights as stipulated by Article 22 of the Constitution".[156] In the opinion of the Constitutional Court, the Supreme Court should have established all the relevant facts that could confirm or refute the explanation mentioned above. This argument seems strong, because YPA employees were placed in a worse position than other citizens of other SFRY republics by being denied the possibility of arguing that their absence was beyond their control.

154 Executive Council of the Assembly of the Republic of Slovenia, Decision No. 22610, dated 27 June 1991.

155 Supreme Court of the Republic of Slovenia, Ruling No. U 1083/92.

156 Constitutional Court of the Republic of Slovenia, Ruling No. Up-77/94 dated 16 September, 1997.

3.2.4 *The Exclusion Clause of Posing a Threat to the Public Order, Security, or Defence of the Country*

As mentioned earlier, in international law citizenship is not a right but an option offered to an individual, or a privilege gained if the individual meets the legal requirements and if the individual interests of a person applying for citizenship concur with the "national interest".[157]

The protection of Slovenia's national interest found expression in an amendment to Article 40 of the Citizenship of the Republic of Slovenia Act,[158] which came into force on 14 December 1991, when the six-month window for submitting applications for citizenship was about to close. The amendment introduced two new paragraphs (Paragraphs 2 and 3) containing exclusion clauses. According to Paragraph 2, applications for citizenship were rejected regardless of whether a person fulfilled other conditions,

> if, since 26.6.1991, the person has committed a criminal offence under Chapter 15 or 16 of the Penal Code of the Socialist Federal Republic of Yugoslavia (Official Gazette of the Socialist Federal Republic of Yugoslavia, No. 44/76, 34/84, 74/87, 57/89, 3/90 and 38/90), directed against the Republic of Slovenia or other values that in accordance with the provision of Article 4, Paragraph 1 of the Constitutional Act Implementing the Basic Constitutional Charter on the Independence and Sovereignty of the Republic of Slovenia are protected by the criminal laws of the Republic of Slovenia, irrespective of where the offence was committed. If criminal proceedings were instigated for the offence, the procedure for the acquisition of citizenship shall be pending until the criminal proceedings are finally finished.

The new Paragraph 3 stipulated that "regardless of whether the person fulfils the conditions under Paragraph 1 of this Article, the application may be rejected if the reasons under Article 10, Item 8 hereof apply to the applicant". In other words, it excluded persons who could present a threat to the public order, security, or defence of the state.[159] Judging by available sources, the reason for amending Article 40 was "changed circumstances following the military assault on Slovenia", since the original text of Article 40 dated from the period when it was

---

157 Supreme Court of the Republic of Slovenia, Ruling No. U 634/95-7. See also Kutoš, Pregled sodne prakse Vrhovnega sodišča RS v zvezi s 40. členom Zakona o državljanstvu, in: Dnevi javnega prava, 1999, p. 633.

158 Zakon o dopolnitvi Zakona o državljanstvu Republike Slovenije, Official Gazette of the Republic of Slovenia, No. 30/1991I.

159 Zakon o dopolnitvi zakona o državljanstvu Republike Slovenije, Official Gazette of the Republic of Slovenia, No. 30/1991I, in connection with Article 10, Para 1, Item 8 of the Citizenship of the Republic of Slovenia Act.

still possible to expect a peaceful resolution to the Yugoslav crisis.[160] By inserting these two additional requirements, the legislator further curtailed the promise given in the Statement of Good Intentions, as well as the provision in Article 13 of the CAIBCC, which did not contain conditions of exclusion.

The new Paragraph 2, which refers to criminal offences against the nation and the state, proved to be completely useless, since the offence had to be committed against the person's own nation and the state. However, at the time of the assault, Slovenia was already an independent state, thus, it was another country and another nation with respect to members of the Yugoslav army. Consequently, all criminal complaints against individuals who were citizens of other republics or citizens of the SFRY were turned down, because one of the elements of the crime (one's own nation or own country) was not established. Instead, all situations that were originally intended to be covered by Paragraph 2 of Article 40, were processed on the basis of the new Paragraph 3, which stipulated the rejection of citizenship if the person posed a threat to the public order, security, and defence of the State. The administrative fact-finding procedures at the Ministry of the Interior responsible for citizenship issues, were, according to Končina, carried out in cooperation with the Ministry of Defence, the Security and Intelligence Department, using the police and physical persons as witnesses.[161] For this purpose, a "blacklist" was compiled, which we will discuss below. The application of Paragraph 3 instead of Paragraph 2 was specious, since it was inconsistent with the reason for including these conditions.[162] Paragraph 2 was added for the purpose of preventing persons who had previously committed criminal offences (during the war of independence) from acquiring citizenship. Paragraph 3, which excluded persons who could pose a threat to the security and defence of the country in the future, should not have been used to do what Paragraph 2 could not (more on this below).

The application of the new Paragraph 3 led to the development of extensive case law. However, neither the Supreme Court nor the Constitutional Court upheld the argument that it was unlawful to apply Paragraph 3 instead of Paragraph 2 when assessing acts committed in the past. The courts only established that general statements used by administrative bodies were not sufficient proof

---

160 Končina, Zakon o državljanstvu Republike Slovenije s komentarjem, 1993, p. 132; Mesojedec Pervinšek, Predpisi o državljanih in tujcih z uvodnimi pojasnili, 1997, p. 27.

161 Končina, Zakon o državljanstvu Republike Slovenije s komentarjem, 1993, p. 136.

162 Dedić, Jalušič, Zorn: The Erased: Organized Innocence and the Politics of Exclusion, 2003, p. 63.

to reject an application for citizenship on the grounds of a threat to the security and defence of the country, and demanded that administrative bodies provide specific explanations of when, where, and in which way the YPA member in question operated against the interests of the Republic of Slovenia.[163] This same standard was to be applied to former YPA assistance staff (nurses, typists, technical staff, flight controllers).[164]

The Regulation[165] on the criteria to establish whether the requirements for gaining citizenship of the Republic of Slovenia through naturalisation had been met (mentioned above) contained a passage that referred to the potential threat to the security and defence of the country. It stipulated that in certain cases one's rank in the YPA, if high enough, could represent a threat,[166] meaning that the very possession of such a rank sufficed to reject the application and that person's circumstances were not assessed at all. Even stricter rules applied to the members of the intelligence services; employment in such a service, regardless of rank, sufficed for the rejection of the application for citizenship.[167] Later on, the practice of the Supreme Court changed. In 1997 it decided that an applicant's YPA rank *per se* did not suffice for the rejection of citizenship, and required that the person's subsequent actions and participation in the assault on Slovenia be investigated.[168] The case law on applications that were denied because of a threat to the public order developed during the period that this provision was in force. Persons who had already been penalised for a single criminal offence, and even some persons who were never prosecuted, were excluded from citizenship.[169]

---

163 Supreme Court of the Republic of Slovenia, Ruling No. U 777/92-6.

164 Supreme Court of the Republic of Slovenia, Rulings No. U 823/93-5, U 1086/95-5, U 778/92-6 and U 1186/92-7. *See also* tudi Kutoš, Pregled sodne prakse Vrhovnega sodišča RS v zvezi s 40. členom Zakona o državljanstvu, in: Dnevi javnega prava, 1999, p. 645.

165 Official Gazette of the Republic of Slovenia, No. 47/1994.

166 Supreme Court of the Republic of Slovenia, Ruling No. U 325/93-6. *See also* Kutoš, Pregled sodne prakse Vrhovnega sodišča RS v zvezi s 40. členom Zakona o državljanstvu, in: Dnevi javnega prava, 1999, p. 645.

167 During that period the situation was very similar to that in Estonia and Latvia, where the Russian members of armed forces and intelligence services were prevented from obtaining citizenship.

168 Supreme Court of the Republic of Slovenia, Ruling No. U 1577/94-7. *See also* Kutoš, Pregled sodne prakse Vrhovnega sodišča RS v zvezi s 40. členom Zakona o državljanstvu, in: Dnevi javnega prava, 1999, p. 646.

169 Supreme Court of the Republic of Slovenia, Rulings No. No. U 317/94-4, U 1686/94-4, U 632/92 and U 688/92. *See also* Kutoš, Pregled sodne prakse Vrhovnega sodišča

Six years later, the Constitutional Court decided that the provision in Article 40, Para 3 of the Citizenship of the Republic of Slovenia Act, which refers to a threat to public order, was unconstitutional. The court's explanation was that this clause was not grounded in a predominant and legitimate public interest that would justify nullifying the protection of legitimate expectations, and that the persons excluded on this ground should have been granted citizenship. The legislative material behind the Act clearly shows that the "legitimate public interest" was to prevent persons who participated in the assault on Slovenia or whose conduct was expressly disloyal at the time when Slovenia was gaining independence from acquiring citizenship; the public interest was defined as the protection of the state, its security, and defence.[170]

3.2.5 The Issue of Retroactive Additional Requirements for Granting Citizenship

Since the amendments to the Citizenship of the Republic of Slovenia Act were added at a time when people were already submitting applications for citizenship and the final deadline to do so was approaching, it is a question whether the retroactive use of the provision in the new Paragraph 3 of Article 40 was legitimate.

- *The Retroactivity of General Legal Acts*

The Constitution of the Republic of Slovenia prohibits the retroactive application of laws, other regulations, and general acts (Article 155, Paragraph 1). It is allowed only under special conditions determined on the constitutional level. In fact, retroactivity essentially contradicts the purpose of general acts (laws, implementing acts), which is to instruct the public how to behave and what to do in specific circumstances. This is also the reason why laws always take effect following the date of their entry into force – it is a prerequisite for legal predictability and reliability, which are the elements of legal certainty. Retroactivity generally contradicts these principles and is therefore not permissible in states ruled by law, because legal subjects could not predict the consequences (penalties imposed by retroactive provisions) at the time when they acted in a specific manner.

Nevertheless, in practice there are situations in which retroactivity does not implicate these concerns, or only does so to a small degree, but a retroactive

RS v zvezi s 40. členom Zakona o državljanstvu, in: Dnevi javnega prava, 1999, pp. 642–643.

170 Dedić, Jalušič, Zorn, The Erased: Organized Innocence and the Politics of Exclusion, 2003, p. 65.

measure nevertheless must be consistent with the Constitution. Such a situation is envisaged by the provision in Article 155, Paragraph 2 of the Constitution, which states that "a law may only establish that certain of its provisions have retroactive effect, if this is required in the public interest and provided that no acquired rights are infringed thereby". The main requirement that must be met in such cases is that a retroactive provision serves the public interest and that it does not interfere with rights that have already been individualised and recognised by way of individual legal acts.[171]

- *The Retroactive Effect of Additional Requirements for Gaining Citizenship*

Several applicants who were denied citizenship appealed to the Supreme Court, the Constitutional Court, or both, objecting to the retroactive effect of the new provisions. The Supreme Court overruled these objections, concluding that the administrative body assessed the application for citizenship based on the provisions that were valid at the time when the decision was issued, as stipulated by the then-valid Administrative Dispute Act, rather than in accordance with the provisions that were valid at the time when the application was submitted. Accordingly, it ruled that the provision did not have a retroactive effect and should not be used retroactively.[172] The Supreme Court referred back to a decision of the Constitutional Court which stressed that, in accordance with Article 15 of the Citizenship of the Republic of Slovenia Act, an applicant becomes a Slovenian citizen on the date when the citizenship certificate is handed to the applicant,[173] and thus his/her rights proceeding from citizenship are protected from that moment onwards.

The decision of the Constitutional Court is consistent with the fact that citizenship has not yet become a right either in domestic or international law, so it is not possible to gain citizenship by way of a lawsuit against the state (except if the person involved is a child who would otherwise become stateless).[174] Citizenship

---

171 Pavčnik, Teorija prava, 1997, pp. 17–173.

172 Supreme Court of the Republic of Slovenia, Ruling No. U 688/92.

173 Constitutional Court of the Republic of Slovenia, Ruling No. U-I-147/92. *See also* Mesojedec Pervinšek, Predpisi o državljanih in tujcih z uvodnimi pojasnili, 1997, p. 51.

174 Although in international law citizenship has not yet been constituted as a right, the states should endeavour to achieve it after the example of the American Convention on Human Rights, which acknowledges this right. In most countries, citizenship is a pre-right, enabling a person to access other rights (i.e. the right to have a right). In Slovenia, this role is played by the status of permanent resident, which enables access to almost the same set of rights as enjoyed by citizens, save for the voting right,

is therefore still considered a privilege granted to a person by an administrative body if he/she meets the legal requirements. The interest of the state here still prevails over the interest of an individual.[175]

The Decision of the Constitutional Court is apparently consistent with Article 155 of the Constitution, which permits a retroactive effect if it serves the public interest and if it does not infringe on acquired rights. Since a person becomes a citizen of the country on the date when he/she receives the citizenship certificate, the rights of citizenship are conferred only on that date and not on the date when the application for citizenship is submitted. Theoretically, the requirements for obtaining citizenship could therefore change countless times during the period between the application date and the date of issuing a citizenship certificate, even if this had negative implications for the individual.

The above discussion begs the question of what the principle of legal expectations means. It guarantees that the state will not arbitrarily, i.e. without solid grounds in the public interest, aggravate a person's legal situation.[176] This principle was emphasised in the dissenting opinion of Judge Krivic, who pointed out that the first version of the Citizenship of the Republic of Slovenia Act enabled the citizens of other SFRY republics who had their permanent residence registered in Slovenia and actually lived there to obtain Slovenian citizenship upon fulfilling the sole requirement of submitting the application by the prescribed date. Article 13 of CAIBCC, from which these persons' right to citizenship proceeded, did not anticipate discretionary decisions by the administrative body; the legislature thus enacted the "expectancy right" according to which people came to rely on validly enacted legal provisions and adapted their conduct thereto. Judge Krivic pointed out that perhaps they would have acted in a different way had citizenship not been guaranteed to them under these particular conditions. The law was amended to the disadvantage of the applicants when many of them had already filed their applications for citizenship and fulfilled the requirements that were valid at that time. In the opinion of Judge Krivic, the state breached the principle of legitimate expectation, but its conduct was not necessarily unconstitutional. In

---

the right to be employed in the state administration, etc. However, the constitution/establishment of this right is important in the countries that do not recognise permanent resident status. In such countries, persons who live there without being citizens of the country are deprived of their "right to have rights". *Cf.* Arendt, The Origins of Totalitarianism, 2003, p. 377.

175 Mesojedec Pervinšek, Predpisi o državljanih in tujcih z uvodnimi pojasnili, 1997, p. 28.

176 Constitutional Court of the Republic of Slovenia, Ruling No. U-I-123/92.

analysing the provisions in Article 40, Para 2 and Article 40, Para 3, Judge Krivic weighed the principle of legitimate expectation against that of the predominant public interest, and concluded as follows:

> … if at the time of gaining independence the state gave an assurance to its residents without citizenship that all of them would gain citizenship, including persons who are potentially dangerous for the state – if, as said, it assured them so at the time when its security and defence had been much more threatened than half a year later, when the amendments to the legislation objected herein were adopted, there seems to exist no solid reason to breach this legal or constitutional promise subsequently, during a period that is more peaceful and secure.[177]

Judge Krivic pointed out that the amended law was passed several months after the assault on Slovenia had ended and after the persons who were affected by this amendment had already adopted certain conducts and approaches that were later "condemned" by rejecting their application for citizenship. However, had they been aware that their specific conduct could prevent them from gaining citizenship, perhaps they would have acted differently.

As mentioned earlier, in 1999 the Constitutional Court Decision[178] only invalidated the part of the provision that referred to the protection of the public order, while the part referring to the security and defence of the state remained in force. Judge Čebulj disagreed with this decision. In his dissenting opinion he stated that the subject of the Constitutional Court's ruling was not the retroactive effect of Article 40, Para 3 of the amended Citizenship of the Republic of Slovenia Act, because this provision did not have a retroactive effect, but whether the subsequently added provision could be applied to applications that had been submitted before the provision came into force.

> As regards this issue, the Constitutional Court should first establish the presence or absence of the prevailing reasons of public interest that would exact the use of the amended provision when assessing applications that were submitted before the provision came into force, and if such reasons did not exist, whether the principle of legal expectations exacts the use of the provision before it was amended rather than the amended provision in cases involving applicants who at the time when they submitted the application met the requirements stipulated in Article 40 of ZDRS [Citizenship of the Republic of Slovenia Act], particularly if at the time when the amended provision came into force the prescribed [sixty-day] period for the issuing of citizenship certificates had already expired.[179]

177 Supreme Court of the Republic of Slovenia, Ruling No. U 688/92.
178 Constitutional Court of the Republic of Slovenia, Ruling No. U-I-89/99.
179 Constitutional Court of the Republic of Slovenia, Ruling No. U-I-89/99.

It is difficult to overlook the fact that many applicants submitted their applications before the amended Citizenship of the Republic of Slovenia Act came into force, and that the provisions changed during the period in which their applications were processed. One can imagine the situation of applicants who submitted their applications between June and October. Since at that time the amendments were not yet in force, all those who met the requirements initially stipulated by Article 40 would have been granted citizenship. However, if the application was not resolved within the legally prescribed sixty-day period, the consequence was that the criteria applied were stricter than those valid at the time when the application was submitted.

To illustrate the implications, let us imagine that two applicants who had been previously prosecuted for comparable criminal offences submitted their applications during this period. One would have been granted Slovenian citizenship, because the certificate was issued before the new provision came into force, while the other would not have been, because his certificate was issued after the new provision came into force (here we assume that the administrative bodies did not intentionally prolong the procedure for problematic applicants knowing that the new provision was on the way and that it would enable them to reject all such applicants). In such a case, the application of the amended law during the administrative procedure would constitute a violation of the constitutional right to equality before the law.

In addition, there is another aspect to the retroactive effect, i.e. the retroactivity proceeding from the method of applying the provision in the new Para 3 of Article 40. When applying the exclusion clause concerning a threat to the security and defence of the country, the Ministry of the Interior assessed the threat posed by the individual in the past (i.e. at the time when Slovenia fought the war for independence) rather than at the time when the application for citizenship was processed.[180] The Ministry should have determined if the person was likely to pose a threat in the future, after he/she became a citizen of Slovenia. Instead, it evaluated the threats posed in the past, meaning that the rejection of citizenship on these grounds in effect penalised the applicant's past conduct.

The amendment to Article 40 of the Citizenship of the Republic of Slovenia Act and the method of its implementation led some to describe the Statement of Good Intentions as a political fraud concocted by those who performed the erasure. Indeed, for the people who were denied citizenship on the grounds of the

180 Dedić, Jalušič, Zorn, The Erased: Organized Innocence and the Politics of Exclusion, 2003, p. 64.

new provisions in Article 40, the amendment annulled the meaning of the Statement of Good Intentions. Its promise of political equality was in reality replaced with a moral (and often prejudiced) assessment of the applicants.[181]

We cannot help but agree that the Statement of Good Intentions was a fraud. Its aim was to attract the greatest possible number of people to vote in favour of Slovenia's independence and it was motivated by apprehension about the outcome of the referendum. The Statement contained so many promises that the majority in the Assembly could justifiably expect high support for independence.[182] The promise of equal treatment and preservation of their acquired rights secured the support of people who were soon after arbitrarily deprived of their status.

3.2.6 The Exclusion Clauses and the Role of Courts

What, then, was the point of the exclusion clause contained in the new Paragraph 3 of Article 40? When it became clear that restrictive provisions which could prevent unwanted persons from obtaining citizenship could not be included in the Citizenship of the Republic of Slovenia Act, the executives at the Republic's Secretariat for Defence and the Secretariat for Administrative Internal Affairs (today the Ministry of Defence and the Ministry of the Interior) began to compile a "blacklist", that is, a list of people who were to be prohibited entry into Slovenia after the country gained independence and who were not entitled to gain citizenship. The list was compiled secretly, based on intelligence service information. It included all the employees of the Yugoslav army and individuals who the government suspected were opposed to the independence of Slovenia, such as people who had contacts with Belgrade-based media.[183]

The criteria were obviously general, and the goal was to create a list of people who were to be removed.[184] The number of people on that list cannot be determined precisely.[185] Various sources suggest that the list was compiled based on citizens' denouncements, meaning that the Secretariats relied on general accusations and did not have credible information on whether or not these persons truly posed a threat to the security and defence of Slovenia. In 1997, the

---

181 "We, the Ethno-Citizens of Ethno-Democracy", in Journal for the Critique of Science, 35 (2007) 228, pp. 60–61.

182 Interview with Lev Kreft, 14 July 2011.

183 *Ibid.*

184 *Ibid.*

185 In 1994, it was said that 235 people were on the list; in April 1995 the figure was said to be 778, and still later 655. The parliamentary Committee for Defence asked the Ministry of the Interior to provide the list, but the request was denied "for operative reasons".

then Minister of the Interior, Mirko Bandelj, publicly admitted that the ban on entering Slovenia for blacklisted people was of "a political nature", that it "was not grounded in regulations and that viewed from the perspective of rule of law and the protection of human rights, it was untenable". Unfortunately, this confession did not trigger a procedure to establish who was responsible for it.[186]

The blacklist was compiled unlawfully. The leading officials at the Ministry of Defence and the Ministry of the Interior were obviously aware of the blacklist's unlawfulness. They thus amended Article 40 to legitimise their activities in spite of the fact that applications for citizenship were already coming in. What is my basis for this argument? As follows from the above explanation of the amendment, the Ministry of the Interior decided to issue said amendment shortly before the expiration of the deadline for submitting applications because of the "events that happened after Slovenia gained independence", and because of the fact that some applicants allegedly "participated directly in the assault on Slovenia", or whose "conduct was disloyal". In the opinion of the lawmakers, they were motivated exclusively by "material benefits", for example, the purchase of the apartments in which they lived,[187] military pensions, etc. to apply for citizenship, while their conduct proved that they were not willing to accept citizenship as "an integral relationship with the state" and that they did not intend to "be subordinate to its sovereignty as loyal citizens".[188]

The amendment went into force very quickly. Rather than observing the common 15-day term between the publication of the law and its entry into force, it went into force a few days after it was passed by the National Assembly, on 14 December 1991, when it was published in the official gazette of Slovenia. At that time, Slovenia's sovereignty was beginning to be recognised internationally, and the three-month moratorium on the independence process was nearing its end. Certain members of the left-wing opposition parties opposed the amendment, maintaining that citizenship had no connection whatsoever with alleged war crimes and that such acts were subject to other sanctions. However, they had no chance of convincing the right-wing parliamentary majority. The situation on

---

186 Mekina, I., The Erasure of the Erasure, in Journal for the Critique of Science, 35 (2007) 228, p. 185.

187 While Slovenia was part of Yugoslavia, a large part of the population lived in publicly owned apartments to which they held the so-called occupancy right. After it gained independence, these apartments were privatised but only persons with Slovenian citizenship had the right to purchase them.

188 Predlog Zakona o dopolnitvah ZDRS z dne 21. 10. 1991 and the Constitutional Court of the Republic of Slovenia, Ruling No. U-I-89/99.

the domestic political stage became tense. Following the ten-day war and international recognition of the new state, the coalition and the opposition could no longer reach any agreement. All the obstacles were removed and the nationalist ideology and exclusionary policies began to flourish.

Article 40 of the Citizenship of the Republic of Slovenia Act thus was amended primarily to enable the achievement of goals associated with the secretly compiled blacklist. Applications for citizenship by blacklisted persons could now be processed—or rather denied—on the grounds of the amended Article 40.

The amended Article 40, which provided the Ministry of the Interior the right to deny applications on the grounds of "the protection of national interest", served as the basis for rejecting 449 applications.[189] Most of the applicants were YPA officers who allegedly actively participated in the assault on Slovenia, civilians who presumably collaborated with the YPA security service, and perpetrators of serious crimes "whose lives so far suggest that they will commit crimes in the future as well".[190] It should be stressed that all the civilians who worked for the Yugoslav army, for example, hospital staff, were also denied citizenship. The analysis of the legal order and practice shows that if the prescribed time limit for resolving applications for citizenship was observed, the applications that had been submitted more than 60 days before the amendment came into force could not be rejected. The Ministry used the right with retroactive effect that was indeed consistent with Article 155 of the Slovenian Constitution, although its consistency with Article 2 of the Constitution and the principle of legitimate expectations is doubtful. By confirming this unlawful administrative practice, the courts helped the Ministry implement the provision. The requirements imposed by the courts were superficial, for example the obligation to specify how a specific action contradicted the interests of Slovenia.

3.3 The Situation of Children

Despite the clarity of the provision in Article 40, Para 4 of the Citizenship of the Republic of Slovenia Act, which regulated the acquisition of citizenship by children under 18 (who could obtain Slovenian citizenship if one of their parents obtained it),[191] its interpretation was sometimes highly unusual in practice.

---

189 Mesojedec Pervinšek, Predpisi o državljanih in tujcih z uvodnimi pojasnili, 1997, p. 28.

190 *Ibid.*

191 Initially the second paragraph, and later the fourth paragraph of amended Article 40 of the Citizenship of the Republic of Slovenia Act.

In accordance with this provision and the related Article 14 of the same act, the parents or guardians of a child under 18 were responsible for submitting the child's application for citizenship. In one such case, the parents submitted the application but the child came of age before the application was resolved. The child was not granted citizenship because, the court reasoned, the conditions of gaining citizenship stipulated in Article 14 did not apply to a person who was no longer underage, so the applicant had to meet the conditions set out in Article 40, Para 1 (registered permanent address, actually living in Slovenia). The child allegedly did not meet these conditions, since it was established that he/she lived with his/her parents in Germany. However, the father of the child obtained Slovenian citizenship after the independence. The Supreme Court ruled that this decision violated the right of the child. The applicant should have been treated as a child even though he/she came of age in the meantime, and the child should have been granted Slovenian citizenship because his/her father was granted Slovenian citizenship.[192]

In a similar example, a child was denied citizenship because his/her application was not resolved within the prescribed 60-day period, and by the time it was finally resolved, the child had come of age. The Supreme Court upheld the complaint and explained as follows:

> If the child was underage at the time when the application was submitted in accordance with Article 40, Para 4 of the Citizenship of the Republic of Slovenia Act, and if the sued party did not resolve the application within the 60-day period but later, when the child had already come of age, and consequently rejected the application on the grounds that one of the conditions set out in Article 40, Para 1 of ZDRS was not met, the constitutional rights of the child and the provisions of the UN Convention on the Rights of the Child were violated, according to which the priority in the procedure should be given to the rights of the child if both parents were granted the citizenship of the Republic of Slovenia. The provisions in the Constitution (Article 56) and in the Convention on the Rights of the Child prevail over the provisions in the Citizenship of the Republic of Slovenia Act and over references to the principle of legality.[193]

The Supreme Court also found a violation of the Convention on the Rights of the Child in a case involving a child who was legally disowned by his/her parents. The child's application was rejected with a formalist explanation; the court stated that according to Article 40, Para 4 of the Citizenship of the Republic of Slovenia Act and Article 14 therein, a child under 18 can only gain citizenship if his/her

192 Supreme Court of the Republic of Slovenia, Ruling No. U 1092/924.
193 Supreme Court of the Republic of Slovenia, Ruling No. U 426/93.

parents, or one of the parents who gained Slovenian citizenship, apply on behalf of the child. The Supreme Court ruled that the law referred to normal situations in which parents exercised their parental rights, but in this case the child's parents had renounced their parental rights and duties. Since the child was not adopted, he/she should have been treated as an independent person, because any other approach would be in contravention of the UN Convention on the Rights of the Child.[194]

3.4 Remedying Certain Shortcomings in the Legislation on Citizenship

Some of the erased firmly believed that they held Slovenian republic citizenship (but could not prove it) so they expected to obtain citizenship automatically, in accordance with Article 39 of the Citizenship of the Republic of Slovenia Act. Since republic citizenship in the former Yugoslavia was not duly recorded, and because these failures could deprive certain people who lived in Slovenia of citizenship, two corrections to the Citizenship of the Republic of Slovenia Act were adopted in 1994[195] to eliminate this shortcoming.[196] The corrections introduced two additional methods of gaining Slovenian citizenship: through an avowal and through a statement. By adopting these two corrections, the government implicitly admitted that the provision in the previous law put people at the risk of becoming stateless. The newly added Article 39a stipulated that a person whose permanent address was registered in the Republic of Slovenia on 23 December 1990, or had actually been living in Slovenia continuously since that date, should be considered a citizen of the Republic of Slovenia if he/she could have acquired Slovenian citizenship pursuant to Article 37 of the Citizenship of the Federal People's Republic of Yugoslavia Act but had instead acquired the citizenship of another republic of the former Yugoslavia by 21 December 1950.[197] The applicant was asked to submit documents that served as a legal basis for acquiring citizenship of another SFRY republic, but if he/she could not produce such documents and unequivocally stated so, his/her statement was taken as proof.

---

194 Supreme Court of the Republic of Slovenia, Ruling No. U 679/93.

195 Zakon o spremembah in dopolnitvah Zakona o državljanstvu Republike Slovenije, Official Gazette of the Republic of Slovenia, No. 13/1994.

196 Medved, From Civic to Ethnic Community?, in Citizenship Policies in the New Europe, 2007, p. 218.

197 Mesojedec Pervinšek, Predpisi o državljanih in tujcih z uvodnimi pojasnili, 1997, p. 20.

This provision was useful for persons of Slovenian ethnic origin who in the past held citizenship of another republic (e.g. because their parents lived in another SFRY republic) but could have gained Slovenian republic citizenship had they requested it. The law therefore somewhat ameliorated the fact that republic citizenship, which in the SFRY did not have a practical application and was thus largely ignored,[198] became the main connecting element for the automatic acquisition of citizenship.

Another additional option was introduced by Article 41.[199] Under this new article, citizenship could be granted to persons who were born in Slovenia and were over eighteen, if one of their parents had Slovenian republic citizenship when they were born but decided that the child should be assigned another republic's citizenship. These persons were asked to declare their Slovenian citizenship in a statement that had to be submitted before they reached the age of 23.[200] This alleviated the situation of younger people who, at the time of Slovenia's independence, were convinced that they would gain Slovenian citizenship automatically, and thus did not apply for it. They learned that they did not have Slovenian citizenship only after the deadline for submitting an application had expired.

3.5 Statistical Data on Citizenships Granted under Article 40 of the Citizenship of the Republic of Slovenia Act and Related Circumstances

Of the total number of applications for citizenship (174168) under Article 40 of the Citizenship of the Republic of Slovenia Act, 170996 persons gained citizenship;[201] this group makes up 8.7 per cent of all the permanent residents of Slovenia (regardless of citizenship). As a rule, these citizens then held dual citizenship, because they also acquired the citizenship of another SFRY successor

198 Jovanović, Državljanstvo socijalističke federativne republike Jugoslavije, 1977, p. 66.

199 Zakon o spremembah in dopolnitvah Zakona o državljanstvu Republike Slovenije, Official Gazette of the Republic of Slovenia, No. 13/1994.

200 Medved, From Civic to Ethnic Community?, in Citizenship Policies in the New Europe, 2007, p. 219.

201 Certain later sources give a higher number – 171,125. *Cf.* Medved, From Civic to Ethnic Community?, in Citizenship Policies in the New Europe, 2007, p. 219.

state in accordance with the continuity principle; release from previous citizenship was not required under Article 40.[202]

Most citizenship certificates were issued by May 1992. 2417 applications were rejected; of these, 449 were rejected based on Para 3 of Article 40. 234 people died before their applications were resolved. 348 applications were rejected because the applicants missed the deadline for submission, which expired on 25 December 1991. In 13 cases the processing of the application was stopped.[203]

The available sources reveal that the number of applications for citizenship exceeded expectations, as the expected number was around 80000. The increase was attributed to the passage of the Housing Act,[204] (dubbed Jazbinšek Act), which came into force on 19 October 1991. According to this law, a person had to be a citizen of the Republic of Slovenia to own real estate in Slovenia.[205] As a matter of fact, 70 per cent of all applications were submitted after the Housing Act came into force.[206] Another wave of applications followed the international recognition of Slovenia. In the opinion of Končina, these were submitted by applicants "who until then believed that Yugoslavia would not break up", but "lost their hope".[207] Another motivation was the fact that the right to withdraw deposits for military pensions and the right to pension bonuses was tied to Slovenian citizenship.[208] However, no one has attributed an increase in applications towards the end of 1991 to an obvious reason: the deadline for submitting applications was approaching as war broke out in the other SFRY republics, so many realised that they could not return to their homes and that as citizens of Slovenia they could help their relatives in war-torn regions survive.[209]

Statements about the reasons that led people to apply for citizenship obviously stress material benefits that people were trying to access by applying for citizenship. This would not be controversial had these statements been uttered

---

202 This rule had exceptions, as all persons whose republican citizenship was not duly recorded had single citizenship after gaining Slovenian citizenship.

203 Mesojedec Pervinšek, Predpisi o državljanih in tujcih z uvodnimi pojasnili, 1997, p. 32.

204 Stanovanjski zakon, Official Gazette of the Republic of Slovenia, No. 18/1991I.

205 Mesojedec Pervinšek, Predpisi o državljanih in tujcih z uvodnimi pojasnili, 1997, p. 32.

206 *Ibid.*

207 Končina, Zakon o državljanstvu Republike Slovenije s komentarjem, 1993, p. 11 and 136.

208 *Ibid.*, p. 12.

209 Interview with Lev Kreft, 14 July 2011.

in a context describing the historical circumstances and facts which characterise a certain period. However, keeping in mind the atmosphere at the time, and given the fact that there were subsequent demands to revoke citizenships granted under Article 40 and that the same reasons were put forward in an attempt to vindicate the erasure (and these pretexts are still in place, as is evident from the government's response to the ECHR ruling), these statements should be read as an expression of intolerance towards the citizens of other SFRY republics, who remained "here" rather than "going back" and who obviously intended to remain in Slovenia in the future as well.

The demographic composition of the group that gained citizenship under Article 40 was as follows: 46 per cent had the republic citizenship of Bosnia-Herzegovina, 34 per cent had Croatian republic citizenship, 13 per cent Serbian, three per cent Macedonian, and slightly less than three per cent Montenegrin; 27 per cent of applicants were underage, and 73 per cent were over 18. Of the total number of citizens of other SFRY republics who were granted citizenship under Article 40, as many as 30 per cent were born in Slovenia. Regarding this group's level of education, 60 per cent had elementary education, 20 per cent vocational education, and ten per cent had secondary school education or higher. Around 20 per cent of the applicants were unemployed.[210] One study showed that around 80 per cent of those who gained citizenship were unskilled workers. In most cases, all family members gained citizenship (but in some instances individual family members were erased). The average duration of residence in Slovenia of persons who gained citizenship was approximately eight years (from five to fifteen years in Slovenia).[211]

The impression gained from the above statistics corresponds to migration trends in the former Yugoslavia. Migrants who moved from other SFRY republics to Slovenia were mainly workers with lower levels of education, most of them coming from Bosnia-Herzegovina. Furthermore, these statistics also offer information on the erased people. As I will describe in more detail later in the text, the proportion of underage persons among the erased (20 per cent) was somewhat lower than the proportion of underage people in the group who gained citizenship under Article 40, but much higher than one would expect (more than 5000 children were erased). The common belief among the general public was that the erased were mainly members of the YPA who allegedly took part in the

---

210 Mesojedec Pervinšek, Predpisi o državljanih in tujcih z uvodnimi pojasnili, 1997, pp. 33–34.

211 Končina, Zakon o državljanstvu Republike Slovenije s komentarjem, 1993, p. 135.

assault on Slovenia. However, the data show that "only" 449 applications were rejected based on Article 40, Para 3, and these were probably persons who were blacklisted. Of these, only the applications rejected on the ground of a threat to the security and defence of the country can be associated with the members of the Yugoslav army, many of who were assistant personnel rather than officers. Given this number and keeping in mind the erased included 5000 children and unskilled immigrant workers from other republics, the generalisation that the erased people (25000 altogether according to the official data of the Ministry of the Interior) were members of the Yugoslav Army and aggressors against independent Slovenia is not grounded in fact.

At the time when Slovenia gained independence, there were around 200000 citizens of other SFRY republics living in Slovenia; around 29000 of them did not gain citizenship. Of these, some submitted applications but were denied (2417). Others did not apply for citizenship for various reasons, either because they were born in Slovenia and thought that they would obtain it automatically, or because they feared that by gaining Slovenian citizenship they would lose citizenship of another SFRY successor state and with it certain rights (e.g. the right to property they possessed there), or they simply did not want to apply for citizenship because they wanted to continue to live in Slovenia as foreigners with a permanent residence permit. Many believed that by taking Slovenian citizenship they would renounce their ethnic origins.[212] Perhaps some among them could colloquially be called manipulators, but that is not a legal category and certainly not a justifiable reason for depriving a person of his/her legal status. Furthermore, there are people who maintain that they applied for citizenship but their applications were never resolved,[213] and others who attempted to apply for citizenship but had their applications refused by government employees under various pretences. Although many persons reported such incidents and said reports are consistent, government representatives still refuse to acknowledge that such incidents ever occurred.[214] For example, many people who attempted to submit applications with the municipal body for internal affairs in Ljubljana stated that they were

212 Interview with Lev Kreft, 14 July 2011.

213 Kogovšek, Izbris kot kršitev pravno zavarovanih človekovih pravic, in: Brazgotine izbrisa, 2010, p. 101.

214 Matevž Krivic, who is authorised by many erased people to represent them, confirmed that eight out of ten people he interviewed on this issue wanted to apply for citizenship. Krivic, Politični zločin, ne "administrativna napaka", in: Pravna praksa 26 (2007) 9, p. 21.

turned down by "a man missing one hand".[215] Such conduct on the part of administration employees was a breach of the General Administrative Procedure Act[216] under which they were obliged to accept the application and set the deadline by which the client had to supply the missing documents. Applicants were asked to submit a birth certificate to prove their republic citizenship and date of birth. This could be issued only by the successor state in which the applicant was born, so if that country was at war or another obstacle arose, the applicant was unable to supply it by the prescribed date. The administrative units and the Ministry of the Interior should have been aware of potential problems, given that communication with administrative units in other republics had been interrupted for months before Slovenia gained independence.[217] Accordingly, this treatment of applicants for citizenship can be understood as harassment. Why it happened remains unexplained to the present day; administration employees and bodies either deny allegations or refuse to comment. Taking into account that the atmosphere in which Slovenia declared independence was suffused with intolerance towards citizens of other SFRY republics, that a large part of the public opposed the granting of citizenship to this group of people,[218] and that the number of applications considerably exceeded expectations,[219] it appears likely that harassment did occur. Moreover, such conduct on the part of administration employees was orchestrated and systematic, so there is little doubt that they were acting in accordance with in-house instructions.

---

215 *Ibid.*

216 Zakon o splošnem upravnem postopku, Official Gazette of the Federal People's Republic of Yugoslavia, No. 52/1956, Official Gazette of the Socialist Federal Republic of Yugoslavia, No. 10/1965, 18/1965, 4/1977, 11/1978, and Official Gazette of the Republic of Slovenia, No. 4/1992.

217 Interview with Lev Kreft, 24 July 2011.

218 A 1990 opinion survey showed that 86% of respondents thought that all Slovenes, Italians, and Hungarians who were living in Slovenia and had Slovenian republican citizenship under the legislation valid at that time, should gain Slovenian citizenship automatically. However, only 64% of respondents thought that members of other Yugoslav nations who were living in Slovenia and had Slovenian republican citizenship should also gain Slovenian citizenship automatically. A similar per cent of respondents (66%) though that members of other Yugoslav nations who lived and worked in Slovenia should obtain Slovenian citizenship if they wished so. Toš, Vrednote na prehodu III. Slovensko javno mnenje 1999–2004 (Values in Transition III. The Slovenian Public Opinion 1999–2004)(2004), question B7.

219 Mesojedec Pervinšek, Predpisi o državljanih in tujcih z uvodnimi pojasnili, 1997, p. 32.

What all erased people have in common is that they did not gain citizenship and that until the end of the period to submit an application for citizenship (or in the case of those who submitted applications, until the date they were notified that they had been rejected) they had equal rights and duties as the citizens of the Republic of Slovenia, except for the right to own property. None of them could be aware at that time how their legal status would change once the deadline expired.

3.6 The Suitability of the Legislation on Citizenship from the Perspective of the Obligation to Submit an Application

The establishment of Slovenia's citizenry was most clearly marked by the distinction made between persons who had Slovenian republic citizenship and those who had citizenship of another SFRY republic. While the former became Slovenian citizens automatically, the latter could gain Slovenian citizenship by a one-time extraordinary (exceptional) naturalisation upon application if they met the legal requirements that, as previously stated, were problematic in many ways. The necessity to apply for citizenship was explained by the principle of freedom to gain or lose citizenship. According to this principle, a person cannot lose Slovenian citizenship against his/her own will, and foreigners cannot be forced to become Slovenian citizens against their will (except when the principle of the prevention of statelessness prevails, for example, in cases involving children without known parents).[220]

While the principle of freedom of choice as such is not questionable, there are several possible ways to implement it, including the institute of an option. In this arrangement, a person who automatically gains citizenship of a country is given the option of taking another country's citizenship by a set date, or to reject the citizenship that was given to him/her automatically. In this arrangement, an individual's will is taken into account while at the same time protecting the person's legal status.

The arrangement chosen by policy makers in Slovenia is indeed one of the possible ways to implement the principle of freedom of choice, but it is problematic with respect to the prohibition of discrimination on the basis of ethnic origin. In fact, by granting citizenship based on continuity with Slovenian republic citizenship—which, in turn, had been obtained based on the *jus sanguinis* principle—the government de facto excluded the members of other Yugoslav nations on the basis of their ethnicity. This could be interpreted as indirect discrimination based on ethnic origin.

---

220 *Ibid.*, p. 12.

Direct discrimination occurs when a seemingly neutral rule or norm has the effect of placing individuals or groups of specific ethnic origin into a situation that is worse than that of other persons or groups who belong to the majority group. Although during the Yugoslav era republic citizenship was not directly tied to ethnic origins, it was predominantly held by members of the majority ethnic group in the republic, so granting citizenship based on continuity with the previous republic citizenship disproportionately affected individuals of non-Slovene ethnic origin.

On the other hand, the principle of continuity, as the antipode of the principle of zero option, has its advantages, particularly when viewed from the perspective of persons who already had Slovenian republic citizenship, as they could not be deprived of it simply because a new state was formed.

3.7 The Suitability of the Legislation on Citizenship from the Perspective of the Principle of Preventing Statelessness

One of the key principles on which the Citizenship of the Republic of Slovenia Act is based is the prevention of statelessness, despite the fact that Slovenia is not a signatory to the Convention on the Reduction of Statelessness.[221] For this reason, two exceptions were added to the fundamental *jus sanguinis* principle: citizenship was granted to children whose parents had no citizenship or whose citizenship is unknown, and to children who were found within the territory of Slovenia (who then obtain citizenship based on the *jus soli* principle). These mechanisms of preventing statelessness are also available to foreigners who apply for citizenship by naturalisation. Those who fulfil all the conditions to gain citizenship by naturalisation are issued an assurance by the Ministry of the Interior that they will be granted Slovenian citizenship if they provide proof of a release from previous citizenship within two years. For applicants who request a release from another citizenship, this is a guarantee that they will not become stateless. The citizenship certificate is then issued when the document proving the release from previous citizenship is provided. If the person fails to provide such a document, the naturalisation procedure is terminated. In accordance with the Hague Convention dating from 1930 (Article 7), a person who applies for release from Slovenian citizenship can request, within one year, a cancellation of the release. This is an assurance that a person who fails to gain another citizenship can preserve his/her previous citizenship. The revocation of citizenship is possible only if the person proves that he/she has dual citizenship.

221 *Ibid.*, p. 13.

The representatives of the Ministry of the Interior have repeatedly argued that Article 40, under which citizens of other republics applied for citizenship (or chose not to apply, or were rejected citizenship), did not put people at the risk of becoming stateless but rather led to dual citizenship.[222] However, several authors argue that what happened in reality was the de facto and de jure statelessness of a certain number of persons.[223]

The argument of the Ministry was that given the legal system of the time, it was legally and theoretically impossible for a person who was a citizen of one of the SFRY republics not to also be a citizen of the SFRY, and the other way round, i.e. to be a citizen of SFRY and not of one of its republics. According to Mesojedec-Pervinšek, if strictly applied, the federal and the republican legislation of the former SFRY prevented statelessness, because every Yugoslav citizen, based on the *jus sanguinis* and in some cases the *jus soli* principle, was guaranteed republic citizenship. Theoretically, this was true. Every Yugoslav citizen had the citizenship of at least one Yugoslav republic, which should have prevented statelessness if successor states based their citizenship legislation on the principle of continuity with republic citizenship. Furthermore, in theory, a person's civil status could not be affected even if the information on a person's republic citizenship was not entered into the relevant register, because the constitution of citizenship depended on the conditions prescribed by law, and not on an entry into a register (initially the population register and then the register of births).[224]

However, the composite citizenship system used in the former SFRY later caused many problems in practice, particularly for the erased people. It was opaque, data were scattered, entries inaccurate and inconsistent, and on top of that some people did not know which population register contained their data.[225] Information on the republic citizenship of persons who were born in Slovenia after 1965 and were assigned citizenship of another SFRY republic was entered into the Slovenian population register, but this information was not consistently forwarded to relevant administrative bodies in other republics or consistently recorded in other republics' population registers. If these persons did not apply for Slovenian citizenship, either due to ignorance or a conviction

222 *Ibid.*, p. 14.

223 Ogradi, Izbrisani državljani SFRJ, 2003, p. 8.

224 Mesojedec Pervinšek, Predpisi o državljanih in tujcih z uvodnimi pojasnili, 1997, p. 22.

225 Medved, From Civic to Ethnic Community?, in: Citizenship Policies in the New Europe (2007), p. 218. Also Rava, EUDO Citizenship Observatory, Country Report: Serbia, 2010, p. 6.

that they would obtain it automatically by birth, they were later erased and found themselves in a Catch-22 situation, because their "home" republics of which they were citizens according to Slovenian records did not have them registered as citizens. The assumption of the Slovenian administrative bodies that these persons held citizenship of another republic thus often proved erroneous. Mesojedec-Privšek also established that individual cases "indicate that in certain countries the persons who until 1991 had been considered the citizens of specific republics, were no longer considered citizens of the successor states" as illustrated by documents issued by the diplomatic and consular representative offices of the countries from which they originated according to the *jus sanguinis* principle.[226]

The situation of persons who were born in Slovenia after 1965 and continued to live there despite not obtaining Slovenian citizenship at birth proved to be especially problematic. While they did not obtain Slovenian citizenship automatically, they failed to apply for it because they thought they already had it. When they learned that they had never obtained Slovenian citizenship, they applied for citizenship through naturalisation. However, one of the conditions these persons had to meet was the submission of proof of release from their previous citizenship.[227] Those who were not registered as citizens in another successor state could not obtain such proof, rendering them unable to fulfil all of the conditions of naturalisation. The situation of these persons raises the issue of statelessness. A systemic solution to this problem was put forward by Mesojedec-Pervinšek who wrote:

> Based on the citizenship-related experience of Slovenia, it can be said that only a fast, efficient and benevolent solution of these issues by all the SFRY successor states, taking into account the principle of continuity in the area of republic and federal citizenship, could contribute to the effective arrangement of the status of affected people.[228]

Under this approach, while sensible in the abstract, the resolution of individual problems required the promptness, efficiency, and integrity of foreign administrative bodies. Hoping for such administrative bodies proved to be a vain exercise, given that the Slovenian administration proved to be precisely the opposite, as the accounts of erased people demonstrate. It was very slow in processing

226 Mesojedec Pervinšek, Predpisi o državljanih in tujcih z uvodnimi pojasnili, 1997, p. 23.

227 *Ibid.*

228 *Ibid.*

applications for citizenship under Article 40,[229] in granting alien status, and later in dealing with the erased people.[230]

Persons who after the dissolution of Yugoslavia did not gain the citizenship of any successor state became either effectively (de facto) or legally (de jure) stateless. The difference between de facto and de jure statelessness has not been defined in international conventions, but it has been defined in legal doctrine. A de jure stateless person is a person whom no state recognises as its citizen in accordance with its legislation.[231] The problem with this definition is that it requires proof of a negative fact, meaning that a claimant is asked to provide statements issued by countries with which he/she could have close ties proving that he/she is not a citizen of those countries. De facto statelessness occurs when a person cannot prove his/her de jure statelessness, and that person does not receive the protection of the laws of the state in which he or she lives. For example, de facto statelessness occurs when someone has citizenship of a specific country but does not have all rights enjoyed by other citizens. This definition is also problematic, since legal doctrine is still not clear on what the elements of effective citizenship are. Nevertheless, effective citizenship could be defined as one that ensures consular protection to an individual, possession of identification documents and a passport recognised by other countries, and the exercising of civil rights in relation to the country of citizenship, such as the right to vote.

As already mentioned, the Yugoslav federal and republican legislation on citizenship would have prevented statelessness had it been consistently implemented. It anticipated nearly all possible situations, so each SFRY citizen had the citizenship of one republic which then enabled him/her to obtain citizenship of the successor state based on the principle of continuity. Therefore, in theory, the erased people should be only de facto stateless. However, some were also de jure stateless. Most often, these were erased persons born in Slovenia after 1965 who had a parent with the citizenship of another republic, so the child was assigned citizenship

229 Letno poročilo Varuha človekovih pravic RS za leto 1995, točka 4.5.1, Državljanstvo.

230 Human Rights Ombudsman of the Republic of Slovenia, Problematika izbrisanih v letnih poročilih varuha, Posebno poročilo, 2004, pp. 25–27.

231 International conventions concerned with the issue of statelessness do not make a distinction between de jure and de facto statelessness; in these conventions, statelessness is defined merely as a situation in which no state recognizes a person as its citizen in accordance with its legislation. The distinction between the two mentioned kinds of statelessness arises from legal doctrine. See Equal Rights Trust, Legal Working Paper: The Protection of Stateless Persons in Detention under International Law, 2009.

of that other republic (by the parents' choice or without consulting the parents). The child's citizenship was then entered into the Slovenian register, but the republic whose citizenship the child obtained was not informed. Furthermore, some records contained the designation "Yugoslav" rather than a specified republic citizenship, or the field was simply left empty. Such persons were de jure stateless for several years before they were able to obtain citizenship of a successor state. If the successor state had a thorough administration, obtaining citizenship was not a problem. If not, the procedure for establishing the republic citizenship may never have been implemented, and consequently a person who was entitled to citizenship based on the continuity principle could not obtain it. Since practice is not always ideal and administrative bodies are not always as efficient as one would hope, many persons found themselves in an impossible situation.

The example most often used to illustrate the de facto statelessness of the erased people is that of people who lived in Slovenia without legal status but obtained the citizenship of another successor state on the basis of their previous republic citizenship. Since these people had often been away from their republic of birth for many years (for some of them, 40 years or more) and they no longer had meaningful ties with it (familial, economic, social ties), they neither wanted nor needed its citizenship nor did they apply for its passport. However, as soon as such a person applies to the embassy of the successor state for these personal documents and obtains them, they are no longer stateless.

3.8 The Suitability of Legislation on Citizenship from the Perspective of the International Obligations of States in the Case of Succession

I mentioned earlier that international legal sources concerned with the issue of citizenship list principles that states should observe, but provide few specifics to be taken into account when drafting laws on citizenship. Two of the key documents, the European Convention on Nationality and the Draft Articles on Nationality of Natural Persons in relation to the Succession of States (hereafter the Draft Articles), did not exist at the time when Slovenia gained independence, and they are still not binding on Slovenia. The 1997 European Convention on Nationality, which Slovenia has not yet ratified, defines in Article 18 the principles that signatory states should observe in the case of succession when drafting its legislation on citizenship, including the principles of the rule of law, the protection of human rights, and the prevention of statelessness.

Particularly important in this respect are the Draft Articles, although the document is not formally binding. It proposes principles that states should observe during the process of succession, with different alternatives depending on the kind of succession (transfer of part of the territory, unification of States, dissolution of a State, and separation of part of the territory). Article 22 stipulates that if a state dissolves, successor states should grant citizenship to all persons who have "their habitual residence in its territory". This is subject to the provisions in Article 8 (1) which stipulate that "a successor State does not have the obligation to attribute its nationality to persons concerned if they have their habitual residence in another State and also have the nationality of that or any other State" and Article 8 (2) which stipulates that "a successor State shall not attribute its nationality to persons concerned who have their habitual residence in another State against the will of the persons concerned unless they would otherwise become stateless". However, in accordance with Article 22 (b) (i), the successor state shall grant citizenship to persons who have no habitual residence in the successor state but have "an appropriate legal connection with a constituent unit of the predecessor State that has become part of that successor State...". Additionally, in accordance with Article 22 (b) (ii), successor states are obliged to give citizenship to "persons concerned not entitled to a nationality of any State concerned under subparagraphs (a) and (b) (i) having their habitual residence in a third State, who were born in or, before leaving the predecessor State, had their last habitual residence in what has become the territory of that successor State or having any other appropriate connection with that successor State".

Article 23(1) of the Draft Articles, stipulates that "successor States shall grant a right of option to persons concerned covered by the provisions of article 22 who are qualified to acquire the nationality of two or more successor States", and Article 23(2) that "each successor State shall grant a right to opt for its nationality to persons concerned who are not covered by the provisions of article 22". We should also draw attention to Article 14, which states that "the status of persons concerned as habitual residents shall not be affected by the succession of States" and that "a State concerned shall take all necessary measures to allow persons concerned who, because of events connected with the succession of States, were forced to leave their habitual residence on its territory to return thereto".

The UN International Law Commission, which prepared the Draft Articles, chose habitual residence as the main principle after reviewing the practice of countries such as the former Czechoslovakia and Yugoslavia, which attributed citizenship based on the narrower principle of continuity with the previous citizenship of federal units. The Commission established that many serious problems were encountered in practice wherever requirements for obtaining citizenship considerably constricted citizenship options.[232] The difficulties were especially great if a state acted contrary to the provisions in Article 14 of the Draft Articles, which were drawn to prevent changes in habitual residents' status as a result of succession.

The model of attributing citizenship based on the habitual residence principle was employed after the dissolution of Austria-Hungary.[233] At the time when Slovenia was preparing to declare independence, its lawmakers were aware that such a model, which includes the right of option, had gained ground in international law and in Central Europe particularly.[234] However, they quickly discarded this solution with the explanation an international treaty (such as the treaties of St. Germain, Rapallo or Trianon) would have been a prerequisite, which allegedly could not be achieved because of the political atmosphere of the time and later because of the wars and ethnic conflicts.

This explanation is untenable. An international treaty is not a prerequisite to attributing citizenship on the habitual residence basis. This model could be adopted unilaterally, and such an approach would have spared time and money for both the government and the affected persons. Since more than 85% of citizens of other Yugoslav republics who had permanent residence in Slovenia obtained Slovenian citizenship under Article 40 upon application, it would not make a sizeable difference if they were all assigned Slovenian citizenship automatically, particularly if they were given the option of renouncing Slovenian citizenship within a specified time period (excluding those whose renunciation would cause them to be stateless).[235] Moreover, viewed from a human rights perspective, the only appropriate approach would have been to assign Slovenian citizenship to all persons who had habitual residence in the territory of the newly independent state. This would eliminate the specious distinction that was made between those with a registered permanent address, those who had a registered temporary address, and those not registered at all despite living in Slovenia for a long period of time and having close ties to the country.

---

232 Item 5 in the Comments to Articles 22 and 23 of the Draft Articles on Nationality of Natural Persons in relation to the Succession of States.

233 *Ibid.*, Item 4.

234 Mesojedec Pervinšek, Predpisi o državljanih in tujcih z uvodnimi pojasnili, 1997, pp. 24–25.

235 Proposals to this effect, which unfortunately were not adopted, were put forward by certain delegates to the Socio-political Chamber at the time when the Citizenship of the Republic of Slovenia Act was undergoing the legislative procedure. Zorn, "We, the Ethno-Citizens of Ethno-Democracy", in: Journal for the Critique of Science 35 (2007) 228, p. 59.

Part II: The Situation of Aliens following Slovenian Secession and the Erasure

"The gateway to the law is open as it always is, and the doorkeeper has stepped to one side, so the man bends over to try and see in. When the doorkeeper notices this he laughs and says, 'If you're tempted give it a try, try and go in even though I say you can't. Careful though: I'm powerful. And I'm only the lowliest of all the doormen".

Franz Kafka, The Trial

1. The Situation of Persons who did not Obtain Slovenian Citizenship

1.1 Transitional Provisions in the Aliens Act

Citizens of other SFRY republics who resided in Slovenia but did not obtain citizenship under the transitional provisions of the Citizenship of the Republic of Slovenia Act found themselves in an ambiguous legal position. Although they were not considered citizens of Slovenia, their status as aliens was not clear.

The law that regulated the status of aliens in Slovenia was entitled the Aliens Act.[236] It superseded the federal Yugoslav Law on the Movement and Residence of Aliens,[237] according to which the status of aliens and immigration policy were the province of federal bodies.[238] The Aliens Act contained provisions on aliens' entry into Slovenia, visas, the acquisition, and revocation of temporary and permanent residence permits, as well as provisions on the forced removal of aliens, the Transitional Home for Aliens, and passports and other documents for aliens.

Most of these provisions related to foreigners who had not resided in Slovenia previously, including those individuals who planned to apply for a residence permit. The other two groups of aliens covered by this law were those persons who had already obtained alien status under Yugoslav law, and citizens of other SFRY republics who did not acquire Slovenian citizenship.

---

236 Zakon o tujcih, Official Gazette of the Republic of Slovenia, No. 1/1991I.

237 Zakon o gibanju in prebivanju tujcev, Official Gazette of the Socialist federal Republic of Yugoslavia, No. 56/1980, 53/1985, 30/1989, 26/1990.

238 Juhant, Upravnopravni vidiki statusnih zadev tujcev, 1996, p. 6.

Citizens of other republics who had a permanent address registered in Slovenia and applied for Slovenian citizenship under Article 40 of the Citizenship of Slovenia Act were covered by Article 81, Para 1. It stipulated that the provisions of the Aliens Act did not apply to this group until their applications for Slovenian citizenship were resolved. Article 81, Para 2 referred to people who did not apply for Slovenian citizenship under Article 40 or were denied it. It stipulated that provisions of the Aliens Act would begin to apply to them within two months of the expiration of the deadline for applications under Article 40, or within two months of the date on which the decision denying their application was issued. Since the six-month deadline for submitting an application expired on 26 December 1991, the provisions in the Aliens Act came into force on 26 February 1992. However, neither the Citizenship of the Republic of Slovenia Act nor the Aliens Act regulated the status of these people during the interim period, i.e. from 26 December 1991 to 26 February 1992. Article 13 of the Constitutional Act contained an important provision that affected their status during this period. According to the provision, those citizens of other SFRY republics who had their permanent residence registered in Slovenia had the same rights and duties as the citizens of Slovenia, except for the right to own real estate until they gained Slovenian citizenship or until the deadline set by Article 81 of the Aliens Act expired. During this period, their status, including the right to enter and reside in the country, was not affected.

However, this provision did not apply to the members of the armed forces and other unlawfully blacklisted persons. According to Končina, persons considered to be active YPA members who participated in the assault on Slovenia were prohibited from entering Slovenia.[239] In other words, the Yugoslav Army employees who left Slovenia when the army withdrew could not return to Slovenia even if they resigned, retired from the army, or had family in Slovenia. If a prohibition on entry was issued, Article 12, Para 1 of the Aliens Act stipulated that such a foreigner could not enter Slovenia even if he/she had formerly held a residence permit.[240]

The general public, including people who were affected by the measure, was not aware of what happened on 26 February 1992. Only government representatives knew that this date was a milestone. Most of the people who were robbed

---

239 Končina, Zakon o državljanstvu Republike Slovenije s komentarjem, 1993, p. 11.

240 Article 12, Para 1 of the 1991 Aliens Act read as follows: "The body responsible for the supervision of aliens crossing the border can refuse to issue a visa to an alien, issue a prohibition on entering the country or prohibit entry even if an alien has a valid visa".

of their legal status were members of the lower working class, and most of them did not read the official gazette of Slovenia or the new legislation. Moreover, even if they had been acquainted with Article 81, Para 1 of the Aliens Act, they would not have been better off; in the best case scenario, it could have provoked them to ask additional questions and ask for a clarification of the provision stipulating that "the provisions of the Aliens Act will begin to be applied" to them on the specified date. As a matter of fact, Article 81 was vague and ambiguous. It was not clear what – if anything – was expected from the citizens of other SFRY republics who did not gain Slovenian citizenship. It was not clear if they had to do something to retain their legal status, or if they did not need to do anything because their status would be regulated automatically. The trained eye of a well-informed person could perhaps spot a difference between the provisions referring to the citizens of SFRY republics and those referring to non-Yugoslav foreigners who had been granted alien status under Yugoslav laws. The latter were protected by Article 82, Para 3 of the Aliens Act, which stipulated that permanent residence permits issued by SFRY under the Law on the Movement and Residence of Aliens[241] continued to be valid for all foreigners who had permanent residence in Slovenia on the day the Aliens Act came into force. In other words, a Frenchman or an Englishman who had the status of an alien in the SFRY did not need to do anything to retain this status. By contrast, no similar provision applicable to citizens of SFRY republics could be found in this law. I will explain the reasons for this difference below.

1.2 The Amendments that Could Have Prevented the Erasure

Documents from the period when the Aliens Act was in preparation show that several amendments to Article 81 were proposed in order to prevent the erasure. Had any of these been adopted, the legal status of citizens of other SFRY republics would have been more clearly defined rather than becoming more complicated. The amendments were proposed by the left-wing opposition parties in the National Assembly. Unfortunately, the proposed amendments were not supported by the parliamentary majority.

The amendments proposed that all individuals whose permanent residence was already registered in Slovenia should obtain permanent residence permits.

241 Zakon o gibanju in prebivanju tujcev, Official Gazette of the Socialist Federal Republic of Yugoslavia, No. 56/1980, 53/1985, 30/1989, 26/1990.

Had they been adopted, the SFRY citizens who did not gain Slovenian citizenship would have been able to retain their legal status.[242]

The first proposed amendment read:

> Citizens of the SFRY who are citizens of another republic and who have not applied for citizenship of the Republic of Slovenia but have employment in Slovenia on the day this law comes into force shall be issued permanent residence permits.

The rationale behind this amendment was that such a provision would somewhat improve the situation of the many workers from other republics who did not necessarily have their permanent residence registered in Slovenia and were consequently not entitled to apply for citizenship under Article 40. The Executive Council of the National Assembly rejected the amendment, arguing that it was not clear whether permanent residence permits should be issued to all citizens of other republics employed in Slovenia or only the citizens who had their permanent residence registered in Slovenia and met the criteria set out in Article 40. If permits were to be issued only for the latter group, the Executive Council would have supported the amendment. As a result, two new amendments were tabled by the opposition parties. The first read:

> Citizens of SFRY who are citizens of another republic and who have not applied for the citizenship of the Republic of Slovenia but have their permanent residence registered in Slovenia or are employed in Slovenia on the day this law comes into force, shall be issued permanent residence permits.

The second, alternative amendment, submitted in case the first one was rejected, read:

> Citizens of the SFRY who are citizens of another republic and who have not applied for citizenship of the Republic of Slovenia but have their permanent residence registered in Slovenia on the day this law comes into force shall be issued permanent residence permits.[243]

The amendments' proponents argued that this was the only appropriate way to fulfil the promise that independence would not affect the situation of the citizens of other republics and that their legal status would not be harmed, as stated in the Statement of Good Intentions and the Agreement signed by all of the political

---

242 Interview with Lev Kreft, Member of the Parliament at the time of passing of the Aliens Act, 14 July 2011.

243 Based on Savanović, Geografska interpretacija izbrisa, 2007, pp. 29–30.

parties in the National Assembly.[244] The first of the two amendments was more inclusive, since it covered those who were employed in Slovenia but had not registered a permanent address as well as those who had. Viewed from the perspective of protecting human rights, it was more appropriate especially because even individuals who had employment were not always able to register a permanent address, for various reasons (e.g. if they lived in a dormitory). Had the second amendment been adopted, it could have prevented the consequences of the restrictive interpretation of the deficient Aliens Act — which, as the Constitutional Court later confirmed, created a legal vacuum — at least for people who had registered their permanent residence in Slovenia. All three chambers of the National Assembly had to pass the amendment for it to be adopted. Two chambers voted against it. In the third chamber (the Socio-political Chamber) the amendment fell one vote shy of being adopted. The outcome of the first round of voting was undecided (19 votes in favour, 19 against, six abstentions) but it was rejected in the second round, 20 votes to 19,[245] despite the fact that it was publicly supported by the Executive Council of the Assembly.[246]

The confirmation of Article 82 of the Aliens Act followed immediately, formally codifying the distinction between various groups of persons who resided in Slovenia lawfully before it gained independence.[247]

The rejection of the amendment was mitigated by promises that this issue would be regulated some other way. At the same session, a resolution proposed by the Social Democratic Party was adopted. It said that, after gaining independence, the Republic of Slovenia would

> launch a process with a view to signing an agreement with other republics of the SFRY on the settlement of issues and the regulation of rights and obligations towards citizens of SFRY who live in Slovenia but will not become its citizens or will apply for Slovenian citizenship, as well as the issues pertaining to the citizens of the Republic of Slovenia who live in other republics of the present SFRY, their rights and obligations (the voting

---

244 This explanation was put forward by Left Kreft who at that time was a delegate in the Socio-political Chamber. Mekina, B., A Monument to the Erased, in: Journal for the Critique of Science, 35 (2007) 228, p. 46.

245 Mekina, B., A Monument to the Erased, in: Journal for the Critique of Science, 35 (2007) 228, p. 46.

246 Savanović, Geografska interpretacija izbrisa, 2007, p. 30.

247 Zorn, "We, the Ethno-Citizens of Ethno-Democracy", in: Journal for the Critique of Science 35 (2007) 228, p. 63.

right, the ownership, real estate, inheritance, employment, health, social and housing rights and the like).[248]

It is not clear whether the resolution was adopted because the majority in Parliament truly believed that such an agreement could be reached soon, or whether it was just a smoke screen. The circumstances suggest the latter.[249] It is important to note that the Slovenian government opted for the unilateral (and exclusive) regulation of citizenship issues even before Yugoslavia disintegrated. The tense relations among SFRY republics had precluded the possibility of reaching any kind of agreement.[250]

The only succession agreement among SFRY successor states was signed in 2001. It primarily covered the issues of debt sharing, state property, and the ownership of banks, while individual rights concerning movable and immovable property were only addressed marginally. Bilateral agreements on social security were signed in 1997 with Croatia, in 2000 with Macedonia, in 2008 with Bosnia-Herzegovina, in 2010 with Serbia, and in 2012 with Montenegro. An interesting detail is that the Macedonian Law on the Movement and Residence of Foreigners,[251] adopted in 1992, contains a provision that is identical to that in Article 81 of the Aliens Act of the Republic of Slovenia. This suggests that the Slovenian administration helped Macedonia draft its legislation and that it "exported" one of its worst practices, enabling Macedonia to carry out its own erasure while failing to resolve the status and rights of erased Macedonian citizens in Slovenia.

1.3 A Mistake or a Deliberate Decision?

The ambiguous and deficient Article 81 of the Aliens Act created an unconstitutional legal vacuum which engendered various arbitrary interpretations. Before I proceed to analyse these interpretations, I would like to focus on the question of whether the lawmakers and delegates to the National Assembly were aware of the consequences of rejecting the amendments. This is closely related to the key question of whether the wording of the Aliens Act and the erasure that followed were mistakes born of inexperience, or intentional and deliberate.

---

248 The Party of Democratic Reform, Session 19 of the Socio-political Chamber (1991), p. 363.

249 Interview with Lev Kreft, 14 July 2011.

250 *Cf.* the Constitutional Court of the Republic of Slovenia, Ruling No. U-I-284/94, paragraph 8.

251 Official Gazette of the Republic of Macedonia, No. 36/1992.

In contrast to Article 82, which contained all the necessary details needed to regulate the status of non-Yugoslav citizens who had already obtained alien status under the SFRY legislation, Article 81 was incomplete and ambiguous in terms of both content and wording. An amendment was clearly required. This implies that the lawmakers knew what the law should have contained to protect the citizens of other SFRY republics and that all the excuses suggesting a lack of awareness were false. Perhaps some members of the government or some delegates to the National Assembly were truly unaware of the flaws in Article 81, and believed that the citizens of other SFRY republics who did not gain citizenship would automatically retain some kind of legal status after the deadlines expired. However, they must have realised their mistake when the legislative and legal service of the National Assembly pointed out the problem and when the amendments were proposed. Nevertheless, the parliamentary majority continued to insist that the disputed provisions would not cause problems while the proposed amendments would only benefit "traitors".[252] The debate provoked by the amendments touched upon every aspect of the Aliens Act, so everyone had a chance to gain a full picture of the situation and learn which criteria SFRY citizens needed to meet to be allowed to enter Slovenia. Moreover, they must have been aware that many persons would not be able to meet the restrictive criteria for obtaining alien status. After all, this was obvious from parliamentary debates that clearly suggest that certain delegates anticipated the erasure and tried to prevent it:

> Those who maintain that by granting citizenship to permanently settled immigrants we would bring upon us, as they say, a too big financial or social burden, simply forget that these immigrants, if they don't gain citizenship, will have to be granted either temporary or permanent residence permits, the rights arising from employment and social security rights. Therefore, the only difference would be their feeling of being threatened, and with good reason, for example, that they will be robbed of the right to vote, and perhaps the right to buy certain kinds of property [...] and that as individuals they will be more vulnerable to all sorts of extortion and persecutions, since under certain conditions it will be possible to revoke their residence permits – unless [...] someone truly believes that at the end of the 20th century it is necessary and possible to organize, in a small and free-thinking republic that through its struggle for self-determination knocks on the conscience of the international public, some kind of new expulsion deportations.[253]

252 Interview with Lev Kreft, 14 July 2011.
253 Mile Šetinc, 19th Session of the Socio-political Chamber, (1991), p. 69. See also Zorn, "We, the Ethno-citizens of Ethno-democracy", in: Journal for the Critique of Science 35 (2007) 228, pp. 61–62.

Unfortunately, "the expulsion deportations" did occur. The decision not to support the proposed amendments enabled the erasure, indicating that it was conscious, informed, and intentional. The only question still unclear was how to implement it, i.e. how to deprive people of their legal status.

2. The In-house Instructions on the Implementation of the Aliens Act and Other Independence Laws

2.1 The In-house Instruction of 26 June 1991 – SFRY Citizens as Aliens

The public, including the citizens of other republics who did not obtain Slovenian citizenship, was not alerted to the new provisions affecting Yugoslav citizens. However, the Ministry of the Interior prepared detailed unpublished in-house instructions[254] on how to handle these people's personal documents and permanent address registrations.

The instructions (also referred to as circulars or dispatches) were sent to the local administrations all across Slovenia that maintained the registers of permanent and temporary residents. The Ministry also organised several consulting sessions to instruct local bodies on how to implement a series of new administrative procedures and services that were established when Slovenia became a sovereign country (for example, how to issue permanent and temporary residence permits).

One day after the Citizenship of the Republic of Slovenia Act went into force on 26 June 1991, the Ministry of the Interior sent out its first set of instructions, in which it drew attention to the changes in the legal status of citizens of other SFRY republics in Slovenia. The circular explained the difference between the two groups of citizens of other SFRY republics. The first consisted of persons who on 23 December 1990 and on the day the Aliens Act came into force had their permanent address registered in Slovenia. This group was entitled to apply for citizenship. The instructions stressed that, in accordance with Article 13 of the Constitutional Law, they had the same rights and obligations as the citizens of the Republic of Slovenia. The second group consisted of citizens of other SFRY republics who registered their permanent address in Slovenia after 23 December 1990 or who only had temporary residence. This group was not eligible to apply for citizenship. The persons in the latter group were to be treated as aliens with

254 I obtained the in-house instructions (circulars) of the Ministry of the Interior on 5 May 2009 by submitting a freedom of information request.

unregulated status in all administrative procedures such as the registration and de-registration of addresses and the issuing of ID cards, passports, or other personal documents.[255] The Ministry further drew attention to the transitional provisions in the law on the passports of citizens of Slovenia. The provision relevant to citizens of other republics stipulated that Yugoslav passports issued under the Law on the Passports of SFRY Citizens[256] would be in use for two years after the new law came into force. The instructions were marked as preliminary and possibly subject to changes. The circular also announced a second consulting session scheduled for the following week.

2.2 In-house Instruction of 30 July 1991 – A Moratorium

One month later, in the wake of the Brioni Declaration that ended the hostilities of the Yugoslav National Army against Slovenia (signed by Slovenia and the SFRY on 7 July 1991), and the three-month moratorium on the implementation of the Declaration of Independence, the Ministry of the Interior issued a new set of instructions. The moratorium required a modification of one of the guidelines in the previous circular: citizens of other SFRY republics who registered their permanent or temporary address in Slovenia between 23 December 1990 and 25 June 1991 were to be treated as citizens of SFRY and not as foreigners (as the first in-house circular stated) and their status could not be changed unless they so chose. The rules applicable to the other group (persons who registered their permanent address in Slovenia before 23 December 1990) did not change.[257]

What this meant in practice was that people in both groups could continue to exercise all the rights they had enjoyed until then (e.g. unemployment benefits), that their legal status in Slovenia was unchanged, and that they could not (yet) be expelled from the country. If they had registered a temporary address,

---

255 The in-house instruction of the Ministry of the Interior to all local administration bodies entitled *Izvajanje Zakona o tujcih in Zakona o potnih listinah državljanov Republike Slovenije* (The Implementation of the Aliens Act and the Passports of Citizens of the Republic of Slovenia Act, No. 0016/8-S-010/14-91 dated 26 June 1991.

256 Zakon o potnih listinah državljanov SFRJ, Official Gazette of the Socialist Federal Republic of Yugoslavia, No. 30/1979 in 53/1985.

257 The in-house instruction of the Ministry of the Interior to all local administration bodies entitled *Izvajanje Zakona o tujcih in Zakona o potnih listinah državljanov Republike Slovenije – spremembe stališč izdanih pod No. 0016/8-S-010/4-91 z dne 26. junija 1991* (The Implementation of the Aliens Act and the Passports of Citizens of the Republic of Slovenia Act – changes to the instructions No. 0016/8-S-010/4-91 dated 26 June 1991, No. 0016/8-S-010/4-91 dated 30 July 1991.

they continued to be treated as SFRY citizens with temporary residence in Slovenia. The instruction also said that local administrative bodies in Slovenia were obliged to issue new passports to SFRY citizens at their request, in accordance with the Law on the Passports of SFRY citizens.

The above rules were in place as long as the moratorium lasted; once it expired, the status of SFRY citizens radically deteriorated regardless of whether or not they were born in Slovenia, had jobs or families there, or whether their personal situation required them to remain there.

2.3 The In-house Instructions of 5 February and 18 February 1992 – The Unlawful Invalidation of Documents and Restrictive Conditions on Work Visas

In the meantime, the government and the leading officials at the Ministry of the Interior were preparing for the administrative processing of persons who had not applied for citizenship, or applied for it but were denied. The provisions in Article 81, Para 2 of the Aliens Act were to be applied to this group beginning on 26 February 1992, but the unclear wording and ambiguities as to the law's practical implementation necessitated clarifications. The Ministry accordingly organised another consultation session held on 23 January 1992 and produced another set of detailed in-house instructions. The report on the meeting dated February 1992 reveals the instructions that were dispatched to local administrative bodies but were not made public. The instructions primarily explained the rules to be applied when issuing visas, temporary and permanent residence permits, revoking residence permits, expelling foreigners from the country, and handling their personal documents.

Certain rules were stricter than the conditions set out in the Aliens Act. For example, the instructions said that a work visa could be issued for a maximum of three months, while Article 7, Para 3 of the Aliens Act stipulated that a work visa would be issued for the duration of the employment contract, or for the period during which a foreigner would perform a specific job, but in no case should its validity exceed the validity of the foreigner's passport. On the other hand, there were several rules that were less strict. For example, Article 6, Para 4 of the Aliens Act stipulated that a visa could be issued only to foreigners who had valid passports, while the instructions said that a work permit could be issued to a foreigner without a valid passport but the administrative body was obliged to advise the foreigner to obtain a passport as soon as possible. All of these instructions had implications for the erased people, such as those who had to re-apply for work permits and temporary or permanent residence permits. The last instruction in this series was of particular importance. It stated that

> when processing requests relating to alien status, it is necessary to establish whether the person has personal documents (an ID card, a passport, a weapon permit) issued by interior affairs bodies in the Republic of Slovenia. If a person possesses such documents, they must be confiscated, but only if a person applies for alien status. As a rule, a passport should be confiscated and destroyed, and the person should be instructed to obtain a passport from his/her own country; only exceptionally may a foreigner's passport be issued.[258]

This circular was sent to the local bodies before the erasure, so it applied not only to the people who were later erased but to all SFRY citizens who did not gain Slovenian citizenship and were therefore considered ineligible to reside in Slovenia. Moreover, the measure quoted above was not prescribed by law. The handling of passports issued under the SFRY legislation was addressed in the Passports of the Republic of Slovenia Act,[259] which was part of the independence legislation. It stipulated that Yugoslav passports would remain in use for two years after the new law (the Aliens Act) came into force, meaning that they expired on 26 June 1993 at the latest. Yugoslav passports had to be exchanged for Slovenian passports at the expiration of the two-year period at the latest, while new Slovenian passports could be issued only to Slovenian citizens. Citizens of other republics who did not gain Slovenian citizenship (regardless of whether or not their previous passport had been issued in Slovenia) could only obtain a foreigner's passport if they met the requirements set out in Article 44. In other words, the law on Slovenian passports did not distinguish between Slovenian citizens and the citizens of other SFRY republics who did not gain Slovenian citizenship. This differentiation was introduced by the Ministry of the Interior and it was not based in law. The testimonies of the erased people demonstrate that the instructions were consistently observed in practice.

Had the rule of law been observed, a separate law would have been passed regulating the passports of SFRY citizens who did not gain Slovenian citizenship. It should have specified in detail when and why their passports expired. It could have prescribed the same deadline (two years) as for Slovenian citizens. Every

258 The in-house instruction of the Ministry of the Interior to all local administration bodies entitled *Zakon o tujcih – zaključki s posvetovanja z dne 23/1-1992* (The Aliens Act – conclusions of the consultation meeting on 23/1-1992), No. 0016/9-S-26/3-92 dated 5 February 1992.

259 Zakon o potnih listinah državljanov Republike Slovenije, Official Gazette of the Republic of Slovenia, No. 1/1991I.

holder of such a passport should have received a notification specifying the date of expiration, instructions on how to apply for a new passport or a foreigner's passport before the expiration date, and the conditions for obtaining a new passport. If a passport holder failed to take all the necessary steps, the relevant body should have launched a legal procedure to obtain a ruling as a basis to invalidate the passport. Such a decision should have contained the reasons for its invalidation and information on the right to appeal. In this way, the rights of individuals would have been protected as required by the rule of law, and particularly the principle of trust in law.

The issue of ID cards was addressed by new legislation only in 1997, meaning that Yugoslav ID cards were valid until their expiration date. Accordingly, no special provision referred to the ID cards of citizens of other republics who did not gain Slovenian citizenship, but the in-house instruction of the Ministry was clear on this issue: if such a person turned to an administrative body, his/her ID card was to be invalidated.

Since the people who did not qualify for citizenship were no longer legally allowed to live in Slovenia but still had jobs in Slovenia, employers had to invent other ways to legalise their employment. One option was a work visa. The in-house instruction dated 18 February 1992 advised local administrative bodies to issue a work visa at a request of a company to all foreign workers who had a valid Yugoslav passport. When applying for a work visa, the company had to specify the duration of the period for which the visa was requested, but the instruction specified that, "until the new labour legislation is passed", as a general rule the work visa should not be issued for more than three months.

A foreign worker who did not have a valid Yugoslav passport could be issued a foreigner's passport.[260] As proceeds from the in-house instructions, this rule was introduced on the initiative of construction companies whose contracts abroad depended on workers who did not gain Slovenian citizenship, so they were concerned that these workers would encounter difficulties when crossing the border.

The above instruction explains why some erased people were able to retain their jobs although they had no legal status or valid personal documents. That said, the restrictive requirements for a work visa, its short validity, and the resulting need for repeated renewals explain why these persons were more likely to

260 The in-house instruction of the Ministry of the Interior to all local administration bodies entitled *Problematika tujcev, zaposlenih v gradbenih podjetjih – stališče* (The issue of aliens employed by construction companies – a stance), No. 0016/4-1255-8 dated 18 February 1992.

lose their jobs than Slovenian citizens (I assume here that the reason was not general xenophobia on the part of the employers).

3. The In-house Instructions on the Erasure from the Register of Permanent Residents

3.1 The In-house Instructions of 28 February 1992 – The Erasure, the Invalidation of Passports, and Deportations

The Ministry's in-house instructions contained a maximally restrictive interpretation of Article 81 of the Aliens Act. According to this interpretation, the citizens of other SFRY republics with permanent residence in Slovenia who did not apply for Slovenian citizenship lost the right to reside in the country on 26 February 1992, the day when the provisions in the Aliens Act came into force. Those who applied for citizenship and were denied had to leave Slovenia within two months of being notified.

On 27 February 1992, one day after the two-month period expired, another in-house instruction was dispatched advising local administrative bodies to begin 'fixing' the status of all persons covered by Article 81, Para 2 of the Aliens Act.[261] These were people who had resided in Slovenia lawfully until 25 February 1992 and, in accordance with the Constitutional Law, had the same rights and obligations as Slovenian citizens. On 26 February they lost the right to reside in Slovenia and had to re-apply for a temporary or permanent residence permit. To be granted a permit, they had to meet the same requirements as other foreigners who were non-Yugoslav citizens. The instructions were sent only to the administrative bodies, although the obligations referred to third persons. In other words, only the local administrations were informed that these persons were obliged to start resolving their new status, while the people affected by the provision were not.[262] In addition, the local administrative bodies were instructed to bring the

---

261 The in-house instruction of the Ministry of the Interior to all local administration bodies entitled *Izvajanje Zakona o tujcih – navodilo* (The implementation of the Aliens Act – an instruction), No. 0016/4-1496-8 dated 27 February 1992.

262 Some have argued that the people who were erased had two months to arrange their status, that is, starting on 25 December 1991 when the deadline for the applications expired. It is true that Article 81 defined this period as a transition, but it did not include any provision imposing the resolution of their status. It is evident from the dispatches that the obligation to resolve one's status was defined only on 27 February 1992 when the two-month period had already expired. The assertion is therefore false.

data in the register of permanent residents "in line" with the interpretation of Article 81, Para 2 of the Aliens Act.

> In parallel [...] it is necessary to begin to sort the records. To this end, a project has been launched to set up online records of foreigners, and adequate training will be provided. This will take place by region and you will be informed about it in time.[263]

This instruction is crucial to understanding the erasure. The persons affected by this measure would not have needed to regulate their status had the government not deprived them of it arbitrarily and without advance notice. While the annulment of their status constituted the erasure in the wider sense of the word, "the sorting of records" was its technical implementation. Accordingly, the residence registrations of all Yugoslav citizens who did not apply for Slovenian citizenship were marked as terminated on 26 February 1992. The residence of persons who applied for citizenship but were denied expired two months after the denial was issued. The register also contained a box for the entry of a new permanent address. These entries were completely arbitrary. The administration employees entered the name of an SFRY republic, mainly based on the republic citizenship of the person in question, or, to be more precise, based on their own assumptions. Most of the erased people continued to live in Slovenia because they were not notified that their legal status had been invalidated.

The Ministry's leading officials were aware that most of the people whose residence registration was terminated would not meet the criteria for obtaining alien status under the Aliens Act. This is obvious from another passage of the above-mentioned instructions, in which State Secretary Slavko Debelak wrote:

> Many problems can be expected to emerge during that period [of sorting the records] in connection with people who will become foreigners on 28/2/21992 [sic!] and who have not applied either for temporary or for permanent residence permits.[264]

The fact that the government and the State Secretary decided to rob these persons of their legal status while being fully aware of the resulting problems suggests that the restrictive interpretation of the provisions in the Aliens Act was intentional. Instead of attempting to prevent the anticipated problems, they adapted the steps they took to be able to tackle these problems. One such move was the unlawful invalidation of personal documents:

---

263 The in-house instruction of the Ministry of the Interior to all local administration bodies entitled *Izvajanje Zakona o tujcih – navodilo* (The implementation of the Aliens Act – an instruction), No. 0016/4-1496-8 dated 27 February 1992.

264 *Ibid.*

> We would like to point out that their [foreigners'] papers, even if issued by relevant bodies in our country and still valid, shall cease to be valid due to the changed status of these persons.[265]

This recalled an earlier instruction of the Ministry that ordered local administrative bodies to confiscate and destroy these persons' ID cards and passports.[266]

The next measure taken to resolve the expected problems was deportation—meaning that the apprehensions of an opposition MP about "expulsion deportations" came true. The in-house instruction dated 27 February 1992 reveals that the deportations were planned before the erasure itself was carried out. It states that no official decision on the cancellation of a residence permit was required if a foreigner entered Slovenia without a passport, visa, entry permit, or residence permit; such a person could simply be "taken to the border [by the police] to cross over without any decision issued by the administrative body".[267] It should be noted that citizens of other SFRY republics who lived in Slovenia did not need to present these documents when they entered Slovenia, because at the time Slovenia was still part of Yugoslavia and there were no borders between the republics. It is interesting that the police resisted such "deportations to the state border". The dispatch said that "police units insist that in such cases an administrative body has to issue a decision on the cancellation of residence permits". However, the Ministry made it clear that such an interpretation was "not consistent with the law". Its intention was to force local administrative bodies to persuade the police to deport people without a ruling. The testimonies of the erased people show that many people were expelled (or "transported to the state border") without prior court proceedings and without a court ruling.

3.2 The In-house Instruction of 15 June 1992 – The Removal of Individual and Household Records

More detailed instructions on how to treat SFRY citizens and sort records were given at the consultation session on 28 May 1992, followed by written instructions in the form of a circular dated 15 June 1992. Since registers of permanent

265 *Ibid.*

266 The in-house instruction of the Ministry of the Interior to all local administration bodies entitled Zakon o tujcih – zaključki s posvetovanja z dne 23/1-1992 (The Aliens Act – the conclusions of the consultation on 23/1-1992), No. 0016/9-S-26/3-92 dated 5 February 1992.

267 *Ibid.*

residences were kept digitally and manually, the instructions referred to both types of data. Upon establishing that

> a person is not a citizen of the Republic of Slovenia [...], he/she is to be instructed to regulate his/her alien status and his/her records are erased from the register of permanent residents. The change of status must be duly noted in the digital record and in all records maintained by local administrative bodies. As to the manual register of permanent residents, the box "Official note" will read "became a foreigner" accompanied by the date when the person's status was changed. The personal records are to be removed from the register and placed in a separate register of persons who were released from Slovenian citizenship. The box "Type of change" in the family record will read "became a foreigner" and family members whose status has changed are to be erased from the family records. If all family members have become foreigners, this must be noted in the 'Official note' box along with the date, and the household record is to be removed and placed in a separate register of households that have moved elsewhere or ceased to exist.[268]

This circular, too, contained instructions on the destruction of personal documents, mentioning ID cards in particular:

> An ID card issued in the Republic of Slovenia is to be destroyed. The record of issuing the ID card is to be removed from the register of ID cards and destroyed.[269]

The invalidation and destruction of ID cards was not based on a law or an executive act. It should be noted that the records were removed and placed in the register of persons who were dismissed from Slovenian citizenship. In effect, the erasure was tantamount to cancelling a person's citizenship status – and the authorities were aware of this.

An analysis of the terminology used in this in-house instruction reveals that the authorities tried to present the erasure as a purely administrative act with no connection whatsoever to the people whose lives it affected. At the same time, it reveals a discrepancy between the records and reality of which the government employees must have been aware. The instruction referring to household records that were to be "removed and placed in a separate register of households that moved elsewhere or ceased to exist" is particularly conspicuous. The fact is that most families did not move away, and by no means ceased to exist. On the contrary, they continued to live in Slovenia without legal status. They ceased to exist

---

268 The in-house instruction of the Ministry of the Interior to all local administration bodies entitled *Zaključki s posvetovanja, ki je bilo dne 28/5-1992 za referente, ki delajo na področju registra stalnega prebivalstva* (The conclusions of the consultation session held on 28 May 1992 for employees working with registers of permanent residents), No. 0016/2-S1.-92 dated 15 June 1992.

269 *Ibid.*

in the registers of the administrative bodies, but were present in real life and had to struggle to keep their homes.

The same circular explains when a person became a foreigner (i.e. when the annulment of his/her legal status came into effect). Persons who met all the criteria for gaining citizenship in accordance with Article 40 of the Aliens Act but did not apply for citizenship became foreigners on 26 February 1992, or on the day when they regulated their alien status, whichever was earlier. Persons who applied for citizenship and were denied became aliens two months after being notified of the decision, regardless of whether they appealed, as according to the Administrative Dispute Act an appeal cannot suspend the execution of such a decision. Persons who registered a permanent or temporary address in Slovenia after 23 December 1990 were not entitled to apply for citizenship, so they became foreigners on the day Slovenia gained independence, i.e. on 26 June 1991.[270] The instruction dated 15 September 1995 additionally specified that if a pending application for citizenship was terminated, the person became an alien when the decision on the termination of the procedure was finalised, i.e. on the day the decision was handed to the person.[271]

The instructions also reveal how exactly the act of erasure from the register of permanent residents was carried out in practice. As a matter of fact, there were several interpretations of the erasure. The Ministry of the Interior insisted that no erasure took place, as the records were only "transferred" from the register of permanent residents to the register of aliens, and that this procedure was based on the Law on Residence and Population Registers.[272] Another explanation was that the register of permanent residents was initially maintained manually and later digitised, so at the time of the erasure these records were designated as "dead" but remained part of the register.[273]

---

270 The in-house instruction of the Ministry of the Interior to all local administration bodies entitled *Zaključki s posvetovanja, ki je bilo dne 28/5-1992 za referente, ki delajo na področju registra stalnega prebivalstva* (The conclusions of the consultation session held on 28 May 1992 for employees working with registers of permanent residents), No. 0016/2-S1.-92 dated 15 June 1992.

271 A letter from the Ministry of the Interior to all local administration bodies entitled *Začetek veljavnosti določb Zakona o tujcih – 81. člen*, No. 0012/8-252-206 dated 15 September 1995.

272 Zakon o evidenci nastanitve občanov in o registru prebivalstva, Official Gazette of the Socialist Republic of Slovenia, No. 6/1983, 26/1990.

273 Hot, Reševanje vprašanja izbrisanih, 2004, p. 14–15.

The latter explanation, which was also corroborated by the Constitutional Court Rulings No. U-I-284/94 and No. U-II-1/04, is consistent with the in-house instructions mentioned earlier. Even today, erased persons can obtain a printout of past registrations of permanent residence from the register. Regarding the alleged "transfer" of records to a register of aliens, the Constitutional Court ruled that the Aliens Act did not mention any register of aliens without permanent residence permits, so the records of citizens of other SFRY republics could not be transferred to such a register.[274]

To sum up, the erased persons were mainly members of the lower working class and their children. They were not aware of the seriousness of their situation, the approaching deadline that had major implications for their status, or the consequences of a lapse in citizenship. They knew nothing about the administrative "cleansing", either during the period when the preparations for it were underway or later, when it was accomplished. Even months later, many were not aware of it unless they found out by chance, for example, when they wanted to extend their driver's licenses or sought medical assistance.

Given the employment and education demographics of the erased group, it is evident that the erasure had a class aspect to it: the people who were erased were members of a social class that was identified as disposable.

The instructions discussed above had the practical effect of creating a group of people who were later named "the erased". The latest data by the Ministry of the Interior obtained from an in-house inspection of records in January 2009 show that this group comprised 25671 people. As mentioned in the previous chapter, 29000 people who were citizens of another SFRY republic but lived in Slovenia were denied Slovenian citizenship. This yields a difference of around 3300 people, or, in other words, 3300 of the 29000 non-Slovenian SFRY citizens are not considered erased. It is assumed that these persons left Slovenia or deregistered their residence there of their own will before 26 February 1992.

4. The Consequences of the Erasure

4.1 Disregard for the Situation of Citizens of Other SFRY Republics in Slovenia

The result of the erasure and the interpretation of Article 81, Para 2 of the Aliens Act described above was that citizens of other SFRY republics were deprived of their legal status and were obliged to acquire it anew as if they had never been

274 Constitutional Court of the Republic of Slovenia, Ruling No. U-II-1/04.

Slovenian residents, while foreigners who wished to enter the country for the first time and reside there could do so.[275] While the Aliens Act was apparently neutral and applied to all aliens without discrimination, it discriminated against the citizens of other SFRY republics in practice because it did not take into account the fact that they had acquired the right to reside in Slovenia before the country became independent. Similarly, it did not take certain other circumstances into account that made the acquisition of permanent or temporary residence permits under general conditions very difficult for this group. Disregard for their specific position was one of the reasons why the Constitutional Court ruled that the Aliens Act was unconstitutional (more on this in Part IV).[276]

Article 19 of the Aliens Act stipulated that a person could obtain a temporary residence permit on the grounds of schooling, specialisation, employment, medical treatment, professional activity, marriage to a partner who was a Slovenian citizen, ownership of a property in Slovenia, rights arising from work in Slovenia (e.g. pension), or another justified reason. Accordingly, temporary residence permits were issued mainly to erased people whose partners were Slovenian citizens and those who had employment.

The condition for obtaining a permanent residence permit under Article 16 of the Aliens Act was, in addition to the criteria listed above, three years of residence in Slovenia on a temporary residence permit.[277] However, erased people did not meet this condition because registrations of permanent residence from the period preceding the erasure were not taken into account.[278] To be more precise, it began to be taken into account only later, based on Government Decision No. 260-01/91-2/5-8 dated 3 September 1992 (more on this below). Persons who could not prove that they had sufficient means to support themselves could not obtain either temporary or permanent residence permits. This proved to be an insurmountable difficulty for erased people who were unemployed or unable to work unless a third person (a family member, an acquaintance, etc.) provided

---

275 This conclusion was also confirmed by the Constitutional Court, Ruling No. U-I-284/94, paragraph 14.

276 Constitutional Court of the Republic of Slovenia, Ruling No. U-I-284/94.

277 The Government later adopted Decision No. 26001/912/58 dated 3 September 1992, which said that the three-year residence requirement was to be considered fulfilled if the person had his/her permanent address registered in Slovenia for at least three years and actually lived in Slovenia before "the provisions of the Aliens Act" came into force.

278 Confirmed by the Constitutional Court of the Republic of Slovenia, Ruling No. U-I-284/94, Paragraph 14.

for their subsistence.[279] A temporary residence permit was also unavailable to the following groups: persons who were expelled or removed from the country, or were prohibited from being present in the country, as long as the prohibition was in place; international offenders; persons without identification papers; persons with invalid identification documents; and persons who came from regions plagued by infectious diseases and had no proof of vaccination.

The requirement that the person had to enter the country lawfully with a passport, as specified in Article 13 of the Aliens Act, posed an additional difficulty. The erased people did enter the country lawfully but not necessarily by presenting their passports, since they arrived in Slovenia when it was still part of Yugoslavia and thus did not need a passport to enter. Moreover, even if they had valid passports issued under SFRY legislation, these were invalidated and destroyed when they presented them to the Slovenian administrative bodies, who subsequently instructed them to obtain passports from their "own" countries. In other words, they were treated just like all other foreigners in the country despite their unique situation. For many erased persons, obtaining a passport or other required documents (birth certificate, proof of a clean criminal record) was practically impossible because of the war raging in the Balkans at the time.[280] The certificates and other required papers could not be older than several months, which presented an additional problem; procedures were protracted, so the same documents had to be produced time and again as they became outdated before the procedure was completed.[281]

These difficulties led to the Constitutional Court's Ruling No. U-I-284/94, which stated that the Aliens Act, in terms of content, was not in line with the situation of citizens of other republics and that consequently its provisions could not be applied to this group of people, not even by employing legal analogies.[282]

Some administration employees attempted to help the erased residents, but they were forced to breach the law to do so. For example, in one case a statement

279 Pistotnik, The Erasure as a Testing Ground for European Migration Policies, in: The Scars of the Erasure, 2010, p. 72.

280 Ogradi, Izbrisani državljani SFRJ (2003), p. 25.

281 Pistotnik, The Erasure as a Testing Ground for European Migration Policies, in: The Scars of the Erasure, 2010, p. 72.

282 Constitutional Court of the Republic of Slovenia, Ruling No. U-I-284/94, Paragraph 13.

by a person who worked illegally was accepted as proof that he had sufficient means to support himself.[283]

Persons who did not meet the requirements for obtaining a residence permit were forced to live for years without legal status. For those who managed to obtain a temporary residence permit, the situation improved temporarily, but once the permit expired they had to go through the whole procedure again, ensuring that anxiety was always there. A relatively favourable aspect of the law was that the required length of residence in Slovenia on a temporary residence permit was initially three years. This requirement was changed in 1997, when the Act Amending the Aliens Act introduced the requirement of eight years of residence in Slovenia prior to obtaining a permanent residence permit.[284]

4.2 A Communication to the Government of 4 June 1992 – "Ignore the Acquired Rights"

The consequences of the erasure during the first few months following its implementation are also evident from a letter dated 4 June 1992, addressed to the Government and signed by Igor Bavčar, the Minister of the Interior at the time.[285] In it, the Minister informed the government that as a result of the "operationalisation" of Article 40 of the Citizenship of the Republic of Slovenia Act, approximately 40000 people had become foreigners in Slovenia "by force of law or as a consequence of rejected citizenship". These people then attempted to acquire legal status. Thus, 800 applications for permanent residence were submitted by 1 June 1992. By the same date, the City of Ljubljana municipal body alone issued 5000 temporary residence permits. In the words of the Minister, applicants for residence permits were motivated by substantial reasons such as having resided in Slovenia for a significant amount of time, employment, marriage to a partner who had Slovenian citizenship, the desire to secure the ownership rights to a property, and the like. Acquired rights were another important motivator. However, these often conflicted with the legal requirements for obtaining a residence permit. For example, an unemployed person had the right to unemployment

283 Pistotnik, The Erasure as a Testing Ground for European Migration Policies, in: The Scars of the Erasure, 2010, p. 72.

284 Zakon o spremembah Zakona o tujcih, Official Gazette of the Republic of Slovenia, No. 44/1997.

285 A letter from the Ministry of the Interior to the Government of the Republic of Slovenia entitled "*Open issues related to the implementation of the Aliens Act*", No. 0016/1-S-010/3-91 dated 4 June 1992.

benefits before the erasure, but was no longer able to exercise this right afterwards. On top of this, such a person did not have sufficient means to support himself/herself, thereby failing to meet another condition for obtaining a residence permit.

The Minister also described a "special problem with processing the applications for permanent residence" which was a consequence of two legal stances that gained currency. According to the first, which took into account the rights acquired before 23 December 1990 and 25 June 1991, persons who "under the previous legislation had their permanent residence registered in the Republic of Slovenia" should have retained their permanent resident status regardless of their change of status in accordance with the Aliens Act. The second stance was that the provision in the Aliens Act prevailed, so the permanent residence permit could be obtained only by persons who resided in Slovenia for three years on a temporary residence permit. Minister Bavčar proposed that the government should adhere to the latter legal opinion and "ignore the acquired rights".

He supported this proposal with several arguments, mentioning draft laws on the social protection and employment of foreigners and resulting rights (to which persons with permanent residence permits were also entitled). He also pointed out that the first legal stance was problematic because once permanent resident status was granted, it was difficult to revoke it. He illustrated why that would be problematic with the example of personae non grata — "repeat offenders, violators of the public order and peace and certain persons who once belonged to the YPA"—who, in his opinion, should not have obtained permanent resident status. The Minister, however, failed to mention that this group constituted a tiny minority and that the people affected by the erasure mainly came from the lower working classes. He also added that Slovenia had observed the principle of individual free will and had respected "all the rights" of the citizens of other SFRY republics. Citizenship-wise, his assertion was partly true, but it fell short of reality regarding permanent resident status. The letter mentions only one argument that could be interpreted as supporting the first legal stance, that is, that these persons, "due to long-standing residence in Slovenia, lost contact with their countries of origin, hence their substantial ties to Slovenia".[286] Obviously, the Minister did not find this argument important enough to change his convictions and recognise the need to respect acquired rights.

The letter was sent to the government three and a half months after the erasure, meaning that the interpretation of the relevant provisions in the Aliens Act

286 *Ibid.*

could not have been changed even if the government had wished to do so. At any rate, the government must have been acquainted with the implementation of the erasure, so it is safe to assume that it agreed with the interpretation. It should also be noted that Minister Bavčar was a member of the government and although the instructions to local authorities were signed by Slavko Debelak, a Secretary with the Ministry of the Interior, they definitely had Minister Bavčar's approval.

The letter is a valuable source for yet another reason. It contains key information about differing opinions within the state administration and about the arguments provided in support of each. In addition, it produced a specific result. On 2 September 1992 the government adopted Decision No. 260-01/91-2/5-8 stipulating that the requirement of a three-year uninterrupted residence in Slovenia on a temporary residence permit should be considered fulfilled if a person "[has] had their permanent residence registered for at least three years and actually lived here [in Slovenia] before the provision in the Aliens Act went into force".[287]

It is obvious that the decision was a compromise between the differing legal opinions presented by Minister Bavčar. However, only one group of affected people had their acquired rights recognised in this way: those who had registered their permanent residence three years before the Aliens Act's provisions came into force. Individuals who had permanent resident status for less than three years were left out. It is not possible to glean from the explanation accompanying the Decision which circumstances were taken into account when prescribing the three-year requirement and why the rule was not applied to all people who had permanent residence in Slovenia on 23 December 1990. The explanation suggests that the compromise was of a general nature and rather hasty.

> The independence legislation of the Republic of Slovenia relating to interior affairs took into account to the greatest extent possible the rights of the citizens of other republics of the former Yugoslavia which arise from the international convention and inter-state agreements. The independence legislation (particularly Article 40 of the Citizenship Act and Article 81 of the Aliens Act) enabled these people to freely choose their status.

Indeed, this part of the explanation contradicts the content of the decision. If the independence legislation had truly respected all the rights of these individuals, why was it then necessary to issue a decision that interfered with the law and changed its interpretation by dismissing one of the legal conditions for acquiring a permanent residence permit?

---

287 The Decision of the Government of the RS 260-01/91-2/5-8 dated 3 September 1992. See also a dispatch by the Ministry of the Interior to all local administration bodies Zakona o tujcih (The Aliens Act), No. 0016/4-6744-8 dated 16 September 1992.

In 1992, 1468 permanent residence permits were issued based on this decision (which was not published, leaving the people who were affected uninformed of these developments); 763 were issued in 1993, 361 were issued in 1994, 312 were issued in 1995, 640 were issued in 1996, and 1259 were issued in 1997. Altogether 4893 permanent residence permits were issued on this basis.[288] The Constitutional Court later ruled that by adopting the above-mentioned decision the government encroached on the domain of the judiciary. The ruling stated that "the government does not have legal permission to determine a manner in which a legal provision will be implemented by issuing a decision as an individual act". Instead of issuing a decision, it should have "proposed to the legislator how to regulate the legal status" of citizens of other republics.[289] Let me add that it would have been more effective to amend the Aliens Act so as to enable the acquisition of permanent residence permits for the elapsed period at least by all citizens of other SFRY republics who had permanent residence registered in Slovenia on 23 December 1990, or even better, all those who had valid permanent residence permits until 25 June 1991. Had the government decided to do so, it would have precluded the ECHR Judgment in 2012.

4.3 Informing the Public about the Erasure

Representatives of the Ministry of the Interior, of the government, and other high officials rejected the objections that members of the public were not informed about their impending loss of status and their options to apply for citizenship both publicly and in certain official documents. They argued that the information was initially spread by means of the mass media and billboards, later followed by personal invitations. Certain local administrations, for example, in Ljubljana, Maribor, and Koper, used phone calls to invite people to fix their status, or invited them to do so by unregistered or registered post, as prescribed by the General Administrative Procedure Act. All of this was supposedly done in addition to publishing the information in the official gazette of the Republic of Slovenia, which, according to the government, would have sufficed in itself.[290]

I will not waste time trying to explain how it could possibly suffice to publish the information that a person's legal status is to be annulled in the official gazette.

288 Constitutional Court of the Republic of Slovenia, Ruling No. U-I-284/94, Para 3.

289 *Ibid.*

290 For example, the answer of the Government of the Republic of Slovenia regarding the acceptability and justifiability of the complaint in the case *Makuc and others v. Slovenia* (now *Kurić and Others v. Slovenia*), dated 26 October 2007, Para 27.

Instead, let me investigate the two methods of informing the public mentioned above. The first was information in the media about the Citizenship of the Republic of Slovenia Act and its conditions for obtaining citizenship. This information was published in the second part of 1991 when the submission of applications for citizenship was already underway. It reached quite a large number of people, given that the majority of those who were entitled to apply for citizenship under Article 40 submitted applications.

The second phase of informing the public, allegedly involving personal invitations, took place after 26 February 1992, when the erasure had already been implemented and people had already been deprived of their legal status. Some responded to the letters sent out by local administrative bodies, others did not. The bulletin *Okno uprave* ("Window of Administration", a bulletin of the Association of Professional Workers in Interior Administration) reveals the manner in which the public was informed and the responses. The issue dated 28 March 2003 featured an interview with Slavko Debelak, a State Secretary with the Ministry of the Interior at the time of the erasure, who signed most of the in-house instructions on the erasure, as well as interviews with other employees who implemented the erasure in practice. One employee working for the local administrative body in Ljubljana stated:

> At the (then) City of Ljubljana Secretariat for Internal Affairs we ordered a print out of all persons who did not have Slovenian citizenship (republic citizenship under the old legislation) and did not submit applications for Slovenian citizenship within the prescribed deadline. We sent out invitations to all of them and informed them of the changes that were a result of Slovenia's independence. We sent out around 7000 invitations: most of these were returned with the remark "unknown" or "moved", while approximately 2000 were delivered to the recipients; between 500 and 700 people responded. We devoted attention to every one among them, we took into account the fact that some regions were mired in war and that they could not bring all the documents. Their response was mainly affirmative and those who decided to remain in Slovenia sorted out their status – in one way or another.[291]

The testimonies of many erased persons from the Ljubljana district (and other parts of Slovenia) discredit the statement above; they were not able to resolve their status for years or even an entire decade. Those who did not receive an invitation to visit a local administration office learned about the erasure when they tried to fulfil an administrative obligation, for example, to renew their driver's licenses or some other document, enrol in a secondary school or a university

291 Lumbar, Vabila, 2003.

course, or when they stopped receiving cash benefits.[292] Certain erased people stated that they declined to accept the invitation or did not respond to it deliberately because they heard from others that their documents would be invalidated.

The invitations were a decoy, a deceitful tactic used by administrative employees to attract people to the local office, ostensibly to "resolve their status", but the actual result of the person's visit to the local administration was precisely the opposite.[293]

4.4 Invalidation of Identification Documents and Difficulties with Acquiring Legal Status

Those who responded to the invitation or turned to the local administration office at some later point in time had already been deprived of their legal status. To obtain a temporary residence permit, they had to fulfil the same conditions as other foreigners who were entering the country for the first time. When an erased person turned up at a local administrative office, he/she was asked to present identification documents; if he/she did so, their documents were invalidated.[294] The erased person was then informed that he/she had lost his/her legal status and was instructed to acquire alien status. The responsibility for legal status was therefore placed on the victims of the erasure.[295]

The employees then informed the erased person about his/her options and the documents that he/she had to submit to obtain legal status. One of the documents required was a passport of the country whose citizen the erased person presumably was (the authorities made assumptions about his/her citizenship[296]). This meant that the erased person had to exit Slovenia to obtain the passport. However, in most cases the country of citizenship required proof of one's registration of permanent residence to issue a passport. Certain countries (Croatia in particular) did not impose strict requirements and accepted fictitious

292 Zdravković, The Struggle Against the Denial of Citizenship, in: The Scars of the Erasure, 2010, p. 257.

293 Dedić, Jalušič, Zorn, The Erased: Organized Innocence and the Politics of Exclusion, 2003, p. 105.

294 Pistotnik, The Erasure as a Testing Ground for European Migration Policies, in: The Scars of the Erasure, 2010, p. 65, note 12.

295 Dedić, Jalušič, Zorn, The Erased: Organized Innocence and the Politics of Exclusion, 2003, p. 97.

296 Pistotnik, The Erasure as a Testing Ground for European Migration Policies, in: The Scars of the Erasure, 2010, p. 65.

registrations at a friend's or relative's address as proof.[297] Other countries compounded the problems faced by erased people by asking them to submit proof that they had de-registered their permanent residence in Slovenia before allowing them to register a permanent address in that other country; erased people could not produce such proof because they had not actively de-registered their permanent address in Slovenia.

For some individuals, these administrative obstacles were insurmountable. They fell into a vicious circle, left without identification documents and were unable to obtain them either in Slovenia or their country of origin.

The time gaps between the disintegration of Yugoslavia, the establishment of successor countries, and those countries' adoption of new citizenship legislation caused further problems. For example, Bosnia-Herzegovina only established unified passports in 1997; until then, the Federation of Bosnia and Herzegovina and the Republika Srpska had separate passports. Certain regions were struggling with wars that closed down state offices and destroyed records, so no documents, certificates, or extracts could be issued.

A newly introduced visa for the citizens of all the successor states except Croatia also posed a great obstacle. To obtain documents from their country of origin, erased people could not avoid travelling there, because the successor states did not have diplomatic or consular offices in Slovenia at the time. Those who managed to retain their SFRY passports or obtained a foreigner's passport in Slovenia (which enabled a one-way journey only) could leave Slovenia, but they could not re-enter without a visa. Some were helped by friends, relatives, and various humanitarian organisations (including churches) who procured the papers in their countries of origin so they did not have to leave Slovenia. There were even companies that offered document procurement services for a fee.[298] Once consular offices were established in Slovenia, the passports could be obtained there without leaving the country. However, the rules were soon changed and a residence permit in Slovenia became a condition for obtaining a passport through the consulate.

The erasure, inconsistent legal provisions, the absence of diplomatic and consular offices and diplomatic relations among countries, and the risk of not being able to re-enter Slovenia once they left the country forced erased people to circumvent the law or even to resort to unlawful methods to resolve their status.

297 In one case, the Croatian authorities accepted the residential address in Slovenia where the person applying for a Croatian passport had lived before the erasure.

298 Pistotnik, The Erasure as a Testing Ground for European Migration Policies, in: The Scars of the Erasure, 2010, p. 66–67.

Throughout this time, the authorities and the public at large made statements along the lines that these people "came from somewhere else" and therefore could "as well return there".[299] Needless to say, this was far from true. Many of the erased people were born in Slovenia and had spent their whole lives there, and many moved to Slovenia decades before the erasure—it was not merely the place where they had their permanent address, it was their habitual place of residence and they intended to continue to live there.

4.5 The Expiration of Driver's Licenses

In 1991, the Amendments to the Road Traffic Safety Act were passed.[300] Article 6 stipulated that driver's licenses issued under the SFRY legislation could remain in use for three years after the Amendments were passed,[301] until 25 June 1994. However, erased people who attempted to replace their driver's licenses within the three-year period could not be issued new licenses, as they did not have legal status or valid identification documents. In 1998 a new Road Safety Act was passed,[302] allowing foreign driver's licenses to be exchanged for Slovenian licenses under certain conditions. Article 135 of this law stipulated that foreigners who had been living in Slovenia for more than six months could apply for the replacement of a foreign driver's license with a Slovenian license within one year of the commencement of their residence in Slovenia without taking a driving test. This law came into force on 1 May 1998, and erased people could use the provision if they obtained a residence permit after 1 May 1998, if it was valid for more than six months, and if they had a valid driver's license issued in another country. The time window was very short, so many erased people missed it. This meant that an erased person whose driver's license expired could only obtain a new Slovenian driver's license by taking a driving test, incurring additional expenses.

4.6 Implications for Employment

The erasure had many implications for the employment of affected persons. The act that became applicable for the erased people's employment was the

---

299 *Ibid.*, p. 67.

300 Zakon o varnosti cestnega prometa, Official Gazette of the Socialist Republic of Slovenia, No. 5/1982, 40/1984 in 29/1986.

301 Zakon o spremembah in dopolnitvah Zakona o varnosti cestnega prometa, Official Gazette of the Republic of Slovenia, No. 1/1991.

302 Zakon o varnosti cestnega prometa, Official Gazette of the Republic of Slovenia, No. 30/1998.

Employment of Aliens Act. It was passed in July 1992[303] and stipulated that aliens who wanted to work in Slovenia had to apply for a work permit.[304] Article 23 of this act stipulated that a personal work permit of unlimited duration could be obtained only by citizens of other republics who had an open-ended employment contract on the day the law came into force and had worked in Slovenia for at least ten years before that date. Those who had jobs but had worked in Slovenia for less than ten years before that date, or had temporary employment contracts, or were daily migrant workers, or received unemployment cash benefits, could obtain personal work permits for one year.

Persons who were denied Slovenian citizenship on the grounds of posing a threat to public order or crimes against the country and the nation were not entitled to apply for a work visa under the Aliens Employment Act. This provision was not grounded in a persuasive reason (why would a person who was convicted of a minor crime be completely excluded from the labour market?), and the law did not give the decision-making body the option of exercising discretion or applying the principle of proportionality. Obviously, the provision was aimed at preventing these people from living in Slovenia in the future.

The Aliens Employment Act further imposed on employers the obligation to send a written notice to those of their employees who were citizens of other former republics, informing them about the provisions that affected them. Citizens of other republics who did not apply for a work permit or were denied lost their jobs. Under Article 26, Para 1 of the Aliens Employment Act, their employment ended on the day that the decision on the termination of employment became valid. Citizens of other republics who were granted work permits could retain their jobs, and employment was one of the conditions for obtaining a residence permit. Persons who obtained personal work permits with unlimited validity therefore had free access to the labour market, and the permit was valid even if the person lost his/her job. The situation of those who held personal work permits with limited validity was more uncertain: once the work permit expired, its renewal depended on the willingness of the employer to retain the employee in question. Erased people who were employed at the time of the erasure could obtain work permits if they or their employers applied for it within the prescribed amount of time. They could therefore retain their jobs, and this also enabled

303 Zakon o zaposlovanju tujcev, Official Gazette of the Republic of Slovenia, No. 33/1992.

304 This was not a novelty; the same requirement existed in the equivalent SFRY law. *See* Official Gazette of the Socialist Federal Republic of Yugoslavia, No. 11/1978, 64/1989.

them to obtain temporary residence permits in accordance with the Aliens Act. In this way at least some of them were able to gain legal status.

It should be noted that after becoming a sovereign country, Slovenia made a transition to the market economy and at the same time lost markets in other SFRY republics. This produced a serious economic crisis and consequently a high unemployment rate; many erased people were affected. In other words, erased people often lost their jobs because they were unable to meet the conditions for obtaining a work permit, but the loss of one's legal status did not automatically cause the loss of one's job.[305] Nevertheless, the restrictions on obtaining personal work permits placed people in an uncertain situation and caused them concern as to whether they would be able to renew their work visas after one year. Their employers had additional expenses and had to overcome various administrative hurdles to retain erased workers.

The conditions that had to be fulfilled to obtain a work permit represented a serious obstacle for citizens of other former republics who did not gain Slovenian citizenship, because the law did not take their specific situation into account. The requirement of ten years of prior employment in Slovenia was exaggerated and arbitrary. The law did not make clear why someone who had worked in Slovenia for ten years before the Aliens Employment Act came into force was entitled to a personal work visa of unlimited validity, while someone else who had worked in Slovenia for a shorter amount of time was not. Once again, this reflects the fact that the requirements imposed by the Aliens Employment Act caused many erased persons to lose their jobs.

The Aliens Employment Act thus further complicated the situation of erased people, as it prevented many of them from retaining their jobs and forced them to accept jobs in the informal economy (e.g. construction, cleaning, etc.). This is how one erased woman described her life:

> All this time I was without status, had nothing. I worked 23, 30, 34 hours in a row. Without a pause! I finished at one job and went to the next, and so on. I was cleaning, including master cleaning, in companies, apartments, all of that illegally. All of that in order to make a living for my small children (Indira, 48).[306]

305 This is the opinion that was shaped by the case law. The Ruling by the Higher Court in Koper No. I Cp 739/2005 and the Ruling by the Higher Court in Ljubljana No. II Cp 4395/2009.

306 Kogovšek, The Erasure as a Violation of Legally protected Human Rights, in: The Scars of the Erasure, 2010, p. 122.

People without work permits also did not have the legal means to claim other rights arising from work, for example, the right to health care and insurance, fair working conditions (including restrictions on the length of a workday), and equal payment for equal work. If, for example, they were not paid for their work, they could not take the case to court because they did not have a work contract. Moreover, the years they spent working illegally did not count towards their retirement, because they were not paying contributions. Some of these individuals lost a decade or more of work that could have counted towards retirement.

> I was born in Slovenia and I was living in Slovenia. In 1982 or 1983 I started my first business, metal products manufacturing. I had to close the company in 1995, because I was erased by the Chamber of Commerce, because I didn't have Slovenian citizenship. I've had a regular job only since 2006. I lost 12 qualifying years because of the erasure (Tomislav, 59).[307]

Since work is how one earns a livelihood, restrictions on their access to the labour market constituted a very serious blow for most of the erased people. The inability to earn a livelihood affected every area of their lives. It is obviously impossible to say whether all active people who were erased would have had jobs if they had retained their status. However, they would have had – or should have had – access to the labour market under the same terms as the citizens of Slovenia even as foreigners with permanent residence permits. Article 8 of the Aliens Employment Act posed another problem for erased people. It stipulated that an open-ended personal work permit could only be issued to a foreigner who had lived in Slovenia for more than ten years on a permanent residence permit. This meant that an erased person without a job first had to obtain a permanent residence permit and then wait for another ten years to be entitled to apply for a personal work permit.[308] An open-ended personal work permit based solely on the permanent residence permit was not introduced until 2000.[309] In other words, erased people had no access to the labour market until 2000 unless they had already secured a job for which they could obtain a limited-term work permit. As a consequence, they could not register with the Employment Service and lost

307 *Ibid.*

308 Note that until 1997 when the amendments to the Employment of Aliens Act (Zakon o spremembah Zakona o tujcih, Official Gazette of the Republic of Slovenia, No. 44/1997) were passed, a foreigner could obtain a permanent residence permit after living in Slovenia for three years on a temporary residence permit, but in 1997 this limit was increased to eight years.

309 *See* Article 10, Para 9, of the Aliens Employment Act (Zakon o zaposlovanju in delu tujcev, Official Gazette of the Republic of Slovenia, No. 66/2000).

the rights arising from work to which they were entitled before the erasure (e.g. unemployment cash benefits and benefits paid while waiting for employment; for example, one of the appellants in the *Kurić and Others v. Slovenia* case lost the right to parental compensation). The Aliens Employment Act of 1992 has never been referred to the Constitutional Court. If it had been, the chances are that it would have been found unconstitutional, similarly to parts of the Aliens Act.

When analysing the consequences of the erasure from the perspective of the protection of human rights, for example, the right to access work, it is necessary to take into account the *non sequitur* argument which posits that causes and effects must be sufficiently linked to establish causal connection. Not all life events that followed in the wake of the erasure were its direct consequences; some could have occurred even if people had retained their permanent resident status.[310] That said, one should not be misled into thinking that the absence of legal status is a legitimate explanation for the loss of rights. The argument that a person had no legal status was often an expedient excuse to prevent him/her from accessing certain rights. Human rights violations often involve a pattern of chain reasoning: someone is deprived of his/her legal status, so he/she can no longer exercise his/her rights according to the legislation in force, but the authorities refer to the legislation to argue that the person must have legal status in order to be granted his/her rights. In this way, an apparently lawful exclusion may be explained by the fact that the person has no residence permit in the country, or had no permit to enter it, or the like.[311] To be able to rebut the *non sequitur* argument, it is necessary to understand how chain reasoning works. In the case of erased people, the argument claims that they were excluded from specific rights not because they were erased but because they did not have legal status. However, since it was precisely the erasure that robbed these people of their legal status, such an argument is untenable.

4.7 The Difficulty of Retaining the Right to Tenancy

Upon losing their legal status, erased people also lost the right to access accommodation. Before the erasure, under the 1982 Law on Housing Relations,[312] most

---

310 Kogovšek, The Erasure as a Violation of Legally protected Human Rights, in: The Scars of the Erasure, 2010, p. 85.

311 Chain reasoning is especially frequent when regulating access to economic and social rights; for more on this, *see also* Cholewinski, Irregular migrants, 2005, p. 31.

312 Zakon o stanovanjskih razmerjih, Official Gazette of the Socialist Republic of Slovenia, No. 35/1982.

of them had held the right to tenancy in socially owned apartments, or apartments owned by the companies for which they worked, or by the military.[313] When Slovenia became a sovereign country, these apartments were put on sale and the tenants could buy them on favourable terms. However, erased people were excluded from this opportunity. Before the erasure, they could not buy the apartments because their real right to property was suspended (although their other rights and obligations remained intact during the same period). After the erasure, they were excluded by the provisions in the Housing Act passed in 1991,[314] which stipulated Slovenian citizenship as a condition of this right. The question here is whether the provisions in the Housing Act were in line with the later Agreement on Succession Issues.[315] Article 6, attachment G of that agreement stipulates that the housing rights in the legislation of each successor state should be afforded equally to all citizens who were SFRY citizens and therefore held such a right without differentiation. According to this provision, the right to buy a socially owned apartment in Slovenia should also have been granted to tenants who did not gain Slovenian citizenship.

Since these people could not buy socially owned apartments, they had no choice but to rent during the period from 19 October 1991 (the day the Housing Act came into force) to 26 February 1992 (the date of the erasure). Their tenancy rights expired on the day of the erasure, in accordance with Article 141 of the Housing Act.

> We were not left without our apartment, we stayed in it, as it was owned by my husband's former employer. We got the offer to buy the apartment, but since we did not have a permanent residence permit [sic!], we couldn't do it. Now we pay rent, 140 euros plus expenses. And we only have one room, 39 square meters in size (Jasna, 61).[316]

After the erasure, erased people could not sign a rental agreement, so some were evicted from their apartments, or had their apartments confiscated or appropriated in some other way while they were away (e.g. after they were expelled from the country). In accordance with Article 126 of the 1991 Housing Act, tenants who chose not to buy the apartment or signed a rental agreement but moved out had the right to indemnification for any money they had invested in the

313 The transfer of property rights was based on Article 11 of the Housing Act (SZ), Official Gazette of the Republic of Slovenia, No. 18/1991I.

314 Stanovanjski zakon, Official Gazette of the Republic of Slovenia, No. 18/1991.

315 Official Gazette of the Republic of Slovenia, No. 20/2002.

316 Kogovšek, The Erasure as a Violation of Legally protected Human Rights, in: The Scars of the Erasure, 2010, p. 128.

apartment, regardless of their reason for not buying it. The Supreme Court confirmed that circumstances related to citizenship or legal status did not affect their right to indemnification.[317]

After the erasure, erased people were completely dependent on their acquaintances or relatives for accommodation; the only other possibility was to rent an apartment without a contract. Those who were not able to earn a livelihood (e.g. because of illness) were the most vulnerable. Many became homeless; they moved from one dwelling to another or lived in makeshift homes or outdoors.[318] Their vulnerability was exacerbated by the fact that they could not apply for not-for-profit apartments because these were only available to Slovenian citizens. This provision is inconsistent with the Council's Directive 2003/109/ES[319] that stipulates that not-for-profit accommodation should be accessible to foreigners with long-term resident status, which is equivalent to permanent resident status in Slovenia. The citizens of other SFRY republics with a permanent address in Slovenia were unjustifiably excluded from the right to buy apartments under favourable terms, because as citizens of the SFRY they, too, contributed to the taxes used to construct the buildings, which was paid for from the state budget.

An issue that remains unresolved to the present day is the validity of rental contracts signed between apartment owners and erased people that were not cancelled when the latter left Slovenia or were expelled. This issue will have to be resolved if the tenants ever appear in court to claim the rights that arise from these contracts.

4.8 The Right to Education

The children of erased parents (who were robbed of legal status along with their parents) could, as a rule, exercise their right to elementary school education up to the age of 15, as no legal status was required to enrol in school. Despite this, some of them had difficulty enrolling,[320] although problems were more frequent with secondary and university-level education. A young woman testifies:

317 Supreme Court of the Republic of Slovenia, Ruling No. II Ips 397/94.

318 Stories by the erased people, *You Cannot Fight the System Alone* and *I Was Lucky* in Kogovšek and Petković (eds.) The Scars of the Erasure, 2010.

319 The Council Directive 2003/109/ES dated 25 November 2003 on the status of citizens of third countries who are long-time residents UL L 16, 23. 1. 2004, p. 44.

320 Kogovšek, The Erasure as a Violation of Legally protected Human Rights, in: The Scars of the Erasure, 2010, p. 120.

> I then went to enrol in school. They wanted my citizenship and documents, but I couldn't show them anything, so I couldn't enrol. It was 1992, I was 15 at that time. [...] I was already accepted as I had passed the exams, but when I wanted to register I couldn't, because I didn't have the documents. [...] So we were all tense, nervous, I didn't know who to turn to, we had money problems, who could help us and where, nobody wanted to help, I mean, nobody understood. I cried, I cried all the time. I pleaded, as I said, I pleaded at the administrative unit, but no. They were indifferent, I told them I couldn't go to school. "Yeah", he said, "you need a document", they said. So I said, "Then give me the document and I'll go". How without a document? You go and try to cross the border without a document. I, too, cannot go to school without a document. And in the school, they said, "Unfortunately, we cannot accept you". I cried so much. I turned to the Centre for Social Work, and a lady there told me, "You're young, you can work". I said, "Madam, how can I work? What with? I have no documents" (Jana S., 30).[321]

Young people without legal status could not enrol in a higher-level educational institution. The 1996 Vocational Education Act[322] stipulated that foreigners could enrol in schools in Slovenia under the same terms as Slovenian citizens if an agreement on reciprocity was signed between Slovenia and the student's home country. If such an agreement did not exist, they had to pay for schooling. In other words, foreigners had to present an identification document when enrolling, which the people who were erased could not do. Had they been allowed to retain their permanent resident status, they could at least have paid tuition and enrolled in secondary or higher-level courses. Since Article 1 of the Convention on the Rights of the Child defines a child as a person up to 18 years of age, the right to education of all erased children up to 18 who were denied access to school was violated. According to the European Convention for the Protection of Human Rights and Fundamental Freedoms and the International Covenant on Economic, Social and Cultural Rights, young people over 18 also have the right to education.

4.9 Arrests

Judging by the testimonies of erased people, the right to freedom and security and the right to freedom of movement were the most critical rights. Many erased persons reported extensively on events that may be interpreted as violations of these rights. For example, if they were stopped by the police and asked to produce an identification document which they did not possess, they were transported

321 *Ibid.*, p. 120–121.

322 Article 9, Para 4 of the Vocational Education Act (Zakon o poklicnem in strokovnem izobraževanju), Official Gazette of the Republic of Slovenia, No. 12/1996.

to the Transitional Home for Aliens (later renamed, more to the point, Centre for the Removal of Aliens, and still later, for the sake of political correctness, the Centre for Aliens). The accounts of the erased people vary; some spent only one night in the Centre and were released through the intervention of lawyers, acquaintances, or relatives, while others stayed there for longer periods of time.

> I went to the eye doctor to treat my eye, and they gave me eye drops. When I went to collect these eye drops, I was stopped by the police and had to show my ID card. I had on me also that piece of paper, for aliens. And the Bosnian passport that had already expired. Anyway I was already officially a Slovenian citizen. I explained it to them and told them to call and check, because it was a working day, afternoon, around half past one. They didn't bother but took me directly to the minor offence judge. The judge did not call me in at all, but I stayed in the corridor all the time and a policeman guarded me. Only the second policeman went inside, then came out and brought the papers, and then they took me downstairs. When I heard that I was sentenced to expulsion from the Republic of Slovenia, I went mad and I hit my head with the glass there, on Mala ulica 3. […] They tied me up and beat me. Then they took me to the Medical Centre to have my wound stitched. From the Medical Centre they took me to that freaky place in Šiška [the Transitory Home for Aliens on Celovška Street]. I was detained all night; there were many people there; people were sleeping on the floor. I don't know when they took me there – I was in shock, I only know that it was in the night. They let me go when my friends called the social workers who presumably – I didn't know it – repeatedly called the police all night. They faxed them my certificate of Slovenian citizenship (Rifet, 45).[323]

Others were detained in the Centre for Aliens for much longer, and found themselves in extremely vulnerable situations.

> In 1995 two policemen stopped me in the street to check my identification. They asked for my documents, and I told them that I didn't have any. They took me to the police station in Polje where they kept me for four hours. Then they took me to court and I was sentenced to pay 8000 tolars for illegally residing in Slovenia. From there they took me to the Centre for Aliens. They didn't explain anything and I didn't get any paper saying what it was all about. I was not given a chance to go to the apartment where I lived to collect some necessary things like clothes. I was locked in the room overnight, and in the morning a social worker and an inspector arrived. They gave me a document confirming that I was detained in the Centre for Aliens. One month later I got a one-way passport; that document was valid for 48 hours, to leave Slovenia. They took me to the Dolga vas border crossing along with another person, gave me a bus ticket to Belgrade and 50 German marks. I didn't make it to Serbia because I didn't have an entry visa, so I got off the bus. The road took me to Budapest to the Yugoslav Embassy, where they required 500 forints for a Serbian visa and told me that the waiting time to get a visa was 6 months. I couldn't take that option. I spent two days at the railway station in Budapest,

323 *Ibid.*, p. 92.

> where the police again checked my identification and I was detained for 8 hours. The Hungarian police then took me to the Dolga vas border crossing, where the Slovenian police waited for me and took me to Prosenjakovci to the Centre for Aliens. I spent three months in Prosenjakovci and was then moved, because of my poor health (asthmatic), to Ljubljana, to the Transitory Home for Aliens on Celovška 166. I stayed in the Transitory home for Aliens, open department, from 15 May 1995 until the end of 2001. I had permission to go out, to stay at home for a week now and then, but even on these days I had to report to the Home every day at 22h. In the beginning of 2002 I was released after my friend guaranteed that he would take care of me. I remember that at the time when I lived in the Centre, 40 percent of people there, I reckon, were people from former Yugoslav republics, I suppose that many of them were erased too. I also remember a mother with a child who told me that at that time she had been living in the Home with her child for 8 years (Almir, 55).[324]

The relevant provision in Article 5 of the ECHR stipulates that it is lawful to deprive a person of his/her freedom if this is done to prevent him/her from unlawfully entering the country, or as part of an effort to deport or extradite that person. The question is whether the right to freedom of movement of the erased persons who were placed in the Centre for Aliens was violated. To answer this question, it is first necessary to clarify if an erased person could be considered a person against whom action was being taken with a view to deportation or extradition, i.e. if he/she was detained "with a view to extradition".[325]

In Slovenia, the expulsion procedure was launched during the time following the erasure as a side sanction of expulsion from the country[326] imposed in criminal proceedings, or on the basis of a sanction of extradition from the country imposed in proceedings for a minor offence. In both cases, the ruling had to be issued by a court, the criminal court in the former case and the court for minor offences in the latter. However, as described in more detail in the next subsection, many erased persons were expelled from the country by the police as instructed by the Ministry of the Interior; the instructions said that SFRY citizens who did not obtain Slovenian citizenship could be taken to the state border based on Article 28 of the Aliens Act in force at that time.

Since erased persons were unlawfully deprived of their status, their residence in Slovenia should have been considered lawful. Accordingly, all detentions of

324 *Ibid.*, p. 93.

325 Leach, Taking a case to the European Court of Human Rights, 2001, p. 128.

326 A secondary penalty in the criminal law is a type of penalty that can be imposed only in connection with the main penalty. The secondary penalty of an alien's expulsion from the country was abolished under the new Penal Code (Official Gazette of the Republic of Slovenia, No. 55/2008).

erased people, including in the Centre for Aliens, which were based solely on the fact that they did not have legal status as a result of the erasure were unlawful. In all such cases, the erased person's human rights were violated regardless of whether or not there was a court ruling. The fact that the Slovenian authorities considered them persons without legal status was a direct consequence of the erasure that had unlawfully robbed them of that legal status. This was particularly unacceptable after the Constitutional Court issued its Ruling No. U-I-284/94 establishing that erased people were deprived of their permanent resident status unlawfully, as all further measures taken by the state in connection with it, including detentions in the Centre for Aliens, were also unlawful.

It is obvious that many cases of detention or restrictions on the movement of erased persons did not lead to their expulsion from the country; had such an intention been present, they would have been expelled immediately rather than detained. Rather, these were instances of prolonged arbitrary persecution and an unjustified encroachment on personal freedom. The testimonies of erased persons reveal that detentions in the Centre for Aliens occurred most frequently during the 1990s; during the following decade, only a few such cases were recorded, with the last case dating from 2008.[327] The fact that detentions were not rare is confirmed by an in-house instruction of the general police headquarters sent to all police stations in 2002:

> In procedures involving the citizens of countries that are successors to the former SFRY who do not have a valid residence permit in Slovenia, police officers are required to first check the central register of permanent residents (the RISK transaction). This check is necessary to establish whether the alien has already submitted a permanent residence application in accordance with the Act Regulating the Legal Status of Citizens of Former Yugoslavia Living in the Republic of Slovenia (Official Gazette of the Republic of Slovenia No. 61/99). If such an application has been submitted but not yet resolved, it is not allowed to take measures against illegal residence, and it is not allowed to place him/her in the Centre for Aliens.[328]

By analogy, it is possible that the police believed that such a measure was allowed in the case of erased persons who did not apply for citizenship. Needless to say, their assumption was wrong. The lawfulness or unlawfulness of the detentions was not connected to applications for citizenship. The above-mentioned instruction reveals that the authorities were aware at least of the fact that the detentions

327 Kovač, Izbrisanih ne izganjajo – ali pač?, in: Pravna praksa 27 (2008) 15, p. 23.

328 Dispatch of the Uniformed Police Directorate, part of the General Police Directorate (State Border and Foreigners Section) sent to all Police Directorates in the RS, No. M0001755, dated 19 March 2002.

were arbitrary, but they nevertheless found an (unlawful) excuse for them. The detention of erased people in the Centre for Aliens was in contravention of Article 5 of the European Convention on Human Rights. However, the Convention only came into force in Slovenia in 1994. Thus, detentions that occurred before that date and were on-going on the day when the Convention came into force in Slovenia cannot be considered violations of the ECHR, although they do represent a violation of the rules of international customary law in the area of human rights that is based on the Universal Declaration of Human Rights (Article 3).

4.10 Expulsions

Article 9 of the Universal Declaration of Human Rights prohibits arbitrary expulsions from the country. Article 13 of the International Covenant on Civil and Political Rights states the following:

> An alien lawfully in the territory of a State Party to the present Covenant may be expelled therefrom only in pursuance of a decision reached in accordance with law and shall, except where compelling reasons of national security otherwise require, be allowed to submit the reasons against his expulsion and to have his case reviewed by, and be represented for the purpose before, the competent authority or a person or persons especially designated by the competent authority.

The expulsions reported by many erased people were a result of the unlawful cancelling of their legal status. During the first few months following the erasure, the police carried out expulsions based on the in-house instruction of the Ministry of the Interior.[329] It should be noted, however, that in many cases the police obtained a court ruling before expelling an erased person from the country. Some expulsions fell short of completion as evident from the testimony below.

> In 1994 I was stopped by a policeman quite by chance. He asked me to show my documents and took me to the police station in Vošnjakova. [...] It was some time after nine in the morning. I was kept there until three in the afternoon. Without any explanation. I didn't know the reason, didn't know why. I asked them but they said nothing. Then two police officers came to the waiting room and said that they had to take me [to the court for minor offences]. When I came to the judge she started to ask questions, how and what and all that. And in the end she read the document that she wrote and said that I was expelled and that they had to take me to Albania. And at that time I had to pay for the transport. I paid it – I remember it well – it was 34,000 tolars. [...] My wife brought me money. I gave them my whole salary. I felt like I wanted to die. Then, incidentally, I knew one gentleman, a police officer, so I described the situation to him and

329 The in-house instruction by the Ministry of the Interior, No. 0016/4-1496-8 dated 27 February 1992.

asked if something could be done. "Yeah, man" said he, "do you have proof, any proof, that you live here in Slovenia?" So I said: "Yes, of course I have, I have an apartment here, a wife, I have everything here, man. I've worked in Slovenia for 10 years. I have all these certificates, but I don't have them here. Would you be so kind", I said, "and take me to my apartment?" "Yes", he said, "I will". And he took me. He asked the judge and she said: 'Okay, take him. But bring him back'. I took all the documents that were needed and showed them everything. […] Who I am and what I am. Then the judge threw the ruling into the dustbin. But she didn't give the money back to me. […] And I was released and went home. From that day on I didn't dare go out on the street (Božo, 45).[330]

Certain erased people who managed to return to Slovenia after their first expulsion from the country were expelled repeatedly. Those who were expelled without a court ruling did not receive any official paper, so to prove that the expulsion had happened they needed the testimony of a family member.

In 1993 the police […] came to our house and put all of us, the whole family, in the police van, took us to the border with Hungary and left us there without any explanation. Since we didn't know what to do, we came back illegally to Slovenia across Croatia, and went home. A month or two later the police officers […] came again and again took the whole family to the Hungarian border. We again returned illegally to our home in Ljubljana. But because of these two deportations we were afraid that they would attempt it again, so in 1993, together with our relatives, we decided to flee across Austria and go to Germany, to Düsseldorf, where we registered as refugees from Slovenia and Macedonia. (Samir, 57)[331]

Rumours about the expulsions spread quickly, so those who feared it began to hide from the police and avoid public places.

At that time the policemen came often and knocked on the door. Close to us, some 200 meters away, is a dormitory unit, and it often happened that three or four Black Marias with police officers came in the morning and at night to fetch people. We were wondering what was happening, if they were fighting each other again or what. Later, we were told that these Black Marias came to fetch people and take them to the border. I don't know how my father found out about it, but he went into hiding, because the police often came to his door. Actually, for three years he lived without leaving the apartment. Like the Japanese during the Second World War. He hoarded food, cans, and he had stale bread and many other things (Begeš, 89).[332]

330 Kogovšek, The Erasure as a Violation of Legally protected Human Rights, in: The Scars of the Erasure, 2010, p. 94–95.

331 *Ibid.*, p. 95.

332 *Ibid.*, p. 96.

To answer the question of whether the expulsions of erased people constituted violations of their human rights, it is necessary to begin with the unlawful cancellation of their legal status in Slovenia. Since the Constitutional Court ruled that erased people should have retained permanent resident status, their forced removal from the country would only have been lawful if it was a sanction imposed by the court and if their residence permits had first been revoked. Therefore, the expulsions constituted a violation of the right to be protected from arbitrary expulsion from the country. Furthermore, in its Ruling No. U-I-284/94, the Constitutional Court held that that erased people could not be sentenced to expulsion from the country before their status was regulated, since that could mean a violation of the right to the protection of private and family life codified in Article 8 of the ECHR.

4.11 The Right to the Protection of Private and Family Life and the Role of the European Court of Human Rights

In its judgment in the case of *Kurić and Others v. Slovenia*, the European Court of Human Rights confirmed that the authorities encroached on erased people's right to private and family life.[333] It established that the applicants had their private or family lives or both in Slovenia in the meaning of Article 8 of the European Convention on Human Rights, that the erasure was an encroachment on this right, and that the effects of the erasure had not abated due to the "repercussions of the erasure and the prolonged refusal of Slovenian authorities to comprehensively regulate the applicants' situation".[334] In accordance with the case law, the Court also judged whether the measure was lawful, whether the authorities pursued a legitimate aim, and whether it was a necessary measure in a democratic society (the test of proportionality).

With regard to the erasure's lawfulness, the Grand Chamber concurred with the conclusions of the Constitutional Court of the Republic of Slovenia. It confirmed that based on the provisions in the independence legislation and particularly Article 81 of the Aliens Act, erased people could not expect that as aliens they would be deprived of their legal status without prior notification. The Court also did not overlook the fact that in implementing the erasure, the administration employees adhered to unpublished in-house instructions that were not accessible to applicants. It concluded that the Slovenian legislation and in-house

333 Grand Chamber of the ECHR, *Kurić and Others v. Slovenia*, complaint No. 26828/06, the ruling dated 26 June 2012, paragraph 336.–362.

334 *Ibid.*, paragraph 336.–340.

instructions behind the erasure did not meet the standards of foreseeability and accessibility that had developed in the case law, and thus ruled that the encroachment on applicants' rights protected by Article 8 of the Convention was unlawful.[335]

The Court further ruled that by adopting the independence legislation, the State pursued a legitimate aim of defining its citizenship and protecting national security,[336] but the measure of erasure was not necessary in a democratic society. The applicants had enjoyed a wide range of economic and social rights in Slovenia of which they were deprived by the erasure. As a consequence, they suffered serious and lasting problems. The consequences of the erasure were by no means proportional to the legitimate aim of the State, so the Court ruled that Article 8 had been violated.[337]

5. The Role of the Supreme Court in Confirming the Erasure

An analysis of the Supreme Court case law relating to the appeals of erased people during the period from 26 February 1992 to 4 February 1999, when the Supreme Court first asked the Constitutional Court to rule on the constitutionality of issues related to the erasure, shows that during this period the Supreme Court of Slovenia fully followed the above-mentioned interpretation of the law and acted as a servant for the executive branch of the government. The Supreme Court thus contributed to the perpetuation of the situation, which lasted until the Constitutional Court issued its ruling.

How is it possible that the Supreme Court, given the arguments put forward by the appellants, did not decide to forward the Aliens Act to the Constitutional Court to judge its constitutionality? One of the rulings of the Supreme Court shows that the appellant expressed his disagreement with the explanation of the Administrative Court that the execution of the erasure by official duty without an adequate administrative procedure was in accordance with Article 81 of the Aliens Act. In the appellant's opinion, the erasure should have been carried out based on an administrative procedure in which the appellant had the right to participate. The appellant requested the Supreme Court to submit Article 81 of the Aliens Act to the Constitutional Court and obtain its opinion on the interpretation of this provision. The Supreme Court ignored the request and instead confirmed the interpretation of the administrative bodies and the

---

335 *Ibid.*, paragraph 343.–349.

336 *Ibid.*, paragraph 353.

337 *Ibid.*, paragraph 360.–362.

Administrative Court, as it had many times before and would many times again. Moreover, it said that it "did not have any reservations" as to the correctness of the legal opinions regarding the date when the Aliens Act's provisions were to begin to apply to persons who were citizens of another SFRY republic, and when their records were to be removed from the population register.[338] In several rulings, the Supreme Court concurred with the Ministry of the Interior that the restrictive interpretation of Article 81 of the Aliens Act was correct and that the erased people were obliged to reapply for temporary residence permits.[339] Only after the Constitutional Court issued its ruling and proclaimed the Aliens Act unconstitutional did the Supreme Court change its stance. A ruling in the case of an erased person who applied for a permanent residence permit accordingly stated the following:

> Since the Constitutional Court of the RS [...] stated in its ruling No. U-I-284/94 dated 4 February 1999 that the Aliens Act was in contravention of the Constitution of the RS because it did not define the conditions under which citizens of other SFRY republics could acquire a permanent residence permit in Slovenia, and because the disputed ruling and decision [of the Ministry of the Interior] arise from an unconstitutional provision, the ruling of the first instance court had to be changed in such a way that the appeal is upheld and the decision of the Ministry is repealed.[340]

After the Constitutional Court issued its ruling, a specific case law was developed related to the complaints that the erased people filed with the Ministry of the Interior. The Supreme Court adopted the opinion that the Ministry should have considered complaints about erasure from the register of permanent residents as an application to issue a confirmation of permanent residence from the said register. The decision of the Ministry to refuse to issue such an extract from the official record should have been considered an administrative act that could be challenged in an administrative dispute. The Supreme Court further decided that the administrative body should have enabled the erased people to argue the facts on which their erasure depended. These facts should have been established according to the evidence provided in the procedure, while also taking into account the right of the complainant to participate in the procedure.[341] This

338 Supreme Court of the Republic of Slovenia, Ruling No. U 680/958.

339 Supreme Court of the Republic of Slovenia, Ruling No. 884/928. A similar argument can be found in Supreme Court of the Republic of Slovenia, Ruling No. U 1342/96.

340 Supreme Court of the Republic of Slovenia, Ruling No. I Up 12/2004.

341 Supreme Court of the Republic of Slovenia, Ruling No. I Up 486/99. See also Supreme Court of the Republic of Slovenia, Ruling No. I Up 278/99, I Up 562/99, I Up 501/99 and I Up 1162/2002.

opinion, which was based on Articles 171 and 143 of the General Administrative Procedure Act adopted in 1986,[342] was closer to that of many individuals whose appeals were initially rejected by the Supreme Court: that the erasure should have been implemented based on the individual administrative procedure and that it should have observed the right of the individual to complain and to participate in the procedure.

6. Conclusions

The main conclusion that proceeds from my reconstruction of the erasure is that it was a meticulous and orchestrated act and that its consequences were completely ignored. It is clear that the people who designed and implemented the erasure knew precisely what they were doing, that they did it consciously and that it can by no means be interpreted as a mistake. Another surprising conclusion is that the in-house instructions were in contravention of the law in many ways, but the employees of the administration nevertheless implemented them uncritically. In so doing, they violated the erased people's rights and contributed to the ECHR's judgment. In Part III I explain how these violations of human rights could happen, the motives behind the erasure, and the factors that led to it.

342 Zakon o splošnem upravnem postopku, Official Gazette of the Socialist Federal Republic of Yugoslavia, No. 47/1986.

Part III: The Elements of Totalitarianism as a Precondition for Collective Violations of Human Rights

The man from the country had not expected difficulties like this, the law was supposed to be accessible for anyone at any time, he thinks [...] The doorkeeper gives him a stool and lets him sit down to one side of the gate. He sits there for days and years.
Franz Kafka, The Trial

How could so many people be erased, and human rights be violated on such a massive scale? Given the extent and implications of the erasure, the number of people affected, and their prolonged suffering, there is no doubt that what happened should be designated as a mass violation of human rights. This designation also applies to the response of those who took part in the erasure and of society as a whole. Certain elements were present that characterised other serious and mass violations of human rights, such as the crimes committed in Yugoslavia's successor states in the 1990s, or in authoritarian systems such as Nazi Germany, which deprived Jewish persons of their citizenship. Although the implications and consequences of the latter were incomparably more horrendous, the circumstances that enabled these crimes and contributed to them were similar to those surrounding the erasure.

A few crucial questions can serve to pinpoint the similarities between these atrocities: What made the erasure possible? Why did the government decide to deprive a group of people of their legal status? Why did the government employees fulfil the unlawful instructions of the Ministry of the Interior uncritically? Why, once the act was accomplished, did state officials deny it or attempt to justify it? And why did they enjoy the broad support of the public? The answers are linked to certain traits of the erasure that are also inherent in other mass violations of human rights. Behind all of them stand nationalist ideologies, the imagined Other, an identity grounded in a historical sense of victimhood, the inability/unwillingness to submit one's own acts to moral judgement, the inability to face one's own past, and the pathology of organised innocence. I explain these concepts in detail below.

1. Nationalism and the Creation of the Other

The motivation behind the erasure is closely connected with the concept of "nationalising nationalism" and the inherent paradox of a modern nation-state. Hannah Arendt writes that when a nation-state is established, the founding nation declares both its sovereignty and its commitment to human rights, but the two are incompatible because sovereignty implies that the sovereign is not bound by any universal law.[343] In line with this reasoning, my thesis is that the Slovenian nation-state was established to serve the needs of a Slovenian ethnic group rather than its citizens. After Slovenia became a sovereign country, the Slovenian ethnic group was homogenised and protected from discrimination; in the process, a symbolic Other was created and excluded from society and the state. I will proceed to explain how and why homogenisation took place, why the Other[344] was created and what the role of nationalism was.

1.1 Nationalising Nationalism

In Part II of the book I discussed the proposed amendments to the Aliens Act that, if passed, could have prevented the erasure. This unusual rejection of the amendments without any serious discussion can be explained by the simple fact that the majority in the National Assembly had already made up its mind; all attempts to persuade it to pass the amendments were thus doomed to failure.[345]

The formal and legal preparations to establish the nation-state rested on the nationalist ideology which pervaded the entire political apparatus of the time. It was the main driving force behind the ethnic homogenisation, foundation, and later the existence of a new state "created as the state of a specific nation and for that specific nation".[346] Its borders corresponded more or less to the boundaries delineating the territory inhabited by the Slovenes (they were the same as the

---

343 Arendt, The Origins of Totalitarianism, 1973, p. 230.

344 The concept of "the Other" is borrowed from anthropology. In connection with the erasure, it denotes an inhabitant of Slovenia who is of non-Slovenian ethnic origin and has not gained Slovenian citizenship. I use this general concept because I do not want to reproduce the more specific expressions that were used to denote erased people.

345 Bajt, More Than Administratively Created "Foreigners", in: The Scars of the Erasure, 2010, p. 196. *Cf.* Mekina, B., A Monument to the Erased, in: Journal for the Critique of Science 35 (2007) 228, p. 46.

346 Bajt, More Than Administratively Created "Foreigners", in: The Scars of the Erasure, 2010, p. 195–196.

post-war People's Republic of Slovenia, which formed part of the FPRY). Its citizenry was defined in a manner that made it possible to reject individuals who were considered "not acceptable" (as they were designated traitors or aggressors against Slovenian statehood). The erasure was one of the instruments employed to homogenise the nation and an expression of the nationalist ideology that guided the independence process.

Nationalism can be expressed in various ways. Smith gives the following meanings of the term: "1) a process of formation, or growth, of nations; 2) a sentiment or consciousness of belonging to the nation; 3) a language and symbolism of the nation; 4) a social and political movement on behalf of the nation".[347] Nationalism in Slovenia should be understood primarily as the expression of a nationalist ideology that is focused on the nation and its welfare, or to be more precise, national autonomy, national unity, and national identity. In such a constellation, the nation is usually perceived as a group of people defined by certain objective (e.g. language, religion, territory, institutions) and subjective factors (e.g. the sense of belonging).[348]

The motives for the erasure were frequently attributed to nationalism or even racism; the two are interrelated. Veronika Bajt writes that racism was not generally accepted as a motive because it was understood in the sense of classic 19th century biological (scientific) racism, rather than cultural or (neo)racism in which biological differences have been substituted with an obsession with cultural differences.[349] Another brand of discrimination that can underlie the erasure is classism, given that the affected group was mainly composed of members of the lower working class. Racism and nationalism should be understood as connected phenomena because the logic behind the exclusion of the Other is the same in both. In the case of the erasure, it led to the exclusion of migrants, including Roma people and Muslims.[350] However, there are differences between nationalism and racism. Unlike racism, nationalism first tries to assimilate the Other through the forced "homogenisation of the national community within the borders of a nation-state".[351]

From a legal perspective, the homogenisation of the national community in Slovenia was implemented in two steps. The first was the automatic assignment of Slovenian citizenship to individuals who had previously held Slovenian republic

347 Smith, Nationalism: Theory, Ideology, History, 2001, p. 6.
348 *Ibid.*, p. 11.
349 *Ibid.*, p. 195–196.
350 *Ibid.*, p. 196.
351 *Ibid.*

citizenship, which in turn was essentially based on the principle of blood ties. In other words, most of the population that had Slovenian republic citizenship were ethnic Slovenes. In this way, the authorities reinforced the centrality of the Slovenian ethnic identity to citizenship; the national community was equated with the ethnic community. By automatically granting citizenship based on the principle of continuity, Slovenia became the *de facto* state of all Slovenes rather than of all its citizens regardless of their ethnic origin.[352] This is indeed a contradiction, because automatisms should, by definition, ensure some kind of neutrality. In this particular case, however, the principle of continuity operated expressly as an excluding principle because of the previous method of assigning citizenship during the Yugoslav era.[353]

The second step of homogenisation was extraordinary naturalisation, i.e. the option of applying for citizenship under favourable terms as stipulated by Article 40 of the Citizenship Act. Extraordinary naturalisation can therefore be understood as an element of "nationalising nationalism" that attempts to assimilate the Other. This process also included other elements of nationalisation, for example, the linguistic homogenisation that found expression in the proposal that knowledge of Slovenian should be a requirement for obtaining citizenship. A Slovenian citizenry consisting of such a "homogenised" national community did not leave any room for the Other. The supposed unacceptability of the idea that the Other should live side by side with the Slovenes was best illustrated by MP Andrej Šter's argument against the amendment to the Aliens Act (it is the only argument *against* the amendments recorded in the parliamentary minutes). The MP, who later even set up a website entitled "The Truth About the Erasure" to contest Constitutional Court decisions, opposed the amendment because it "introduces into the legal order an explicit disorder and uncertainty, because it introduces a category that is otherwise unknown, an in-between category".[354] Needless to say, the argument was incorrect because the legal order had long since known the category of persons with permanent residence permits which, as the proposers

352 Bajt, More Than Administratively Created "Foreigners", in: The Scars of the Erasure, 2010, p. 201.

353 In Yugoslavia, shifting from one to another republic citizenship was possible and quite simple (see Part I). However, since republican citizenship did not have any significance with regard to individual rights, and since all SFRY citizens had the same status wherever they lived, people rarely chose to change their republican citizenship. There was simply no need to do it.

354 Mekina, B., A Monument to the Erased, in: Journal for the Critique of Science 35 (2007) 228, p. 46.

of the amendment advocated, should have encompassed all the citizens of SFRY who did not gain Slovenian citizenship. The category was also included in the draft Aliens Act discussed at that time.

The MP's statement betrays a typical totalitarian element characteristic of the phenomenon of organised innocence and apologetic references to the legal order as a kind of superior force (more on this below). With the homogenisation of the national community, the predicate for the erasure was in place, or in Bajt's words, it was an "excommunication *sui generis* that 'homogenized' the nation-state practically overnight".[355] The erasure of the Other who could not be assimilated thus became one of the elements of nationalising nationalism in Slovenia.[356] It is also suggested by statements that labelled the erased people "disloyal national traitors who did not want to accept Slovenian citizenship when it was 'offered' to them".[357]

It is significant that the number of applications for Slovenian citizenship under Article 40 was twice that expected by the government and that 171000 people were granted Slovenian citizenship while only several thousand were rejected it.[358] Indeed, the government rejected those applications that *could* be rejected, but it had to grant citizenship to the vast majority of people who applied for it and fulfilled the relatively undemanding criteria. This provided the designers of citizenship policy and the proponents of the erasure with an expedient answer to the objections that the erasure constituted a violation of human rights. Their argument ran along the lines that given all the "benevolence"[359] the government showed by granting (or more accurately, "being forced to grant") citizenship to so many people and admitting the non-Slovenes among the Slovenes, it cannot be reproached for the removal of the Other who chose not to seise the opportunity. This suggests that the erased people can also be seen as scapegoats for

---

355 Bajt, More Than Administratively Created "Foreigners", in: The Scars of the Erasure, 2010, p. 199.

356 The testimonies of the erased people include accounts of other nationalising practices. One such example was a squabble over the name of a newborn child that the employee attempted to "Slovenise" while the father insisted on the original, Serbian form. Bajt, More Than Administratively Created "Foreigners", in: The Scars of the Erasure, 2010, p. 191, 212.

357 *Cf.* Bajt, More Than Administratively Created "Foreigners", in: The Scars of the Erasure, 2010, p. 213.

358 Mesojedec Pervinšek, Predpisi o državljanih in tujcih z uvodnimi pojasnili, 1997, p. 32.

359 Dedić, Jalušič, Zorn, The Erased: Organized Innocence and the Politics of Exclusion, 2003, p. 17.

all the granted citizenships. The grievances came to light later through repeated demands to revise granted citizenships and the designation "new citizens".

1.2 The Identity of the Historical Victim and the Creation of "the Other"

Nationalist discourse and the process of creating the Other drew on the classic nationalist myth of historical victimhood. In that myth, the Slovenian nation is a victim that has suffered under totalitarian regimes for centuries while never oppressing others; any occasional violence by Slovenians was directed towards fellow countrymen and was to be blamed on the external totalitarian powers that brought about such behaviour.[360] The identity of the innocent victim served as an explanation for feelings of being threatened, which supposedly gave the nation an absolute right to protect itself and the newly established country from the Other that could endanger it. Since Slovenia sought independence from Yugoslavia, it was the citizens of other SFRY republics who were designated as the Other (with Yugoslav People's Army members considered particularly dangerous). To this end, the public discourse that supported activities in the run-up to independence was dominated by anti-Balkan state-building mythology and ideology,[361] bolstered by matching rhetoric that only escalated when sovereignty was achieved. Slovenia was presented as a civilised pro-Western country in contrast to the Balkans, which were portrayed as barbaric and occupying a lower position on the civilisational ladder, an obvious expression of cultural racism. The image was reinforced by citing wars and crimes in the Balkans, while the erasure in Slovenia was presented as a "lesser evil".[362]

An identity based on victimhood may explain the politics of exclusion, but it can by no means justify it; nor can it absolve anyone of responsibility. Jalušič writes that the

> victim identity is not only dangerous but also incapable of producing an independent political community that can accept responsibility for itself or others as long as it falls back upon its own ill-fate and vulnerability.[363]

360 Bajt, More Than Administratively Created "Foreigners", in: The Scars of the Erasure, 2010, p. 214. *See also* Dedić, Jalušič, Zorn, The Erased: Organized Innocence and the Politics of Exclusion, 2003, p. 16.

361 Dedić, Jalušič, Zorn, The Erased: Organized Innocence and the Politics of Exclusion, 2003, p. 100.

362 *Ibid.*, p. 56.

363 *Ibid.*, p. 16.

She draws attention to Israel and its political elite which, despite the horrific experience of the Jewish people and 50 years of statehood, is not capable of taking political responsibility but continues to pursue a politics of war and to legitimise it with a victim identity.[364]

The inherent paradox of the nation-state is the phenomenon that Hannah Arendt considered the main totalitarian threat after Auschwitz: when a nation establishes a state, it excludes from its protection all minorities and all those who are without their own state through the process of homogenisation and by preventing access to citizenship and rights.[365] Thus, it annuls the ideals that form the foundation of a state that respects human rights. This phenomenon is evident in many new nation-states that transitioned from a single-party system to parliamentary democracy in the early 1990s. Before the transition, many of these countries boasted strong movements for human rights, so it was reasonable to expect that the newly sovereign states would respect human rights. However, these expectations were already betrayed in the process of defining the citizenry, since many persons were excluded.[366] The nationalism that leads to the establishment of a nation-state brings national sovereignty and the human rights of the minorities into conflict. Stripping a minority of its citizenship or other legal status is one of the main instruments used in the totalitarian politics[367] that are obviously perpetuated to some extent even once the nation-state is established.

2. Elements of Totalitarianism

2.1 The Problem of Thoughtlessness

What caused the erasure? What led the government to abuse the law so radically and what led the government employees to consistently observe orders that were not legally sound? Did they truly harbour such hate for the immigrants? Were they motivated by nationalist sentiments? Were they essentially bad and evil-thinking people?

An analysis of the motivation of the persons who committed the erasure shows that nationalism, which was based on a victim identity and resulted in the

364 *Ibid.*

365 Jalušič, Renouncing the Political Capacities, in: Journal for the Critique of Science 35 (2007) 228, p. 100.

366 Dedić, Jalušič, Zorn, The Erased: Organized Innocence and the Politics of Exclusion, 2003, p. 10, 11.

367 Jalušič, Renouncing the Political Capacities, in: Journal for the Critique of Science 35 (2007) 228, p. 101.

exclusion of the Other, was an important social and political factor but not the main reason for the erasure, or any other mass violation of human rights for that matter. Violations of rights, crimes, and wars do not occur simply because an old, subdued ethnic intolerance suddenly bubbles to the surface. Just as anti-Semitism was not the main force propelling the Holocaust,[368] nationalism and racism were not the main forces behind the erasure. Moreover, it would be dangerous to put all the blame for the erasure on nationalism, because that could encourage the apologists of exclusionary politics to invoke nationalism as a justification for exclusion and explain such exclusion with the need to protect a specific nation-state territory for the benefit of one's own people.[369]

Mass violations of human rights have different causes. Observing Adolf Eichmann during the trial in Jerusalem, Hannah Arendt noted that the man who had organised the transportation of Jews to the concentration camps did not really hate Jewish people – he had some Jewish friends or relatives, others he held in deep respect and still others were his colleagues at work.[370] He did not nurture nationalist or racist emotions strong enough to make him commit a crime. He was motivated to accomplish his task by something completely different – pure ambition, a strong desire to advance his career and improve his social standing.[371] To achieve this, he was willing to obey orders regardless of moral concerns, and was not able or willing to recognise the immorality of his acts as a result. Hannah Arendt therefore concluded that, rather than being an embittered man driven by hate, Eichmann was banal – an everyday man of mediocre talents who, in striving to please his superiors, ignored the ethical dilemmas and began to behave like a cog in a machine composed of many other cogs.[372] "Everyone pulled the levers of that vast machinery, so at the end of the day all that was needed was to press the button and the process unfolded almost on its own".[373]

While some Nazi officials may have been motivated by ethnic hatred, the reasons that led many others to take part in the Holocaust were very banal; they were mired in thoughtlessness, that is to say, in their own inability and unwillingness to judge the morality of their conduct. Arendt described Eichmann and

368 Arendt, The Origins of Totalitarianism, 1973, p. 39.

369 Jalušič, Renouncing the Political Capacities, in: Journal for the Critique of Science 35 (2007) 228, p. 98.

370 Arendt, Eichmann in Jerusalem, 1994, p. 29.

371 *Ibid.*, p. 33.

372 *Ibid.*, p. 26.

373 Mekina, B., A Monument to the Erased, in: Journal for the Critique of Science 35 (2007) 228, p. 51.

other government employees with Eichmann's mentality as a new species of criminals who do not commit a crime out of hatred but as part of the new "form of government" with a constant, dangerous totalitarian potential.[374]

Some of the circumstances described above also characterise the erasure. The testimonies of erased people show that, while some government employees did indeed make nationalist remarks, most of them were neutral in executing their tasks; it was not possible to glean any nationalist motive from their conduct or words. Accordingly, when responding to accusations related to the erasure, their defence was predominantly that they were simply fulfilling their tasks and implementing the law while trying to help the erased people as best they could. These claims bore no indication of hatred, but they reflected the inability and unwillingness of these employees to make a moral/value judgment regarding their own conduct. An absence of reflection and non-recognition of the ethical dilemma is also evident from the interviews published in the state administration's bulletin and from certain scholarly articles, which reveal the employees' indignation and distress at the accusations. In one such text, civil servant Ivanka Medvešček analysed the erasure in detail and described several cases processed by the office for which she worked. While she recognised the flaws in the legal basis of the erasure, she failed to assign responsibility, even in part, to government employees and instead dismissed insinuations to that effect as offensive and discrediting.[375]

What blocked people's ability to think and to judge the morality of their own conduct? Why did this ability fail when it was most needed? Why did the government employees fail to prevent a mass violation of human rights, even though a commitment to respect human rights was one of the foundations of the new state?

The provision in the Constitution that stipulates that human rights must be respected is by no means a guarantee that the principle will be fully implemented. The level of respect for human rights depends on completely different social factors, not on what is written in the Constitution. In Slovenia, these factors were nationalism and the corresponding atmosphere that created a specific mentality which made people ready to commit violations, take part in them, or tolerate them.[376] Moreover, many people were not simply ready to follow unlawful orders; they apparently agreed with them and approved of them. For this reason,

---

374 Arendt, The Origins of Totalitarianism, 1973, p. 478.

375 Medvešček, Pravni položaj prebivalcev Slovenije po razpadu skupne države, 2005, pp. 81, 82, 119.

376 Jalušič, Renouncing the Political Capacities, in: Journal for the Critique of Science 35 (2007) 228, p. 99.

the perpetrators of the erasure remain unable to accept responsibility for what happened. Another reason for this is that the social circumstances that made the violations possible are still in place, as is evident from the persistent justification and normalisation of the erasure[377] to this day. The social patterns that motivate the violations do not disappear when the act is accomplished, but survive it, and can potentially lead to new violations in different forms.[378] In the case of the erasure, the violations of rights continued while the implementation of the Constitutional Court's ruling was postponed, and more recently with negative reactions to the ECHR judgment in the *Kurić* case.

It is evident from the above that certain elements of totalitarianism persisted in independent Slovenia despite its new democratic order, and that their presence is not predicated on any specific political system. The essential characteristic of these totalitarian elements is that they destroy the basic prerequisites for autonomous action in people,[379] such as the ability to think, make a critical judgment, evaluate the situation, mount opposition, or engage in a discussion—all of which are necessary to political engagement. People's inability to think and act survived the transition to the new political system, producing new forms of exclusion.[380]

2.2 The Non-Recognition of the Ethical Dilemma and Dehumanisation

Thoughtlessness in the sense of an inability and unwillingness to judge the morality of one's own conduct prevented the government employees who implemented the erasure from perceiving the ethical dilemma that they were embroiled in. It reduced them to ethically neutral bureaucrats interested only in procedural efficiency and the fulfilment of administrative instructions rather than human fates.[381] Bauman's analysis of the Holocaust, where the non-recognition of the ethical dilemma was much more explicit, showed that, to eliminate moral reservations when committing violence or breaching rights, three main conditions must be fulfilled: (1) the violations committed by the administrative staff must be authorised (ordered) by superiors; (2) the tasks must be routinised by carefully dividing work among individual officials (to prevent them from grasping the

377 *Ibid.*, p. 110.

378 *Ibid.*

379 *Ibid.*, p. 105.

380 Such phenomena could also be termed democratic deficit or liberal deficit.

381 Bauman in Dedić, Jalušič, Zorn, The Erased: organized Innocence and the Politics of Exclusion, 2003, p. 110.

complete picture to which they contribute through their actions, thus diverting their attention from the ultimate goal and directing it instead to the means of achieving that goal, which becomes a goal in itself);[382] and (3) the victims whose rights are violated must be dehumanised through ideological processes such as those described earlier in the text, for example by turning them into the Other. Bauman was thus able to explain how ordinary people in Germany turned into mass murderers.[383]

All three of these preconditions were fulfilled before the erasure was implemented. The violations were ordered by the Ministry of the Interior and the employees received precise instructions on how to interpret the Aliens Act and how to "cleanse" the manual and digital registers of individual and households records. The tasks were divided up: employees dealing directly with foreigners invalidated their personal documents, the courts issued rulings on expulsions, the employees working for the Ministry of Defence confiscated Yugoslav People's Army-owned apartments, and the police stopped people in the streets and transported them to the detention centre or the state border. At the same time, erased people were dehumanised in the eyes of the public (aliens, non-Slovenes, people from the Balkans, southerners, aggressors, national traitors, and disloyal speculators who did not want Slovenian citizenship, to name just a few of the labels they were given in public discourse).[384] The bureaucracy dehumanised erased people by defining them precisely in its in-house instructions, turning them into an *object*, an object to be separated from the rest of the population. These people could then be approached neutrally, as *cases* rather than human beings.[385] Dehumanised and depersonalised, they ceased to be neighbours, colleagues, or respected members of the local communities in which they lived; they became mere *aliens*.[386]

2.3 Depriving People of Legal Status to Dehumanise Them

Depriving persons of their legal status based on an arbitrary interpretation of the Aliens Act was a severe means of dehumanisation. It placed erased people

382 *Ibid.*, p. 110.

383 *Ibid.*

384 *Cf.* Dedić, Jalušič, Zorn, The Erased: Organized Innocence and the Politics of Exclusion, 2003, p. 62.

385 Dedić, Jalušič, Zorn, The Erased: Organized Innocence and the Politics of Exclusion, 2003, p. 111.

386 *Ibid.*

outside the law, that is, in a situation worse than that of a criminal suspect, because the latter is still prosecuted within the framework of the law.[387]

Depriving a group of their status is a frequently used tool for dehumanisation. At the moment, such a process is underway in Israel, where Palestinians are deprived of legal status en masse. In the Third Reich, Jews who were forced to emigrate or were expelled were first deprived of citizenship and then of their property. Romania, which was considered the most anti-Semitic state in pre-war Europe and had always "outstripped" Germany in this sense, deprived all Romanian Jews of their citizenship in 1940 and later adopted other anti-Semitic laws (note that in the 19th century, the world powers attempted to bring Romania to recognise its Jewish population as Romanian citizens, without success).[388] The revocation of citizenship (or rejection of citizenship) has therefore always been one of the first measures followed by others that are even worse. For example, Jews were not expelled from Germany immediately. What has come to be known as the final solution followed after other, less harsh measures failed to produce the desired effect. The revocation of citizenship in this process was one of the first means of dehumanisation which enabled the authorities to treat these people as they pleased.[389]

The erasure partly followed the same pattern. Once the targeted people were deprived of legal status, the authorities were able to proceed with other measures – persecution, expulsion, and prevention from exercising many of their rights. It should be noted that the erasure from the register of permanent residents and Slovenia's citizenship policy were intertwined. The erasure would not have happened if an exclusive citizenship policy had not been in place, because people would have gained citizenship and retained their legal status. The opposite is also true – it would not have been possible to completely exclude these people from citizenship without erasing them. Had they not been erased, they would have retained their permanent resident status, which would have, in turn, enabled them to exercise all the rights needed to lead a normal life, integrate into society, access

387 Arendt, The Origins of Totalitarianism, 1973, the Chapter on the Decline of the Nation State.

388 Arendt, Eichmann in Jerusalem, 1994, p. 190.

389 *Cf.* Goldston, Holes in the Rights Framework, in: Ethics and International Affairs 20 (2006) 3. It is a singular paradox that ever since 1948 Israel has been depriving Palestinians of citizenship (*cf.* Shiblak, Stateless Palestinians, Forced Migration Review 26 (2006). The Jewish state therefore implements policies that lead to statelessness similar to those to which Jewish people themselves were subjected before WWII.

employment, and earn a livelihood. All of this would have made their access to citizenship through naturalisation easier.

The erasure thus started with the rejection of applications for citizenship. The conditions for obtaining citizenship through extraordinary naturalisation enabled the rejection of certain applications and thus contributed to the erasure. The citizenship policy that established a distinction between the principle of continuity and extraordinary naturalisation paved the way for the erasure. This is the reason why the deprivation of legal status was an act comparable to those frequently used as a means of discrimination against unwanted population groups.

In public discourse in Slovenia, the notions of citizenship and permanent residence are often confused. Consequently, in an effort to articulate their legal demands as clearly as possible, both erased people and their supporters have strictly insisted on the distinction between the two terms, stressing that in the legal sense they strove to regain the previously held permanent resident status to which they were entitled. This primarily strategic approach may, however, obscure the wider significance and implications of citizenship. In the strictly formal sense of the word, citizenship is a legal tie between an individual and the state that imposes certain rights and obligations on both parties. In the wider sense, however, it designates full membership in a community, ensuring a person a specific position within it. Therefore, the insistence on the distinction between citizenship and permanent residence may have an unwanted side effect – it may preclude criticism of ethnicity-based citizenship and divert attention from other, similar exclusion processes motivated by the same reasons (such as those determining attitudes towards Roma people, people without documents, etc.).[390]

Once dehumanised, erased people were placed outside the legal framework of the country, meaning that they were robbed of the opportunity to voice their concerns, be heard, and participate equally in society. Vlasta Jalušič writes that the most severe consequence of denying someone their human rights is the loss of freedom, life and equality, and of the possibility to be visible and be heard; people "cease to be politically relevant" and are reduced to a state of bare life,[391] to *hominess sacri*,[392] i.e. to being outcasts. They thus become people who are at the

390 *Cf.* Kurnik, The Erased Go to Heaven, in: Journal for the Critique of Science 35 (2007) 228, p. 140.

391 Dedić, Jalušič, Zorn, The Erased: Organized Innocence and the Politics of Exclusion, 2003, p. 15.

392 According to Agamben, *homo sacer* is an image of bare life caught in sovereign exile that can be killed but cannot be sacrificed. Agamben, Homo Sacer, 2004, p. 94.

same time within and outside the boundaries of law.[393] A legal status grants the individual "the right to have rights;"[394] it is a meta-right on which all other rights depend in the contemporary organisation of the state. It is the reason why this right is the first to be taken away by governments with totalitarian or autocratic aspirations.

2.4 Double Dehumanisation

In systems that harbour elements of totalitarianism, the dehumanisation process affects the perpetrators as well as the victims. Both sides are robbed of the basic prerequisites for action and political thinking, the only difference being that the perpetrators dehumanise themselves willingly by renouncing their potential for acting and reasoning: instead of being ethically and politically responsible persons, they begin to behave like "cogs in a machine".[395] The resulting bureaucratic mechanism first enables the perpetrators to arbitrarily dehumanise people, then to deny any intention of harming anyone, and finally to argue that they did nothing wrong and prove their innocence[396] by saying that all they did was "execute the law". In such a bureaucratic environment people who in fact possess the ability to think, act, and take responsibility for their actions, begin to behave irresponsibly. That is precisely what the ideology of modern nation-states strives to achieve – to declare that people's ability to act is unnecessary, undesired, and redundant.[397] Without this, exclusionary policies cannot be implemented.

The dehumanisation process establishes the conditions for the orchestrated innocence of the entire community. Fundamental personal values are inverted, causing people to lose their ability to judge, so acts and events that were unimaginable in the past become imaginable. They are no longer condemned by anyone, not even those who opposed them earlier.[398]

Hannah Arendt was the first to use this term *homo sacer* in this meaning of the word. I am grateful to Vlasta Jalušič who alerted me to this fact.

393 *Cf.* Flander, Homines sacri, in: Pravna praksa, 28 (2009) 14, p. 18.

394 Dedić, Jalušič, Zorn, The Erased: Organized Innocence and the Politics of Exclusion, 2003, p. 15.

395 Jalušič, Renouncing the Political Capacities, in: Journal for the Critique of Science 35 (2007) 228, p. 102.

396 *Ibid.*

397 *Ibid.*

398 *Ibid.*

3. The Inability to Confront the Past

3.1 "We Were Only Implementing the Law"

The response to accusations of mass violations of the human rights of erased people suggests that the circumstances that contributed to the erasure continue to exist. The community and the political elites are not willing to accept the facts, admit that violations did occur, and take their share of responsibility for it. Such conduct is typical of environments that experience mass violations of human rights. In most cases, the perpetrators first defend themselves by saying that they were only implementing the law. This is precisely what many Slovenian government employees said in response to journalists' questions about the circumstances that led to the erasure (note that Slovenian prosecutors have not yet posed such a question, and perhaps never will)[399] References to the law were and are still used as a circular justification, with the implementation of the law presented as something enforced from without, or as an objective process that has a life of its own and exists beyond the sphere of human will or influence.

However, in reality, the government employees were not implementing the law to which they refer, because what they were doing was not written in that law, or rather, the law was ambiguous in this respect. They were actually implementing the orders of their superiors – and they obeyed these without a hint of anguish about their unlawfulness. Their inability to judge the morality of their own conduct found expression on two levels: as an inability to judge the legality of their own acts, and as an inability to recognise the moral dubiousness of their conduct, despite the fact that it led to mass violations of human rights. Government employees strove to prove that they were only a cog in a machine that worked independently of them and that anyone in a similar situation would have done the same, which they believed absolved them of responsibility.[400]

3.2 Attributing the Responsibility to the Victims, Redirecting Attention, and Denying the Crime

One method frequently used to justify the erasure was the shifting of responsibility to the victims. It can be seen in explanations to the effect that erased people had the opportunity to apply for citizenship but chose not to do so, that they had the opportunity to regulate their status but failed to do so (with government

399 Mekina, B., A Monument to the Erased, in: Journal for the Critique of Science 35 (2007) 228, p. 49. *See also* Tršinar, Izbrisani, in: Okno uprave, 2003.

400 Tršinar, Izbrisani, in: Okno uprave, 2003.

employees being ready to "help" anyone who wanted to try), or that they were not entitled to Slovenian citizenship because they took part in the assault on Slovenia or were criminals or the like.[401] In other words, these explanations refer to circumstances that may or may not have been true, but are ultimately irrelevant, since the sole purpose of such apologies is to defend the perpetrators against the accusations and absolve them of responsibility. This is comparable to saying that a rape victim instigated the crime by wearing provoking clothes, or that a woman's sharp tongue triggered domestic violence.

Redirecting attention to unimportant issues is another telltale sign that someone wants to evade responsibility. Examples include "erased people only wanted to get compensation payments", or that criticism was in fact equivalent to "throwing mud at the state of Slovenia",[402] or calling those who drew attention to the violations "defamers of and traitors to the country".[403] Both the government and government employees frequently resorted to sheer denial of the erasure.[404] For example, they claimed that what happened was not an erasure but a "transfer" of data[405] that did not rob affected people of their right to continue living at the previous address.[406] They also claimed that the employees only observed "the principle of free will"[407] which prohibits the enforcement of a legal status on anyone against their will. It was (and still is) a systematic approach that can primarily be understood as "organised lying".[408] For example, the substitution of the term "erased people" with "persons whose registration of residence was terminated

401 Kogovšek, The Erased People Yesterday, Today and Tomorrow, in: The Scars of the Erasure, 2010, p. 14. *See also* Gregorčič, Phantom Irresponsibility, or Fascism in Disguise, in: Journal for the Critique of Science 35 (2007) 228, p. 123.

402 Gregorčič, Phantom Irresponsibility, or Fascism in Disguise, in: Journal for the Critique of Science 35 (2007) 228, p. 123.

403 Dedić, Jalušič, Zorn, The Erased: Organized Innocence and the Politics of Exclusion, 2003, p. 8.

404 Mekina, B., A Monument to the Erased, in: Journal for the Critique of Science 35 (2007) 228, p. 49.

405 Hot, Reševanje vprašanja izbrisanih, 2004, pp. 14–15.

406 The response of the Government of the Republic of Slovenia concerning the acceptability and the grounds of the appeal against the lawsuit in the case *Makuc and Others v. Slovenia* (now *Kurić and Others v. Slovenia*), dated 26 October 2007, paragraph 43.

407 The argument was frequently used by the main proponents of the erasure, Andrej Šter and Slavko Debelak. Tršinar, Izbrisani, in: Okno uprave, 2003.

408 Dedić, Jalušič, Zorn, The Erased: Organized Innocence and the Politics of Exclusion, 2003, p. 9.

because of the implementation of Article 81 of the Aliens Act" downplays the violation of the law and makes it more readily acceptable to the general public.

These processes are very similar to what happened in Serbia and other post-Yugoslav countries during the post-war period. When a Serbian television station broadcast a documentary about the massacre in Srebrenica, the majority of the audience responded with indignation or frivolous comments rather than seriously discussing who was responsible for the crimes.[409] The genocide in Srebrenica is downplayed in Serbian public discourse, much like the erasure in Slovenia: it is not referred to as a genocide, the number of victims is understated by a factor of up to ten, and responsibility for the massacre is attributed to the Dutch battalion.[410] In the case of the erasure, which – let me point out again – can by no means be compared to the crimes mentioned above, media reports either triggered hate speech or went unnoticed. Responsibility for the erasure (and for indemnification) was attributed to all kinds of factors and never to the perpetrators, and there was even a broad willingness to attribute it to the erased people themselves.

3.3 Non-Punishment

The state institutions and the judiciary of countries that experience wars or mass violations of human rights are typically unwilling to confront these issues.[411] Slovenia is no exception in this respect. The unconstitutional conduct of Slovenian political elites has never been referred to court, and the perpetrators were not prosecuted for their conduct. As Marta Gregorčič says, the key people responsible for the erasure "still working at their old professions in the political and economic elite".[412] Similarly, many people who took part in the Holocaust worked for the state for many years, pursuing "blooming careers".[413] Most of the people who participated in the erasure now occupy important positions in the state administration to which they have been promoted since then.[414] All the key perpetrators

409 Jalušič, Renouncing the Political Capacities, in: Journal for the Critique of Science 35 (2007) 228, p. 96.
410 *Ibid.*
411 *Ibid.*
412 *See also* Gregorčič, Phantom Irresponsibility, or Fascism in Disguise, in: Journal for the Critique of Science 35 (2007) 228, p. 123.
413 Arendt, Eichmann in Jerusalem, 1994, p. 17.
414 The Prime Minister at the time of the erasure is today an MP in the European Parliament. The Minister of the Interior at the time of the erasure was later first an MP in the Slovenian Parliament, then the Minister for European Affairs (1997–2002),

continue to participate in public life, sit in front rows at national celebrations, and are treated with great respect.

Given the all-around involvement of the entire state apparatus in the erasure, it is possible to say, in Hannah Arendt's words, that if Slovenia "had been too sensitive about employing officials with a compromising [...] past, there might have been no administration at all".[415] Government members and state employees responded to reproaches as if they were "untouchable". They interpreted accusations as an attack on the foundations of Slovenia's sovereignty and independence, and appealed to "patriotic" citizens to join them in their opinion,[416] thus gaining broad public support that helped them evade responsibility and remain unpunished. Their explanation was that, in a country like Slovenia, violations of human rights such as those of which they were accused were altogether impossible, and cited various historical circumstances and myths as proof.[417]

3.4 Organised Innocence

Organised innocence, which includes the evasion of responsibility, feigned ignorance, and the use of myths,[418] expresses the inability and unwillingness of a community (and its political elites) to confront its own past, bring the facts to light, accept responsibility, identify the factors that contributed to the crimes, and deal with their consequences.

Denial, self-justification and contextualisation are three methods of achieving organised innocence. They suggest that the perpetrators are unable to confront past crimes.[419] With the first method, the perpetrators refuse to speak about the crime, attempt to forget or hope that the "skeletons in the cupboard" will somehow vanish. The second approach involves attempts to vindicate the crime by citing

---

and finally the Chairman of the Executive Board of the Istrabenz oil company. The Secretary with the Ministry of Defense of the time was later a lecturer/professor at the Faculty of Criminal Justice and Security and the Faculty of Administration, where he taught, among other things, citizenship law. I selected these examples because of their visibility and importance of the functions these persons performed at the time of the erasure, after it and today, but the list is much longer.

415 Arendt, Eichmann in Jerusalem, 1994, p. 18.

416 Dedić, Jalušič, Zorn, The Erased: Organized Innocence and the Politics of Exclusion, 2003, p. 18.

417 *Ibid.*, p. 16.

418 Jalušič, Renouncing the Political Capacities, in: Journal for the Critique of Science 35 (2007) 228, p. 104.

419 *Ibid.*, p. 99.

propaganda or powerlessness ("we were only implementing the law"); responsibility can also be attributed to lawmakers ("the legislator should not have created a legal vacuum"). The third method, which is the most dangerous of the three, contextualises the crime and condones it by listing the reasons that supposedly justify a specific act (e.g. "erased people are aggressors and speculators"). This method is the most problematic, because it enables future acts of exclusion to be legitimised: if the violence is not too severe or too "uncivilised", contextualisation can make exclusion appear unproblematic, so that it can eventually be normalised.[420] The goal is invariably the evasion of responsibility, which is achieved by establishing collective responsibility and organized innocence: if someone can be held responsible, it is all of us, and therefore no one in particular.[421]

My claim is therefore the opposite of the notion that "evil" autocratic leaders abuse their power to commit crimes, while the "people" (including government employees) are innocent, misled or unable to do anything but stand by and watch helplessly.[422] It is necessary to recognise that part of the responsibility always lies with the people, or rather the individuals as citizens, particularly those who actively participate in the crime by carrying out the orders (even if only as cogs in a large machine). They are responsible for surrendering to organised innocence, an "a priori construct providing an ideological shield that protects one from responsibility". Organised innocence encompasses not only the masses, but also the intellectual elite that largely produces it. It has a dual function: it enables individuals to indulge in non-thinking and renounce their ability to judge, as well as to refuse to act or to accept any responsibility.[423]

Thoughtlessness and the unwillingness to identify evil is what prevents one from resisting amoral orders.[424] In connection with the erasure, the state officials' and employees' ability to think was reduced to references to the relevant law, as if it were the Bible of law or the Constitution rather than an insignificant administrative rule that has no bearing whatsoever on the rights and obligations of individuals. The unwillingness to recognise the evil nature of the erasure is obvious from the fact that the employees working for the local administration offices had the best insight into the situation of Yugoslav citizens and knew exactly what the impact of the erasure on their lives would be. Accordingly, they were aware, or at least should have been aware, of the amorality of the act and of the specific

---

420 *Ibid.*, p. 110.
421 *Ibid.*, p. 99.
422 *Ibid.*, p. 102.
423 *Ibid.*, p. 100.
424 Jalušič in: Arendt, Vita Activa (1996), p. XXIII.

interpretation of the Aliens Act decreed by the Ministry of the Interior. However, instead of resisting, they *pretended* that their conduct was based in law.

It is interesting to see how these employees responded to the ruling of the Constitutional Court that clearly exposed the part played by the bureaucrats and the government in the erasure. Their reaction was one of great indignation. They were exasperated, angry, and some even complained about being forced to justify themselves to their families and explain that, in reality, things were not as they were being presented.[425] In other words, they were incapable of understanding the significance of their role and attributed the responsibility to others. Their behaviour is surprisingly similar to that of Eichmann who said that he was not a "master of his own deeds" and that "he was unable 'to change anything'".[426] But it is not important at all, says Hannah Arendt, what someone else would do in the same situation; what counts is what you did.

4. Other Motives behind the Erasure

Recognition of the true nature of organised innocence (as a bureaucratised society's mode of operation) should not blind us to other motives behind the erasure. It served many goals, and its causes and motives were accordingly complex. As other authors have established, nationalist or racist ideology is not in itself strong enough of a motive to trigger violence. However, either of the two can be used as a mask to conceal other motives, such as the confiscation of property and land.[427] This theory proved correct in the case of German Jews, who were first deprived of citizenship and then of property. Similar motives are also suggested by the circumstances surrounding the erasure.

4.1 Revenge

At the time when Slovenia sought independence, relations between the Yugoslav republics and their leaders were at a low point. Slovenia's relations with Serbia were particularly poor, because Serbia and the Yugoslav People's Army posed the greatest threat during Slovenia's open preparations for secession. Their relations deteriorated further, first when the army intervened, causing a ten-day war in Slovenia, and then when armed conflicts and wars broke out in other Yugoslav

425 Tršinar, Izbrisani, in: Okno uprave, 2003.
426 Arendt, Eichmann in Jerusalem, 1994, p. 136.
427 Levi in: Jalušič, Zlo nemišljenja, 2010, p. 79.

successor states.[428] It is impossible to ignore the influence that this atmosphere had on how the Slovenian government formulated its citizenship policy, regardless of whether the threat was real or imagined. For the Slovenian government, the atmosphere provided a sufficient basis to opt for a more restrictive type of citizenship policy than what might have been chosen in different circumstances. Therefore, I propose that the erasure may have been an act of revenge by the Slovenian government for bad relations among the republics. However, with the international public paying close attention to the developments in Yugoslavia, it was not possible to take revenge directly on the real target, and the anger was redirected towards weak individuals. These mainly innocent victims could easily be set apart as a group using simple criteria (registered permanent residence and non-acquisition of citizenship). Taking revenge on the real target was out of the question, because the Slovenian government was hoping to win international recognition for the new state and accordingly did its best to avoid the war. The chosen method of revenge was less violent than a military assault, but its goals were just as inhumane. It was revenge for a feeling of historical victimhood, enabled by non-thinking and organised innocence syndrome. A desire for revenge is evident from the stigmatisation of the erased people as aggressors and from unjustified generalisations that equated them with YPA officers who allegedly threatened Slovenia with weapons and even expressed such threats publicly.[429]

4.2 Material Motives

The reasons for the erasure also included material motives. Thanks to a restrictive citizenship policy, the cancellation of their legal status, and difficult access to all kinds of residence permits, erased people could be robbed of all social benefits arising from the legislation. In addition, they were prevented from enjoying the two main material advantages of the privatisation process – purchasing socially owned apartments under favourable terms and obtaining state-issued certificates.

---

428 *Cf.* Mesojedec Pervinšek, Predpisi o državljanih in tujcih z uvodnimi pojasnili, 1997, and Končina, Zakon o državljanstvu Republike Slovenije s komentarjem, 1993.

429 A comparison with Rwanda is interesting in this context. In Rwanda, the genocide was committed against the local Tutsi population who did not have anything to do with the Rwandan Patriotic Front's aggression, committed by Tutsis from Uganda. The genocide against the local Tutsi was committed when local Tutsis were declared the supporters of the aggressors and internal enemies. For more on this, see Dedić, Konstrukcija kolektivnih identitet in genocid v nekdanji Jugoslaviji in Ruandi, 2008.

Much like the majority of the Slovenian population, erased people lived in socially owned apartments when Slovenia gained independence (or, more precisely, the apartments were the property of municipalities, state bodies, and socially owned companies). In accordance with the Housing Act passed in 1991,[430] the holder of the tenancy right could buy his/her apartment under favourable terms on the condition that he/she was a Slovenian citizen. Consequently, erased persons were excluded from this right. Moreover, if they failed to sign a rent agreement for the apartment in which they lived (but could not buy), they had to move out. The pointlessness of denying them this right was obvious from the fact that many of these apartments remained empty for years. Non-citizens were also excluded from the distribution of social capital through state-issued certificates (Article 31 of the Ownership Transformation of Companies Act).[431]

In the next step of the post-independence process, SFRY citizens who did not gain citizenship were deprived of all the social benefits to which other non-Slovenian citizens who have permanent residence in Slovenia are entitled. The awareness that the acquired rights proceeding from their permanent residence in Slovenia until then would grant them access to social benefits was obviously strong. This fact was pointed out by Igor Bavčar, then Minister of the Interior, in a letter to the government dated 4 June 1992. It can be understood as an additional argument in support of his proposal that the government should "ignore" the acquired rights of the former permanent residents. In his letter, the Minister did not forget to hint at the problems that might arise if permanent residence permits had to be revoked,[432] which can be understood as an additional argument to persuade the government that it was sensible to prevent those people from accessing material benefits.

Certain social benefits are tied to on-going insurance payments (e.g. medical insurance) and others to contributions paid in the past (pension insurance); erased people were prevented from accessing both. Without legal status and valid documents, they could not be insured nor could they access pensions and disability benefits. Those who regained their legal status could receive disability or old-age pensions, but only under the condition that they fulfilled a minimum number of years in the system. If not, all past contributions were lost.

430 Stanovanjski zakon, Official Gazette of the Republic of Slovenia, No. 18/1991I.

431 Zakon o lastninskem preoblikovanju podjetij, Official Gazette of the Republic of Slovenia, No. 55/1992.

432 A letter from the Ministry of the Interior to the Government of the republic of Slovenia entitled "Open issues relating to the implementation of the Aliens Act", No. 0016/1S010/391 dated 4 June 1992.

Erased people not only lost access to state benefits paid from the funds to which they themselves had contributed in the past, but they also had to bear additional costs, such as fees paid to regulate their legal status, travel expenses to other parts of Yugoslavia to fetch documents, fees for official translations of documents and certificates from other countries, the cost of the Slovenian language exam that was required for citizenship through naturalisation, administrative taxes, judicial taxes, the costs of legal counselling, and last but not least, the fines paid for residing illegally in Slovenia and without valid documents.[433] Material gains proceeding from the erasure went to transportation companies, state bodies, courts, interpreters, and lawyers. In other words, erased people were not only prevented from accessing the socially owned property to which they were entitled by virtue of the principle of equality, but they also had to spend a large additional sum if they wanted to remain in Slovenia or return to the country.[434]

Material motives were also implicated in the treatment of Jewish people before and during WWII. As mentioned above, the first measure to affect the Jews was the revocation of citizenship. It was revoked by the 11th Decree supplementing the Law on Citizenship of the German Reich, dated 25 November 1941. It stipulated that:

> A Jew loses German citizenship:
> a) on the day this Decree comes into force if he has habitual residence abroad at the time when this Decree comes into force,
> b) if after this Decree comes into force he establishes habitual residence abroad, with the date the habitual residence is transferred abroad.[435]

Paragraph 1 in Part III stipulated:

> Based on this Decree, the property of the Jews who lost German citizenship becomes the property of the Reich on the day the person lost citizenship.[436]

Needless to say, Jews did not leave voluntarily (and even if they had, their departure would not have been a sufficient reason to revoke their citizenship). They were first persecuted and encouraged to emigrate, and later deported. This was

---

433 Zorn, Registered as Workers, Erased as non-Slovenes, in: The Scars of the Erasure, 2010, p. 40.

434 *Cf.* Mekina, I., The Erasure of the Erasure, in Journal for the Critique of Science 35 (2007) 228, p. 182.

435 Translated into English by the author.

436 Based on Alexy, A Defence of Radbruch's Formula, in: Recrafting the Rule of Law, 1999, pp. 18–19.

taken as a change of their habitual residence, thus fulfilling the condition for dispossession.

5. The Disintegration of Yugoslavia as a Contributing Factor

It is often erroneously argued that people were erased because they did not acquire Slovenian citizenship. In reality, the non-acquisition of Slovenian citizenship was simply a criterion that could be used to delimit this group and that could be exploited later to argue that the erasure was based in law. Similarly, the cause of the erasure was not the military assault on Slovenia by the former Yugoslavia. Rather, the dissolution of Yugoslavia and Slovenia's independence should be understood as an opportunity for the government to implement a measure that until then had been unimaginable. The erasure would have been difficult to implement if the country had not disintegrated, because the indefensibility of the move would have been clear at a glance. If the Slovenian government set apart a group of people based on ethnic or any other obvious criterion and then deprived its members of legal status, the move would have been difficult to conceal and vindicate in front of both the international and domestic public.

5.1 State of Exception

The theory that Yugoslavia's disintegration enabled the erasure can be explained by Giorgio Agamben's theory of the state of exception. In essence, this theory describes the modern totalitarian regimes of the 20th century as systems that exploit the state of exception to create a legally supported civil war. This enables the physical removal not only of political opponents but of entire categories of the population which for one reason or another have failed to integrate into a given political system. The state of exception can take on various forms, ranging from the suspension of the Constitution or constitutional rights, sometimes in combination with the transfer of full authority to the executive branch of the government (as when a state of emergency is proclaimed), to less obvious forms, when the Constitution is left in place but certain constitutional provisions are not applicable in exceptional situations.

The state of exception can emerge in two ways: through the agency of the constituent power or of the constituted power.[437] In the case of the erasure, both powers were at work. Gaining independence was a unique state of exception achieved through the use of the constituent power, which then led to the

437 Agamben, State of exception, 2005, p. 38.

suspension of the former social order and the establishment of the new one. Once the new order was established, another state of exception – the treatment of the Other – emerged. It targeted a specific group of the population that, according to the authorities, could not be homogenised within the country. The new order was maintained by the constituted power, which oversaw the expulsions and the continuous denial of rights.

During states of exception, the discrepancy between the norms and their practical application is at its greatest. The force of law is taken away from the laws – the laws are valid but do not have the force of law. Instead, the force of law is attributed to acts that are not legally valid.[438] I will take as an example the Aliens Act. Its vagueness rendered it practicably unworkable, and the reason for this was the legal vacuum created by the lack of clarity in the law itself. The force of law was therefore transferred to the unwritten interpretations of the Aliens Act in which the law was enforced according to norms that it did not contain. The force of law was further ascribed to the in-house instructions which filled the legal vacuum created by the Aliens Act, and later to the government's Decision of 1992 that changed the requirements for obtaining a permanent residence permit in Slovenia.[439]

Agamben explains that the state of exception is a space that is outside the law, meaning that the acts committed within that space are also outside the law.[440] Schmitt would not agree with this, as in his view the so-called pure violence that occurs in the state of exception cannot be beyond the law, because the law has foreseen it precisely by excluding it from the law.[441] Furthermore, according to Schmitt, every exception must have a corresponding rule, although there are situations in which the difference between exception and rule is obscured, and the state of exception becomes the rule. The erasure placed erased people in precisely such a situation. They found themselves outside the law, in a state of exception, because the rules of democracy and respect for human rights were suspended in relation to them with the establishment of the new state. They came to be governed by a parallel system that was outside the law, and for those who could not regain their status, the state of exception became the rule. It was possible to move in and out of the state of exception: a person who acquired a temporary residence permit came close to leaving the state of exception – i.e. to possessing

---

438 *Ibid.*

439 Decision No. 26001/ 912/ 58 of the Government of the Republic of Slovenia dated 3 September 1992.

440 Agamben, State of exception, 2005, p. 50.

441 *Ibid.*, p. 54.

a legal status – but only temporarily. Any failure to renew one's temporary residence permit relegated one back to the state of exception, which for these people again became the rule.

In the past, the interpretation of the state of exception proceeded from the literal meaning of the word, i.e. it denoted a state that is exceptional and signalled a temporary deviation from the rule. Over time, however, the arbitrary introduction of the state of emergency (one that was not induced by a military assault), without going so far as to necessitate the suspension of the Constitution, became one of the main elements and operational methods of modern social systems, including democratic post-totalitarian systems which retained elements of totalitarianism. For example, this can be implemented through the introduction of various temporary or exceptional measures which then turn into permanent features of the system, or by obscuring the dividing lines separating the legislative, executive, and judiciary branches.[442] In the case of the erasure, the executive, legislative, and judicial branches of government worked in unison. The executive branch prepared the laws, the legislative branch approved them, sometimes without much debate, and the judicial branch helped to implement them. For a long time, the Constitutional Court contributed to this state of affairs. It received the first request to assess the constitutionality of the Aliens Act in 1994, the year it was established, but it only processed that request a full five years later.[443]

There is a revealing comparison to be made between the erasure and another modern phenomenon of the state of exception which was introduced in the US after the terrorist attacks of 11 September 2001: the Patriot Act, which suspended the right of terror suspects to be treated as prisoners of war or as criminal suspects. Agamben pointed out that the novelty in the Patriot Act was the radical erasure of the legal status of the individual in order to produce a legally unnamed being that cannot be classified. He used the same word as we do – erasure. He noted that imprisoned terror suspects were placed in an area outside the law and outside judicial control,[444] which is similar to what happened to erased people.

---

442 *Ibid.*, pp. 2 and 7.

443 The initiative filed soon after the Constitutional Court was established in 1994 was processed only by the next generation of constitutional judges. This suggests that the initiative was not dealt with because of reasons internal to the Constitutional court. We will probably never know what happened, because the judges of the time remain silent on this topic. However, the passivity of the Constitutional Court during the first few years following its establishment perpetuated the isolation of the victims of the erasure.

444 Agamben, State of exception, 2005, pp. 3–4.

Agamben compared the prisoners' situation with that of the Jews in Nazi concentration camps. Erased people can also be compared to them in certain respects, although one should invariably stay aware of the differences in the seriousness and horror of the two situations.

5.2 The Theory of Shock

The fact that the erasure could happen only thanks to the dissolution of Yugoslavia is perhaps even better explained by the theory of shock, which is the economic version of the state of exception. This theory was developed and advocated by Milton Friedman of the University of Chicago and was lately intensively discussed by Naomi Klein in her book The Shock Doctrine. The latter posits that shock therapy in the form of a temporary but significant reduction of public expenses can reduce public debt, the amount of money in circulation and inflation. The public experiences these measures as a shock, because the scope of goods and services provided by the state is essentially reduced, and the state of shock is an opportunity to introduce extreme neoliberal measures, privatise public property, and reduce the role of the state. It can also be used to enable repression and exclusion, since the population, reeling from the shock, is largely incapable of resistance.[445]

The state in which erased people found themselves was similar to the state of shock described above, and it is what in fact *enabled* the erasure. The shock doctrine can be effective in any political system, but it flourishes in systems that depend on repression for their survival.[446] In Slovenia, the repression affected the erased people. The first shock that paved the way for the erasure was Slovenia's secession and the dissolution of Yugoslavia; it created a chance for the government to formulate the citizenship and migration policies that enabled the erasure. In this sense, the shock can be interpreted as a sudden and drastic social change, which ushers in the kinds of measures that would not be possible without a state of exception. Similar shocks are coups d'état, wars, financial crises, etc. Had Slovenia not become a sovereign country, it would have been difficult to deprive a group of people of legal status (or at least it would not have gone unnoticed). The creation of a new state created ideal circumstances for the Slovenian government to get rid of the undesired population group.

The shock took place on a systemic, macro-level when the group of people was deprived of legal status, although not all of them were necessarily aware of it. The

445 Klein, The Shock Doctrine, 2007.
446 *Ibid.*

next shock took place on an individual, micro-level when the members of this group learned that they had been robbed of their legal status. It filled them with fear, they felt threatened, and this rendered them incapable of resisting further similar measures. It blunted them, or made them fearful or "nervous", as some of them put it,[447] making them incapable of struggle. What they experienced was in fact unimaginable until it actually happened.

Why was an individual shock indispensable to the success of the measure? According to Klein, Milton Friedman predicted that the speed, suddenness, and extent of the economic changes would cause a psychological response in the public that would facilitate adaptation to the system.[448] However, for the success of such an operation, macro-level changes alone do not suffice; additional individual measures are needed to incapacitate individuals and destroy their ability to comprehend the world around them. As instruction guides on interrogation say, in the course of an interrogation a person enters a period of psychological shock or paralysis resulting from the trauma of the interrogation that seems to destroy the surrounding world and an individual's position in it.[449] Individual resistance is thus prevented, while on the level of society this translates into an inability to resist by the population as a whole. The erasure had a similarly destructive effect on individuals and many of them could not find their way out of the situation into which they were forced for years. Several years passed before they organised themselves, got to know and meet each other, and became aware that their situations were not isolated cases. The collective awareness of the erased people as a group was shaped as late as around 2002, when the Association of the Erased Residents of Slovenia was established.[450] Their chances of self-help were also thwarted by certain measures that are regretfully reminiscent of the techniques of intimidation used by CIA, e.g. night-time or early-morning surprise arrests.[451] Some were intimidated at their homes,[452] while others experienced other kinds

447 Lipovec Čebron, Erased Rights, Invisible Diseases, in: The Scars of the Erasure, 2010, p. 154.

448 Klein, The Shock Doctrine, 2007, p. 7.

449 *Ibid.*, p. 16.

450 During the early 1990s, only a few erased persons were aware of the extent of the phenomenon. Among them were former members of the YPA who knew each other well and exchanged information early on; they later jointly turned to the Helsinki Watch – Association for Human Rights for help.

451 *Cf.* CIA, Human Resource Exploitation Training Manual, 1983.

452 The Dabetić family, for example, suffered serious police violence after a neighbour denounced them, saying that they were hiding rebels in their house. The police broke

of police violence, harassment, inhumane and humiliating treatment, or long detention in the Centre for Aliens. All this exacerbated their shock and created an atmosphere in which people felt frightened and incapable of resistance. The question posed by the Uruguayan writer Eduardo Galeano, who wondered, "How can this inequality be maintained if not through jolts of electric shock?"[453] seems to be pertinent to the case of the erased people. In the context of the erasure it would read: when can people be deprived of their legal status and persuaded to disappear if not when the new state and its citizenry are created and the whole project is veiled in secrecy and intimidation?

6. The Totalitarianism of the Law

6.1 Introduction: The Law (Statute) as a Tool

The last part of my endeavour to explain how the erasure could happen is dedicated to the role played by the law. In the western intellectual tradition, which enables the implementation of totalitarian measures despite democracy's hegemony, the law plays a crucial role. It is an especially expedient tool when a large part of the political or social community needs to be prevented from thinking or when thinking needs to be proclaimed redundant. While the Nazis ruled by way of decrees[454] that were invested with the power of law, the public officials in Slovenia ruled by way of in-house instructions that were not invested with the power of law.[455] In Nazi Germany, not one of the regulations defined the "final

into their apartment overnight and intimidated one of their adult sons by holding a gun to his head and ordering him to crawl on his knees across a distance of more than 2 km between the apartment and the house where his parents lived. The police fired more than 30 shots in front of the house, damaging the water tank and many other objects. When they entered the house, they pointed the guns at the parents, blinded them with the spotlight and ordered them to reveal where they kept the rebels. The parents answered that they never had contact with rebels and that the grandfather of the family was a well-known Partisan hero. After some time, the police officers accepted the explanation and left the house without explanation. See the statements by Velimir Dabetić in the complaint to the ECHR in the case Kurić and others v. Slovenia (complaint No. 26828/06).

453 Klein, The Shock Doctrine, 2007, p. 7.

454 Arendt, The Origins of Totalitarianism, 1973, p. 216.

455 The in-house instructions have no effect on third parties and cannot impose any obligations or rights on them (*Cf.* Kerševan, Uradništvo med strokovnostjo in navodili, in: Podjetje in delo 32 (2006) 67, p. 1275). However, the employees had to observe the instructions. The provision stipulating that a civil servant may refuse to execute

solution". Similarly, not one of the regulations in Slovenia stipulated that anyone should be deprived of legal status. Nevertheless, both regimes strove to provide legal "cover" for the violations of human rights, raising apprehensions about the use of law to justify violations. The Nazis' use of legal documents (laws and decrees) to commit crimes against the Jews was, in the opinion of Arendt, a symptom of German pedantry and thoroughness, and in addition, it lent the crimes an aura of legality.[456] Similar pedantry can also be identified in the implementation of the erasure. Many of the internal instructions ordering and coordinating the erasure reveal the efforts to carefully time and orchestrate actions to ensure that the measure was implemented simultaneously across the whole country and in the same manner.

The law (and many legal experts) played a disgraceful role in the erasure. It was used as a disguise, as a pretence that could be invoked at any time, and as a means of implementing the erasure. The legal professionals and all others who invoked the law (the Aliens Act and the Residence and the Population Register Act) behaved as if it were a divine force (rather than a result of human negotiations and agreements) upon which they themselves had no influence. This was the opposite of the truth: certain legal experts who were delegates to the National Assembly or representatives of the Ministry of the Interior first supported or approved the Aliens Act, then implemented its provisions and finally saw to it that all their subordinates followed suit. They themselves created an ambiguous law – and it was precisely this ambiguity that later enabled arbitrary interpretations.

6.2 The Elements of Totalitarianism in the Law

The above indicates the presence of certain elements of totalitarianism in the Slovenian legal system, which is an issue that deserves special attention. The basic problem with the laws that contain elements of totalitarianism is their lack of integrity. This arises from the two opposing sets of goals such laws pursue: one is the consistency of a norm, legal hierarchy, and internal harmony; the other is blind adjustment to the arbitrary political demands of the government in

an order or instruction if such an order forces him/her to commit an unlawful act, and that he/she is obliged to refuse it if it leads to a criminal act, was only introduced later (Article 94 of the Civil Servants Act). However, they should have behaved in accordance with this principle and refused to obey the unlawful in-house instructions that ordered the erasure.

456 Arendt, Eichmann in Jerusalem, 1994, p. 148.

power.[457] In regards to the erasure, the question of whether or not to recognise acquired rights posed a dilemma, with the latter option eventually prevailing.[458] In a totalitarian law, every legal norm has another "shadow" norm (the in-house instructions in the case of the erasure), and the first norm is valid only if the second norm endorses it. The presence of "shadow" norms and the possibility of arbitrary interpretations corresponding to the particular needs of the government in power make a totalitarian law whimsical and unpredictable. In other words, contrary to the idea of a constitutional democracy where changes in the law are supposed to take place to bring the law in line with constitutional principles, changes in totalitarian law reflect a certain secret pattern that appears chaotic and unpredictable.[459]

6.2.1 The Basic Norm

In a totalitarian law, the basic norm is not a constitution in the sense in which Kelsen used the word, but something that is above the constitution; it can be the will of the ruling elite, the wishes of the leader, or some other interest that is considered the highest source of law. The origin of the basic norm varies from one totalitarian regime to the next and it may or may not be visible. Intellectuals frequently assist in implementing the goals dictated by the source of the basic norm. They make use of various tools to fulfil the task – they may formulate a new law or re-interpret an existing one, make use of the mass media, propagate dogmatic statements, or advise intimidation and punishment. This leads to a false collective awareness and acceptance of the basic norm and will as the highest power.[460]

The same process can be observed in relation to restrictive citizenship policies and the erasure. The basic norm was evident from phrases such as "the national interest" and "natural law", which supposedly justified the removal of one part of the population. The basic norm, the main goal of which was to remove the Other from Slovenian society, was put into practice not only with the help of legal professionals as its implementers, but also the entire intellectual and political elite, with few exceptions. They put their knowledge and experience at the

457 Podgorecki, Totalitarian Law: Concepts and Issues, in: Totalitarian and PostTotalitarian Law, 1996, p. 7.

458 A letter by Igor Bavčar, i.e. the Ministry of the Interior, addressed to the Government of the Republic of Slovenia, entitled "Open issues regarding the implementation of the Aliens Act", No. 0016/1S010/ 391 dated 4 June 1992.

459 Podgorecki, Totalitarian Law: Concepts and Issues, in: Totalitarian and PostTotalitarian Law, 1996, p. 7.

460 *Ibid.*

disposal of the government when the independence legislation had to be written and corresponding in-house instructions were formulated. The intellectual elite also assisted the government whenever the public needed to be persuaded that the erasure was necessary, or whenever it had to be justified, or when postponing the redressing of wrongs. To promote its exclusionary policies, the government used most of the mechanisms mentioned above, ranging from intimidation and punishment (e.g. fines for unlawfully residing in the country) to the use of mass media and the persistent repetition of dogmas. Gradually, almost the entire public was convinced that the erasure was the only possible option and that it was a just act emanating from some higher will.

6.2.2 The Supremacy of the Basic Norm over the Constitution

In totalitarian societies, the constitution is typically seen as a compulsory veneer, with the rights enshrined in it appearing as a list of wishes rather than something that must be respected. It is offered up as proof that the citizens do indeed enjoy all the rights listed therein, but in reality it is the norms in the "shadow" constitution that are in force, i.e. those that the ruling elite is willing to accept. The constitution is understood as just one of many elements that should be taken into account and not as the supreme document to which everything else should be subordinated.[461] This is how the constitution was perceived in the case of the erasure, too.

Another frequently discussed concept related to the erasure was the "natural" law that supposedly explained why the rulings of the Constitutional Court were inherently wrong. The rulings were criticised for not taking into account the "natural" law that bestowed upon the Slovenian ethnic group a natural right to freely choose who is entitled to obtain Slovenian citizenship and to exclude all others. This stance covered up for the understanding that the Constitution's primary role is to protect the perceived "us" and not the perceived "them". The same view was shared by part of the public, as demonstrated by a public opinion survey in 2008. In this survey, 86 per cent of respondents thought that the rulings of the Constitutional Court should be observed unconditionally, but when asked if the same principle applied to the rulings concerning erased people, only 71 per cent agreed.[462] This means that 15 per cent of respondents either thought

461 Podgorecki, Totalitarian Law: Concepts and Issues, in: Totalitarian and PostTotalitarian Law, 1996, p. 11.

462 Kogovšek, The Erased People Yesterday, Today and Tomorrow, in: The Scars of the Erasure, 2010, p. 10.

that the Constitutional Court's rulings concerning erased people did not need to be respected, or they did not know how to answer this question. The respondents who said that the rulings concerning erased people should not be observed but on the whole recognised the obligation to go along with the decisions of the Constitutional Court obviously thought, much like the government representatives, that the authority of the Constitution and of the Constitutional Court as its interpreter was restricted to the cases that they personally agreed with. Individuals and government representatives who hold such views deny the authority of the Constitution in situations that contradict their wishes, which they see as a basic norm placed above the Constitution.

6.2.3 *The Servility of the Law*

In a legal system that contains elements of totalitarianism, laws are not seen as having the independent value of a norm. Consequently, laws are observed only if they reinforce the basic norm, which is not of a legal but of a political nature, and they can be supplemented with executive acts that are invested with the power of law despite contradicting the law. Moreover, all laws have a shadow law, meaning that they are valid only if they are not at variance with their shadow law. "Shadow" laws are not accessible to the public. Only certain higher governmental circles have access to them and they are usually distributed as circulars, executive acts, in-house guidelines, or instructions issued from the political centre.[463]

Typically, the ruling elites perceive these secret laws as entirely natural, indeed so natural that they do not see the need to make them public.[464] Accordingly, legal issues in systems with totalitarian elements are regulated by "shadow" laws, while the public constantly receives discreet warnings that the official laws are unreliable, as they can be modified at any time according to the needs of the government.[465]

These elements of totalitarianism are evidently present in the laws and other legal regulations that affected erased people. The more the law was publicised and the more debate it triggered, the slighter its influence on the legal situation of erased people was, and vice versa. The most debated and the best-known law was the Citizenship of the Republic of Slovenia Act. The requirements for obtaining

---

463 Podgorecki, Totalitarian Law: Concepts and Issues, in: Totalitarian and PostTotalitarian Law, 1996, pp. 12–13.

464 *Cf.* Arendt, The Origins of Totalitarianism, 1973, p. 462.

465 Podgorecki, Totalitarian Law: Concepts and Issues, in: Totalitarian and PostTotalitarian Law, 1996, p. 14.

Slovenian citizenship were reproduced in the print media, public debates flared, and the opposition to extraordinary naturalisation was loud. The Aliens Act, which had far more implications for people who did not gain citizenship, was practically never mentioned.[466] Moreover, even if it had been discussed, those to whom its provisions applied would not have been better off, because the law was vague. One could say that it screamed for the supplements that eventually arrived in the form of in-house instructions (shadow laws) that filled the vacuum created by the Aliens Act. The in-house instructions were inaccessible to those whose legal status was affected by them, as these were not public documents. "Real power begins where secrecy begins".[467]

The opposition between a law and its shadow law also comes to light in the regulations and the case law relating to people who were denied entry to Slovenia because their applications for citizenship were rejected due to a threat to public order, security, or the country's defence. When granting citizenship, the Ministry of the Interior had to choose between two options. The Secretary at the Ministry of the Interior, Slavko Debelak, described these as follows:

> The Ministry of the Interior is now faced with a dilemma: should it comply with the law – law being a relative matter and a reflection of our time – or also pay heed to some sort of public interest. Our decisions are brought in accordance with the Act on General Administrative Procedure, which clearly states that our decisions shall not contradict public interest. You know what the opinion of the public is. In a few moments I am going to show you the letters we are receiving. People are literally denouncing the arrivals to us. And hence we are faced with the dilemma. If we stick solely to the law, which is adapted to the conditions that arose after the aggression, we will clash with public interest, which would consequently bring about more damage than following certain things to the letter.[468]

Debelak's dilemma therefore was whether to obey the law that granted citizenship to everyone who met the requirements (which would have been in harmony with the professed democracy and commitment to human rights), or to take into account the alleged "demands" of the people, which Debelak called "the public interest". However, this should not lead the reader to conclude that the law, or rather the manner in which it was implemented, served the majority of the public. The will of the people was in line with the wishes of the political elites, so it

466 Mekina, B., A Monument to the Erased, in: Journal for the Critique of Science 35 (2007) 228, p. 46.

467 Arendt, The Origins of Totalitarianism, 1973, p. 403.

468 Mekina, I., The Erasure of the Erasure, in: Journal for the Critique of Science 35 (2007) 228, p. 181.

could be used as an excuse to argue that the citizenship policy, such as it was, was the will of the people and that the government was only implementing their will. As a result, declarations of a threat to the public order, security, and defence of the country were applied arbitrarily. This was a consequence of the adapted interpretation of the law. Debelak also described the adaptability and servility of the law.

> A legal system is inevitably the product of politics [...]. Precisely the issues that are currently not resolved in an appropriate manner compelled us to interpret the law in the way that reflects the situation that befell Slovenia.[469]

6.2.4 *The Role of the Bureaucracy as a Method of Governing by Decree*

In systems with totalitarian elements, the bureaucracy plays a key role, since it implements the desired policies. Moreover, by virtue of its very nature, bureaucracies operate in a manner that is close to totalitarianism. Podgorecki writes that bureaucracies are partly totalitarian even in democratic systems, because their ideal is a completely rational and thoroughly impersonal approach. While they adhere to a strict hierarchy, organisation, and routine division of work, bureaucracies are in fact completely anarchic. The purpose behind complete rationality and impersonality (naturally, the two are purely theoretical notions) is to ensure the impartial treatment of clients. However, such an approach can also be destructive, because bureaucrats who do not show interest in the situation of their clients and treat them robotically, as cases rather than people, make the bureaucracy even more of an all-encompassing system, force clients to be subjected to the system, and assert the superiority of official institutions. In this way, they contribute to the described dehumanisation and depersonalisation. Individuals are approached as objects that need to be broken, because in totalitarian systems the bureaucracy operates to the benefit of the ruling elite. The clients do not perceive bureaucrats as people who are there to offer them protection, but as people who pose a threat and with whom one must struggle to survive. Bureaucracies which operate in totalitarian ways have an absolute power over individuals and they interfere brutally with their lives and privacy.[470] To be able to cope, the individuals must adapt to the expectations of the system.[471]

---

469 *Ibid.*

470 Arendt, The Origins of Totalitarianism, 1973, p. 245.

471 In psychological terms, employees who form part of the structure of a totalitarian bureaucracy project their own suffering (caused by aggression) onto others. The attitude of bureaucrats towards their clients reflects the attitude of their superiors towards

These elements of totalitarianism within a bureaucracy can be seen clearly in the treatment of erased people. They were exposed to intense dehumanisation and depersonalisation in the bureaucratic procedures that they were forced to navigate. They were treated as objects, they were first deprived of their legal status and then forced to reacquire it as required by the system, while the system did not show much interest in accommodating their personal situations. Government employees deprived erased persons of their legal status regardless of the impact this had on their lives. The approach followed a hierarchical organisational pattern: the process was broken down into individual tasks that assured a routine division of work in line with the totalitarian ideology. The testimonies of erased people point to many totalitarian elements in the administrative procedures at the local government offices. Some erased people reported that their applications for citizenship were never processed,[472] while others said that they inquired about the regulation of their status but the government employees, obviously positioned lower in the bureaucratic hierarchy, did not want to help them or misled them by giving out false information.[473]

The argument that the government, with the help of the bureaucracy, wanted to crush the erased people, is also corroborated by the fact that the Ministry of the Interior, as it admitted itself, did not notify these people that they had been deprived of their status, but it did notify "dormitory unit managements and HR departments in companies for which these people worked".[474] The denial of the right to be notified of one's own legal status is itself a serious violation of human rights, while the notification of third parties, such as an employer or a landlord on whom erased people depended for their livelihood or housing, deprived erased people of their independence.

6.2.5 *The Participation of the Judiciary in the Repression*

In systems with elements of totalitarianism, the government is only nominally divided into legislative, executive, and judicial branches; this division does not

---

themselves. Podgorecki, Totalitarian Law: Concepts and Issues, in: Totalitarian and PostTotalitarian Law, 1996, pp. 14–16.

472 Kogovšek, The Erasure as a Violation of Legally Protected Human Rights, in: The Scars of the Erasure, 2010, pp. 102–103. *See also* Lipovec Čebron, The Metastasis of the Erasure, in: Journal for the Critique of Science 35 (2007) 228, p. 78, note 18.

473 A story of an erased person entitled "I missed Slovenia, I was born there", in: The Scars of the Erasure, 2010, p. 193.

474 Krivic, Politični zločin, ne "administrativna napaka", in: Pravna praksa 26 (2007) 9, p. 21.

exist in reality. Usually in such systems the judiciary has no power to control the other two branches of government, and serves only as a supplementary mechanism of oppression. This may be achieved by appointing incompetent judges, by limiting their term in office, supervising their work, or assigning cases to specific judges only. In some cases, courts even process cases in accordance with the instructions of the leading party or the government. Another role of the judiciary in such environments is to select the norms that will and will not be observed, to re-interpret them in the manner endorsed by the government, or to extend their validity beyond the limits of the legal regulations.[475]

The transition from a one-party to a multi-party system in Slovenia created all the necessary conditions for the independent work of the judiciary: judges were given unlimited terms in office, the Constitution defined the branches of government and gave autonomy to each, a system of checks and balances was put in place, and the Constitutional Court was established as the highest guardian of constitutionality, basic human rights, and freedoms. Despite all of these efforts, the elements of totalitarianism persisted, enabling the judiciary, including the Supreme Court, to act as they did. In procedures concerning the acquisition of citizenship and regulation of erased people's status, the Supreme Court acted as a proxy for the executive branch of the government. It only corrected the restrictive administrative practices of the Ministry of the Interior minimally, and failed to deal with important issues such as the retroactive application of declarations of a threat to the public order, security, and defence of the country. Despite the unconstitutionality of the Aliens Act, the court confirmed the practice of local administrations that deprived people of their status. Justice was restored only with the rulings of the Constitutional Court, which is not part of the judicial branch of government.

The uncritical rulings of the Supreme Court on the unconstitutional legislation and in-house instructions reveal totalitarian elements that were overruled by the Constitutional Court only in the late 1990s, which eventually proved that the political system as a whole did in fact contain the elements of constitutional democracy. Dyzenhaus's term for legal systems that allow such practices is "wicked legal systems". During apartheid in South Africa, when the government was passing conspicuously discriminatory laws, courts facing this dilemma took varied approaches. Some adhered strictly to the laws that prohibited the political organisations of the Native South Africans, while others applied the tradition of

475 Podgorecki, Totalitarian Law: Concepts and Issues, in: Totalitarian and PostTotalitarian Law, 1996, pp. 18–19.

common law, which enabled them to circumvent the discriminatory laws and deliver precedential judgments.[476] Slovenia lacks a tradition of common law, but the courts had another instrument at their disposal that could have been used if they had not been heavily indoctrinated: they could have invoked the Constitution or forwarded unjust laws to the Constitutional Court (established in 1994) for assessment.[477]

6.2.6 *Apparent Legality*

In totalitarian law, the laws are not applied in accordance with their original purpose or in the way they are written. This means that two parallel legal systems exist: one creates the illusion of the rule of law, and the other produces legal insecurity and unpredictability by allowing the abuse of those laws. Public discussions revolve around the former, phony legal system, while the latter is never addressed in public; it is a subject of discussion in private circles whose members trust each other. It catches public attention and provokes scepticism only when a society undergoes sudden changes.[478]

The erasure was shrouded in nominal legality for a long time. The government referred to the law persistently, even well after the Constitutional Court ruled that the erasure was unlawful and the Aliens Act was unconstitutional. An important tool in creating the illusion of lawfulness was the careful selection of words and the omission of the names of the public officials who passed the law, ordered the erasure, and implemented it. Erased residents were "the citizens of other republics whose registrations in the register of permanent residents expired because

476 Dyzenhaus, Recrafting the Rule of Law, 2010, p. VII.

477 An argument in defence of the Supreme Court and other courts would be that in Slovenia, the assessment of constitutionality is abstract and mainly reserved for the Constitutional Court (for further information on the dilemmas as to the suitability of abstract and concrete assessment of constitutionality, see Sadurski, Rights Before Courts, 2008, pp. 19–20). However, this argument would apply only to the period after 1994 when the Constitutional Court Act was passed. Before that, there was no Constitutional Court in Slovenia and the constitutionality of individual acts could have been assessed by the Supreme Court. Once the Constitutional Court was established, the Supreme Court and other courts had the option of terminating the proceedings and forwarding the Aliens Act to the Constitutional Court. These courts did not use this option which, in my opinion, constitutes a serious professional mistake.

478 Podgorecki, Totalitarian Law: Concepts and Issues, in: Totalitarian and PostTotalitarian Law, 1996, p. 19–20.

of the implementation of Article 81 of the Aliens Act".[479] Residence registrations thus appeared to have expired of their own, by some automatism, without anyone intervening or having anything to do with it, as if the law had passed itself without anyone being responsible for it. This formulation was in use until the end of 2008, with the sole purpose of maintaining an image of complete legality. In 2008 the government's narrative changed slightly, and the obligation to implement the ruling of the Constitutional Court temporarily acquired an important place on the political agenda (I will elaborate on this later in the text).

As is typical of totalitarian regimes, there were two legal realities at the time of the erasure: officially, registrations expired "because of the implementation of the Aliens Act", but secretly there was a legal vacuum caused by the Aliens Act which produced an arbitrary interpretation. The latter was brought to light thanks to the sudden social changes that came in the wake of the first systemic ruling of the Constitutional Court in 1999 and the increased visibility of erased people, which was a result of their self-organisation.

6.2.7 Legitimisation

A typical trait of totalitarian regimes is that the population of a country acquiesces to a specific method of governance and to the rule of the specific elite, but has no respect for it. In this way, it tacitly endorses the government and ensures its legitimisation. The reasons which lead to such a situation are diverse; they include the conviction that resistance would not bring about any change, fear that the situation would only deteriorate further, a lack of experience in fighting injustice, a lack of allies among other oppressed groups, a lack of hope that the international community (or someone else) would exert pressure on the government, a fear of further repression, the conviction that fate cannot be changed, and so on. Each of these reasons can be strong enough to paralyse the population and prevent resistance. In the next step, the population begins to perceive the government and its politics as natural, as something that cannot be changed. When this natural legitimacy is achieved, there is no longer an urgent need for excessive

479 For example, the answer of the Government of the Republic of Slovenia concerning the acceptability and justifiability of the complaint over the admissibility ruling in the case *Makuc and Others v. Slovenia* (now *Kurić and Others v. Slovenia*), dated 26 October 2007.

oppression to maintain the status quo – totalitarian propaganda can accomplish the task on its own.[480]

These factors can be identified in the context of the erasure. They were present during the 1990s and they have persisted to the present day. They rendered the erased people passive and unable to resist. It is evident from the fact that, of the 25000 erased people in total, only a small group is prepared to appear in public and speak about the erasure. Others are held back by the fear that the situation will only deteriorate, the conviction that it is impossible to win a victory over the state, a lack of experience with activism, a lack of support from other communities/groups in Slovenia, and the absence of determination on the part of the international community to take a more decisive approach and exert pressure on the Slovenian government. Those who managed to regain their status relatively early on are now mostly reluctant to maintain contact with the erased people as a group. Such behaviour helped legitimise the politics that led to the erasure and reduced the chances of resolving the problem. During the 1990s, being erased appeared to these people as their destiny, a given, natural state against which it was not possible to fight and which had to be taken as something self-evident that could not be altered by their individual will. This almost enabled the politics that brought about the erasure to reach the stage of "natural legitimacy" (particularly after several botched attempts to implement the rulings of the Constitutional Court). What eventually prevented it and saved the erasure from being collectively forgotten was the activism of erased people and various non-governmental organisations (NGOs). In 2012, it resulted in the historical ruling of the European Court of Human Rights. This change was possible because the elements of totalitarianism did not prevail completely, because the international system for the protection of human rights worked, because civil society activism was allowed and because the governments in Slovenia succeeded each other quickly enough to finally push the erasure and the implementation of the rulings of the Constitutional Court to the top of the political agenda.

6.2.8 *The Instability, Unpredictability, and Retroactivity of the Law*

Law that nurtures the elements of totalitarianism does not ensure stability.[481] Since the laws that were related to erased people are totalitarian in their essence, the instability was directly experienced by erased people. If the laws covering

480 Podgorecki, Totalitarian Law: Concepts and Issues, in: Totalitarian and PostTotalitarian Law, 1996, p. 21–22.

481 *Ibid.*, p. 25.

their legal status had ensured stability, their situation would not have changed or worsened when Slovenia became a sovereign country. But it did, first when two categories of the population were defined with regard to access to citizenship, and then when their acquired rights were taken away from them. The instability of the laws came to light when former citizens became disenfranchised aliens practically overnight. Totalitarian elements also frequently encroach on the basic rules of the predictability of law and the prohibition of retroactivity. My analysis earlier in the text demonstrated that this happened in the context of the erasure. Moreover, the 1999 Act Regulating the Legal Status of Citizens of Former Yugoslavia Living in the Republic of Slovenia also contained a retroactive provision stipulating that permanent residence permits could be issued to citizens of Yugoslavia's successor states who had been actually living in Slovenia since the erasure in 1992. Erased people, on the other hand, could not change whether they lived in Slovenia after the erasure or not retroactively, nor could they influence their status in any way.

7. Conclusions

The elements of totalitarianism in the legal system surrounding the erasure confirm that such elements are not present only in one-party or autocratic systems, but in all systems. As Podgorecki says, in post-totalitarian democracies the laws are definitely passed more openly, but it seems that the totalitarian bureaucratic machinery that executes them still functions in a similar manner as before the transition.[482]

In implementing the erasure, the law was used in an arbitrary and totalitarian manner to discriminate and exclude undesired persons. These practices should be alien to the rule of law, but were instead understood as an expression of justice. If the law is exploited to realise intentions that are not in harmony with the basic principles of justice and then used as an excuse for crimes or violations, we are obliged to identify that practice and reject it. The legal experts and others who shape people's lives through the laws that they formulate, pass, and implement must accept responsibility, monitor the impact of every law on people's lives, continually assess if these impacts are just, and particularly if the laws ensure justice for marginalised social groups. If they fail to fulfil these tasks, the legal experts and the laws they create will continue to contribute to the preservation of the elements of totalitarianism which in the long term will make us all "superfluous".[483]

---

482 *Ibid.*, p. 29.
483 *Cf.* Arendt, The Origins of Totalitarianism, 1973, p. 443.

their legal status and [illegible] their situation would not [illegible]

[illegible] non-Slovenia [illegible] because [illegible] did not [illegible] two [illegible]

Part IV: The Erasure, Constitutionality, and the Rule of Law

Over many years, the man watches the doorkeeper almost without a break. He forgets about the other doormen, and begins to think this one is the only thing stopping him from gaining access to the law. Over the first few years he curses his unhappy condition out loud, but later, as he becomes old, he just grumbles to himself.

Franz Kafka, The Trial

1. Introduction

In this part of the book I examine the Constitutional Court's role in solving the issue of the erasure and its consequences, and the meaning of the Constitutional Court's rulings from the perspective of individual constitutional principles.

To answer these two crucial questions, I analyse sixteen Constitutional Court rulings. In selecting the rulings, my starting point was the erasure in a wider sense, and I thus also include rulings that are only indirectly related to it. In addition to the two most renowned rulings of the Constitutional Court, to which I later refer as "fundamental" (Rulings U-I-284/94 and U-I-246/02), I also take into account a less widely known ruling (Ruling U-I-295/99), as well as all of the rulings of the Constitutional Court on the complaints lodged by erased people concerning the erasure, their unregulated status, and the rights that they were no longer able to exercise after they lost their permanent residence permit in Slovenia (Rulings Up-333/96, Up-60/97, Up-20/97, Up-152/97, Up-336/98, Up-119/99 and Up-211/04). In addition, I discuss all rulings related to the proposed legislative referendums on erasure-related issues (Rulings U-II-3/03-15, U-II-1/04, U-II-3/047, U-I-257/03-14 and U-II-1/10-25). I also analyse a petition for a referendum on the revocation of citizenships granted under Article 40 of the Citizenship of the Republic of Slovenia Act, since this proposal was motivated by the same nationalist ideology that was behind other requests for referenda related to the erasure.

In general, the Constitutional Court played a positive and decisive role in the legal resolution of the erasure. However, I also discuss whether its rulings on the issue reveal any negative or restrictive aspects. The Constitutional Court rulings mainly contained congruent instructions for the legislator, the purpose of which was to eliminate the violations in a constitutional manner, but their content was not completely unambiguous.

I analyse the Constitutional Court rulings by individual constitutional issues, as this enables me to avoid organising them monotonously by chronological order and discussing the constitutional issues that appear in several rulings multiple times. For the sake of clarity and for reference, I include Table 1 with the rulings listed in chronological order.

Table 1: The Constitutional Court Rulings related to the erasure

No.	Ruling No.	Date	Type	Subject	Relevant articles of the Constitution
1.	U-I-266/95	20 November 1995	A petition by the National Assembly to assess the constitutionality of the request for a referendum	Revocation of citizenship granted under Article 40 of the Citizenship of the RS Act	Article 2 – the rule of law (the principle of legal certainty) Article 34 – the right to personal dignity and safety Article 35 – privacy and personality Rights
2.	U-I-284/94	4 February 1999	A petition for the assessment of constitutionality	The erasure, the legal vacuum in the Aliens Act	Article 2 – the rule of law (the principle of legal certainty) Article 14, Para 2 – equality before the law
3.	Up-333/96	1 July 1999	A constitutional complaint	The erasure, issuing of a driver's license	Article 14, Para 2 – equality before the law Article 22 – equal protection of rights
4.	Up-60/ 97	15 July 1999	A constitutional complaint	The erasure	Article 14, Para 2 – equality before the law Article 22 – equal protection of rights

No.	Ruling No.	Date	Type	Subject	Relevant articles of the Constitution
5.	Up-20/ 97	18 November 1999	A constitutional complaint	Advance military pension payment	Article 22 – equal protection of rights
6.	Up-152/ 97	16 December 1999	A constitutional complaint	Advance military pension payment	Article 22 – equal protection of rights
7.	U-I-295/ 9913	18 May 2000	A petition for the assessment of constitutionality	Stricter exclusion criteria for issuing permanent residence permits in the Act on the Regulation of the Status of Citizens of Other State Successors to the Former SFRY than in the Aliens Act.	Article 2 – the rule of law (the principle of legal certainty) Article 14, Para 2 – equality before the law
8.	Up-336/ 98	20 September 2001	A constitutional complaint	Income support	Article 14, Para 2 – equality before the law Article 22 – equal protection of rights
9.	U-I-119/ 99	23 May 2002	A petition for the assessment of constitutionality	Driver's license	Article 2 – the rule of law (the principle of legal certainty)

No.	Ruling No.	Date	Type	Subject	Relevant articles of the Constitution
	U-I-246/02-28	3 April 2003	A petition for the assessment of constitutionality	The retroactive effect of permanent residence permits; forced removal of foreigners; the criteria for determining a vague legal concept of actually living in Slovenia; the deadline for the submission of applications	Article 2 – the rule of law (the principle of legal certainty) Article 120, Para 2 – the legality principle (the principle of the subordination of the administrative authorities to the Constitution and laws)
11.	U-II-3/03-15	22 December 2003	A petition of the National Assembly to assess the constitutionality of the request for subsequent legislative referendum	The unconstitutional consequences as a result of the rejection of the law at the referendum; the deadline for the submission of the application/proposal	Articles 16 and 22 of the Referendum and People's Initiative Act
12.	U-I-257/03-14	26 January 2004	A petition of the National Assembly to assess the constitutionality of the decision to call a subsequent legislative referendum	The obligation to call a referendum	Article 90. Para 2 – the obligation of the National Assembly to call a referendum

No.	Ruling No.	Date	Type	Subject	Relevant articles of the Constitution
13.	U-II-1/ 04	26 February 2004	A petition of the National Assembly to assess the constitutionality of the decision to call a preliminary legislative referendum	Permanent residence permits; the renewal of the procedure; the exclusion of the possibility to exercise certain rights; the exclusion of the right to damage payments; the determination of new criminal offences	Article 2 – the rule of law (the principle of legal certainty) Article 14, Para 2 – equality before the law Article 15 – judicial protection, the violation of human rights and redress for the violation of Article 26 – right to compensation, Article 28 – the principle of legality in criminal law
14.	U-II-3/ 04-7	20 April 2004	A petition of the National Assembly to assess the constitutionality of the decision to call a preliminary legislative referendum	The clarity of the referendum question, abuse of the institute of referendum	Article 16 of the Referendum and People's Initiative Act
15.	Up-211/ 04-21	2 March 2006	A constitutional complaint	Actually living in Slovenia	Article 22 – equal protection of rights
16.	U-II-1/ 10-25	10 June 2010	A petition of the National Assembly to assess the constitutionality of the decision to call a subsequent legislative referendum	The emergence of unconstitutional consequences; the principle of proportionality; the weighing of rights	Article 2 – the rule of law Article 3, Para 2 – the principle of the separation of powers Article 14, Para 2 – equality before the law Article 34 – right to dignity and safety

2. Constitutional Issues and the Erasure

2.1 The Rule of Law and the Erasure

Many Constitutional Court rulings on erasure-related issues found violations of the principles of the rule of law. The rule of law refers to a form of state organisation that emerged in response to other state forms (e.g. the police state) that did not subject their operation to regulation by the legislature.[484] The principle of rule of law consists of the following elements: the separation of powers; the protection of individual freedoms; the adoption of laws in a parliament elected by the people in democratic elections; the subordination of the executive and judicial branches of the government to law; the restriction, measurability, and predictability of the state's conduct with regard to its citizens; legal certainty, or the principle of trust in the validity and durability of laws; the prohibition of retroactive laws; the principle of proportionality (prohibiting excessive encroachment on human rights and fundamental freedoms); clear and distinct regulations; a well-developed and independent judicial system; the option of judicial control over administrative provisions; the option of constitutional appeals; the principle of *nullum crimen sine lege* and other guarantees in criminal proceedings; and the principle of fair treatment in judicial proceedings and proceedings before other state bodies.[485] Pavčnik also mentions the equal and foreseeable treatment of subjects, along with legal remedies that can be used both to exercise a right and to realise an obligation.[486]

In connection with the erasure, the most important principles are legal certainty, legality, and equality before the law, the principle of clarity, and the separation of powers. In the next two chapters I examine the violations of these principles caused by the erasure in the wider sense of the word, that is, the erasure as the cancellation of one's legal status.

2.1.1 The Principle of Legal Certainty

The principle of legal certainty demands that individual decisions made by the authorities be lawful, adopted without reservations, and not be transitional in nature; in other words, decisions should be stable.[487] Furthermore, it also prohibits

484 Pavčnik, Narava pravne države in njene prvine, in: Pravna država, 2009, p. 30.
485 Šturm (ed.), Komentar Ustave Republike Slovenije, 2010, pp. 54–55.
486 Pavčnik, Narava pravne države in njene prvine, in: Pravna država, 2009, p. 32.
487 Constitutional Court of the Republic of Slovenia, Ruling U-I-266/95, paragraph 11.

the retroactive implementation of laws.[488] Historically, the principle originated in the areas of civil and contract law and gradually gained ground in public law as well, first when judging specific legal acts (decisions), then general legal acts (laws and regulations).[489]

In connection with the erasure, the most important aspect of the principle of legal certainty is the assurance that a state will not take any action that is detrimental to an individual's circumstances unless doing so advances a legitimate government interest. Taking this into account, the Constitutional Court found that the principle of legal certainty was violated in seven of the sixteen rulings analysed here. It found such a violation as early as 1995 (Ruling U-I-266/95), when it assessed the constitutionality of the referendum on the revocation of citizenship granted under Article 40 of the Citizenship of the Republic of Slovenia Act. It concluded that the revocation of citizenship constitutes an encroachment on one's acquired rights, since citizenship, once granted in accordance with the constitution and relevant statutes, is a constitutionally protected right. The revocation of citizenship would have essentially interfered with the relationships of rights based on valid laws and arising from citizenship.[490] Moreover, as Boštjan M. Zupančič (then Constitutional Court judge, now a Slovenian judge at the European Court of Human Rights) stressed in the concurring opinion, persons who gained citizenship under Article 40 of the Citizenship of the Republic of Slovenia Act, to which Article 13 of UZITUL explicitly refers, were the "constitutive bearers of Slovenian statehood", who had the right to vote in the referendum on sovereignty and independence, by virtue of which they were "the sovereign people mentioned in Article 3, Para 2 [of the Constitution] that established the state of Slovenia". These are persons, he emphasised, "who in accordance with Article 13 of the Constitutional Act and Article 40 of the Citizenship Act were citizens of the Republic of Slovenia, which is therefore their country".[491] The Constitutional Court thus prevented a referendum which, given the hostile atmosphere at the time, could have led to the revocation of citizenship. Had the revocation of citizenship been approved at the referendum, all the people who had already gained citizenship would have been deprived of it, meaning that they, too, would have been erased. Their situation would have then been the same as that of the individuals who did not apply for Slovenian citizenship or had been denied it.

488 Šturm (ed.), Komentar Ustave Republike Slovenije, 2010, p. 57.

489 *Ibid.*

490 Constitutional Court of the Republic of Slovenia, Ruling U-I-266/95, paragraph 13.

491 Concurring opinion of Judge Boštjan M. Zupančič to Constitutional Court of the Republic of Slovenia Ruling No. U-I-266/95.

The Constitutional Court's assessment of the constitutionality of the erasure itself was based on the principle of legal certainty. In the constitutional complaint submitted on 14 November 1994, the complainants claimed that several articles of the Aliens Act were unconstitutional. This included Article 81, which covered the status of the citizens of other SFRY republics, and Articles 13 and 16, which determined the requirements for the acquisition of temporary and permanent residence permits (i.e. the requirements that erased people were expected to meet). Four years later, the Constitutional Court rejected the legal framework for regulating the status of erased people proposed by the parliamentary majority and the Ministry of the Interior. The court began by noting that the situation of the citizens of other SFRY republics who did not acquire Slovenian citizenship was unique, and that the law should have taken this into account. In other words, the legislature should have included special provisions, either in the Aliens Act or in a separate law, to regulate the status of these people. Since their situation was uniquely different from that of foreigners from third countries (before Slovenia became independent, they were citizens of the country in which they lived), the Constitutional Court found that the provisions in Articles 13 and 16 of the Aliens Act regarding foreign nationals from third countries should not have been applied to the citizens of other SFRY republics.[492] The Court concluded that, after the expiration of the deadlines determined in Article 81, Para 2 of the Aliens Act (see part III), the citizens of other republics found themselves in an "uncertain legal situation", and that the wording of Article 81 was such that "these people had no way of knowing what their status as aliens would be and which provisions of the [Aliens] Act would apply to them".[493] The following explanation captures the essence of the legal uncertainty faced by erased people:

> The principle of the protection of legal certainty guarantees to the individual that the state will not make his/her legal position worse without a justified reason. It was quite justified for the citizens of other [SFRY] republics who did not opt for Slovenian citizenship not to expect that they would be given the same status as foreigners who were entering the Republic of Slovenia for the first time, or that they would be deprived of their permanent residence permits, and this without any notice whatsoever. In the [legal] acts connected to the independence process, Slovenia as a future state undertook to guarantee the protection of human rights and fundamental freedoms to all persons in the territory of the Republic of Slovenia regardless of nationality, without any discrimination, in conformity with the Constitution of the Republic of Slovenia and applicable international law [...] Citizens of other republics who did not opt for citizenship of

492 Constitutional Court of the Republic of Slovenia, Ruling U-I-284/94, paragraph 14.
493 *Ibid.*, paragraph 15.

> the Republic of Slovenia or whose application was rejected could, with reference to the above-mentioned acts connected to Slovenia's independence process, quite rightly expect that this circumstance would not essentially worsen their position and that they would continue to have permanent residence in the Republic of Slovenia if they so wished. Said persons could quite rightly expect that the conditions which would enable them to continue to have permanent residence in the Republic of Slovenia would not be more rigorous than those set in reference to the acquisition of citizenship by Article 13 of the [Basic Constitutional Charter] or Article 40 of the [Citizenship Act], and that their legal status would be regulated in accordance with international law.[494]

This explanation shows that a chasm existed between the justifiable expectation of the citizens of other SFRY republics that they would retain their permanent resident status, and the unanticipated expectation of the authorities that, as these persons were supposedly the legal equivalents of foreigners from third countries, they should apply for a residence status. The expectations of the citizens of other republics were based on the independence legislation (described in Part II), which promised a great deal and assured non-discriminatory treatment and respect for the human rights of all permanent residents. Their impression of being legally secure was reinforced by other circumstances, e.g. by the fact that their personal ID numbers were registered in Slovenia, that they were entitled to vote in the referendum on sovereignty, that some of them were born in Slovenia, etc. However, none of these factors had any influence whatsoever on their status. Thus, the Constitutional Court decided that by leaving the legal status of erased people unregulated, the principle of legal certainty had been violated.[495]

The next question is whether the Constitutional Court's decision would have been the same if certain missing elements had filled the legal vacuum. For example, if the Aliens Act had contained a clearer provision that, once the deadline expired, the citizens of other SFRY republics would be considered aliens with an unregulated status, that they would then be obliged to regulate their status as stipulated by the Aliens Act, and if they failed to do so, their residence in Slovenia would be terminated by a decision containing legal advice on their right to appeal. However, given the explanation of the ruling above, we can assume with great certainty that the Constitutional Court's decision would have been the same.

The fact that erased people were not issued an official decision and could not appeal against the erasure or obtain judicial protection only made a bad situation worse. The main reason why the Aliens Act was unconstitutional was that their

494 *Ibid.*, paragraph 16.
495 *Ibid.*, paragraph 15.

status remained unregulated and that they were equated with foreigners entering Slovenia for the first time. In other words, even if the law had regulated such a deprivation of status in detail, including procedural guarantees, the act would still have been unconstitutional.

The above ruling of the Constitutional Court was implemented by passing the Legal Status Act.[496] It contained an exclusion clause (Article 3) stipulating the conditions under which a permanent residence permit could not be issued. A comparison of this article and the exclusion clauses in the Aliens Act of 1991 defining whose residence permits should be revoked[497] shows that the exclusion clauses in the law regulating the status of erased people were more severe than those applicable to foreigners from a third country. When deciding whether to grant a residence permit to a foreigner from a third country, the relevant state body had the option of discretion. This option was not included in the case of erased people; if the exclusion clause applied, the state body had no choice but to deny the application for a residence permit. In principle, the fact that exclusion clauses were included in the text is not at issue, since the grounds for exclusion, i.e. the possibility of revoking a residence permit, would have existed even if erased people had retained their permanent resident status. However, the stricter conditions were disputable, since, as the Constitutional Court stated in Ruling U-I-295/99, "when regulating their status, the starting point should be the legal status that they should have", that is, the status of permanent residents, or more precisely, foreigners with permanent residence permits. Therefore, the same conditions should have applied to erased people. The Constitutional Court concluded that any legal arrangement that ignored this point of view would be "in conflict with the principle of legal certainty, which guarantees to the individual that the state will not make his/her legal situation worse without a justified reason".[498]

The legislature also violated the principle of legal certainty by not including the option to regulate one's status retroactively in the Legal Status Act, e.g. for

496 Zakon o urejanju statusa državljanov drugih držav naslednic SFRJ v Republiki Sloveniji, Official Gazette of the Republic of Slovenia, No. 61/1999.

497 Article 24 of the Aliens Act (Official Gazette of the Republic of Slovenia, No. 1/1991I), which comprises negative conditions, stated: "The permanent residence permit of a foreigner can be revoked if [...] he or she was convicted of a crime and sentenced to imprisonment for at least three years; [...] if he or she was sentenced to imprisonment on multiple occasions, for a total duration of more than five years".

498 Constitutional Court of the Republic of Slovenia, Ruling No. U-I-295/99.

the period which started on the date of the erasure. In its Ruling U-I-246/02, the Constitutional Court pointed out that

> the principle of legal certainty, as one of the elements of the principle of rule of law under Art. 2 of the Constitution, requires that the position of the persons mentioned not remain unregulated for such a long period of time. Permanent resident status is an important prerequisite for the exercise of certain rights and legal benefits that erased persons could not exercise due to the legally unregulated state of affairs.[499]

This means that the unconstitutionality arising from the violation of the principle of legal certainty should have been eliminated in accordance with this principle. This could only have been achieved by recognizing the permanent resident status of erased people for the duration of their erasure. Furthermore, the unconstitutional situation should have been resolved entirely and not only in part, as partial redress necessarily means that an unconstitutional element remains in place. Accordingly, Point 8 of the Constitutional Court's ruling imposed on the Ministry of the Interior the obligation to "issue [erased people] supplementary decisions on the establishment of their permanent residence in the Republic of Slovenia from 26 February 1992 onwards" (for more on the significance of these decisions and regulation of erased people's status for the past period, see part V).

The above was not the only way in which the principle of legal certainty was violated. The legislator did not take into account the diversity of legal situations in which erased people found themselves after the erasure. It set a general condition, the vague legal concept of "actually living in Slovenia", without defining any criteria to establish when this condition was met.[500]

Furthermore, the principle of legal certainty was also violated when a three-month window was set to submit applications for a permanent residence permit. The Constitutional Court ruled that this period was too short, that when "determining the time limit [...] the legislature should also have considered personal and other circumstances that could impede the timely filing of an application by entitled persons", that "due to the fact that their legal position was unregulated for a long period of time, citizens of other Republics could not have expected that such a short time limit would be prescribed for the regulation of their status", and "in particular, they could not have envisaged that not applying within such a short period would result in a loss of the right to acquire a permanent residence permit". The Constitutional Court further stressed that "it was also in the

---

499 Constitutional Court of the Republic of Slovenia, Ruling No. U-I-246/02, paragraph 15.

500 *Ibid.*, paragraph 30.

interest of the State to have fewer persons with unregulated legal status living in Slovenia",[501] meaning that the deadline should have been long enough to enable the erased people to meet it.

Ruling U-I-119/99 found that the principle of legal certainty was violated because the legislature did not regulate the replacement of driver's licenses, as did Ruling No. U-II-1/04, which found that certain parts of the question to be asked at a preliminary legislative referendum requested by the then-opposition parties, the Slovenian Democratic Party and New Slovenia, were unconstitutional. In the latter case, the Constitutional Court concluded that the petition for a preliminary legislative referendum aimed to interfere, in the most severe manner, with the principles of the rule of law. When assessing the consistency of this request with the Constitution, it found a series of problems ranging from the petitioners downplaying the erasure by calling it "the transfer from the register of permanent residents to the register of aliens without permanent residence" (which did not exist) to the addition of a criterion of exclusion, i.e. that a person who rejected the invitation of the Presidency of Slovenia to leave the YPA could not be issued a permanent residence permit.[502]

If the content of any law were similar to that of this referendum, it would constitute interference with the legal status of the erased people in a manner irreconcilable with the principle of legal certainty (Such a law would also be explicitly totalitarian). Thus, the Constitutional Court declared that the content of the referendum was unconstitutional (for more on the proposed referendums and their conformity with the Constitution, see the section on the referendums below).

2.1.2 The Principle of Legality

The principle of legality posits, among other things, that the state administration is bound by the Constitution and the laws. It is defined in Article 120, Para 2 of the Constitution ("Administrative authorities perform their work independently within the framework and on the basis of the Constitution and the laws"). In other words, administrative bodies cannot perform any action not explicitly stipulated by law (i.e. the regulations adopted by a democratically elected legislature); the laws determine the scope of their powers. Administrative law was developed precisely with this aim in mind – to place restrictions on administrative bodies and to define their powers.[503] This means that the executive branch of

501 *Ibid.*, paragraph 34.

502 Constitutional Court of the Republic of Slovenia, Ruling No. U-II-1/04.

503 *Cf.* Kerševan, Vladavina prava in upravno pravo, in: Pravna država, 2009, p. 150.

the government can operate only as provided by law and not in accordance with its own regulations. For these reasons, the principle of legality is related to the principle of the separation of powers and the principle of democracy.[504]

In its rulings on various issues related to the erasure, the Constitutional Court established that the principle of legality was violated twice: first when the erasure took place and then again when the criteria to assess whether applicants met the condition of actually living in Slovenia were set.

The representatives of the government and the state administration, as well as certain intellectuals, had argued for years (and some individuals continue to argue today)[505] that the erasure was a lawful act based on Article 5 of the Rules on Permanent Residence Registration and Cancellation Form, Personal and Household Records and the Manner and Maintenance of the Register of Permanent Residents[506] (hereafter: the Rules). The Rules were passed in 1992 based on the Residence Registration Act.[507]

The Rules stipulated that the register should only contain records on the citizens of the Republic of Slovenia who had their permanent residence registered within a certain municipality. In its answer to a complaint requesting that the constitutionality of the Rules be assessed, the government insisted that the records on citizens and foreigners should have been kept separately, and that by "transferring" the records from the register of permanent residents to the "register of aliens", the administrative bodies only sought to bring the registers in line with the Rules.[508] The measure was implemented *ex proprio motu*, and therefore no administrative procedure was launched and no decisions issued which could

---

504 Šturm (ed.), Komentar Ustave Republike Slovenije, 2010, p. 869.

505 Website Resnica o izbrisu (*The Truth about the Erasure*), http://izbrisani.siol.net/vs.htm, which only publishes documents in support of the erasure, including many letters from Andrej Šter in response to the former Constitutional Court judge, Matevž Krivic.

506 Pravilnik o obrazcu za prijavo oziroma odjavo stalnega prebivališča, o obrazcu osebnega kartona in kartona gospodinjstev ter o načinu in vzdrževanju registra stalnega prebivalstva, Official Gazette of the Republic of Slovenia, No. 27/1992.

507 Zakon o evidenci nastanitve občanov in o registru prebivalstva, Official Gazette of the Socialist Republic of Slovenia, No. 6/1983; Official Gazette of the Republic of Slovenia, No. 26/1990, 11/19911, 4/1992.

508 Constitutional Court of the Republic of Slovenia, Ruling No. U-I-284/94, paragraph 2. See also the response of the government of the Republic of Slovenia of 10 September 1998 in the procedure of constitutional review of paragraph 1 of Article 16 and paragraph 2 of Article 81 of the Aliens Act, in the Ruling of the Constitutional Court of the Republic of Slovenia No. U-I-284/94.

be appealed in court. As stated in the government's response to the action against Slovenia brought by *Kurić* before the ECHR, this measure was not a mistake but an act that brought the register in line with the state of affairs that existed after the implementation of the Aliens Act.[509]

In explaining the presumed legality of this measure, various authors adhered to the formalised administrative approach. They argued that entering a record into or erasing a record from a register were administrative acts that did not affect the status of a person. In other words, it was merely a method of recording information about a specific fact in an official register maintained in accordance with the law. According to the government, the law stipulated that an alien's record could only be entered into the register of permanent residents if he/she had been issued a citizenship certificate or an administrative permit for permanent residence in the Republic of Slovenia. Such entries and erasures were simply administrative acts that did not influence the legal status of a person; they merely recorded the change of that status.[510] Their effect was therefore of a declarative rather than a constitutive nature. This means that a foreigner retained the right to permanent residence even if he/she had no record in the register of permanent residents, and vice versa, that a foreigner who lost the right to permanent residence could not regain it simply by being entered into the register of permanent residents. Since the records were allegedly merely brought into line with the actual state of affairs and transferred to another register, the government maintained that the affected persons were not deprived of their right "to continue to live at the address where they lived until that time".[511]

These arguments were often used to justify the conduct of the state administration and to prove that erasure from the register of permanent residents could by no means affect the rights of these people. Erasure from the register of permanent residents was therefore described as a consequence of the rules on how administrative records were to be maintained, or the rules that regulated the obligation of registering and cancelling a permanent address.

---

509 The response of the Government of the Republic of Slovenia about the admissibility of a complaint in the case *Makuc and Others v. Slovenia* (now *Kurić and Others v. Slovenia*), of October 26, 2007, p. 11.

510 Kerševan, Upravnopravni vidik odškodninske odgovornosti države v primeru "izbrisanih", in: Pravna praksa 28 (2009) 19, p. 6.

511 The response of the Government of the Republic of Slovenia about the admissibility of a complaint in the case *Makuc and Others v. Slovenia* (now *Kurić and Others v. Slovenia*), of October 26, 2007, p. 11.

These arguments are legally wrong. If erasure from the register did not affect the status of these persons but was a consequence of their loss of status, then it should have been preceded by some lawful event that caused the loss of status. However, there was no such previous event: the Aliens Act did not define the future legal status of affected people, nor were they issued any document evincing the change of their status. The change was not based on a general legal act that could have applied to them as a group. Nor was it based on individual legal measures issued to every affected person. The only – unlawful – previous step that influenced their status was the arbitrary *interpretation* of Article 81, Para 2 of the Aliens Act, or, to be more precise, the way in which the legal vacuum was filled by ascribing to the provision a meaning that it did not have. What the Aliens Act stipulated was that its provisions would become applicable to a specific group of people at a certain point in time. However, this did not imply that they would no longer have a legal status and that would need to reapply for it – that was an arbitrary attribution of meaning. To the contrary, the same provision could also have been interpreted to mean that, at a certain point in time, the status of this group of people would change from that of citizens with a registered permanent residence to that of foreigners with permanent residence permits. (This would have been similar to what happened to all other foreigners living in Slovenia when it became a sovereign country). The administrative legal theory that claims that the data was deleted merely to reflect a lawful fact is therefore not sustainable for the simple reason that no such fact existed.

Similarly, the argument that the harmonisation of the registers was based on Article 5 of the Rules is false. The Rules only contained the following provisions:

1. The register of permanent residents contains data on the citizens of the Republic of Slovenia who have their permanent residence registered within the municipality.
2. The relevant body shall add a note recording a temporary absence of over three months of any citizen of the Republic of Slovenia who travels abroad, and a note recording any denial of the registration of permanent residence in accordance with Article 6, Para 4 of the Population Register Act.

There is obviously no trace of any provision in this or any other article of the Rules that could have served as a legal basis for the erasure of the citizens of other SFRY republics who had a registered permanent residence. Moreover, even if such a provision had existed, the Rules were merely a general legal act issued by the Minister of the Interior as a representative of the executive branch of the government; only a law could have authorised the erasure.

Another question here is what the legal basis was for formulating Article 5 of the Rules and for stipulating that only records on the citizens of the Republic of Slovenia were to be entered into the register of permanent residents, excluding the records of foreigners with permanent residence permits. The Population Register Act that served as the basis for the Rules referred to the *members of the public*, that is, to all persons who have a registered permanent residence in a specific municipality, including foreigners. In this way, the Rules were in contravention of the law.

All of the above leads to the conclusion that the legal basis of the erasure was supposed to consist of an unlawful rule book and the unlawful in-house instructions, that is, documents issued by the executive branch of the government for its own use — which is tantamount to "governing by decree". An in-house instruction should not have influenced the rights and obligations of third persons, especially since the addressees of the instructions were administrative bodies.[512] It should certainly not have been the legal basis for the erasure from the register of permanent residents. The constitutionality of the erasure was disputable, both the wider sense of the word (stripping people of their legal status) and in the narrower sense (erasure from the register). By depriving these persons of their legal status and erasing them from the register of permanent residents, the authorities encroached on many acquired rights of the people who were erased.[513]

Given the magnitude of the task, which necessitated the concerted actions of hundreds of civil servants and their superiors in accordance with the in-house instructions of the Ministry of the Interior, it is interesting that none of the people involved are known to have displayed any signs of doubt as to the lawfulness of the measure they were implementing (Many still do not). It is unacceptable that they did not oppose the implementation of the unlawful instructions and that they did not demand to know which law endorsed such instructions. Undoubtedly, we should allow for the possibility that some of them had suspicions about the lawfulness of their actions, and that they later tried to mitigate the consequences by helping erased individuals to reacquire their status. However, no serious resistance on the part of civil servants can be identified, so there is nothing to indicate that they followed the instructions against their will.

The absence of the slightest hint of resistance is particularly perplexing because, as a rule, administration employees seek to know the legal basis of every administrative task they perform, even routine tasks such as issuing any kind of certificate on civil status or signing a document in a specific corner of the paper.

512 Kerševan, Uradništvo med strokovnostjo in navodili, in: Podjetje in delo 32 (2006) 67, p. 1275.

513 *Cf.* Ogradi, Izbrisani državljani SFRJ, 2003, p. 27.

In this case however, they did not ask about the legal basis of erasing people from the register of permanent residents, punching holes in their valid personal documents, and contacting the police to carry out the expulsions. Their conduct is even more puzzling considering that the Population Register Act in force at the time stipulated that a record in the register of permanent residents could only be erased after the relevant administrative body had first conducted a procedure to establish the facts of the case (verifying that the person did not live at the address registered as his/her permanent residence) and then issued a final decision. Article 4 of the Population Register Act further stipulated that a person could only be erased from the register of permanent residents if he/she had died, moved away from the territory of the RS, his/her Slovenian citizenship was terminated, or if he/she was deregistered on the basis of a final decision. Even though the Population Register Act did not provide for any other kind of erasure from the register of permanent residents, this did not deter the administration employees from carrying out the erasure. Furthermore, Article 8 of the act stipulated that, once it was established that the person did not live at his/her registered address and a final decision to erase his/her record from the register had been issued, the authorities were obliged to notify that person about his/her right to a legal remedy. However, the administration employees did not find it unusual that no legal remedies were envisaged when they erased people as "a consequence of the implementation of Article 81 of the Aliens Act" (a favourite expression of the administrative employees) – clearly, no one thought this to be necessary.

Thus, the Constitutional Court established in Ruling U-I-284/94 that the administrative bodies should not have erased people "ex officio, without any decision or notification addressed to the person concerned", because "there was no statutory basis whatsoever for them to do so". In fact, it concluded that the Population Register Act that was invoked by the Government in its explanations, "does not contain any provisions on the removal of permanent residences from the register on the basis of the Act itself".[514] Although this ruling did not formally establish that Article 120, Para 2 (the principle of administration in accordance with the constitution and laws) had been violated, the violation is apparent from the fact that administration had no legal basis for its acts.

In Ruling U-I-246/02, the Constitutional Court formally declared that the principle of legality had been violated. It stated that Article 1 of the Legal Status Act was incongruous with Article 120, Para 2 of the Constitution, because it did

514 Constitutional Court of the Republic of Slovenia, Ruling No. U-I-284/94, paragraph 14.

not define the criteria for establishing whether the condition of actually living in Slovenia was fulfilled. It stressed that

> the principle of legality not only determines the framework and basis for the operation of administrative bodies, but also ensures that their operation is transparent and foreseeable, which increases legal certainty. At the same time, this principle is important for the effective protection of the individual's rights and legal interests, including effective control of the constitutionality and legality of individual administrative acts.

2.1.3 The Principle of Equality and the Role of the ECHR

The principle of equality which, along with the principle of the rule of law and the welfare state, effectuates the constitutional principle of justice, posits the right to equality in law and before the law, i.e. when the laws are made and when they are applied.

In accordance with this principle, when drafting legislation the legislature should determine if two groups of people, however they may be classified, are so similar as to justify the same legal approach, or so different that different approaches are required. The legislature has a degree of discretion to enact different regulations for different groups if solid reasons for this exist. However, there are restrictions: the differing regulation must not have an adverse effect on a large number of people, it must be well founded, and must not encroach on other human rights.[515]

In the case of the erasure, the Constitutional Court found a violation of Article 14, Para 2 of the Constitution, which defines the principle of equality before the law. It compared the situation of the citizens of other SFRY republics with permanent residence in Slovenia who did not acquire Slovenian citizenship with that of foreigners from third countries who had acquired permanent residence permits in Slovenia during the Yugoslav era. To establish how similar the two groups were, it is necessary to compare their situation before and after Slovenia became independent. While the citizens of other SFRY republics were equal citizens before independence, foreigners from third countries had the status of aliens with permanent residence permits and were therefore not entitled to all the rights of a citizen. After Slovenia gained its independence, Article 82, Para 3 of the Aliens Act regulated the situation of foreigners from third countries. Their permanent residence permits remained valid, meaning that the continuity of their legal status was recognised. On the other hand, the citizens of other SFRY republics who, until the expiration of deadlines determined in Article 81, Para 2

515 Šturm, Komentar Ustave Republike Slovenije, 2010, pp. 175–176.

of the Aliens Act, had the same rights as citizens of the RS, were expected to re-apply for a legal status as if they were entering the country for the first time. This means that, unlike foreigners from third countries, the continuity of their legal status was not recognised.

The Constitutional Court established that the legislature took the permanent residence of one group into account, but not that of the other. This conclusion then led to the question of whether the legislature had violated the principle of equality in addition to the principle of the protection of legal certainty.[516] The Court's reasoning was as follows:

> The principle of equality as defined in paragraph 2 of Article 14 of the Constitution does not require equality before laws only for the citizens of the Republic of Slovenia, but applies to all persons whose legal position is regulated by law. Article 13 of the Constitution provides that foreigners in Slovenia shall, in accordance with international agreements, have all the rights guaranteed by the Constitution and laws, except for those which belong only to Slovenian citizens on the basis of the Constitution and the laws. To comply with the principle of equality, a statute must regulate identical actual states or identical legal positions equally. The legislator must have real and sound reasons for each instance of a difference in regulation. This means that the legislator must not act arbitrarily when regulating legal relations. Thus, there must be a sound reason for differentiation which derives from the nature of the matter.[517]

The Constitutional Court established that, by only regulating the legal status of persons who had lived in the country as foreigners before Slovenia was independent, but not that of the citizens of other SFRY republics who had also lived and had their permanent residence registered in Slovenia, the legislature placed the citizens of other SFRY republics in a worse legal situation than foreigners from third countries. This differentiation was not based on any

> real and justified reason [...] which could justify why the transitional legal position of citizens of other republics who had registered their permanent residence in the Republic of Slovenia and who legally resided in its territory should be essentially different from the legal position of those persons who had already gained the status of a foreigner with a permanent residence permit before Slovenia became independent.[518]

This position can additionally be supported by the following *a maiore ad minus* (*a fortiori*) argument:[519] if the persons who had held foreigner status before

---

516 Constitutional Court of the Republic of Slovenia, Ruling No.U-I-284/94, paragraph 14.

517 *Ibid.*, para. 17.

518 *Ibid.*, para. 18.

519 From greater to smaller. Pavčnik, Teorija prava, 1997, p. 384.

Slovenia became independent had the right to the continuity of their legal status, than the persons who were citizens before Slovenia became independent were all the more entitled to this right, especially if both groups met the two main requirements, i.e. having their permanent residence registered in Slovenia and actually living in Slovenia.[520]

Members of the lay public frequently claimed that the citizens of other republics were treated better rather than worse than aliens from third countries, since unlike the latter they could gain citizenship through extraordinary naturalisation. While it is true that they were entitled to apply for citizenship, it should be pointed out that the issue of unequal treatment was not connected in any way to the option of gaining citizenship. It only concerned the preservation of the permanent resident status of those SFRY citizens who did not gain Slovenian citizenship.

Thus, the Constitutional Court concluded that the legal vacuum or the failure to regulate the legal status of erased people constituted not only a violation of the principle of legal certainty, but also a violation of the principle of equality defined in Article 14, Para 2 of the Constitution.[521] The conclusion that the erasure was a discriminatory measure which violated Article 14 of the European Convention on the Protection of Human Rights and Fundamental Freedoms was confirmed in 2012 by the Grand Chamber of the ECHR, which fully agreed with the argument of the Constitutional Court of the RS.[522]

The Constitutional Court reiterated its position in 2004 in its judgment on a totalitarian proposal for a preliminary legislative referendum (Ruling U-II-1/04). According to its reasoning, the principle of equality was violated specifically by the proposed addition of an exclusion clause to the requirements for gaining Slovenian citizenship. The suggestion was that persons who did not follow the invitation of the Presidency of the RS to leave the Yugoslav People's Army within a prescribed time should not be entitled to gain citizenship. This proposal involves argument regarding supposed loyalty discussed above, which is frequently used to explain exclusionary politics.[523] The Constitutional Court held that it was in

520 *Cf.* Bugarič, "Preneseni", dejstva, interpelacija, in: Dnevnikov Objektiv, 2009.

521 Constitutional Court of the Republic of Slovenia, Ruling No. U-I-284/94, paragraph 18.

522 ECHR GC, *Kurić and Others v. Slovenia*, application No. 26828/06, judgment of 26. 6. 2012, paragraphs 383–396.

523 *Cf.* an argument of loyalty described in Part II on citizenship policies.

obvious contravention of the Constitution, primarily the principle of legal certainty and the principle of equality.[524]

The violation of the principle of equality continued with the adoption of the Legal Status Act in the wake of the first fundamental ruling of the Constitutional Court in 1999. Article 3 contained the exclusion clause mentioned above. As described in the section on the principle of legal certainty, the requirements in the Legal Status Act were stricter than the general requirements applicable to foreigners in the Aliens Act. The Constitutional Court noted that the proposed text of the act originally contained requirements identical to those in the Aliens Act, but the government subsequently adopted an amendment stipulating much stricter requirements. The Constitutional Court established that "no reasons which could justify [stricter requirements] can be found in the legislative material. This consequently means that the principle of equality defined in Article 14, Para 2 of the Constitution has been violated".[525]

The right to equality before the law defined in Article 14 of the Constitution can be found in another form in Article 22 of the Constitution, which stipulates that "everyone shall be guaranteed equal protection of rights in any proceeding before a court and before other state authorities". This means that the courts and other bodies are not allowed to treat people differently by reaching different decisions in comparable cases, while the parties to proceedings must be guaranteed equality. The proceedings must be fair, unbiased/unprejudiced and appropriate in terms of content.[526]

For the situation and rights of erased people, Article 22 of the Constitution was significant primarily because the unconstitutionality of the Aliens Act was established a full seven years after the erasure. Previously, all bodies and courts including the Supreme Court had upheld the legislation that enabled the erasure in their rulings. The moment the Constitutional Court issued the fundamental ruling that the erasure and the act of stripping people of their legal status were unconstitutional, a constitutional path opened up for erased individuals to claim the rights to which they would have been entitled had the legislation been appropriate and had they been able to retain permanent resident status. Those who had tried to claim their rights first through an administrative procedure and then through judicial protection could now appeal to the Constitutional Court and request, referring to Article 22, that the systemic judgment

524 Constitutional Court of the Republic of Slovenia, Ruling No. U-II-1/04, paragraph 30.
525 Constitutional Court of the Republic of Slovenia, Ruling No. U-I-295/99-13, paragraph 13.
526 Šturm (ed.), Komentar Ustave Republike Slovenije, 2010, pp. 238–239.

(i.e. that the revocation of status was unlawful and unconstitutional and that erased people were entitled to the rights arising from permanent residence) be applied to their individual cases. The Constitutional Court did so in Rulings Up-20/97, Up-60/97, Up-152/97, Up-336/98 and Up-333/96.

2.1.4 The Principle of Clarity

In explaining its interpretation of the Aliens Act, the government frequently asserted that the legal status of the erased people was terminated *ex lege*, i.e. by force of law, without state bodies being obliged to issue any decision.[527] For years after the erasure, the authorities termed this group "people whose registration of permanent residence expired because of the implementation of Article 81 of the Aliens Act". The question here is how this position was defended and whether Article 81 of the Aliens Act did indeed stipulate that permanent residence registrations expire. As a matter of fact, the only clear conclusion to be drawn from Article 81 was that "the provisions in the Aliens Act" would become applicable to these persons after the deadlines specified in the article expired.

The above formulation gives rise to another question: whether it is compatible with the principle of clarity as a sub-principle of the rule of law. One way to establish whether or not a legal norm is in harmony with the rule of law is to evaluate it using the principle of determinability.[528] For many years, the authorities insisted that the purpose of Article 81, Para 2 of the Aliens Act and what the legislature "had in mind" when formulating it was clear. It was allegedly clear that the provision on the applicability of the Aliens Act meant that the erased people had to re-apply for their status. However, the Aliens Act did not contain any such provision; it was the administrative bodies that adopted and applied such an interpretation. It is unclear if the article that enabled that interpretation was in harmony with the principle of determinability.

In the view of professor Kerševan, what the legislature had in mind or wanted to achieve by a specific provision is not essential to its implementation. His reasoning is that, as a rule, when interpreting the law the legislator as a collegial body cannot be asked for an explanation of what it had in mind or what the purpose of a specific provision was. Moreover, the collegial decision-making process implies that the law has a uniform goal and purpose. Kerševan thus concludes

527 *E.g.* The response of the Government of the Republic of Slovenia about admissibility of a complaint in the case *Makuc and Others v. Slovenia* (now *Kurić and Others v. Slovenia*), of October 26, 2007, p. 11.

528 Dyzenhaus, Recrafting the Rule of Law, 1999, p. 5.

that "in terms of content, the law expresses as much of the will of the legislator as unambiguously stated in its provisions", while everything else is left to the interpretation of the administrative bodies and the courts. Furthermore, says Kerševan, what is crucial for the rule of law is that a law, as an abstract legal act, should primarily determine the fundamental goals and the framework of the operation of the executive branch of the government.[529] This means that from the perspective of the principle of rule of law, it is pointless to attempt to establish what the legislature had in mind when it adopted Article 81, Para 2 of the Aliens Act in that specific form. However, the provision should have been sufficiently unambiguous so as to clearly delineate the framework within which the administrative bodies should operate. This condition was not fulfilled because the provision was too general, thus causing a legal vacuum without defining the responsibilities of the administration.

Kerševan further says that the law does not conceal "more meanings or content than written in its norms that would enable one to glean its 'real' meaning by way of logical deduction, or its 'correct' application in individual examples".[530] Regarding the legal situation of the citizens of other SFRY republics, the Aliens Act contained precisely the amount of meaning and content expressed in its provisions. It stipulated that, once the deadlines expired, these people would come under the jurisdiction of the Aliens Act. All further meanings were interpretations of the administrative bodies that went beyond acceptable limits, since the provision in the Aliens Act did not say that affected people would have to re-apply for their status, beginning with an application for a temporary residence permit.

We can thus conclude that Article 81, Para 2 of the Aliens Act did not respect the principle of clarity, while the authorities abused the general nature of the provision by arbitrarily interpreting the law in a manner that was convenient for them at the time. In this sense, the conduct of the authorities, and of the Ministry of the Interior in particular, was not only unconstitutional but also explicitly totalitarian.

2.1.5 *The Separation of Powers*

Governing in accordance with the principle of the separation of powers[531] as defined in Article 3, Para 2 of the Constitution means that the discrete branches

529 Kerševan, Vladavina prava in upravno pravo, in: Pravna država, 2009, p. 153.

530 *Ibid.*, p. 154.

531 In this chapter I deal with the separation of powers only insofar as it relates directly to the erasure. The principle of separation of powers and the position of the

of the government each perform their function as determined by the constitution. The basic branches of the government – the legislative, the executive, and the judicial branches – are supplemented by independent bodies such as an ombudsman, a court of audit, and a constitutional court, and by institutes such as a referendum.[532] None of them is superior to any other in the system as a whole.[533]

The rule proceeding from this principle is that those who set the rules must be separate from those who execute the rules.[534] In the case of the erased people, this principle was violated in many ways. The first mistake was that the law did not contain a sufficiently clear legal provision determining how the citizens of SFRY should be treated, so the executive bodies undertook the task of filling the intentionally created vacuum (through in-house instructions) in order to make it possible to implement the law. The Constitutional Court found that this violated the separation of powers. In Part III of the book I mentioned the government's Decision No. 26001/912/58 dated 3 September 1992. It stipulated that, when processing applications for permanent residence under the Aliens Act, the requirement of continuously living in Slovenia (which those erased people who obtained temporary residence permits could not meet) should be considered fulfilled if the erased person had his/her permanent residence registered in Slovenia and had actually lived at that address before the provisions in the Aliens Act became applicable to him/her.

The opinion of the Constitutional Court was that the government was not authorised to use an in-house instruction to define the manner of implementation of statutory provisions.[535] Neither was it empowered by statute to impose a regulation different from that provided by law. In accordance with Article 120 of the Constitution, the administrative bodies are bound by the Constitution and the laws, so the Government cannot change the content of legal and constitutional provisions by issuing an executive act. The Constitutional Court accordingly established that "when the Government found that in practice the [Aliens Act] could not be applied to the citizens of other SFRY republics, it should have

---

Constitutional Court is also examined in part 2.5. (The Role of the Constitutional Court and Constitutional Review).

532 For more details on the separation of powers see: Šturm (ed.), Komentar Ustave Republike Slovenije, 2010, p. 103–109.

533 Krivic, V sistemu deljene oblasti ni najvišjega organa (2011), unpublished paper for Dnevi javnega prava, 8 June 2011.

534 Krševan, Vladavina prava in upravno pravo, in: Pravna država, 2009, p. 146.

535 Constitutional Court of the Republic of Slovenia, Ruling No. U-I-284/94, paragraph 14.

proposed to the legislator to regulate their legal position, and should not have used a resolution to interfere with the legislative power".[536]

2.2 Referendums and the Erasure

2.2.1 Introduction

A referendum is an instrument that enables voters to make direct decisions concerning the Constitution, pending and extant legislation, or important social issues.[537] In Slovenia, the institute of referendum is regulated by the Constitution and the Referendum and Popular Initiative Act. From the perspective of constitutional law, the referendum is relevant not only because it is guaranteed by the Constitution but also because all decisions taken at a referendum can be disputed before the Constitutional Court,[538] similarly to decisions adopted by an indirect representative body (i.e. the National Assembly). A referendum question can be related to an amendment to the constitution or to a given piece of legislation. This chapter examines the case of a legislative referendum related to the erasure.

So far, five legislative referendums directly or indirectly connected to the erasure have been proposed. One was related to the proposal to revoke citizenships granted under Article 40 of the Citizenship Act, but the Constitutional Court decided that it was inconsistent with the constitution. Four referendum proposals concerned the erasure directly, one of which was successful; the Constitutional Court could not prevent it because the then President of the National Assembly, Borut Pahor, submitted the request too late.[539] Of the three referendums that were prevented, two were intended to back up legislative proposals that stipulated unconstitutional requirements for the regulation of erased people's status, and one to back up the draft law by which the Constitutional Court's Ruling No. U-I-246/02 would be implemented. Three of the proposed referendums were preliminary legislative referendums (intended to take place before a law would

---

536 *Ibid.*

537 Šturm (ed.), Komentar Ustave Republike Slovenije, 2010, p. 804. Also Kaučič, Ustavna zasnova referenduma, in: Pravnik, 49 (1994) 1–3, p. 17.

538 *Cf.* Constitutional Court of the Republic of Slovenia, Ruling No. U-II-3/03-15, paragraph. 21.

539 The referendum question related to the so-called technical law on the implementation of Item 8 of the Constitutional Court's Ruling No. U-I-246/02 obliging the Ministry of the Interior to issue supplementary decisions to the erased people who had already obtained permanent residence permits recognizing their permanent residence in the Republic of Slovenia from 26 February 1992 onwards.

be adopted), and two were subsequent legislative referendums (intended to take place after the law would be adopted).

Table 2: Referendums in Slovenia

Date	Content	Turnout	In favour	Against
8. 12. 1996	Voting system	37.90	/[540]	/
10. 1. 1999	Financing of TET 2	27.33	19.76	78.04
17. 6. 2001	Treatment of infertility	35.66	26.38	72.36
19. 1. 2003	Privatisation of the railways	31.10	47.17	50.84
19. 1. 2003	Telecommunications	31.10	76.72	22.15
23. 3. 2003	Accession to the EU	60.44	89.64	10.36
23. 3. 2003	Accession to NATO	60.43	66.08	33.92
21. 9. 2003	Opening times for shops	57.90	28.83	71.17
4. 4. 2004	Technical law on erased people	31.45	3.82	94.68
25. 9. 2005	Public radio-television I	30.71	50.30	48.92
11. 11. 2007	Insurance companies	57.98	28.88	71.12
22. 6. 2008	Provinces	10.98	63.09[541]	36.91
6. 6. 2010	Arbitration Agreement	42.66	51.54	48.46
12. 12. 2010	Public radio-television II	14.78	27.67	72.33
10. 4. 2011	Mini-jobs	33.99	19.93	80.07
5. 6. 2011	Illegal work	40.44	24.59	75.41
5. 6. 2011	Pension reform	40.46	27.95	72.05
5. 6. 2011	Archives	40.42	29.12	70.88
25. 3. 2012	Family Code	30.31	45.45	54.55
8. 6. 2014	Archives[542]	11.74	32.63	67.37
20. 12. 2015	Marriage and family relations act[543]	36.38	36.49	63.51

540 The answers offered were not "yes" and "no" as three referendum questions were posed.
541 The outcome of a referendum is an average of outcomes at individual locations. Source: National Electoral Commission.
542 This was the first referendum that took place under the new rules where a 20 per cent quorum for the "no" votes (i.e. 20 per cent of all eligible voters) would have to be achieved for the no vote to be valid. The quorum was not achieved therefore the law that was subject to referendum entered into force.
543 The quorum was achieved and the law did not enter into force.

Altogether, fourteen nationwide referendums have been held in Slovenia between 1991 and 2015, as shown in Table 2. The referendum on the erasure that was eventually held because the request to assess its constitutionality was submitted too late concerned the implementation of the "technical" law (for more, see below). It vindicated only a few of the advantages of the referendum as an instrument and confirmed many of its weaknesses.

The turnout at the referendum was 31% of registered voters, which is a below-average participation compared to the turnout at other referendums (the average turnout is 35.74 %). In other words, if only one-third of all registered voters take part in a referendum, the outcome does adequately reflect the predominant will of the people. Moreover, in this particular referendum 94.68% of the participants voted against the implementation of the law, which is a peculiar outcome, since so many votes "against" had not been recorded at any other referendum in Slovenia. The outcome of a referendum is a very complex issue to discuss and goes beyond the purposes of this book, so I will only present a few central dilemmas concerning referendums in Slovenia and in Europe, using the referendums related to the erasure as an example.

2.2.2 *The Advantages and Weaknesses of a Referendum*

A referendum as a form of direct implementation of power has an indisputable basis in the Constitution, but experience shows that referendums have both advantages and disadvantages. The advantages of the referendum include the legitimacy of adopted decisions; people can identify with decisions adopted at a referendum because they have a chance to co-decide; the decisions are accompanied by a public debate; decisions taken at a referendum better represent the will of the people; referendums prevent apathy and people's alienation from decisions adopted by a representative body; referendums presumably meet the needs of the public interest and prevent decisions that run counter to it, while at the same time maximising human potential thanks to the participation of such a large part of the population in the management of public issues.[544] However, the advantages listed above also suggest certain weaknesses. The most serious flaw of referendums is their adverse effect on the situation of minorities.[545]

---

544 Gallagher, Uleri, The referendum experience in Europe, 1996, p. 16.
545 *Ibid.*

Being numerically inferior, minorities are easily outvoted and accordingly do not have a good chance of succeeding. The majority, on the other hand, generally does not have a sufficient understanding of the minority's situation, so it simply exploits its numerical predominance to the detriment of the minority. It should also be noted that citizens often do not have robust knowledge about, much less an informed opinion on, the diverse issues on which they vote, or in other words, their opinions do not result from a careful weighing of relevant information. Another weakness of the referendum is that it may undermine representative democracy and the power of elected government representatives. Finally, rather than seeking consensus on a specific issue, a referendum enforces a specific decision.[546]

The referendum on erased people demonstrated many of the weaknesses of referendums, while failing to utilise their advantages. Erased people were a minority, and an unjustifiably stigmatised one at that. Needless to say, they did not have the slightest chance of succeeding in this or any other referendum. The Slovenian legal system did incorporate a safety mechanism at the time – an assessment of whether a referendum could have unconstitutional consequences (more on this below) – but the fact that the subject is the situation of a minority is not sufficient in itself to prevent such a referendum.

Another weakness that came to light in the referendum on the "technical" law[547] was the complexity of the subject. It was difficult to understand. More importantly, both possible outcomes of the referendum were unfavourable to erased people, meaning that the question was inappropriate, since it did not offer the option of any answer other than "yes" or "no". Following the referendum result the proposed law was not put into practice because it was rejected at the referendum, so it seemed that the obligations stated in the Constitutional Court's ruling were destined not to be fulfilled. However, even if the law had been confirmed, the situation of erased people would not have improved because the law that was supposed to implement it was more restrictive than the

546 *Ibid.*, p. 1.

547 The "technical law" was aimed at implementation of point 8 of the Constitutional Court Ruling No. U-I-246/02, in which the Constitutional Court ordered the Ministry of the Interior to issue to those erased persons, who already acquired permanent residence permits, retroactive supplementary decisions recognizing their permanent residence from the day of the erasure onwards. The contents of the "technical" law are described in detail under 3.2.1.

Constitutional Court ruling. The question is whether the voters truly understood the referendum question and the effects of their choice, or whether they perhaps voted against erased people without being aware that, by circling the "no" option, they were doing them a favour.

The experience of other countries shows that overly complex questions are not suitable for referendums. A 1983 study on the informedness of voters in Switzerland showed that only one out of six Swiss voters matched the ideal of a well-informed citizen who can give solid grounds for his/her choice, while a study conducted in 1993 showed that only half of the voters were well informed.[548] This, of course, means that the other half was not well informed on the issues on which they voted, or at least such was the situation in the early 1990s. The ability to make an informed decision in a referendum depends on the voters' education, the complexity of the referendum question, and their personal interest in the subject, while general interest in politics and trust in state institutions further increases voters' informedness.[549] If the voters' knowledge of a subject is poor, they may easily find themselves confused by opposing arguments showered on them by the competing sides during the run-up to the referendum, so they are more likely to opt for caution and choose to reject whatever is asked from them in the referendum (this phenomenon is known as *Neinsager*).[550]

The referendum on the "technical" law ran a similar course. The probability that the voters were poorly informed on the issue was quite high, since many legal issues that had serious implications for the referendum were not discussed in-depth in the campaign — indeed, many were too complicated even for the people who campaigned for the referendum. The campaign itself was saturated with populist arguments that obfuscated the controversial issues instead of illuminating them, diverting attention from their essence. Campaigners appealed to patriotic feelings, engaged in stigmatisation and generalisations, and fomented a feeling of "threat" posed by "aggressors". Indeed, the campaign was antagonistically reduced to the question "are you for or against erased people?" It is not surprising that the voters, or rather those voters who took part in the referendum, almost unanimously voted "against". Other countries experienced similar difficulties with referendums dealing with excessively complicated issues. Furthermore, such issues do not arouse interest in voters, resulting in low

548 Trechsel, Kriesi, Switzerland: The Referendum and Initiative as a Centrepiece of the Political System, in: The referendum experience in Europe, 1996, p. 197.

549 *Ibid.*, p. 198.

550 Gallagher, Uleri, The Referendum Experience in Europe, 1996, p. 235.

turnout.[551] Indeed, studies show that some voters shape their opinions on emotionally loaded subjects early on, so referendum campaigns do not have much influence on them.[552] This is somewhat contrary to the *Neinsager* phenomenon, but the history of referendums confirms both phenomena.

The fact that the issue regulated by the "technical" law had already been decided by the Constitutional Court was not insignificant. It meant that this was in effect a referendum on the Constitutional Court's ruling. The campaign by the referendum's proponents was indeed based, among other things, on the position that the ruling was wrong, meaning that the referendum actually encroached on the competence and the authority of the Constitutional Court. On the other hand, the supporters of erased people were asked to boycott the referendum, which may be another reason why such a high percentage voted "no". It is also possible that a certain number of "well-informed" participants voted against the law because it was truly unfavourable to the erased people, or because they wanted the Constitutional Court's ruling to be implemented directly, rather than indirectly by way of the "technical" law.

Given the low turnout, the referendum did not meet the legitimacy criterion: there are good reasons to conclude that it did not succeed in overcoming the general indifference of the population or make them identify with the problem and its solution, which are the goals that a referendum should pursue.

It proceeds from the above that the goal of this referendum, much like that of many others, was not of the kind that should be pursued in a referendum (e.g. to secure legitimacy for certain crucial national decisions). Referendums may fulfil certain other functions, one of which is to reinforce the position taken by its proposer.[553] While both possible outcomes of the referendum on the "technical" law were unfavourable to erased people, it was a good opportunity to mobilise the right-wing parties. Their participation in the referendum campaign (based on the unjustified stigmatisation and stereotyping of erased people and opposition to the resolution of the Constitutional Court) consolidated the right wing and contributed to its victory at the next parliamentary elections. In addition, the right-wing parties used the outcome of the referendum as proof that their ideas had wide support. The left-wing parties, on the other hand, paid for their failure

---

551 *Cf.* Morel France: Towards a Less Controversial Use of the Referendum, in: The Referendum Experience in Europe, 1996, p. 79.

552 Trechsel, Kriesi, Switzerland: The Referendum and Initiative as a Centrepiece of the Political System, in: The referendum experience in Europe, 1996, p. 198.

553 Prim. Gallagher, Ireland: The Referendum as a Conservative Device, in: The Referendum Experience in Europe, 1996, p. 94.

to prevent the referendum (for missing the deadline to file a petition with the Constitutional Court) with defeat at the parliamentary elections.

According to some authors, choices taken at referendums are partly influenced by the positions adopted by political parties. Accordingly, supporters of a specific party generally make choices that are in line with the party's position. However, this thesis is not fully applicable to all situations. In addition to political parties, other interest groups also take part in campaigns, and parties are often internally divided over the subject of a referendum. A party's position has also lost some of its significance because today people no longer identify with political parties as strongly as they did in the past.[554]

This factor also played a part in the referendum on the "technical" law. While left-wing parties publicly advocated for the need to resolve the issue of the erasure, their behaviour was discordant and unconvincing. They thus passively enabled the triumph of the right-wing. This led to the complete politicisation of the topic and the stigmatisation of erased people. The position of the centre-left parties did not have much significance, because they failed to mobilise their voters to take part in the referendum. The centre-left parties' passivity and unconvincing campaign in fact signalled that their support for erased people was not in earnest, which was also corroborated by their passivity in solving the problem later on. A strong political will to resolve this issue was first expressed only in 2008, and even that resolution came from a handful of representatives of the left-centre government, to be more precise, from the Minister of the Interior, Katarina Kresal. The referendum on the "technical" law in 2004 therefore showed that political parties on the left and right and their voters could be unified around such questions, and also how easily racism and political radicalism can blend.

The outcomes of referendums are, as a rule, generally favourable to the opposition.[555] The referendum on the technical law confirmed this (as did most of the other referendums proposed by the opposition). Moreover, the proposer of a referendum has generally succeeded in Slovenia. Proposers have an edge over others since they are more engaged in the campaign; and given that the institute of the referendum is an expedient instrument, it is not surprising that opposition parties often make use of it, as they did in Slovenia in connection with the erasure. A referendum was on the table whenever the coalition took a step towards resolving the issue, and it was proposed on both occasions when the centre-left

---

554 *Ibid.*

555 Summarized after Gallagher, Ireland: The Referendum as a Conservative Device, in: The Referendum Experience in Europe, 1996, p. 101.

coalition attempted to adopt a law to regulate it. The right-centre coalition did not do anything similar during its term in office (2004–2008), since the law it proposed was unsuitable and it did not garner the requisite two-thirds majority.

Research also shows that conservative forces have often implemented their will through referendums more effectively than would have been possible through the means of representative democracy.[556] This conclusion is also partly true of Slovenia, where certain liberal ideas were rejected at referendums, for example, access to IVF for single women, reshaping the status of public television, the family code, same-sex marriage, etc. Conservative forces use their mobilisation skills to spread populism and thus prevent certain far-reaching reforms that they find too progressive.[557] The restitution of erased people's status was one such idea that seemed too progressive. On the other hand, some argue that people are more progressive than the representative legislative bodies, which are generally composed of middle-aged men with an above-average income, so referendums could also have a progressive effect and could pave the way for reforms regardless of the wishes of circumspect legislators. There is empirical data to confirm both theories,[558] but the referendum on the "technical" law confirmed the former. In this case, the people demonstrated greater conservatism than their political representatives.

Given all these factors and the partial predictability of the outcome, a referendum is an ideal tool in the hands of the authorities or individual interest groups to legitimise specific policies.[559] The same holds true in this specific case. The referendum on the "technical" law was used by the then-opposition parties to legitimise their views on the issue of the erasure (regardless of the low turnout) and they used its outcome for many years as proof of what "real public opinion" on this issue was.

2.2.3 The Limitations of the Referendum

Slovenian legislation placed no restrictions on legislative referendums until 2014. Until then, Article 90, Para 1 of the Constitution stipulated that a legislative referendum can deal with any issue that is regulated by law. A preliminary legislative

556 *Ibid.*

557 Trechsel, Kriesi, Switzerland: The Referendum and Initiative as a Centrepiece of the Political System, in: The Referendum Experience in Europe, 1996, p. 203. *Cf.* Gallagher, Uleri, The Referendum Experience in Europe, 1996, p. 235.

558 Gallagher, Uleri, The Referendum Experience in Europe, 1996, p. 235.

559 *Ibid.*, p. 240.

referendum that met all of the conditions could have only been prevented by the Constitutional Court if an eligible party had requested constitutional review in accordance with Article 21 of the Constitutional Court Act. The only existing restriction on referendums at the time was that imposed on subsequent legislative referendums. Article 21, Para 1 of the Referendum and the People's Initiative Act stipulated that the National Assembly may request a decision from the Constitutional Court within seven days of the submission of a request for a referendum, if it deems that the referendum result could have unconstitutional implications. This provision conferred on the Constitutional Court the power to assess whether the non-entry into force of the law in question would "truly affect very important constitutional rights [so] that this would warrant – on weighing the affected constitutional goods – an intervention into the constitutional right to a referendum".[560]

When assessing whether a referendum could have unconstitutional consequences and weighing whether it was justified to interfere with the "right" to a referendum, the Constitutional Court first had to establish which constitutional values or rights would be affected if the right to a referendum was respected, and then decide which rights should be given priority. In so doing, the Constitutional Court did not judge the suitability of a specific legal provision, since it was not authorised to do so either within the framework of judging the constitutionality of laws or within the framework of responsibilities stipulated by Article 21, Para 1 of the Referendum and People's Initiative Act.[561]

In line with these rules, the Constitutional Court judged that two referendum questions related to the erasure were inconsistent with the Constitution,[562] as well as one referendum question related to the revocation of citizenship granted under Article 40 of the Citizenship of the Republic of Slovenia Act. In the first case, when it assessed the request for a subsequent legislative referendum on the "technical" law, the National Assembly filed the request with the Constitutional Court one day late (the prescribed deadline was seven days and the request was submitted on the eighth day). The Constitutional Court established that the prescribed seven-day period was mandatory and that it did not have the authority to ignore the fact that the deadline had been missed, so the referendum was

560 Constitutional Court of the Republic of Slovenia, Ruling No. U-II-1/10-19, paragraph 18, and Ruling No. U-I-47/94.

561 Constitutional Court of the Republic of Slovenia, Ruling No. U-II-1/10-19, paragraph 19.

562 Constitutional Court of the Republic of Slovenia, Ruling No. U-II-1/04 and U-II-3/04.

held. It adopted the stance that the only reason for accepting a late request by the National Assembly would be serious unconstitutional consequences caused by the referendum.[563]

The Constitutional Court established that the proposed law implemented, in a somewhat narrower scope, Item 1 of the Constitutional Court's Ruling U-I-246/02 as specified in Item 8 of the same ruling. In addition, it established that the deadline for the implementation of the ruling had already expired. Thus, a rejection of the law at the referendum would only prolong the unconstitutional situation that began when the deadline expired.[564] Therefore, the Constitutional Court held that if the "technical" law was rejected in a referendum, the Constitutional Court's ruling would still be binding. A potential rejection of the law did not have any implications for Item 8 of the Ruling, and the duty of the National Assembly and the Ministry of the Interior to implement it would not expire as a result.[565] Accordingly, it established that a potential rejection of the "technical" law at a referendum would not cause a violation of human rights, rejected the late petition, and the referendum was called.

Six years later, in 2010, a request for another subsequent referendum was rejected. The referendum aimed to overturn the unacceptably overdue Act Amending the Act Regulating the Legal Status of Citizens of Former Yugoslavia Living in the Republic of Slovenia (amendments to the Legal Status Act), which was passed with the purpose of implementing the Constitutional Court Ruling. The National Assembly filed a petition with the Constitutional Court – this time, within the prescribed period – to decide if the referendum could have unconstitutional consequences. The Constitutional Court assessed whether the issues regulated by this law were directly related to an already established unconstitutionality that was to be eliminated by the amendments to the Legal Status Act, and weighed the "right" to a referendum against the constitutional rights that the referendum could violate. It first pointed out that, as long as the unconstitutional situation established in the ruling of the Constitutional Court was not eliminated, the legislation continued to be in contravention of the Constitution. It went on to establish that the non-implementation of the ruling of the Constitutional Court was in itself

---

563 Constitutional Court of the Republic of Slovenia, Ruling No. U-II-3/03-15, paragraph 15.

564 *Ibid.*, paragraph 19.

565 *Ibid.*, paragraph 23.

> a new violation of the Constitution, namely Article 2 and the second paragraph of Article 3 thereof. The weight of all these violations is all the more important, as seven years have passed since the second decision (No. U-I-246/02) [...] any prolongation of the unconstitutional situation already entails unconstitutional consequences in terms of the first paragraph of Article 21 of the [Referendum and the People's Initiative Act] (particularly emphasized in Decision No. U-II-3/04), which means that the review which was requested of the Constitutional Court this time had actually already been carried out. With the further passage of time, considering that the legislature has not responded for an additional six years despite the clear warnings of the Constitutional Court, this unconstitutional situation has only deepened. It has become intolerable.[566]

Upon establishing that the proposed law would eliminate the unconstitutional situation and that it could not be eliminated in any other way, it concluded that the referendum would have unconstitutional consequences and that the right to a referendum should in this case be subordinated to the principle of the rule of law (Article 2 of the Constitution), the right to equality before the law (Article 14, Para 2 of the Constitution), the right to personal dignity and security (Article 24 of the Constitution), the right to the elimination of human rights violations (Article 15, Para 4 of the Constitution), and the authority of the Constitutional Court (Article 2 and Article 3, Para 2 of the Constitution). It pointed out that it was obvious from the response of the persons who had proposed the referendum to the National Assembly's petition that they were not proposing it because they found the amendments to the Legal Status Act unsuitable, but because they opposed the content of the Constitutional Court ruling itself. The referendum would thus have decided on the "rulings and the authority of the Constitutional Court", which was unacceptable.[567] This was the third time that the Constitutional Court indirectly pointed out the danger of abusing legislative referendums – first in Ruling U-I-3/03, when it warned against the danger of referendums proposed with the purpose of postponing the implementation of the Constitutional Court's ruling, then in Ruling U-II-3/04, when it warned against the abuse of preliminary legislative referendums if such referendums were called during the legislative procedure and if their purpose was to enact a regulation that was different than that prescribed by draft law, and finally in Ruling U-II-1/10-19 described above.

This should be understood as a serious warning and as an appeal for caution, to prevent the referendum from becoming a means of settling political accounts

566 Constitutional Court of the Republic of Slovenia, Ruling No. U-II-1/10-19, paragraph 37.

567 *Ibid.*, paragraph 45.

or a means of circumventing the rulings of the Constitutional Court. The proposed referendums threatened to turn the institution into the opposite of what it was meant to be and (since there is no quorum prescribed for the outcome of a referendum to be valid) make a small part of the population a tool in the hands of the political elite to achieve its particular political interests. In this sense, a referendum could acquire elements of totalitarianism through the attempts to undermine the authority of the Constitutional Court.

The issue of restrictions on referendums is not insignificant, given that recently they have often been the subject of Constitutional Court rulings.[568] The concurring opinion of Judge Jadranka Sovdat to Ruling U-II-1/1019 reveals additional information on the principles observed by the Constitutional Court when applying Article 21 of the Referendum and People's Initiative Act and weighing the right to a referendum against the rights with which it interferes. According to Judge Sovdat, the test used when weighing these rights consists of three questions:

> "1) Which constitutional values are identified that stand against the right to vote in a referendum, 2) What weight are they attributed, and 3) What are the reasons why some are attributed greater weight than others?"[569]

Sovdat also points out that the right to a referendum cannot be given priority simply because all registered voters can take part in the decision, while the rights against which it is weighed are those of a narrower group of people (If the opposite was the case, says Sovdat, the Constitutional Court would not need to consider the case at all). Concern that a referendum could threaten the rights or legal status of minorities supports her position.

Since 2014 the Slovenian Constitution prohibits referendums on laws that address unconstitutionality in the field of human rights. A constitutional amendment passed for this purpose is a partial response to the concern that referendums on the rights of minorities should not be allowed.[570] This is particularly important since, owing to the lack of historical experience and a tradition of referendums during the era preceding the country's independence,[571] proposed referendums often related to subjects that were not suitable for this

568 *E.g.* Rulings U-II-1/06, U-II-1/09 dated 5 May 2009, U-II-2/09 dated 9 November 2009 and U-II-3/11 8 dated December 2011.

569 Dissenting opinion of Judge Jadranka Sovdat to Constitutional Court Ruling No. U-II-1/10-19.

570 *See also* Hot, Reševanje vprašanja izbrisanih, 2004, pp. 34–37.

571 *See* Kaučič, Ustavna zasnova referenduma, in: Pravnik, 49 (1994) 13, p. 17.

kind of decision-making (the latest examples are two referendums on the rights of same-sex couples).

Contrary to the Slovenian experience, the literature on referendums in Europe shows that not many referendums in European countries were related to the rights of minorities. In fact, the most similar referendums concerned women's right to vote in Switzerland, the prohibition of abortion in Ireland, the prohibition on constructing minarets and the mandatory expulsion of migrants who committed criminal offences in Switzerland and, more recently, same-sex marriage-related referendums in several European states. Referendums are not a tool intended for regulation of the rights and the status of minorities; they serve to determine the will of the people when it comes to basic questions of statehood (the constitutional order, membership in certain international organisations, or unions such as the EU, etc.).[572] Theoretically, anything can be the subject of a referendum, but some limits are necessary, in line with constitutional democracy.

Gallagher proposes two conditions that can be of help in delimiting what constitutes an appropriate subject for a referendum. The first is that a referendum should only pose questions that can be answered with a simple yes or no, not questions that require negotiations, compromises or a search for complex solutions. The second is that the issue should have implications for the entire population of a country, regardless of political affiliation.[573] The erasure obviously does not meet either of these requirements. It is a complex issue that requires complex solutions. At the same time, it affected a relatively small group of people who, when opposed by the majority, will easily be outvoted in every such referendum.

2.2.4 The Significance of a Referendum for Constitutional Democracy

Although a referendum is a useful instrument for determining the extent of support for key political decisions, constitutional democracy requires that certain constitutional limits are imposed on it if other interests or rights are to be protected. It is not insignificant that the greatest interest in referendums is expressed by people with the lowest level of education who show the least interest in political issues and have the lowest trust in politicians.[574] This is one of the reasons why referendum decisions are subject to the same constitutional restrictions that are in place for legislatures.

572 These are two most common subjects of referendum decision-making in Europe. Gallagher and Uleri, 1996, p. 231.

573 *Ibid.*, p. 245.

574 *Ibid.*, p. 249.

The Constitutional Court drew attention to this in connection with the first request for a subsequent legislative referendum on the erasure, despite rejecting the request to assess its potential unconstitutional consequences because it was submitted late. The Court pointed out that its rulings and the Constitution are binding not only on the legislature, but also on citizens when they exercise power directly by deciding about a specific law at a referendum. In the opinion of the Constitutional Court, the subject of a referendum thus cannot be a law that implements a ruling of the Constitutional Court, or a regulation that is inconsistent with the Constitution, or a regulation which, if rejected, could lead to an unconstitutional situation. A referendum is similarly unacceptable if its purpose is to postpone or prolong the implementation of a Constitutional Court ruling; the failure to implement such a ruling indisputably leads to an unconstitutional situation, which can only be prolonged by the potential rejection of the law at a referendum.[575]

The necessity of constitutional restrictions on the referendum was stressed by Judge Jan Zobec in his concurring opinion to Ruling U-II-1/1019. In his words, the survival of democracy critically depends on the "immunity sub-system", and an important part of this sub-system is "a release valve consisting of the constitutional prohibition on a referendum – and even more so when a referendum petition aims at disregarding a decision of the Constitutional Court". In Zobec's words, "the idea that the people [...] decide on the 'validity' of a decision of the Constitutional Court is fundamentally constitutionally wrong", especially "if it is accompanied by the overt intention of the proposers of the referendum to manipulate the legislature's obligation arising from a decision of the Constitutional Court". Needless to say, I absolutely agree with his view.

The Constitutional Court defined the essence of constitutional democracy and its relation to decisions taken by the majority in its Ruling U-I-111/04 dated 8 July 2004. It stated that the values protected by the Constitution, human rights, and freedoms in particular, can prevail over the democratically adopted decisions of the majority. In the concurring opinion to Ruling U-II-1/10-19, Judge Zobec said that if a referendum is to decide on a right on which the Constitutional Court has already stated its position, and if the proposed law eliminates an established unconstitutionality in accordance with the Constitution, then such right not only prevail over the "human right" to a referendum but completely annul it. The right to a referendum simply does not extend that far. Judge Zobec

575 Constitutional Court of the Republic of Slovenia, Ruling No. U-II-1/10-19, paragraphs 21 and 22.

even thinks that to allow a referendum in such a case could in the long run threaten the existence of the Constitutional Court.[576]

His view is completely correct; all provisions in the Constitution, and particularly those that define the principle of the separation of powers and the protection of human rights and fundamental freedoms, would be reduced to mere program norms, or the principles of desired behaviour (as in totalitarian systems, see Part IV of the book). They would collapse the moment the majority voted against them "democratically" at a referendum. That, in turn, would annul the authority of the Constitution and constitutional democracy with it. The adjective "constitutional" in the collocation "constitutional democracy" therefore implies that there are restrictions on any democratic exercise of power, regardless of whether it is executed directly through a referendum or indirectly in the form of acts by the representative body. This means that democracy as an expression of the majority's will is limited, while unlimited democracy would be totalitarian. It means that "the judgment on whether the decisions taken by the majority are correct are subordinate to the fundamental reservation, that is, whether such decisions are in line with the Constitution".[577]

2.3 The Right to Compensation and the Role of the ECHR

The right to compensation for the damages caused by the state bodies that erased a number of individuals from the register of permanent residents is a constitutional issue as well as an issue of civil law. I discuss this right as it was recognised to the erased people only by the European Court of Human Rights two decades after the erasure. Before that this right was denied to them even though it is defined with the Slovenian Constitution. Article 26, Para 1 of the Constitution reads:

> Everyone has the right to compensation for damages caused by unlawful actions in connection with the performance of any function or other activity by a person or authority performing such a function or activity within a state or local community authority or as a bearer of public authority.

This provision proceeds from the obligation of the state to ensure legal security in principle and in practice. It is in fact a concretisation of the principles of the rule of law that the authorities are obliged to respect in accordance with the

576 Dissenting opinion of judge Jan Zobec to the Constitutional Court Ruling No. U-II-1/10-19.

577 Teršek, Legitimnost kot prvina političnih in pravnih konceptov sodobne ustavne demokracije, 2008, p. 340.

Constitution, laws or lawful regulations. If their conduct is in contravention of this, they must compensate the damages caused by their conduct, as I will show below.

The right to compensation for damages is connected to the constitutional guarantee of the judicial protection of human rights and fundamental freedoms and to the right to the elimination of the consequences of their violation defined in Article 15, Para 4 of the Constitution. The right to compensation for damages is secondary to the government's obligation to ensure the constitutionality and lawfulness of its operations, but if the authorities fail to fulfil this duty, the right to compensation is exercised "as the *ultima ratio* of the rule of law".[578]

To exercise the right to compensation for damages and to establish who caused the damages, three conditions need to be met: (1) that the damages occurred in the course of the performance of duty or the conduct of a bearer of public authority; (2) that they were incurred due to unlawful conduct, and (3) that it was an act committed by a person or a body who performs this duty.[579]

In the case of the erasure, two of these conditions were definitely fulfilled. The damages were incurred in connection with the conduct of a state body. The essential question concerns the second condition – whether the act was unlawful. Here, two things are crucial: the failure of the legislature to regulate the status of erased people, and the conduct of the administrative bodies that erased the people from the register of permanent residents. There is no doubt whatsoever that the act of erasing persons from the register of permanent residents was unlawful, given that it had no legal basis.[580] It was unlawful at the time, even though the Constitutional Court only established this seven years later in Ruling No. U-I-284/94.

The legislature's failure to regulate the legal status of erased people was the subject of various court proceedings.[581] According to Supreme Court case law, Article 26 of the Constitution establishes that the state is liable for failing to pass a certain law only when this duty clearly derives from an EU directive, the

578 Šturm, Komentar Ustave Republike Slovenije, 2010, p. 295.

579 Ibid., pp. 295–297.

580 *Cf.* Kerševan, Upravnopravni vidik odškodninske odgovornosti države v primeru "izbrisanih", in: Pravna praksa 28 (2009) 19. See also Krivic, Slabo prikrito in po vsebini zgrešeno izpodkopavanje odločbe Ustavnega sodišča, in: Pravna praksa 28 (2009) 20, pp. II–III; Kovač, Kogovšek, Formalizem ali smrt, in: Pravna praksa 28 (2009) 20, pp. VI–VIII; Vuksanović, Protipravnost kot eden od elementov odškodninske odgovornosti do izbrisanih, in: Pravna praksa 28 (2009) 20, pp. IV–VI.

581 *E.g.* ruling II Ips 342/2004 of the Supreme Court of the Republic of Slovenia.

Slovenian Constitution, a law or a Constitutional Court decision. Even in these cases, the cause of the damage must be clearly due to the failure of the state to pass such a law.[582]

Therefore, in the view of the Supreme Court, there was no unlawfulness arising from the legislature's failure to pass such a law at the time when Slovenia became a sovereign country, since allegedly not a single regulation listed in the judicial practice of the Supreme Court imposed this obligation. In connection with the erasure, the unlawful situation supposedly first arose in connection with the Constitutional Court's Ruling U-I-246/02, after the six-month period stipulated by the Constitutional Court to implement its decision expired. Accordingly, damage claims by erased persons should supposedly have a causal connection with this failure to pass a law, meaning that it would not be possible to claim compensation for damages caused by the erasure in the 1990s.

It strains reason to think that the Supreme Court only deals with normative unlawfulness, but not with the unlawfulness of the act that deprived people of their legal status, which is essential to establish liability for damages. Moreover, it is not possible to support this position of the Supreme Court. In this case, the normative obligation to regulate the legal status of the citizens of other SFRY republics undoubtedly existed. It is true that this obligation did not proceed explicitly from the Constitution, but it did proceed from it indirectly by way of the principle of equality before the law and the principle of the protection of legal certainty. Therefore, the failure to pass a normative act, which led to a violation of the Constitution, should be considered to meet the condition of unlawful conduct for the purposes of liability for damages.

Until recently, the condition of unlawful conduct and the manner in which it has been interpreted in judicial practice posed a serious obstacle for erased people in their attempt to exercise their right to compensation. This was due to the position taken by Slovenian courts and the Supreme Court in particular. Erased people suffered the greatest part of their total damages during the 1990s. Over time, the options to reacquire legal status generally increased, and the damages ceased to increase accordingly. Other major obstacles to claiming compensation by way of regular, judicial proceedings were the dismissal/absence of primary legal protection and statutory limitations on claims for damages.

The failure to seek primary legal protection means that the right to compensation for damages is not recognised if the affected person did not exercise his/her right to appeal. The right to appeal or to any other legal remedy defined in

582 Higher Court Celje, Judgment No. Cp 386/2009.

Article 25 of the Constitution therefore implies the obligation of the affected person to use the remedies available.[583] In specific terms, since at least one person in Up-60/97 successfully used legal remedies against the erasure and the loss of his/her legal status,[584] legal remedies in accordance with Article 25 of the Constitution were allegedly available to everyone, so all erased people could allegedly have used them. In my opinion, this position is unacceptable, given that the government and the Ministry of the Interior insisted for years that their conduct was lawful and shifted the burden of reacquiring legal status to the thousands of erased people who were struggling for their bare existence. Moreover, the position is explicitly disproportional from the perspective of the equality of statuses: erased people were deprived individuals who found themselves confronting the state, which used every available means of repression to achieve its aims.

The second serious obstacle to obtaining compensation for damages before the Slovenian courts was the time limitation on the validity of damage claims. Damage claims for the erasure expired after a general three-year period commencing on the day that the person learned about the damage or about the person/body that caused the damage, or five years after the damage occurred (Article 352, Paras 1 and 2 of the Code of Obligations; Article 376 of the Obligation Relationships Act). The case law on damage claims by erased people reveals a unified position: the date on which the period for damage claims began was held to be the publication date of the Constitutional Court's Ruling No. U-I-284/94, i.e. 12 March 1999. In the view of the courts, all of the erased people learned that the state's conduct was unlawful on that date. The courts set this date based on the judgment of whether erased people behaved with due care (in accordance with Article 18, Para 1 of the Obligations Relationships Act,[585]) i.e. with regard to when a person could and should learn that the state's conduct was unlawful and not with regard to when the unlawful act actually happened.[586]

---

583 Šturm (ed.), Komentar Ustave Republike Slovenije, 2010, p. 300.

584 The person lodged an action to start the administrative dispute, then appealed to the Supreme Court, and finally started a constitutional dispute in which he proved that his record was erased unlawfully. This led the Constitutional Court to order the Ministry of the Interior to re-enter the person's data into the register.

585 Zakon o obligacijskih razmerjih, Official Gazette of the Republic of Slovenia, No. 29/1978 as amended.

586 Higher Court Maribor, Judgment No. I Cp 2556/2007, Higher Court Ljubljana, Judgment No. II Cp 1291/2008, Higher Court Ljubljana, Judgment No. II Cp 725/2008, Higher Court Ljubljana, Judgment No. II Cp 1589/2009, Higher Court Ljubljana, Judgment No. II Cp 4277/2009, Higher Court Ljubljana, Judgment No. II Cp 3978/2009,

Judging by the available information, only in one case did the courts use a different approach to define when the period began; on the publication date of the Constitutional Court's Ruling U-I-246/02, i.e. 16 April 2003.[587]

The courts therefore considered that all the erased people, without exception, were obliged to behave with due care regarding their legal status by making inquiries or reading the official gazette, and waiting for the decision of the Constitutional Court. In my opinion, this position of the courts is inappropriate and completely out of touch with reality. It demonstrates a complete lack of awareness of the situation of erased people, many of whom were uneducated, homeless, and in despair. It was disproportional to expect the erased people to read the official gazette and act before the period of limitations expired, when they were deprived of all their rights and were struggling for their bare existence. That prevailed over thoughts of compensation. It is also unrealistic to expect that during the 1990s, when the damage was most intense, erased people should have turned to someone for advice on the possibility of claiming damages. At that time, and until the first ruling of the Constitutional Court in 1999, there was a consensus within the legal field that the conduct of the authorities was lawful and constitutional. Knowing the situation of the erased people, we can conclude that the expectations of the courts were not only unrealistic and disproportional but also in contravention of the principle of the protection of legal certainty. According to this principle, the erased people had the right to expect that the state, which had collectively deprived them of their rights, would at least send out personal notifications to the effect that they were again entitled to their rights. The period of limitations should not have commenced until that happened.

In some cases, erased people received an individual notification of the violations committed against them after they had already acquired a permanent resident permit (for more on this see the next chapter) via a special decision. The issuing of these decisions raised the question whether they had implications for statutory limitations. The position of the Constitutional Court was that individual decisions recognising the erasure and retrospectively reinstating the status of erased people from the erasure onwards do not constitute a new damage liability for the state or a new legal basis for claiming damages.[588]

Higher Court Celje, Judgment No. Cp 386/2009, Higher Court Ljubljana, Judgment No. II Cp 4262/2009, Higher Court Ljubljana, Judgment No. I Cp 1128/2010 and Supreme Court of the Republic of Slovenia, Judgment No. II Ips 315/2010.

587 Higher Court Maribor, Judgment No. I Cp 428/2008.

588 Constitutional Court of the Republic of Slovenia, Ruling No. U-II-1/10-19, paragraph 43.

As none of the erased people succeeded with their claims for damages lodged against the Republic of Slovenia before the national courts, their right to compensation defined in Article 26 of the Constitution has not been respected. The European Court of Human Rights overturned this legal situation. In the *Kurić* case the Grand Chamber of the court awarded compensation to six out of ten applicants. Since it found that the applicants were unable to claim compensation before the national courts due to structural problems in the Slovenian legal system, it ordered the Slovenian state to set up a compensation scheme for the erased persons. The European Court awarded compensation to six of the ten applicants who have already received their permanent residence permits, which were issued only after the first instance ECHR decision. Two other applicants who were issued permanent residence permits before the first instance chamber delivered the judgment were left with a bitter feeling. The chamber no longer recognised them as victims and consequently dismissed their application as inadmissible. The Grand Chamber disagreed with this position but its powers did not permit the chamber's decision of inadmissibility to be changed.

The inadmissibility part of the chamber judgment encouraged the Slovenian authorities to issue permanent residence permits to all those applicants taking part in the application who applied for a permanent residence permit, in order to deprive them of their victim status too, as indicated by the chamber judgment. The Grand Chamber judgment therefore represented a revolutionary turning point: it ruled that issuing permanent residence permits by no means sufficed to remedy convention rights violations and that the applicants also had to receive compensation for damages.

3. Conclusions

The rulings of the Constitutional Court contributed crucially to the development not only of the legal doctrine in relation to the issues discussed in this chapter but also to resolving the problem of the erasure itself. With its principled decisions, it countered the popular and political attitudes towards the erasure. By playing a counter-majoritarian role, it also strengthened itself as an institution. At an international conference organised on the 20th anniversary of the establishment of the Slovenian Constitutional Court, Judge Boštjan M. Zupančič claimed that the Court had "saved the honour of Slovenia"[589] with its decisions

589 Zupančič, "Dvajset let Ustave Republike Slovenije: Pomen ustavnosti in ustavna demokracija", unpublished paper presented at the international scientific conference, 21 December 2011.

on erased people, while Judge Ciril Ribičič included the 2003 Ruling on erased people among his list of "magnificent" decisions precisely because of its counter-majoritarian character.[590] The Court also played an important part from the perspective of the separation of powers. Namely, the separation of powers did not work in the case of the erasure, as all three branches of power acted in a synchronised way. If it was not for the Constitutional Court's ruling, the erasure would probably never have been recognised as unlawful. The significance of its ruling was further corroborated by the European Court of Human Rights, which cited them extensively in its reasoning in the *Kurić* case.

The Constitutional Court therefore without a doubt had an extremely important role in resolving the erasure. However, it should not be forgotten that its rulings also have certain deficiencies, such as insisting on the condition of actually living in Slovenia to obtain a permanent residence permit and inconsistent positions on the meaning of supplementary decisions that will be discussed in Part V. Also, certain events from the Constitutional Court's operations with regard to the complaints concerning the erasure remind us that things could easily have been different. Namely, the first petition for constitutional review of the Aliens Act challenging the erasure was lodged with the Constitutional Court in 1994, while the ruling on the matter was issued only in 1999. The procedure therefore lasted for five years, which is significantly long for that time. In the 1990s, the Constitutional Court was not as overburdened as it is now. The judges who sat in court previously and were assigned the cases as rapporteurs (Matevž Krivic, Tone Jerovšek, and Lovro Šturm) entered a serious dispute about how the petitions lodged by the erased persons should be dealt with. This led to the petitions being set aside in order to "study the matter". In 1997 one of the petitions was rejected for formal reasons while in 1998 the other two were joined and assigned to judge Krivic (who later assisted hundreds of erased persons to regulate their legal status). One week later, on 24 June 1998,[591] the court declared the case admissible, while the decision on the merits was adopted by the new composition of the Court. Namely, in 1998 seven new judges out of nine in total were appointed to office.

590 Ribičič, Človekove pravice in ustavna demokracija, 2010, p. 56–58.

591 Decision of the Constitutional Court of 24. 6. 1998, No. U-I-284/94.

Part V: The Implementation of the Decisions of the Constitutional Court

Finally his eyes grow dim, and he no longer knows whether it's really getting darker or just his eyes that are deceiving him. But he seems now to see an inextinguishable light begin to shine from the darkness behind the door.

Franz Kafka, The Trial

1. Introduction

Building on my analysis of the content of the Constitutional Court's decisions in the previous section, here I will concentrate on their implementation. The first systemic decision of the Constitutional Court (No. U-I-284/94) was implemented in full, but the second decision (No. U-I-246/02) remained unimplemented for seven years. The implementation of the court's decisions, or rather, the absence of a mechanism to ensure their implementation therefore deserves special attention. In this part, I discuss the content of the regulations, both proposed and passed, which guide the implementation of constitutional decisions pertaining to the erasure. I also discuss the reasons why these decisions were not implemented.

2. An Overview of the Implementation of the Decisions

In "The Hollow Hope", Rosenberg notes that the courts can bring up questions that other institutions would prefer to ignore.[592] With regard to the erasure and Slovenia, this statement only applies to the Constitutional Court. In 1999, the Constitutional Court ordered the legislature to put an end to the unconstitutional situation by passing a new law that conforms to the constitution. The legislature responded quite quickly and passed the Act Regulating the Legal Status of Citizens of Former Yugoslavia Living in the Republic of Slovenia. In 2003, however, the legislature failed to pass an appropriate law and the Constitutional Court's second systemic decision remained unimplemented for more than seven years. What other political and social factors are necessary, apart from general legislative and constitutional obligations, for these decisions to be implemented?

592 Rosenberg, The Hollow Hope, 1991, p. 8.

The common duty[593] of all individuals and institutions to abide by the decisions of the Constitutional Court originates in Article 1 of the Constitutional Court Act.[594] The legal consequences of constitutional decisions vary according to type. Declaratory decisions are particularly relevant to us here. These decisions determine that a particular law is unconstitutional or unlawful because it fails to regulate an issue or regulates it in a manner that does not enable annulment or abrogation (Article 48, Para. 1 of the Constitutional Court Act). In such cases, the legislative body or other state institution that passed the unlawful or unconstitutional regulation must eliminate the unconstitutionality by a deadline set by the Constitutional Court (Article 48, Para 2). Failure to comply with Article 48 by disregarding the deadline, that is, failing to adopt a revised version of the law or adopting it after the deadline has passed, is a grave breach of Articles 2 (the rule of law) and 3 of the Constitution (the separation of powers). The Constitutional Court has drawn attention to this issue on several occasions.[595]

The annual reports on the work of the Constitutional Court show that breaches of the duty to implement its decisions are not rare.[596] Several breaches occur every year, with some taking several years to resolve. Although some authors believe that the Constitutional Court should take a more resolute stance on the violations of the Constitution and prevent the National Assembly from interpreting the Constitution according to changing political needs,[597] the Constitutional Court has no means to enforce its decisions. Slovenian constitutionalist Andraž Teršek accordingly argues that this effectively makes the Constitutional

593 The common duty to abide by the decisions of the Constitutional Court is absolute, which does not mean that such decisions cannot be questioned along the lines of constitutional law. Despite the importance of the Constitutional Court and constitutional judgments in the context of constitutional democracy, the doctrine of the separation of powers, which also applies to the Constitutional Court, must be observed as well. Moreover, one must be aware of the danger posed by a shift from "the rule of law to the rule of judges". Krivic, V sistemu deljene oblasti ni najvišjega organa, A lecture prepared for "Dnevi javnega prava" conference, 8 June 2011, un-published.

594 Constitutional Court Act – official consolidated text, Official Gazette of the Republic of Slovenia, No. 64/2007.

595 For instance, the Constitutional Court Ruling No. U-I-114/95, U-II-3/03-15 and U-I-259/01.

596 Annual reports on the work of the Constitutional Court are available at www.ue-rs.si/o-sodiscu/letna-porocila/ (15.01.2011).

597 Jambrek, Ustavna demokracija, 1992, p. 331.

Court a "powerless institution".[598] The Constitutional Court is a supreme authority that acts outside the framework of enforcement. Indeed, for the Court to exert force would run counter to the constitutional order.

The decisions of the Constitutional Court cannot be implemented if they are ignored by the National Assembly or if the government fails to muster sufficient political will to eliminate an established unconstitutionality. The legal framework contains no provision that would enable the Constitutional Court to implement its own decisions, since the assumption is that the relevant state institutions will implement them in accordance with the doctrine of the separation of powers[599]. The only remedy available to the Constitutional Court is the escalation of sanctions, and only in situations where unconstitutionality has already been determined but not yet eliminated.

3. The Implementation of the Constitutional Court's Decisions on the Erasure

In my analysis of the implementation of the Constitutional Court's decisions, I focus mainly on the decisions that determined whether a given regulation was constitutional and lawful. I also address the decisions based on constitutional appeals. I will not discuss the decisions relating to referendums, as their implementation was not in doubt. Every time the Court established that a referendum question was unconstitutional, the referendum was called off, except in one case when the request to assess its constitutionality was submitted too late.

Regarding the two systemic decisions of the Constitutional Court, I seek to establish whether the legislation that was proposed and/or passed was successful in eliminating the unconstitutionality. To do so, I will compare the proposed/passed legislation with the corresponding decision of the Constitutional Court. The text of such a decision is invariably binding. In some cases, even the reasoning of the decision can be binding, if its main text specifically mentions the relevance of specific part of the reasoning.[600] Since the Constitutional Court's decisions on the erasure contain such explanatory texts, they must be included in the analysis.

I also discuss the implementation of a number of Constitutional Court decisions pertaining to constitutional complaints. The doctrine of respect for the

598 Teršek, Legitimnost kot prvina političnih in pravnih konceptov sodobne ustavne demokracije, 2008, p. 266.

599 Čebulj, Posebnosti ustavne pritožbe s področja upravnega prava, in Ustavno sodstvo, 2000, p. 319.

600 Testen, Tehnike ustavnosodnega odločanja, in Ustavno sodstvo, 2000, p. 243.

Constitutional Court's decisions, which is binding on all individuals and institutions, also applies to decisions on constitutional appeals in every area of the law. This includes administrative law, which is especially relevant to the legal context of the erasure. When a decision of either the Supreme Court or the Administrative Court is challenged by the Constitutional Court (or an administrative decision is nullified), the Supreme Court or the Administrative Court (or an administrative body) has to reconsider the case in accordance with the decision of the Constitutional Court.[601] Re-assessing whether the courts applied the directive of the Constitutional Court correctly would go beyond the scope of this chapter. As there is no reason to doubt that the Supreme Court and the Administrative Court abided by the Constitutional Court's decisions, I will focus specifically on whether these decisions were consistently incorporated in the regulations that were meant to implement the two systemic decisions of the Constitutional Court.

3.1 Decision No. U-I-284/94: The Legal Status Act

The implementation of the first systemic decision of the Constitutional Court on the erasure (Decision U-I-284/94, issued on 4 February 1999) was not problematic. The Legal Status Act was passed within the deadline set by the Constitutional Court, on 8 July 1999. One possible reason for such a rapid implementation could have been the pressure from the European Commission exerted during the accession negotiations in 1998.[602] In the same year, the Ministry of the Interior formed a committee with the sole purpose of creating procedures, measures, and a methodology to solve the problem of "foreigners without a legal status" in Slovenia. The committee consisted of the representatives of the Ministry of the Interior, the UN High Commission for Refugees (UNHCR) and the GEA 2000 NGO. On 30 June 1998 the Slovenian government issued a directive ordering the Ministry of the Interior to prepare a draft law. The preparatory studies[603] show that the ministry was aware of the problematic situation of the erased people,

---

601 Čebulj, Posebnosti ustavne pritožbe s področja upravnega prava, in: Ustavno sodstvo, 2000, p. 319.

602 Report of the European Commission on the progress of Slovenia in its accession to the EU, 1998. By referring to the report of the European Commission (EC), I am not contending that the EC was determined to resolve the problem of the inhabitants of Slovenia who had no legal status. Its warnings were indeed mild and only demanded minimal measures. After Slovenia joined the EU, the topic became even less important, because it was perceived as a question of internal governance and thus outside of the reach of the EU.

603 Ogradi, Izbrisani državljani SFRJ, 2003, pp. 39–40.

as well as the reasons that led to their loss of status. Nevertheless, on 24 June 1998, when the constitutionality of the Aliens Act was questioned by the Constitutional Court, the Ministry insisted that its implementation was lawful. It appears that the government and the Ministry were showing a different face to the international community, in light of the on-going EU accession negotiations, than to internal supervisory institutions, for instance the Constitutional Court. This replicated the approach that the government took during the struggle for independence – while it strove to get international acceptance, maintaining an amiable image for the international public, it failed to take responsibility for its internal affairs.

Based on the collected data, the Ministry prepared an early draft of the law, the working title of which was the "Legalisation Act". The proposed solution was based on a person's genuine and effective bond with Slovenia. The people who became eligible to apply for permanent residence permits in Slovenia were divided into two groups: (1) people who held permanent residence permits in Slovenia on 25 June 1991 and lived in Slovenia continuously after the country became independent, and (2) people who had a temporary residence registered in Slovenia on 25 June 1991 and had held employment in Slovenia for a period of no less than ten years, and people who were born or educated in Slovenia and lived in Slovenia continuously after its independence.[604]

Although the government was aware of the problems of the people who were erased from the register of permanent residents and other persons who lived in the Republic of Slovenia without residence permits, and despite the warnings of the European Commission, the Legal Status Act[605] was passed just a single month before the deadline set by the Constitutional Court. There was no single key factor that led to the passage of the law; it resulted from a synergy of external and internal pressures contributed to it (more on this to follow).

While the decision of the Constitutional Court was implemented within the designated timeframe, the content of the Legal Status Act was questionable. An especially positive aspect of the law was that, in addition to the erased people, it also included citizens who were not eligible to apply for Slovenian citizenship under Article 40 of the Citizenship of the Republic of Slovenia Act because they did not have their permanent residence registered in Slovenia, although they actually had lived in Slovenia from 25 June 1991 onwards. Previous legislation did

604 *Ibid.*

605 The original name of the act was Zakon o urejanju statusa državljanov drugih držav naslednic SFRJ v Republiki Sloveniji.

not address the plight of these persons. The authorities were aware of this fact and therefore included them in the group that was to have its status legalised by the new legislation. The key requirement that persons in this group had to satisfy was continuous residence in Slovenia. The legislation was finally fully implemented when this group of people was issued residence permits.

The erased people also had to meet the requirement of continuous residence in Slovenia. The Legal Status Act stated that actual residence in Slovenia following the referendum was a key requirement for eligibility for a permanent residence permit. According to Article 1 of this law, one is eligible to acquire a permanent residence permit if one is a "citizen of another successor state of the former SFRY, who on 23 December 1990 had his/her permanent residence registered in the Republic of Slovenia and has lived in the Republic of Slovenia since that day". What are the reasons for this requirement? Why did the legislature decide that a law meant to redress the violations of constitutional rights should include the additional condition of continuous residence in Slovenia following the referendum? The question is important, as a failure to satisfy this condition was one of the most common reasons for rejecting applications. Furthermore, this requirement was included in every subsequent version of the law, and is still present even after the 2010 amendment, albeit in a somewhat more limited form. While the length of the required period of continuous residence in the country (starting on 23 December 1999) is problematic in itself, the requirement of continuous residence as such is even more so.

An attempt to determine the reasons why this requirement was included in the law leads us to Constitutional Court decision No. U-I-284/94, and the separate concurring opinion of Judge Lojze Ude. The explanatory text of the decision discussing the manner in which the issue was to be regulated stated that the legal consequences of the erasure had not ceased to exist and some people were still without permanent or temporary residence permits. It also included a guideline saying that "the legislative authority needs to take into account all the possible circumstances in which these persons have found themselves as a result of the lack of legal status".[606] This instruction is relevant because, as time passed, the affected people found themselves in a variety of circumstances, so some applications to regain legal status were wrongfully rejected on the grounds of the above-mentioned requirements. Unfortunately, this instruction in the explanatory text of the Constitutional Court's decision was not further elaborated. The

606 Constitutional Court of the Republic of Slovenia, Ruling No. U-I-284/94, paragraph 14.

Constitutional Court stated that the requirements should not be radically different from those for Slovenian citizenship, which included a registered permanent residence and actual residence in Slovenia. The decision's explanatory text was, on this point, contradictory. On the one hand, the Constitutional Court demanded that the various circumstances of the erased people be taken into account. On the other hand, it proposed the condition of having one's permanent residence in Slovenia, which wrongly excluded erased persons who did not meet this condition or had had no way to meet it for an extended period of time.

The legislature consequently included actual residence in Slovenia as a requirement (it even went a step further, and the condition was that one should have been actually living in Slovenia since the day of the referendum). This position followed the independent opinion of Judge Ude, who contended that, when regulating the legal status of citizens of the former SFRY republics, the following should be taken into account:

> Not only whether the persons, at the time of the referendum, held permanent residence in the Republic of Slovenia, but also whether they actually lived in the country after the referendum and independence. The Decision mentions the condition of actual residence in the territory of the Republic of Slovenia as the key requirement for a successful application for legal status in several places (for instance Point 13 of the explanatory text). I am of the opinion that this condition should be particularly emphasised.[607]

The question here is whether this guideline should have been part of the Decision itself if the other judges of the Constitutional Court concurred with his opinion. Judging by the text of the decision, one may argue that other judges did not concur, or if they did, they failed to present their agreement clearly. The most likely possibility is that the other judges disagreed and Judge Ude's opinion was isolated, which is why he wrote a separate opinion (This is, in fact, the main purpose of separate opinions, even if they concur with the decision).[608] It is therefore reasonable to conclude that actual residence in the Republic of Slovenia from the day of the referendum onwards was not demanded by the Constitutional Court. Paragraph 13 of the reasoning reads:

> The said persons registered their permanent residence in the territory of Slovenia in conformity with applicable laws and regulations and actually resided in the territory of Slovenia. Permanent residence and actual residence in the territory of the Republic of Slovenia are the essential circumstances that accord a special legal position to the

607 Concurring opinion of Judge Lojze Ude to the Constitutional Court Ruling No. U-I-284/94.

608 Interview with Ciril Ribičič, former Constitutional Court judge, 25 July 2011.

persons concerned, which is why the provisions of the Aliens Act, which regulate the acquisition of permanent or temporary residence permits, are inappropriate for them. The legislature should have regulated the situation of the persons concerned and/or their transition to the alien status in a special manner in transitional provisions of the Aliens Act or in a special statute.[609]

In this passage, the Constitutional Court clearly focuses on the referendum and Slovenia's declaration of independence as the key moments in the past when the two requirements had to be satisfied in order for a person to be eligible for legal status. It is clearly not referring to the following period, when the unlawfully erased legal status was to be reinstated. The referendum and the re-regulation of legal status were far apart in time, and in the meantime, the personal circumstances of a given individual may have changed to a degree where the condition of actual residence in the territory of the Republic of Slovenia could not be met. Ude's commentary is thus not supported by the Constitutional Court's decision and the legislature had no reasonable cause to add this requirement. When drafting the law, the legislature therefore followed an independent opinion rather than the binding decision of the Constitutional Court that made no mention of this requirement.

The requirement is illogical, since it prevented many erased persons from regaining their legal status. One of the consequences of the erasure was to interrupt actual residence in Slovenia for various reasons. For instance, people were deported from the country, travelled to another ex-Yugoslav republic for personal reasons (to visit relatives, acquire papers they needed to arrange their legal status in Slovenia, etc.), or went abroad for medical treatment or schooling. However, on returning to Slovenia many of them were denied entry due to expired passports or new visa requirements (which they could not meet), or in some cases a direct ban on entry.

Moreover, the condition of actual residence in the Republic of Slovenia was enforced retroactively in 1999. This meant that the erased people had to prove that they had actually lived in Slovenia for a long period in the past, during which time they could not yet have been aware of the requirement that was to be set many years later. Therefore, the requirement was not in compliance with the doctrine of reasonable expectation, because the affected persons had no chance to familiarise themselves with the regulation and then alter their actions to avoid sanctions (i.e. the rejection of an application for a permanent residence permit). The condition of actual residence in the Republic of Slovenia

609 Constitutional Court Ruling No. U-I-284/94, Paragraph 13.

from the referendum onwards hinges upon a past reality that can no longer be altered. For affected persons, the requirement of actual residence in Slovenia was unachievable.

The requirement would not be problematic had the erased people been striving for the recognition of a right that they had not previously held, for instance the right to Slovenian citizenship. However, this was not the case – they were trying to regain a right that they had held in the past, a right which had been taken from them unlawfully and which should have been returned to them in accordance with the decision of the Constitutional Court. It should have been returned under the same conditions that were taken as the basis for the erasure, without adding new requirements to be satisfied retroactively. The persons affected by the erasure were all citizens of the SFRY and they all shared two common traits – they did not gain citizenship of the Republic of Slovenia, but had their permanent residence registered in Slovenia on a specific date. Since no other related circumstances were taken into account at the time of erasure, it seems unreasonable that new conditions should be set for regaining that same legal status. The only additional conditions that could be acceptable would be those required for Slovenian citizenship, that is to say, a registered residence at the time of the referendum and actual residence in Slovenia from the referendum to the erasure, but not from the referendum to the day of the Constitutional Court decision.

One could thus assume that the condition of actual residence in the Republic of Slovenia from the referendum onwards is in breach of the doctrine of the protection of legitimate expectation, which is one of the basic elements of the rule of law dictated by Article 2 of the Slovenian Constitution. With decision U-I-246/02 issued in 2003, the Constitutional Court addressed the problematic nature of this requirement to a limited extent. With the implementation of this decision and the passage of the amendments to the Legal Status Act (which I discuss later on) the issue was taken further towards a solution, though certain problems remained.

The Constitutional Court's instructions to the legislature to redress the injustices caused by the erasure and the revocation of legal status were unclear with respect to the conditions that a person had to satisfy in order to regain his/her legal status and to the moment when the legal status, if granted, became effective. The Constitutional Court's decision No. U-I-284/94 does not explicitly mention when the status should start to be effective, but the wording suggests that the unlawful and unconstitutional circumstances were considered to begin on 26 February 1992. The legislature should therefore have been aware that the legal status should have been reinstated for the relevant period in the past as well.

Decisions stemming from constitutional appeals in the immediate aftermath of the first systemic decision issued in 1994 (i.e. U-I-284/94) confirm that the intention was to reinstate the legal status retroactively, from the day of the erasure. In decisions Up-333/96 and Up-60/97, the Constitutional Court instructed the Ministry of the Interior that the appellants should be re-entered into the register of permanent residents until the law regulating this issue was passed, that is, when their legal status was to be reconsidered. The Constitutional Court did not expressly state from which date this re-entering should be effective, but it did identify 26 February 1992 (the two-month deadline from the final decision on the rejection of citizenship of the Republic of Slovenia) as the commencement of unlawful circumstances. One could thus reasonably assume that the re-entering was meant to be effective retroactively, from 26 February 1992, onward.

It is surprising how far-reaching the consequences of decision Up-333/96 were. When the decision was passed, the Ministry of the Interior sent the local municipal authorities a circular dated 24 September 1999 with a list of all erased people attached, instructing them that the persons on the list should be re-entered into the register of permanent residents if they requested it. Moreover, if requested, a certificate of registered residence, a household record and a driver's license were to be issued if the applicant met all other legal requirements.[610] Decision Up-222/96 and its effects confirm that decision U-I-284/94 cannot be understood in any other way than as intending to regulate the legal status for the past period as well.

The disadvantages of the Legal Status Act were brought to the public eye only in 2002, when an initiative for the assessment of its constitutionality was submitted. This also pointed out the inconsistencies arising from the conflicting decisions passed as a result of the constitutional appeals. In response to the constitutional appeal on the matter of U-I-246/01, the National Assembly stated: "The Constitutional Court decision No. U-I-284/94 does not clarify how the legislature is to remove the listed unconstitutionalities, i.e. retroactively or prospectively".[611]

Regarding decision Up-333/96, the National Assembly stated that the decision "is only effective between the two parties in conflict (*inter partes*) and was

610 A circular of the Ministry of the Interior No. 0302-16/01-209-Sl./99 of 24 September 1999.

611 Constitutional Court of the Republic of Slovenia, Ruling No. U-I-246/02, paragraph 4.

meant only as a transitional solution to the problem of the plaintiff's permanent residence status which is required to issue a driver's license".[612]

In decision U-I-246/02, the Constitutional Court rejected the claims of the National Assembly and the government that the obligation to regulate the legal status of erased people retroactively did not proceed from the 1999 decision. Moreover, the Court asserted that the 1999 decision referred to the whole period during which the status remained unresolved and that it was the legislature's duty to resolve the issue for the whole period in question. It confirmed that this position was also consistent with that taken in the case of relevant constitutional appeals (for instance Up-333/95 and Up-60/97), when the Constitutional Court instructed local authorities to re-enter a person into the register of permanent residents from the day of the erasure onwards, as well as in the cases when the erased persons were granted certain material rights which had been denied to them on the grounds of not having the status of permanent residents in the period following the erasure (decision of the Constitutional Court Up-336/98).

During the legislative procedure, the National Assembly also held a discussion on whether residence in Slovenia after the erasure, but before the acquisition of a permanent residence permit, could be considered lawful. The centre-left party at the time – ZLSD – proposed that this period of residence in the country should be considered lawful residence.[613] The legislature nevertheless passed a regulation according to which the permanent residence permit became valid from the day it was issued, thus ignoring the unique situation of the erased persons compared to foreigners from other countries living in Slovenia.

The Legal Status Act had other flaws. It only gave affected people three months to submit an application. The law also included discriminatory clauses that excluded certain groups. For example, those eligible to apply for a permanent residence permit were, in the first article, defined as "citizens of other successor states", although the decision of the Constitutional Court specifically mentioned "citizens of other republics of the former SFRY". This language was not seen as problematic until the Ministry of the Interior suddenly began to demand that applicants present proof of citizenship of another SFRY successor state.[614] This

612 *Ibid.*

613 The amendment of the ZLSD parliament group dated 6 July 1999, No. 213-04/99-28/3, EPA 749-II.

614 In a few cases, the Administrative Court supported the Ministry's interpretation that citizenship of another successor state of the SFRY was required from an applicant. Whenever the Administrative Court's decisions were revised by the Supreme Court, which happened on two occasions, the decisions were nullified and the case returned

primarily affected persons who did not want to acquire citizenship of another successor state, or could not acquire it because of the doctrine of continuity that left some of them stateless. In addition, some of the erased persons had in the meantime secured citizenship of the EU or some other country, but still wanted to regain their legal status in Slovenia. These two groups were excluded by the text of the law (or, more specifically, its interpretation). These legal shortcomings could have been avoided if the law had been read teleologically to determine whether its intention was to regulate the legal status of only those persons who were able to prove that they were citizens of another SFRY successor state, or if eligibility also extended to stateless persons, or citizens of the EU/other countries. Constitutional Court decision U-I-284/94 mentions citizens of other republics of the former SFRY, which means persons who had citizenship of another SFRY republic on the day Slovenia gained independence. It is thus safe to assume that the Constitutional Court did not intend to exclude stateless persons or citizens of the EU or another country, as any subsequently acquired citizenship of these persons is irrelevant to the implementation of the decisions of the Constitutional Court.

Irrespective of these shortcomings, the Constitutional Court's decision U-I-284/94 and the resulting passage of the Legal Status Act were of the utmost importance to the search for a solution to the problem of erasure. Even before the three-month deadline for applications was nullified as too short by decision U-I-246/02, 12937 applications for a permanent residence permit were sent in under this law, 11746 of which were successful. It is not known how many of these permanent residence permits were issued to erased persons, as the numbers include both erased persons and other residents, but estimates put the number at several thousand.

The 2002 amendment to the Citizenship of the Republic of Slovenia Act is also relevant to the implementation of this Constitutional Court decision.[615] This amendment enabled adult persons who had their permanent residence

---

to the initial stage. As is often the case, the administration followed the literal reading of the law (textualism), although it was clear from the intent of the law that it applied to citizens of other republics of the SFRY, who, at the time, could not have been citizens of successor states of the SFRY, irrespective of which citizenship they acquired later on. The intent of the law could easily be perceived from the text. On why the administrators applied a strict textualist perspective *see* Pečarič, Uradništvo med formalnim in neformalnim vplivom na politiko in državljane, 2008, p. 18.

615 The Act Amending the Citizenship of the Republic of Slovenia Act, Official Gazette of the Republic of Slovenia, No. 96/2002.

registered in the territory of the Republic of Slovenia at the time of the referendum and lived in Slovenia from that day on to apply for Slovenian citizenship under more favourable conditions than through regular naturalisation (the conditions are stated in Article 19 of the amendments to the Citizenship Act). The law did not require the persons applying for citizenship to have foreigner status in the Republic of Slovenia. Approximately 3500 people who did not possess permanent residence permits gained citizenship under this law. The reason for this particular regulation was the not-yet-ratified European Convention on Nationality, which includes the guideline that all persons with a genuine and effective connection with a country must be able to acquire citizenship in that country. The legal bond is thus an extension of the bonds already in place. Moreover, the passage of this regulation was motivated by an attempt to correct the shortcomings of the Legal Status Act,[616] specifically the short, three-month deadline to apply for permanent residence permits which ended on 28 December 1999 and prevented many people from submitting an application. Under the amendments to the Citizenship Act, these same persons could apply for citizenship within a year of the implementation of the law.

3.2 Decision No. U-I-246/02

The Legal Status Act was brought to the attention of the Constitutional Court because of its discussed shortcomings. The Court then established its unconstitutionality in 2003 by decision U-I-246/02. However, the implementation of this decision was not as smooth as that of the related 1999 decision.[617] As presented in Part IV of this book, the most controversial part of the decision was point 8 of the main text, in which the Constitutional Court ordered the Ministry of the Interior to issue a special declaratory (supplemental) decision by which permanent residence permits were to be granted retroactively. In order to implement this decision, three laws were proposed but not passed. The decision was implemented only in 2010, when amendments to the Legal Status Act were passed and the last of the declaratory decisions issued, retroactively reinstating the legal status

616 Ogradi, Izbrisani državljani SFRJ, 2003, pp. 46–47.

617 According to Professor Ciril Ribibič, a former judge of the Constitutional Court who participated in the process leading up to 2003 decision, the judges were convinced that the explanatory text of the decision was correct and convincing and could not raise legal doubts, although they were aware that it would cause controversies. Interview with Ciril Ribičil, 25 July 2011.

of erased persons. I will now proceed to briefly analyse the proposed regulations that aimed to implement the 2003 decision of the Constitutional Court.

The decision of the Constitutional Court imposed two obligations, (1) to pass a new law that would correct the unconstitutionalities established by the Constitutional Court, and (2) to issue declaratory (supplemental) decisions. The Ministry of the Interior took immediate action to satisfy both requirements.[618] This triggered discussions, both in the public and the legal sphere, on whether a pertinent law needed to be in place first, before the declaratory decisions could be issued, or if the Constitutional Court's decision was a sufficient basis.[619] The former, extremely formalistic view ultimately prevailed, and the government prepared proposals for two laws: a "technical" law in response to point 8 of the main text of the decision (in which the Constitutional Court ordered the Ministry of the Interior to issue special decisions to legalise residence in the country from the day of the erasure on for all persons who had already secured a permanent residence permit) and a "systemic" law, which was to implement the other articles of the Court's decision.

3.2.1 The Draft "Technical" Law and the Referendum

The proposed law clearly defined the procedures and requirements for issuing declaratory decisions to establish a person's actual residence in Slovenia. The very title of the law – the Proposal of the Law on the Implementation of point 8 of the Decision of the Constitutional Court No. U-I-246/02-28 –, and its popular name, the "technical law", which gained currency in everyday use, suggest that it was unnecessary. It was the consequence of an extremely formalistic legal approach to constitutional law.

The persons eligible to receive the declaratory decisions were those citizens of other successor states of the former SFRY who had their permanent residence registered in Slovenia on 23 December 1990, and on 25 June 1991, and who had already secured permanent residence permits under the Legal Status Act, the Aliens Act of 1991, or the Aliens Act of 1999. The decisions, which were to be issued

618 On 15 April 2003, the Ministry of the Interior organized a press conference to present the measures. Hot, Reševanje vprašanja izbrisanih, 2004, p. 26.

619 A group of nineteen signatories from different backgrounds pleaded with the President to "exercise his influence and moral authority to ensure that the decision of the Constitutional Court is implemented only after the legislature had passed all the laws and regulations ensuing from that constitutional decision" (the open letter dated 18 April 2003). On 28 August, the Minister of the Interior called a meeting of Expert Council for Public Administration.

ex proprio motu (without the person having to apply for it), were meant to recognise their permanent resident status retroactively, i.e. that a person had lived in the Republic of Slovenia legally from 26 February 1992 on, or from the day of the erasure to the day when he/she regained his/her permanent residence permit.[620] However, the proposed law included a restriction (added during the legislative procedure) that such decisions could not be issued to persons whose actual and continuous residence in Slovenia from the erasure onwards had not been determined at the time when they obtained permanent residence permits.[621]

In this matter, the proposed law was considerably different from point 8 of the Constitutional Court's decision; with this change, the legislature cut down the number of eligible applicants from approximately 12000 to four or five thousand persons.[622] This discrepancy created a seemingly paradoxical situation – the legislature made a radical, unconstitutional change regarding the pool of eligible applicants, but at the same time, it set right a presumed shortcoming of the Constitutional Court's decision according to which all the persons who had obtained permanent residence permits were eligible to receive a supplemental decision irrespective of whether they had actually lived in Slovenia beforehand.[623] In 2010, this dilemma was resolved with the argument that it constituted a remedy of the wrongdoing from a human rights perspective, while legally and formally it created a legal fiction (*infra*).

A further shortcoming of the proposed "technical" law was that persons who secured citizenship of the Republic of Slovenia without first gaining a permanent residence permit (for instance persons who secured citizenship under Article 19 of the amendments to the Citizenship Act), were not considered eligible to receive supplemental decisions. These persons had already had to prove that they had lived in Slovenia from the referendum onwards when they applied for citizenship. As citizenship is a higher level status than permanent resident, the supplementary decision should have been issued for these persons as well on an *a fortiori* basis *(a minore ad maius)*. This flaw originated in point 8 of the decision of the Constitutional Court, which specifically mentions only those erased persons who obtained permanent residence permits.

---

620 Proposal of the Law on the Implementation of point 8 of the Decision of the Constitutional Court No. U-I-246/02-28, dated 9 September 2003.

621 Bojan Bugarič, Transcription of the 30th sitting of the National Assembly of the Republic of Slovenia, 29 October 2003.

622 Hot, Reševanje vprašanja izbrisanih, 2004, p. 32.

623 *Ibid.*, p. 31.

Despite its shortcomings, the technical law was passed on 29 October 2003 (it was vetoed by the National Council on 5 November, and then passed in the National Assembly again on 25 January 2004). However, it was never implemented, as it was annulled in the referendum of 4 April 2004.[624]

On 3 February 2004, the Ministry of the Interior started to issue supplementary decisions in accordance with point 8 of the decision of the Constitutional Court without waiting for the outcome of the referendum. This was in accordance with the Constitution, but inconsistent with the policies of the Ministry at the time, as it was the Minister of the Interior, Rado Bohinc, who was coordinating the process of writing the technical law, which was supposed to be the basis for issuing the decisions.

A public debate ensued, with the majority of the commentators claiming that, because of the wording of Article 153, Paragraph 4 of the Constitution, decisions could not be issued before an adequate legal basis was provided. Others countered by invoking the constitutional right to exercise human rights directly, on the basis of Article 15 of the Constitution.[625]

Ultimately the Ministry of the Interior partially implemented point 8 of the Constitutional Court's decision in 2004. It issued 4034 supplementary decisions instead of the total number of 6381 that should have been issued.

3.2.2 The proposal of the "systemic" law

The draft systemic law[626] was the second of the two measures demanded by the Constitutional Court to correct the unconstitutionalities cited in the first seven

---

624 Timeline of the events leading to the referendum: On 2 December 2003, thirty MPs filed a request for a constitutional referendum on the technical law. On 8 December 2004, the Government proposed to the National Assembly that the Constitutional Court should determine whether a referendum was needed. On 22 December, the Constitutional Court rejected the proposal as too late. On 30 December, the National Assembly called a referendum. A day later, a group of 33 members of parliament demanded the assessment of the constitutionality of the call for a referendum, and proposed that the Constitutional Court should temporarily suspend the call for a referendum. On 26 January 2004, the Constitutional Court rejected the request to reassess constitutionality of the call and ordered the National Assembly to set a date for the referendum. The referendum was thus called for 4 April 2004. *Ibid.*, pp. 32–43.

625 Hot, Reševanje vprašanja izbrisanih, 2004, p. 46.

626 Predlog zakona o stalnem prebivanju tujcev z državljanstvom drugih držav naslednic nekdanje SFRJ v Republiki Sloveniji, ki so imeli na dan 23. 12. 1990 in 25. 2. 1992 v Republiki Sloveniji prijavljeno stalno prebivališče.

points of the main text of its decision. The core requirement for obtaining a permanent residence permit continued to be actually living in Slovenia. However, the requirements outlined in this draft were less absolute, with several exemptions allowed. According to this proposal, the requirement of actually living in Slovenia could be satisfied even if one was absent from the country for a period of time. An absence of less than a year had no bearing on the requirement. If the absence lasted over a year, the requirement was satisfied if:

- the person left the Republic of Slovenia due to serious and well-grounded reasons related to the erasure, in an attempt to ensure a livelihood for himself/herself or a dependent family member;
- the person left the Republic of Slovenia due to a crisis caused by the erasure (for instance, for fear of forced removal from the country due to the unclear legal status of foreigners in the Republic of Slovenia);
- the person left the Republic of Slovenia after the erasure, because he/she was sent abroad by a legal entity in the Republic of Slovenia for work, education, or medical treatment, or if the person was a member of a ship's crew sailing under the flag of the Republic of Slovenia;
- the person was removed from the country on the basis of Article 28 of the Aliens Act of 1999, or Article 50 of the Aliens Act 1999, unless the removal was part of a sentence for another offence or a precautionary measure (this exemption was in compliance with the second point of the main text of the Constitutional Court's decision U-I-246/02);
- the person was denied entry into Slovenia, unless the denial was part of a sentence for another offence or of a few other similar measures (this exemption later proved problematic in practice).

Despite these exemptions, the requirement of actually living in the country was not considered satisfied, (1) if the person moved abroad and failed to notify the relevant public authority, while the manner of moving implied that he/she intended to reside outside the Republic of Slovenia permanently and the case was not covered by the first two points, and (2) if the person left the Republic of Slovenia without notifying the relevant public authority to the country of which he/she was a citizen with the intention of permanent reunion with family members who did not have their residence registered in the country on 24 February 1992, or did but also left the Republic of Slovenia without notifying the relevant authority and in a manner that implied permanent relocation.[627]

627 Paragraph 4 of the proposal of "systemic" law.

The proposed solution was one possible way of implementing the Constitutional Court decision. It was not overly restrictive, and did not exclude many of the erased persons who could reasonably expect to have their legal status reinstated. As I will explain below, the proposed measures were to a certain extent comparable to the requirements listed in the amendments to the Legal Status Act in 2010.

The conditions listed above (i.e. a seemingly permanent relocation) were more restrictive than those generally in place for aliens. Other restrictions included, for instance, the time window of one year for applications to be sent in. Moreover, the proposal included two measures which could be considered unconstitutional: (1) the clause which prevented persons employed in the Yugoslav People's Army (YPA) who did not respond to the call of the Presidency of the Republic of Slovenia on 27 June 1991, and directly participated in the YPA's assault against Slovenia, from regaining their legal status (this requirement is incompatible with the fifth point of the Constitutional Court's decision U-II-1/04; moreover, other sanctions are available in such cases), and (2) the recognition of actual residence in Slovenia only for the period in which actual residence in the country could be proven (this requirement is incompatible with point 8 of the main text of the Constitutional Court's decision U-I-246/02-28). Furthermore, the law significantly restricted compensation claims (these were to be valid only if the claimant had already exhausted all legal means to secure his/her legal status) and excluded claims to reparations for damages unrelated to property, which is a breach of Article 26 of the Constitution.

The proposed law was challenged during the legislative process and a petition for a transitional legislative referendum was launched. The petition included certain solutions that had already been declared unconstitutional by the Constitutional Court in its decision of 26 February 2004. Ultimately, this law, the restrictive conditions of which were supported by the majority in the National Assembly, was not passed due to the general elections.

3.2.3 *The proposal of the "Constitutional" Law*

The attempt to implement the decision of the Constitutional Court during the 2000–2004 parliamentary term therefore failed almost completely, except for the partial implementation of point 8 of the decision. In the autumn of 2004, the centre-right parties came to power. These were the same parties that had actively obstructed the implementation of the Constitutional Court's decisions in the previous parliamentary term by calling referendums and threatening to prosecute local administration employees if they implemented the decisions.[628] In the first year after they came to power, no discernible action was taken to implement the Constitutional Court's decision. At the end of 2005, a proposal to amend the Constitutional Act was drafted. The drafting process was not transparent and the document was not accessible to the public until 10 April 2006, when the information commissioner declared it public on request of the journalist Siniša Gačić and Amnesty International.

The form of the proposed document is telling in itself. The government attempted to promote a regulation to the status of a constitutional document and prevent the Constitutional Court from exercising its authority to assess its constitutionality and legality.[629] It aimed to circumvent the previously issued decisions of the Constitutional Court and regulate the matter in an unconstitutional manner. This was a futile pursuit, because the Constitutional Court has the right to reassess constitutional laws that regulate constitutional matters. It is the content of regulations that counts, not their form.[630]

The intention behind the law should not come as a surprise, as an analysis of the proposed provisions shows a large number of unconstitutional elements on which the Constitutional Court had already issued decisions. These include a restriction on compensations (which would become irrelevant if the ECHR decided on the issue), the option of precluding people who did not respond to the presidency's order to abandon the YPA from regaining their legal status, and mandatorily precluding the members of the YPA who took part in the assault on the Republic of Slovenia from regaining their legal status (i.e. a new attempt to retroactively legitimise the blacklist mentioned earlier in the text). The proposal added new requirements to the existing condition of actual residence in Slovenia. For instance, persons who had not already requested to have their legal status reinstated could no longer start the process. The proposal set a new, short deadline of six months within which an application for legal status could

628 Ribičič, Nevarno ustavno sodišče?, Mladina, 2011.

629 Marijan Pavčnik believes that the outmaneuvering of Constitutional Court's decisions is democratically legitimate. In my opinion, this is a dangerous claim as, under the cover of legitimacy, the constitutional body can meddle with the rights that have previously been considered constitutional and untouchable. Pavčnik, Pravni in ustavni temelji prava, in: Ustavno sodstvo, 2000, p. 422.

630 Krivic, Ustavno sodišče: pristojnosti in postopek, in: Ustavno sodstvo, 2000, p. 64. *Also* Teršek, Legitimnost kot prvina političnih in pravnih konceptov sodobne ustavne demokracije, 2008, p. 26.

be submitted. The possibilities of revising the procedure by which a residence permit or a supplemental decision was issued were also expanded.[631]

According to Article 168 of the Constitution, a two thirds majority is required to pass a constitutional law. Since the opposition parties refused to support such an obviously unconstitutional proposal, its proponents could not secure the majority or hope for success. The legal system was thus spared the harm that it would have suffered had the law been passed, as it would have given legitimacy to the erasure and relieved the authorities and administrators of guilt.

3.2.4 The Legal Status Act – A Long-awaited, albeit Partial, Resolution

A new opportunity to implement the Constitutional Court's decisions arose in autumn 2008 with the new governmental term. The new Minister of the Interior, Katarina Kresal, defined the implementation of the decisions as one of the primary goals of the Ministry. Two sets of measures were prepared: (1) the issuing of the remaining supplementary decisions, which were officially renamed "special declaratory decisions" to avoid ambiguities (in Slovenian administrative law, a declaratory decision is a decision which an administrative body uses to decide on an important legal question which is not covered in the main decision); and (2) the preparation of the law which was to achieve a holistic resolution of the legal status of the erased persons on the basis of the Constitutional Court's instructions, taking legal precedent into account.

As a part of the first set of measures, in 2009 the Ministry amended the special declaratory decisions of 2004. The revised decisions focused on *permanent residence permits* rather than *actual residence* as in 2004. Accordingly, erased persons were recognised as having had permanent residence permits and a permanent address registered in Slovenia from the erasure to the day on which the permits were issued. The issuing of decisions was concluded on 15 March 2010. 6381 special declaratory decisions were issued in total (2313 of which were issued in the second round).[632]

As part of the second set of measures, the Ministry, attempting to implement the first seven points of the main text of the Constitutional Court's decision,

---

631 The proposal of the Constitutional law was analysed in detail elsewhere. Kogovšek, The Erasure: The Proposal of a Constitutional Law as the Negation of the Rule of Law, in: Journal for the Critique of Science 35 (2007) 228.

632 Ministry of the Interior. Issuing of the additional decisions on the grounds of point 8 of the Constitutional Court's decision No. U-I-246/02 from 3 April 2003, report is available on the website of the Ministry.

prepared the amendments to the Legal Status Act.[633] They were passed on 8 March 2010. Thirty MPs from the centre-right parties demanded an additional legislative referendum, but the Constitutional Court feared it would have unconstitutional consequences and rejected it on these grounds (Constitutional Court decision U-II-1/10-19, for more see Part IV). The law did not go into effect until 24 June 2010.

The amendments tackled the unconstitutional elements of earlier legislation and were less restrictive than previous proposals (the "systemic" and the "constitutional" law). Regrettably, they retained the established principle underlying the reinstatement of unlawfully denied statuses: actual residence in Slovenia following the referendum. Absence from Slovenia for up to one year was not considered to be in conflict with this requirement, but a longer absence was justifiable only if the person was exempt according to the new Article 1.č of the amendments to the Legal Status Act:

- If a person left the Republic of Slovenia due to the consequences of the erasure;
- If a person left the Republic of Slovenia for work, studies or medical treatment arranged by a legal entity from Slovenia, or, in the case of minors, by parents or guardians, or if the person was a member of a ship's crew.
- If a person left the Republic of Slovenia because he/she could not meet the conditions to be granted a residence permit, and consequently his/her application was rejected, discarded or the application process was discontinued.
- If a person could not return to the Republic of Slovenia due to the war in the successor states of the former SFRY, or due to health reasons.
- If a person was forcibly removed from the Republic of Slovenia under Article 28 of the Aliens Act[634] or Article 50 of the Aliens Act,[635] except when expulsion from the country was part of a penalty for another criminal offence.
- If a person was barred from entering the Republic of Slovenia, except when the prohibition was part of a penalty for another criminal offence or had other, lawful reasons.

Even though the Constitutional Court, in the second point of the decision, demanded that the legislature only reinstate the status of those persons who had been forcibly removed from Slovenia, the law extended to all persons who were

633 Official Gazette of the Republic of Slovenia, No. 50/2010. Also the revised text (LRSCOS-UPB1), Official Gazette of the Republic of Slovenia, No. 76/2010.

634 Official Gazette of the Republic of Slovenia, No. 1/91-I, 44/97, 50/98 and 14/99 – decisions of the Constitutional Court.

635 Official Gazette of the Republic of Slovenia, No. 64/09 – officially revised text.

absent from Slovenia for reasons beyond their influence. As a matter of fact, there were erased persons who did not fully satisfy the requirement of actual residence in the country from the referendum onwards among the applicants under Legal Status Act. In the absence of clear criteria for assessing the eligibility of a candidate, which was a result of the failure to implement the Constitutional Court's decision, a body of administrative practices and judicial case law was developed. As required by the Constitutional Court, it was not radically different from that developed by the Supreme Court for granting Slovenian citizenship in accordance with Article 40 of the Citizenship of the Republic of Slovenia Act. The core requirement was that an absence from Slovenia of which the authorities were not informed could not exceed one year.[636] A large number of people who failed to satisfy this requirement thus found themselves in a problematic situation. If they were expelled, turned away at the border, or if they were stranded by war in another successor state of the former SFRY, they generally could not return to Slovenia for several years. Even temporary absences (for social visits, funerals, holidays, etc.) often turned into unintended long-term absences because of the war or the new visa policy. People were therefore stranded in these countries for many different reasons, and some could even not apply for a visa, because there were no diplomatic relations between the countries (Serbia was one example – to obtain a visa one had to travel to Budapest). In other cases, borders were non-permeable, or the fighting itself might have prevented people from traveling. Some of the erased persons found themselves on the front lines, which made the possibility of a return to Slovenia appear even more distant, while others spent the war as refugees in EU countries, for instance in Germany. It was very unlikely for an erased person to regain his/her legal status before 1999 (when the Legal Status Act set a brief three-month-long window to submit applications, which could easily be missed) or 2002 (when the Citizenship of the Republic of Slovenia Act (RSCA-Č) was passed, with Article 19 enabling erased people to secure citizenship). People often knew which requirement they could not meet and did not even try to apply, as they would only have incurred pointless expenses for administrative and judicial fees.

Given these circumstances, if the doctrine of the rule of law was to be followed, it was necessary to include other justifiable reasons for an absence from Slovenia in the law. Moreover, in decision Up-211/04-21 of 2 March 2001, the Constitutional Court decided that the particular circumstances of a person, and

636 An additional requirement, that absence of more than a year is only problematic if the relevant authorities were not notified, later disappeared.

the reasons for his/her absence were of crucial importance, so the relevant authorities and the courts had to take a stance on them.[637] In this way the Constitutional Court added other justifiable absences to the list of exemptions, a position that was then adopted by the legislature.

Keeping all of this in mind, we find an inconsistency with the first point of decision U-I-264/02. The decision states that the Legal Status Act was unconstitutional because it did not recognise the erased people's right to have their permanent residence recognised from the erasure onwards. This could also be interpreted to mean that all erased persons should have been granted residence permits, irrespective of any hypothetical absence from the country for whatever reason.

One of the most problematic parts of the law was that it included an irrational eliminatory clause. According to this clause, if an absence from the country was justified under one of the aforementioned five points but lasted more than five years, the first five years were to be counted as actual living in Slovenia, while the next five years were not to be counted unless the person's actions demonstrated an intention to return to Slovenia and continue to reside there. According to a textualist interpretation, this means that the first five years of absence (for instance between 1993 and 1998) were considered justified if the absence fell into one of the exempt categories, but absence in the next five years (1998 to 2003) was only considered justified if an additional requirement, that is, a provable attempt to return to Slovenia, was met. The longest absence that the law considered justified was apparently ten years, as a textualist interpretation of the text does not allow for any other interpretation.

The exemptions were introduced for the benefit of those erased persons who, until that point, could not yet secure legal status due to a prolonged absence from the country. However, the additional requirement nullified the intended purpose of the exemptions. The erasure occurred nearly twenty years before the law was passed, and the majority of affected persons left Slovenia in the first few years following the erasure. If they could not return immediately, they often could not return at all, and many still live abroad. Following the textualist interpretation, many of the erased persons who were supposed to be the primary beneficiaries of the law and the exemptions will not be able to secure legal status because the additional requirement functions as an eliminatory clause. This provision effectively annulled the purpose and the meaning of the law, raising questions of its compatibility with the constitutional framework.

637 Constitutional Court of the Republic of Slovenia, Ruling No. Up-211/04-21.

The reason for this legal definition of the longest possible absence is rooted in the Constitutional Court's decision U-I-246/02 which, in the explanatory text, dictates that apart from the vague requirement of actual permanent residence in Slovenia, the legislature must also determine the "period of absence after which the requirement of actual residence is no longer met".[638] Determining such a timeframe is inherently arbitrary and it enables the introduction of new requirements which could prevent erased persons from regaining their unlawfully annulled legal status. The time span of a person's absence from Slovenia is irrelevant. What really matters is the *reason* for the absence and its prolongation. As most absences were a consequence of the erasure and its effects (only a few people left Slovenia of their own will before the erasure without de-registering their permanent residences, but they are also technically considered erased persons), long-term absences are a direct effect of the inability of the state to resolve the problem quickly. It was not until 1999, or even 2003 that the problem of the erasure was brought to the public eye (the first decision of the Constitutional Court barely had an impact on the public, while the 2003 decision remained unimplemented for many years). During that time, erased people who could not prove their actual residence in Slovenia had very little chance of legally returning to the country and acquiring legal status. They could not acquire legal status as erased persons, but they could do it accordance with the Aliens Act if they met the requirements therein. In other words, once a person moved away from Slovenia, the absence lasted for a long time, with the duration depending on individual circumstances and the legal options for securing legal status in Slovenia. Therefore, the legislature is not free to set the maximum length of absence at its own discretion, but must abide by the doctrine of the rule of law which prohibits arbitrary legal requirements; the latter need to be clearly explained, and the explanation is only possible if the requirements are logical and set with a legitimate goal in mind.

Other explanations can be used to resolve a legal dilemma, for instance a teleological, or *intra legem* argument. The purpose of the law is to implement the Constitutional Court's decision and to enable all of the erased persons to reacquire the legal status that they were unlawfully denied. The law sets the conditions that a person must satisfy in order to be eligible for a legal status, even in cases where the person was absent from Slovenia. Since an absence can exceed ten years, a limit of ten years as a maximum possible absence would raise doubts

638 Constitutional Court of the Republic of Slovenia, Ruling No. U-I-246/02, paragraph 30.

about the rationality of the law, since it would prevent many of the intended beneficiaries from securing legal status. The only interpretation that could comply with the constitution is that this requirement should be ignored. The requirement that persons claiming a justified absence of five to ten years must prove that they have attempted to return to the country is also irrelevant to the core purpose of the law. This requirement, which is extremely difficult to meet, has no connection to the realities of the situation or to the core intent of the law, which is to enable erased persons to acquire legal status regardless of whether or not they have attempted to return. This interpretation could be followed when issuing residence permits. If the Ministry of Internal Affairs or the Administrative or the Supreme Court had doubts about the correctness of the interpretation, they could abort the process and ask the Constitutional Court to assess the constitutionality of the aforementioned requirement.[639]

For those who would be allowed to exceed the longest possible period of absence, the law includes a few positive solutions: (1) it correctly defines eligible persons as persons (the law uses the word foreigner) who, on 25 June 1991, were *citizens of other republics of the SFRY* and not citizens of other SFRY successor states,[640] (2) it provides a legal basis for issuing special declaratory decisions to persons who will be issued a residence permit in the future, in accordance with the 2010 amendments to the Legal Status Act or Aliens Act (Article 1), and (3) it regulates the legal status of erased persons' children born in Slovenia, and the special declaratory decisions to be issued to them (Article 1.a).

The law also identifies the legal basis for issuing special declaratory decisions to those erased persons who were granted Slovenian citizenship without first acquiring a permanent residence permit (Article 1.d). The decisions could be issued on the basis of point 8 of the Constitutional Court's decision, following the *a minore ad maius* doctrine, but the legislature decided to include a clarification of the legal grounding in the law. In this instance, once again, legal positivism dominated over classical legal argumentation and pushed the solution to the erasure to formalistic extremes.

---

639 Judging by the letter sent to the Minister of the Interior, on the topic No. 2140-88/2007/41 (121–06), this position was also taken by former Slovenian Constitutional Court judge Matevž Krivic.

640 The Constitutional Court decided that this change was "actually necessary, since the law now includes the persons who were formerly citizens of other SFRY republics and are now possibly citizens of another, non-successor states, or stateless. Even though this change is not reflected in the title of the amendments to the Legal Status Act, the legal clarity remains intact".

The eliminatory clauses are no more restrictive than those applicable to foreigners in accordance with Article 3 of the Aliens Act. Applications could be submitted within three years of the implementation of the law, while applications for children can be submitted at any point before the child's 21st birthday, if it falls outside of the three-year deadline (Article 8),[641] which is an unusually extensive timeframe. Naturally, such a timeframe is only reasonable if the passage of the law is accompanied by a campaign informing the public of the new legal possibilities, and by a proactive search for potential beneficiaries, which did not occur in this case. It would probably be best not to set a deadline at all. In any case, the law provided the possibility of applying for legal status nearly twenty years after the erasure, which was positive since there were still persons living in Slovenia without legal status, and persons who wished to return to Slovenia after a lengthy absence.

Apart from the aforementioned problems, the amendments to the Legal Status Act are also problematic because the state still refuses to accept its responsibility for the erasure. Instead, the burden of regaining their status is placed on the shoulders of the erased people. The process is long and arduous and it involves considerable expenses in terms of both time and money. Moreover, many applications are still rejected, raising doubts as to whether the law truly serves its purpose, which is to fulfil the constitutional obligation and redress the human rights violations.

3.3 The meaning of the special declaratory decisions

The special declaratory decisions, issued to erased persons with the intent of retroactively recognising their permanent residence permits, are unique in the Slovenian legal system. The legal system only recognises permanent residence permits issued to foreigners with a prospective constitutive effect, while the special declaratory decisions have a declarative, retroactive effect. However, this does not mean that they are not in accordance with the legal system. They address a specific legal situation that is not comparable to the circumstances of any other

641 Regarding the listed decisions, the Constitutional Court determined that while it is not a case of direct removal of unconstitutional elements, as the scope of the law is wider than that required by the Constitutional Court, the law is tackling questions which are "closely connected" with the unconstitutional elements and that tackling of these questions serves to prevent new unconstitutionalities. The Constitutional Court further concluded that the legislature "responded to unconstitutional circumstances in accordance with the constitution". Constitutional Court of the Republic of Slovenia, Decision No. U-II-1/10-19, paragraphs 39 and 40.

group in Slovenia. The special declaratory decisions are a form of reparations with legal, moral, and material effects.

3.3.1 *Legal effects*

The legal effects of the special decisions are reflected in their name; they

> do not constitute a new legal status for the affected persons, but take into account the existing situation to determine the legal status which already existed and should have existed according to the law. [...] The declaratory decisions take legal effect from the day the facts important for the establishment of a legal relationship (*ex tunc*) occurred, so their retroactive effect arises from the specific situation in which a legal relationship which has been formed prior to the issuing of the declaratory decision is determined. Due to the nature of the situation, a permanent residence permit granted to a citizen of another republic who was erased from the register of permanent residence only means that their legal status, or permanent resident permit, is recognized and not established anew.[642]

In decision U-II-1/10-19, the Constitutional Court also explained that the use of a declarative retroactive decision to issue a permanent residence permit to persons who had not actually resided in Slovenia because they were expelled or left because of reasons related to the erasure, is an instance of a legal fiction,[643] a legal fact that is assumed to be true, although it is known not to exist.[644] In this case, the legal fiction consists in issuing a permanent residence permit from the day of the erasure to the day the permit was issued, while recognising a fictitious registration of residence during the same period at the address that was registered at the time of the erasure.[645]

The Constitutional Court concluded that the unconstitutional elements could be remedied in only one way: by issuing permanent residence permits. If the person did not actually reside in Slovenia, the situation can only be resolved retroactively through the use of a legal fiction.[646] As a consequence, the special declaratory decision has two different retroactive effects, which lead to the same legal result. Regarding erased persons who resided in Slovenia from the erasure

---

642 The Constitutional Court of the Republic of Slovenia, Ruling No. U-I-246/02, paragraph 19.
643 The Constitutional Court of the Republic of Slovenia, Ruling No. U-II-1/10-19, paragraph 26.
644 Pavčnik, Teorija prava, 1997, p. 292.
645 Article 1 (2) of the Legal Status Act.
646 The Constitutional Court of the Republic of Slovenia, Ruling No. U-II-1/10-19, paragraph 30.

onwards, the decision establishes the existing situation (it equates the legal situation with the actual situation). Regarding erased persons who did not reside in Slovenia from the erasure onwards, the decision creates a legal fiction, that is to say, it assumes that they lived in Slovenia, although it is known that they did not.[647] The use of a legal fiction, a clearly artificial solution that does not reflect the actual situation, is a consequence of the fact that the problem was repeatedly tackled the wrong way by setting actual residence in the country as a basic requirement. If this requirement was not at the core of the process from the very beginning, and if the wrongdoings of the state were rectified in a way that included compensation for damages rather than just reinstating the status of erased people, there would be no need for a legal fiction.

3.3.2 Moral effects

The moral effects of the special declaratory decisions are closely related to their legal effects, and cannot be entirely separated from their material effects. Regarding the retroactive issuing of permanent residence permits, the Constitutional Court concluded that it is a matter of "moral satisfaction as a special form of removing the consequences of a human rights violation stemming from the erasure".[648] This is not controversial, as the issuing of special declaratory decisions is a form of remedy for the breach of human rights.

The moral effects of the decisions are evident, but we must be cautious not to overemphasise them. The question of whether or not such a moral remedy is sufficient is important because erased persons as a group are still stigmatised by the general public and considered responsible for their situation, although it is clear that the blame does not lie with them. Moral satisfaction cannot be provided by issuing, after a lengthy procedure (sometimes reminiscent of a struggle), a residence permit and a decision with no practical public effect. More should be done for moral reparations. Apart from passing more suitable legislation and additional regulations, the possibility of a public apology on the national level should be considered, for instance by passing a resolution in the National Assembly supported by the other branches of government.

Moreover, the material and immaterial damage caused by the erasure is not compensated by issuing a special decision and establishing that a person had the

647 *Cf.* Independent opinion of Judge Jadranka Sovdat on the Constitutional Court's Ruling No. U-II-1/10-19, paragraph 13.

648 Constitutional Court of the Republic of Slovenia, Ruling No. U-II-1/10-19, paragraph 43.

right to permanent residence from the erasure on. The question is whether the "moral satisfaction" provided meets the requirement of Article 15 of the Constitution, which states that the violations of human rights must be redressed. According to the practice of constitutional law, this provision demands that the state that existed prior to the violation be reinstated. If this is not possible due to the nature of the situation, the affected person has the right to reparations for the damages caused by the unlawful actions of the administrative bodies, as stated in Article 26, Para 1 of the Constitution.[649] The moral satisfaction derived from a special declaratory decision could serve the purpose of reinstating the state that existed prior to the violation of human rights, but since most of the erased people suffered additional damages caused by the revocation of their status, the decision on its own is insufficient, as confirmed by the ECHR in the case of *Kurić and Others v Slovenia.*

3.3.3 *Material effects*

Regarding the need to issue special declaratory decisions, the Constitutional Court insisted that one of the reasons why they were issued was to enable erased people to prove that they had resided in Slovenia since the erasure when exercising their material rights. So, for example, decision Up-333/96 gives the appellant the right to obtain a driving license in Slovenia, Up-336/98 recognises the right to income support, and Up-20/97 and Up-152/97 recognise the right to a military pension.[650] In the opinion of the Constitutional Court, persons who were forcibly removed from Slovenia were prevented from exercising their material rights, although most of the erased persons living in Slovenia did not assert their rights either, as very few were aware of the available legal remedies (including a constitutional appeal).

In decision U-I-246/02, the Constitutional Court expressed its stance on the retroactive exercise of material rights. Decision U-II-1/10-19 further elaborated the issue but also convoluted it to a certain extent. First of all, it again stressed that a legal fiction was needed "to enable foreigners with permanent residence permits in Slovenia to possibly exercise their rights in the Republic of Slovenia".[651] Nevertheless, the legal fiction cannot have other legal consequences and "it cannot,

649 Šturm (ed.), Komentar Ustave Republike Slovenije, 2010, p. 202.

650 The Constitutional Court of the Republic of Slovenia, Ruling No. U-II-1/10-19, paragraph 22.

651 *Ibid.*, paragraph 26.

retroactively, institute a legal relationship which could have potentially existed had the erasure from the register of permanent residents not occurred".[652]

The meaning of this stance can most easily be illustrated with concrete examples. A person who worked for ten years in Slovenia and had his/her legal status revoked, who could not support himself/herself through no fault of his/her own, should, according to Article 25 of the Social Security Act 1992[653], be eligible to receive income support.[654] With the special declaratory decision, which created a legal fiction of permanent residence in Slovenia from the erasure onwards, the person would have grounds to retroactively assert this right, as it is dependent on permanent residence. Based on the Constitutional Court's decisions, the centre for social work could recognise the person's right to the benefit retroactively. If the public authority failed to do so, the person would be eligible to compensation in accordance with tort law and the law on redressing the injustices that the state must pass due to the ECHR decision.

It is not clear if this stance confirms the intent of the special decision explained in the Constitutional Court's decision U/II-1/10-19. There, the Court warned that the special declaratory decisions cannot serve as a basis for "new claims arising from various rights, unless they serve to prove actual residence in the Republic of Slovenia in future proceedings". Does this mean that the special decision can be used only to assert one's rights prospectively?

According to the Constitutional Court's explanation, the special decisions do not encroach on the legislative decisions of the public authorities regarding the individual rights arising from permanent residence. It was possible to challenge these using other legal remedies at the time. As the Court stated, "there were legal remedies available (including constitutional appeal) to counter administrative decisions, and, as evident from the Constitutional Court's decisions [...], individuals who made use of these remedies were able to protect their rights and legal interests".[655] This statement lends itself to an alternate interpretation if we take

652 *Ibid.*, paragraph 30.

653 Social Security Act, Official Gazette of the Republic of Slovenia, No. 54/1992.

654 Employment and Work of Aliens Act, Official Gazette of the Republic of Slovenia, No. 33/1992.

655 The Constitutional Court of the Republic of Slovenia, decision No. U-II-1/10-19, paragraph 30. It should be noted that in this decision, which primarily dealt with the referendum, the Constitutional Court also expressed its opinion on questions that were not posed, nor were they especially relevant to the topic in question. It is a case of *obiter dictum* stance – a stance in the explanatory text that could be omitted, as it does not form the basis for the main decision. The courts are not formally bound

the other positions of the Constitutional Court into account. New rights cannot be constituted and exercised, meaning that, for instance, a person could not exercise the right to enter an employment contract retroactively. On the other hand, the rights that a person already had by virtue of being a permanent resident, for instance income support, can be asserted retroactively.

According to the Constitutional Court's stance on the matter, there is a clear distinction between (1) individuals who used legal remedies and succeeded (for instance in decision No. Up-333/97), (2) individuals who claimed a certain right but whose application was rejected, and who either did not challenge the decision or challenged it unsuccessfully, and (3) individuals who did not claim any rights because they thought that they did not meet the requirements. Judging by the Constitutional Court's stance, it is reasonable to assume that the second group cannot do anything to alter the state of affairs, but it is not clear what the third group could do, although based on previous, related opinions one can assume that these rights can still be asserted.

We can assume that the three groups listed above are now in very different situations. The aforementioned distinction implicitly established by the Constitutional Court is questionable, as it does not take into account the differences between individuals who do not have equal possibilities to make use of legal remedies. This path was inaccessible to a large number of erased persons, which is evident from the very small number of constitutional appeals that involved claims to material rights. This is an additional reason why it was necessary to pass a law to rectify both the material and immaterial wrongs suffered by the erased people without treating them differently. The decision of the European Court of Human Rights made it more probable that such a law would be passed.

4. The Role of State Officials in the Implementation of the Constitutional Court's Decision

The Constitutional Court's decision U-I-246/02 remained unimplemented for seven years, which is a serious breach of Article 2 of the Constitution and, according to the European Court of Human Rights, a breach of Article 13 of the European Convention on Human Rights and Fundamental Freedoms (which protects the right to efficient legal remedies). This period of non-implementation is a consequence of the (lack of) action on the part of different state actors. Of

to this type of opinions, but the opinions are still important and cannot easily be revoked by the courts. Krivic, Ustavno sodišče: pristojnosti in postopek, in: Ustavno sodstvo, 2000, pp. 201–202.

these, the actions of the political elite, prominent representatives of governmental institutions and academics were the most visible publicly. In an attempt to block the decision, the political elite made use of various mechanisms including the referendum, while also launching an uninformed and sweeping campaign to prejudice the public against the erased persons. In so doing, they were supported by legal experts who put their expertise in the service of politics, making a number of legal mistakes in the process. Administrators, particularly in the Ministry of the Interior, also played an important role, but their actions were largely invisible in the public arena, where they were represented by other political actors.

I have already written about the role the civil servants played in the erasure in Part IV of the book. These same administrators – often the same individuals who were employed at a particular public body for decades or who moved from the local councils to the ministries – participated in drafting the solutions demanded by the Constitutional Court. Although the majority of the Constitutional Court's decisions targeted the legislature (except for point 8, which singles out the Ministry of the Interior), it was clear that the laws resulting from the Constitutional Court's decision would be proposed by the government, not by MPs or citizens. This in turn meant that the law was to be drafted by the public administrators at the Ministry of the Interior. In other words, the administrators at the Ministry were ordered to draft the law which was to set right their own wrongdoings from a decade or two earlier.

Given the public response of the civil servants to the Constitutional Court's decision,[656] it would be misguided to expect that the task could be carried out without obstruction. Indeed, the proposal met with internal opposition; the administrators rebelled when the leadership of the Ministry wanted to draft a solution with which they disagreed. According to Mirko Pečarič, public policy is formulated by anonymous public servants irrespective of the leadership of a particular ministry,[657] and the search for a solution to the erasure was no different in this respect.

The comparison of individual draft laws intended to implement the Constitutional Court's decision shows that they all include variations on very similar solutions (certain ministries, seeking a more restrictive solution to the question,

656 For instance, the article published in the newsletter "Okno uprave", with the title Erased on 28 March 2003. This article shows that the civil servants still fully denied responsibility for the unlawfulness of the erasure, and continued to fully agree with the measures of erasure, in spite of the Constitutional Court decisions.

657 Pečarič, Uradništvo med formalnim in neformalnim vplivom na politiko in državljane, 2008, p. 21.

drafted stricter regulations), all "contributed" to by the administrators. This leads to a situation where the leadership of a ministry intent on carrying out a project or a reform that is incompatible with the administrators' wishes cannot rely on the latter's obedience, as it risks that the project will be blocked. Civil servants can be very successful in obstructing a project, as the public administration is increasingly more knowledgeable (it does not change with the government), so it cannot easily be controlled by a minister or his cabinet. Pečarič warns that in cases like these, "bureaucratic sabotage" is common. Obstruction does not take the form of open opposition to the proposal, but the administrators use complex expert arguments that cannot easily be dismissed by the ministers or their cabinet to reduce a proposal to what they see as "reasonable", so that radical political plans lose their edge and become more conservative.[658] Bureaucratic sabotage can vary from very innocent small actions to the complete impediment of a project. "The most serious example of bureaucratic sabotage happens when a large number of administrators act collectively in order to neutralise governmental policy".[659] The implementation of the Constitutional Court's decision was a middle-of-the-road situation; the implementation of the regulations was overseen by the Ministry alone, so the rebellion was restricted to the administrators employed at the Ministry of Internal Affairs. The leadership of the ministry was able to avoid bureaucratic sabotage by relying on external consultants.

5. Social and Cultural Constraints on How the Courts Influence Social Change

Considering the response of the public to the Constitutional Court's decision, it is reasonable to assume that the predominant public opinion on the (un)lawfulness and (un)reasonableness of the erasure was very different from that of the Constitutional Court. Moreover, the opinion held by a large portion of the political elite diverged even further from that of the Constitutional Court. At times, it appeared that only a few individuals and human rights organisations agreed with the decision. The Constitutional Court's decision on the erasure revisited a question that the authorities, the public, and the political elites had tried to suppress. Its demand to redress the injustices brought to light a fundamental dilemma: whether the Court is capable of initiating social change with its decisions, and whether its decisions could bring the public to change its opinion and redress the injustices caused by the erasure.

---

658 *Ibid.*
659 *Ibid.*

There are two ways one can approach this question. On the one hand, the courts can be seen as vital agents of social change, especially when a change does not come on its own or when it is opposed by another branch of government (*dynamic court view*). On the other hand, the courts can be seen as weak actors who lack the financial and coercive means to initiate social change, and are only capable of determining unlawfulness and unconstitutionalities (*constraint court view*).[660]

Drawing on his theoretical analysis, Rosenberg showed that this is a reductive binary. He describes the constraints that prevent the courts from bringing about social change, and the requirements that have to be met to overcome these constraints and to initiate social change.[661] His theory is consistent with the finding in various post-conflict countries that passing a sentence on a war criminal will not help the public face the facts and achieve justice and reconciliation. The concept of transitional justice originates in these circumstances.

Rosenberg tested his theory on several landmark cases in the history of the US Supreme Court, for instance the ban on racial segregation in schools (*Brown v. Board of Education*). The systemic decisions of the Constitutional Court on the topic of the erasure are the Slovenian counterparts of these cases.

The hypothesis that the courts are constrained in their power to bring about social change is rooted in three obstacles: (1) the limited nature of the rights protected by the Constitution, (2) the lack of judicial independence and (3) the inability of the judiciary to develop appropriate policies and its lack of powers to implement them.[662]

The limited nature of constitutionally protected rights prevents the courts from processing a whole array of important demands for social change, as some demands simply cannot be analysed in a constitutional context.[663] Even in the case of the erasure, a great deal depended on the wording of the applications. The Constitution and international law do not protect the right to citizenship nor the right to permanent residence (only the right to the freedom of movement in Article 32 of the Constitution, which could serve as a basis from which the right to permanent residence could be derived). In both key proceedings on the topic of unconstitutionality, erased persons were successful in asserting the constitutional principles of protecting legitimate expectations and equality before the law (at the European Court of Human Rights, they were successful in claiming a

660 Rosenberg, The Hollow Hope, 1991, p. 3.
661 *Ibid.*, p. 10.
662 *Ibid.*
663 *Ibid.*, p. 13.

breach of the right to privacy and family life, the right to efficient legal remedies and the right not to be discriminated against), meaning that the first constraint was not relevant to this case.

The second constraint that can prevent courts from initiating social change is the lack of judicial independence from the other branches of government. An independent judiciary, in this context, primarily means the ability of the court to make decisions that diverge from dominant public opinion.[664] Regarding the erased persons, the ordinary courts were not capable of such independence. They fully abided by the unconstitutional legislation apparently without ever harbouring a hint of doubt, or else they would have invoked the constitutional provisions or suspended the proceedings and referred the Aliens Act to the Constitutional Court for assessment. The Constitutional Court, on the other hand, demonstrated a firm moral standing and the ability to assess the legislation impartially, independent of the dominant public opinion and the stances taken by the authorities and the administrators. Thus, the second constraint that could have made it difficult for the Constitutional Court to initiate social change did not apply either.

Rosenberg's third constraint is the inability of the courts to develop appropriate policies and assure their implementation, particularly when a decision calls for the involvement of other actors, for example the executive and the legislative branch of government. Rosenberg argues that there is not much that courts can do if their decisions are ignored by the government.[665] This was certainly true of the 2003 Constitutional Court decision. The same holds true for the implementation of the Constitutional Court's decision on the erasure, which was almost completely dependent on the government as the proposer of the law, the parliament as the legislative branch and, in the case of point 8 of Decision U-I-246/02, on the Ministry of the Interior. In the case of decision U-I-246/02, the third constraint rendered the Constitutional Court incapable of initiating social change (i.e. of reinstating the legal status of erased people). The same obstacle also halted the implementation of decision U-I-284/94, the legislative and the executive branches refused to act. Nevertheless, the obstacle was ultimately overcome, since the government and the National Assembly eventually implemented the decision, even though it required much more decisive action and a greater degree of change in public opinion than the 2003 decision. What are the reasons for this?

664 *Ibid.*
665 *Ibid.*, p. 19. and 21.

1. Decision of the Constitutional Court U-I-284/94			
Constraints preventing social change		**Requirements that courts have to satisfy in order to initiate social change**	
1. Limited array of Constitutional rights.	×	1. Other actors provide incentives to introduce compliance with judicial decisions.	✓
2. The lack of independent judges.	×	2. Unwillingness to implement a decision incurs high costs which induce relevant actors to take action.	×
3. The inability of the courts to create and implement policies.	✓	3. Judicial decisions are implemented by the market.	×
		4. Judicial decisions serve as a protection or excuse for persons who are crucial for implementation and willing to act.	×

The reason is that in 1999, one of the political requirements needed to overcome the third constraint and implement the decision of the Constitutional Court was met, although the decision did not correspond to the dominant public and political opinion.

According to Rosenberg, there are four requirements of which at least one must be met if the third obstacle is to be overcome. These are as follows: 1) other actors provide incentives that are intended to ensure respect for judicial decisions; 2) the refusal to implement a decision incurs high costs which in turn prompts relevant actors to take action and implement the decision; 3) decisions are implemented by the market; 4) relevant actors use the court's decisions as an excuse or cover to take action. In the case of Slovenia, in 1999 one of these requirements was indeed met.[666]

The Constitutional Court's decision U-I-284/94 from 1999 was implemented before the deadline set by the Constitutional Court thanks to the EU accession negotiations. In other words, the actor that provided the incentive to implement the decision was the European Commission, which included the problem of the erasure when negotiating Slovenia's accession to the EU.[667]

666 *Ibid.*, pp. 33–35.

667 Regular reports of the European Commission on the progress of Slovenia in entering the EU, between 1998 and 2002, available at: www.svrez.gov.si/si/zakonodaja_in_dokumenti/eu_dokumenti/redna_porocila_evropske_komisije_o_napredku_slovenije_pri_vkljucevanju_v_evropsko_unijo/ (20 January 2010).

2. Decision of the Constitutional Court U-I-246/02			
Constraints preventing social change		**Requirements that courts have to satisfy in order to initiate social change**	
1. Limited array of Constitutional rights.	×	1. Other actors provide incentives to induce compliance with judicial decisions.	✓
2. The lack of independent judges.	×	2. Unwillingness to implement a decision incurs high costs which induce relevant actors to take action.	×
3. The inability of the courts to create and implement policies.	✓	3. Judicial decisions are implemented by the market.	×
		4. Judicial decisions serve as a protection or excuse for persons who are crucial to implementation and willing to act.	×

Four years later, when Decision U-I-246/02 was issued, there was no similar incentive. Even though Slovenia was not yet an EU member state, the question of persons without legal status was closed[668] and the country's accession to the EU was almost certain. Since the other three requirements were not met either, the constitutional decision remained unimplemented, rendering the Constitutional Court incapable of initiating social change. It took seven years for circumstances to change and the above-mentioned requirements to be met. After the 2008 elections, when a new Minister of Internal Affairs was named, the Ministry made the implementation of the Constitutional Court's decision one of its primary tasks. The fourth requirement was met: Minister Katarina Kresal and the Secretary of State, Goran Klemenčič, used the decision as cover to draft appropriate regulations.

Both examples – the implementation of the 1999 and the 2003 decision – confirm Rosenberg's theory that "without the presence of at least one of the conditions, court decisions will not produce significant social reform". At the same time, social change can easily be incited if the impediments are overcome and at least one of the four conditions is met.[669]

668 The complete report of the European Commission on the country's progress from 2003 no longer mentions the question of persons without legal status.

669 Rosenberg, The Hollow Hope, 1991, p. 35.

Would social changes in Slovenia have occurred without the Constitutional Court's decision?[670] As in the 1954 case of *Brown v Board of Education,* in which the Supreme Court of the United States ordered the racial desegregation of schools, the Constitutional Court's decisions on the erasure uncovered breaches of constitutionality and legality, kept the issue high on the public agenda, helped change public opinion about the erasure and forced the government and the National Assembly to act.[671] Much like in the US, where the Civil Rights Act of 1964, the Voting Rights Act of 1965 and the Housing Act of 1968 would not have been passed without the Supreme Court's decision,[672] the erasure would not have been resolved to the degree that it was without the Constitutional Court's decision of 2003.

In both cases, a number of years (ten in the USA, seven to eleven in Slovenia) went by before the judicial decision was implemented by the passage of a relevant law. This shows that if courts alone incited social reform, it would occur much sooner than in these examples.[673]

In the USA, very little activity to ensure the implementation of the Supreme Court's decision took place before 1964. It was only in 1963 that President John F. Kennedy sent federal troops to the University of Mississippi to ensure that black students could attend classes. At that point, nine years had passed since the Supreme Court issued its decision and the legislation that formally equated the rights of all citizens regardless of race had yet to be passed. Much as in the case of the erasure, the government and the legislature had to actively intervene for desegregation to take place.[674] The glorification of the role played by the Constitutional and Supreme Courts and the presentation of these courts as strong actors who incite social change (in accordance with the *dynamic court view*) can be misleading. The courts could not have produced a direct impact without additional activity on the part of the other branches of government (as the *constraint court view* predicts), at least in the analysed settings.[675] In cases like these, judicial decisions are an important, but by no means the only agent of social change.

---

670 *Ibid.*, p. 8.
671 *Ibid.*, p. 41.
672 *Ibid.*
673 *Ibid.*, p. 49.
674 *Ibid.*, pp. 55–56.
675 *Ibid.*, p. 70.

6. The Principle of Ensuring Respect for the Constitutional Court's Decisions

The implementability of the Constitutional Court's decisions depends on the "legal and political consciousness of the representatives of the other branches and types (legal and political) of government".[676] Since court decisions, particularly declaratory decisions, cannot guarantee their own implementation, various theories have evolved on the characteristics that constitutional decisions should have in order to maximise the probability of being implemented. This goal can be achieved by exercising judicial self-restraint, by abstaining from politics, and by constant care to ensure that the court does not exceed its prerogative.[677] Alternatively, it can also be achieved by raising the general political and legal culture in the country, ensuring the quality and persuasiveness of constitutional decisions,[678] or ensuring that the contents of these decisions are aligned with legitimate public interests,[679] as the probability of a decision being implemented is negatively correlated with the controversy surrounding it. Legal correctness, reliability, and the legitimacy of the constitutional decisions increase the authority of the Constitutional Court and, in turn, the probability of its decisions being implemented.

Does the fact that the Constitutional Court's decisions must be based in the public interest mean they have to be aligned with what Cerar termed the "value system" of a community? In most cases, the answer is yes, except when the Constitutional Court is forced to act as a *correcteur* of the democracy of the "masses".[680] The erasure was such a situation, similar to that of other minority groups.[681] However, the public reaction showed that the Court's decisions were

---

676 Cerar, (Ne)političnost ustavnega sodstva, in: Ustavno sodstvo, 2000, p. 362.

677 Šinkovec, Samoomejevanje ustavnih sodišč, in: Dnevi javnega prava, 1998. Šturm, Vloga ustavnega sodstva v sistemu delitve oblasti in oblike za ustavnosodno presojo aktov zakonodajne oblasti, in: Dnevi javnega prava, 1998, p. 214. Cerar, Slovensko ustavno sodišče – med pravom in politiko, in: Dnevi javnega prava, 1998, p 118.

678 *Cf.* Teršek, Legitimnost kot prvina političnih in pravnih konceptov sodobne ustavne demokracije, 2008, p. 266.

679 *Cf.* Pavčnik, Pravni in ustavni temelji prava, in: Ustavno sodstvo, 2000, p. 422.

680 Cerar, (Ne)političnost ustavnega sodstva, in: Ustavno sodstvo, 2000, p. 373.

681 The protection of the constitutional rights of minorities is a generally recognised and unquestionable task of the Constitutional Court. Nevertheless, a due measure of caution is in order so that the Constitutional Court does not encroach on the constitutional authorities of the legislature. Krivic, V sistemu deljene oblasti ni najvišjega organa, a paper written for the Days of Public Law, 2011, un-published.

not in accordance with the "value system" of the community. The public largely failed to perceive the essential meaning of constitutional decisions that were undoubtedly passed with the interests of the public in mind, as they were striving for equality and the protection of legal expectations, principles that bear on all of us. Nevertheless, the public challenged the authority of the Constitutional Court through populism, generalisations and the stigmatisation of erased people. It is not always possible to act in alignment with the dominant system of values. If it was possible, the Constitutional Court would not be needed at all, it would not have to decide on such a wide array of questions, or it would make decisions by consensus.[682] The Constitutional Court often has to make decisions that are contrary to dominant social opinions, which is indeed the essence of constitutional democracy – the core constitutional values dominate over the decisions of a parliamentary or referendum majority.[683]

7. The Meaning of the ECHR *Kurić and Others v. Slovenia* Case for Constitutional Democracy

The often-mentioned decision of the European Court of Human Rights in the case of *Kurić and Others v Slovenia* resulted from an appeal filed on 4 July 2006 by eleven erased residents of Slovenia (one passed away in the course of the proceedings). The appeal includes a detailed account of the erasure and descriptions of the individual legal and material situations of the appellants. The appellants claimed that their rights had been violated by the erasure and that the state was unwilling to redress this in a satisfactory manner.[684] On 31 May 2007, the ECHR overturned part of the appeal on procedural grounds, but the breach of four articles of the Convention (Articles 8, 13 and 14 of the European Convention on Human Rights and article 1 of the first Protocol) came under consideration.

On 13 July 2010, the Chamber of seven judges decided that Slovenia's failure to implement the Constitutional Court's decisions was a breach of Articles 8 and

682 Teršek, Legitimnost kot prvina političnih in pravnih konceptov sodobne ustavne demokracije, 2008, p. 267.

683 Ribičič, Človekove pravice in ustavna demokracija, 2011, p. 111.

684 The appellants argued that the state was in breach of the following articles of the convention: Article 2 (the right to life), Article 3 (the prohibition of torture), Article 4 (the prohibition of slavery and forced labour), paragraph 1, Article 6 (the right to fair trial), Article 8 (to right to private and family life), Article 13 (the right to effective legal remedies), Article 14 (the prohibition of discrimination) and Article 1 of Protocol 1 (the right to property).

13 of the Convention. The state was ordered to pass appropriate general and individual regulations to rectify the situation. The Court recognised that eight of the appellants had had their rights violated. It rejected two appeals as the appellants' right to permanent residence in Slovenia had already been recognised retroactively, and they were no longer considered victims of the erasure.

This was only a partial victory, as the Court's view was that the return of legal status was sufficient reparation for the past misconduct of the state. The appellants appealed against the part of the decision that rejected two appellants. The state also appealed against the decision as a whole (to its detriment as it turned out, much like in other proceedings before the ECHR in the past), claiming that the Constitutional Court's decision had been implemented by the amendments to the Legal Status Act.

As the proceedings continued, the state granted the six remaining appellants permanent resident permits in an attempt to eliminate their status as victims. For some of them, this was the end of a procedure that had lasted several years. One of the appellants, for instance, won the administrative conflict against the Ministry of the Interior twice before securing a permanent residence permit, while another succeeded only after the matter was brought before the Constitutional Court, which upheld the appeal and passed the matter back to the Ministry. Regarding the victim status, the state relied heavily on past cases against Latvia, in which the state offered to reinstate the legal status of the appellants (as a general rather than an individual option), which the Court considered to be sufficient reparation.[685]

On 26 June 2012, the Grand Chamber of the ECHR passed a new landmark decision, which identified a breach of the right not to be discriminated against (Article 14 of the Convention) in addition to the breaches of the right to the protection of privacy and family life (Article 8 of the Convention) and the right to effective legal remedies (Article 14 of the Convention). Six appellants were granted reparations for immaterial damages, to be paid within three months of the ruling; the payment was indeed effected on 14 September 2012. Reparation for material damages was to be settled after the three-month period, to accommodate potential agreements between the state and the appellants. In the pilot judgment procedure, the Court ordered the state to prepare a reparation scheme for all erased persons.

685 ECHR, *Shevanova v Latvia*, Application No. 58822/00, decision of 7 December 2007, paragraphs 46–50.

The ruling is a pilot judgment,[686] meaning that the Court identified structural problems in the Slovenian legal system that led to the situation and could give rise to thousands of similar appeals. The pilot judgment is a special procedure that the ECHR uses when a large number of similar appeals arise from the same systemic problem.[687] The procedure was created on the recommendation of the Council of Ministers on 12 May 2004.[688] The court first determines that the Convention was violated in a particular case, identifies the shortcomings of the national legislation that may have led to the violation, and instructs the member state on how to correct the shortcomings and create a national system for processing similar cases in the future. The intent of the pilot judgment procedure is to help the member states remove structural weaknesses that bring about legal actions with the same content.[689] The legal basis for the implementation of a pilot judgment procedure is Article 45 of the Convention, which states that the signatory states are obliged to respect the ECHR decisions. According to a new interpretation of this article, the signatory states are also required to identify and remove the structural problem that causes the legal breach. The first and the most renowned pilot judgment was issued by the ECHR in *Broniowski v Poland*,[690] which dealt with the right to compensation for revoked property rights.[691] In the Slovenian context, *Lukenda v Slovenia* is a relevant decision,[692] where the ruling was brought by the Chamber of seven judges rather than the Grand Chamber, as is more common in the pilot judgment procedures.[693]

Procedural questions are important for a ruling. The ECHR identified a breach of Articles 8, 13 and 14 of the Convention only in the case of six out of ten appellants. Two appeals were rejected as the appellants failed to satisfy the criteria for victim status, while another two were rejected as the appellants failed to exhaust all legal remedies available on the national level.

686 Ribičič, Evropsko pravo človekovih pravic, 2007, p. 122.

687 Lazarova Trajkovska, Pilot Judgments Procedure before the European Court of Human Rights, 2012, p. 5.

688 *Ibid.*

689 ECHR, The Pilot Judgement Procedure, Information note issued by the ECHR Registrar.

690 Grand Chamber of the ECHR, *Broniowski v Poland*, Application No. 31443/96, decision of 22 June 2004.

691 A summary of *Broniowski* case is available in: Ribičič, European Human Rights Law, 2007, pp. 156–161.

692 ECHR, *Lukenda v Slovenia*, Application No. 23032/02, decision of 6 October 2005.

693 Independent opinion of Judge Zagrebelsky on *Lukenda v Slovenia* ECHR case, Application No. 23032/02 of October 6, 2005.

The first procedural question referring to victim status and, by extension, access to compensation, will already be analysed in the chapter on compensations. The second important procedural question, which led to two failed appeals, is the exhaustion of the available legal remedies on the national level. During the proceedings, the Government kept insisting that the appellants failed to exhaust the available remedies. Among other things, the Government claimed that, as the Constitutional Court's decision was not implemented for seven years, any of the appellants could have filed a constitutional appeal (as some of the other erased persons did) and been re-entered into the register of permanent residents. Moreover, the Government claimed that the appellants could have started an initiative for the reassessment of constitutionality of the laws that they found controversial.[694]

The Grand Chamber determined that the Constitutional Court had already passed the *erga omnes* decisions and that six appellants' legal status was reinstated in lengthy administrative and legal proceedings. The Court emphasised that the constitutional decisions had not been implemented, which damaged the trust in the feasibility of further individual constitutional appeals.[695] The fact that the appellants spent several years in a situation of vulnerability and legal uncertainty was considered an important circumstance.[696] Taking into account the facts of the case, including the general lengthiness of proceedings, the feeling of powerlessness and frustration – a consequence of the prolonged inactivity of the state – the Court decided that the six appellants, who had already been granted permanent residence permits, did not have to file individual constitutional appeals it order to satisfy the requirement of exhausting all possible legal remedies available on the national level.[697] Furthermore, they did not have to demand an abstract reassessment of the controversial legal acts, as this would entail a repetition of past proceedings in the Constitutional Court.[698] Only two out of the ten appellants had not yet obtained permanent residence permits, nor had they tried to obtain them due to difficult living circumstances and a lack of information. The Grand Chamber did not accept their arguments. It decided that since the

694 Response of the Government of the Republic of Slovenia regarding the justifiability of the appeal against the legal action in *Makuc and others v Slovenia* (now *Kurić and others v Slovenia*).

695 Grand Chamber of the ECHR, *Kurić and Others v Slovenia,* Application No. 26828/06 of 26 June 2012, paragraphs 298 and 299.

696 *Ibid.*, Paragraph 302.

697 *Ibid.*, Paragraphs 304 and 305.

698 *Ibid.*, Paragraph 307.

two appellants, in contrast to the other appellants, failed to file an application for permanent residence permits and thus failed to exhaust the available national legal remedies, they showed insufficient interest in their legal status and were rejected.[699] It is evident from the main text that this decision was adopted in a close vote of 9:8. The outvoted judges warned of inconsistencies as a result of the decision in independent opinions: if the Court decided that legal remedies on the national level were insufficient or not available, it should have rejected the state's claim that the two appellants had not exhausted them.[700]

In several parts of the decision, the ECHR followed the decisions of the Constitutional Court in terms of content, which clearly shows the influence of constitutional courts on the practice of the European Courts. The ECHR's decision confirmed the thesis that issuing a permanent residence permit does not, on its own and without additional reparations, meet the requirement of fairness and cannot be sufficient reparation for the damage caused. The Court's instructions to the state to create a reparations scheme for erased people is also important in terms of respect for the Slovenian Constitution, especially articles 26 and 15, which guarantee the right to compensation and to have human rights violations redressed. In the context of the constitutional appeals by erased persons, these articles were not given due weight by the Constitutional Court. The European Court of Human Rights thus made an important contribution to the observance of constitutional principles in Slovenia.

8. The Compensation Scheme

Based on the ECHR pilot judgment, the Republic of Slovenia established a compensation scheme for erased people on 21 November 2013 by passing a Compensation Act.[701] According to this act, only two groups of erased persons are eligible for compensation: first, those erased persons who have already obtained either a permanent residence permit in Slovenia or Slovenian citizenship and second, those who applied for permanent residence or for citizenship before 2010 but were denied. The scope of beneficiaries was criticised as too narrow, as

---

699 *Ibid.*, Paragraphs 289–294.

700 Partially dissenting opinion of judges Bratza, Tulkens, Spielmann, Koval, Kalaydjieva, Vučinić, Rajmondi; paragraph 4.

701 Zakon o povračilu škode osebam, ki so bile izbrisane iz registra stalnega prebivalstva (ZPŠOIRSP), Official Gazette of the Republic of Slovenia, No. 99/13.

it unjustifiably excludes all other erased persons.[702] First, the scope excludes all persons who filed an application for a permanent residence permit and whose applications are still pending, despite the fact that this group also expressed their interest to continue to reside in Slovenia and should be entitled to compensation. Second, the critics stated that the beneficiaries should include all erased persons, as they were all erased unlawfully in the same way, without differentiation according to their individual circumstances, meaning that they all suffered harm as a result of the erasure.[703] Furthermore, differentiating between the persons who managed to obtain a residence permit and those who did not creates a situation in which one group benefits from all possible remedies (i.e., residence permit and compensation), while another group receives no remedy whatsoever.

The Slovenian authorities justified this definition of the scope of beneficiaries by stating that only those erased persons who expressed their interest to continue to reside in Slovenia are eligible for compensation.[704] The authorities were inspired to come up with these criteria by the ECHR *Kurić* judgment, in which the court rejected the claims of two of the applicants who had never filed an application for permanent residence permit in Slovenia. The court concluded they did not exhaust previous domestic remedies available and that they clearly had no interest in continuing to reside in Slovenia.[705] The fact the authorities simply applied this argument to the general compensation scheme in order to limit the scope of beneficiaries is problematic. It needs to be underlined that the two applicants were not granted compensation not because they were not erased, but because they did not exhaust all domestic remedies, which is a procedural and admissibility condition for the application to be substantially examined by ECHR. This procedural requirement has no relation with the national law and should not be a basis for unjustified discriminatory treatment within the community of erased persons. Moreover, the Court held that if the two applicants had in fact submitted an application for permanent residence, they would have been entitled to complain to the European Court about the violation of their rights under the ECHR irrespective of whether their application was accepted or whether they had challenged the negative decision before the domestic court.[706]

702 See Rule 9 submission of the Peace Institute to the Committee of Minister at the Council of Europe, 28 May 2013.

703 *Ibid.*

704 Draft Act on Compensation for Damages for Persons who were Erased from the Register of Permanent Residence, 25 July 2013.

705 ECHR, *Kurić and Others v. Slovenia*, para. 292.

706 *Ibid.*

The second key element of the compensation scheme is the amount of compensation. Under Article 7 of the Compensation Act, each eligible person is entitled to a lump sum of EUR 50 per month of the erasure. The amount of compensation is defined in a simple administrative procedure and does not require the applicants to submit any proof, while the eligibility for compensation is assessed by the administrative office. If the damages exceed the total amount of compensation awarded in the administrative procedure, the applicants may claim additional compensation before the courts, provided that they are able to prove additional damages caused by the erasure. However, the compensation claimed before the courts can in no case exceed twice the amount already awarded by the administrative office, meaning that the total amount cannot exceed EUR 150 per month of the erasure (Article 12). The amount of compensation that an erased person can claim from Slovenia is therefore significantly lower than the amount awarded by the ECHR to the six applicants. The compensation scheme has consequently been criticised as insufficient, inappropriate, and unlikely to pass the scrutiny of the Committee of Ministers, which, however, declared by Resolution CM/ResDH(2016)112 of 25 May 2016 that all the measures required by the ECHR judgment have been adopted and closed the examination of the case.

In addition to the lump sum that can be increased in case of expenditures for medical treatment and schooling, the Compensation Act includes eight additional measures for erased persons. These measures are:

- payment of contributions for mandatory health insurance: non-citizens who only have a permanent residence permit are not eligible for free health insurance, this provision fills this gap for erased persons;
- admittance to and priority treatment in social care programs;
- relief in claiming rights from public resources: compensation does not count towards income in determining eligibility for social assistance and other state benefits;
- state scholarship: non-citizens with a permanent residence permit are not eligible for state scholarships, this measure fills this gap for erased persons;
- equal treatment with citizens of the Republic of Slovenia with respect to housing: non-citizens currently do not have access to public non-profit rental housing, this provisions fills this gap for erased persons;
- access to the educational system: non-citizens currently do not have access to the public educational system free of charge under equal conditions as citizens, this measure fills this gap for the erased persons;

- inclusion and priority treatment in programs of assistance for the integration of foreigners who are not citizens of EU member states, in cultural, economic, and social life in the Republic of Slovenia.

The additional measures can certainly alleviate hardship in the case of individuals in situations when they will be able to make use of them. However, these additional non-monetary measures cannot compensate for the insufficient amount of damages awarded by the law.

Part VI: A Comparison of the Erasure and Exclusion Politics in Other Countries in Times of Succession

He doesn't have long to live now. Just before he dies, he brings together all his experience from all this time into one question which he has still never put to the doorkeeper. [...] 'What is it you want to know now?' asks the doorkeeper, 'You're insatiable'. 'Everyone wants access to the law', says the man, 'how come, over all these years, no-one but me has asked to be let in?'
Franz Kafka, The Trial

1. Introduction

As mentioned briefly in Part III of this book, deprivation of legal status is a common measure used by countries for the purpose of excluding various minorities from the rights and benefits granted to citizens or other persons with a regulated legal status. Generally, depriving minorities of their legal status was a means of dehumanising them, which enabled further and even more serious violations of rights. The German Reich, which deprived Jewish people of their status, is an example of such a state.[707] There are numerous similar examples of minorities losing their legal status in the recent past that occurred in circumstances of state succession. Thus, I examine whether the erasure is a unique measure of its kind in Central and Eastern Europe, and how it is distinct from other, similar measures. I analyse the manner in which the other successor republics of former Yugoslavia (Croatia, Bosnia and Herzegovina, Serbia, Montenegro, and Kosovo) and the newly formed European states which declared independence in the same period as Slovenia (Estonia, Latvia, Lithuania, the Czech Republic, and Slovakia) determined their citizenship policies. All of the countries mentioned here were established as nation-states, imposed different legal conditions and excluded certain groups from the possibility of acquiring the citizenship of the newly formed country. Whether or not they resolved the status of the people who did not acquire citizenship is another story.

707 To see the regulations which led to Jewish people's loss of citizenship in the Third Reich, see Chapter V.

2. The Successor States of Former Yugoslavia

2.1 Croatia

While Croatia was still a member of the SFRY, the process of acquiring Croatian citizenship was regulated similarly as in Slovenia, according to the *jus sanguinis* and the *jus soli* principles. However, it was possible for every citizen of the SFRY to acquire Croatian republic citizenship irrespective of their birthplace, residence, or nationality[708].

Citizenship in Croatia is understood as a status deriving from ethnic affiliation. It is defined in the Law on Croatian Citizenship,[709] enacted when Croatia declared its independence on October 8, 1991.[710] This law was based on two key principles: the principle of continuity with citizenship of the Socialist Republic of Croatia, and the principle of Croatian ethnicity. Thus, people with citizenship in the former republic of Croatia became citizens of the Republic of Croatia *ex lege*, and all other residents became aliens independently of how long they had resided in Croatia. They could apply for Croatian citizenship through the naturalisation procedure and were required to meet five conditions specified by Article 8 of the law: i) a five-year period of residence in Croatia, ii) renouncing all other citizenships or submitting proof that renouncement would be possible after acquiring Croatian citizenship, iii) proficiency in the Croatian language and Latin script, iv) proof that the applicant's behaviour expressed respect toward the legal order in Croatia, v) acceptance of "Croatian culture".

Many permanent residents who held the citizenship of other Yugoslav republics were not allowed to acquire Croatian citizenship because they could not meet these conditions. The condition of renouncing all other citizenships was particularly difficult to meet, as Croatia was at war with the Federal Republic of Yugoslavia, which consisted at that time of Srpska Krajina (the state of Serbian people in Croatia), Macedonia, Serbia, Montenegro, and Bosnia and Herzegovina. The persons interested in obtaining citizenship in Croatia were citizens of exactly these countries. In addition, the Ministry of Internal Affairs, which was in charge of deciding applications for citizenship, was not obliged to provide

---

708 Law on the Citizenship of the People's Republic of Croatia, Official Gazette of the People's Republic of Croatia, No. 23/1950, and Law on the Citizenship of the Socialist Republic of Croatia, Official Gazette of the Socialist Republic of Croatia, No. 32/1977.

709 Official Gazette of the Republic of Croatia, No. 53/1991.

710 After a three-month moratorium on declaring independence expired on 25 June 1991, the referendum on Croatia's autonomy and independence was held on 19 May 1991.

reasoning in the citizenship decisions that it issued regarding the applications from 1991 to 1993. This enabled arbitrary decision-making.

The ethnocentric attitude of the legislation was expressed in those provisions of the law that enabled ethnic Croats who were registered in Croatia but did not hold Croatian citizenship to acquire citizenship by submitting a written statement claiming they considered themselves Croatian citizens (Article 30, Paragraph 2 of the Law on Croatian Citizenship). The law also facilitated naturalisation for emigrants and their descendants: ethnic Croats without a registered residence in Croatia were also able to acquire citizenship by means of a simple statement (Articles 11 and 16 of the Law).

A problem occurred when an applicant was not a citizen of any of the republics and claimed to be of Croatian origin. In such cases all Yugoslav documents showing that the person was considered a Croat were accepted as proof. Sometimes, even more unusual documents were accepted, such as certificates of the Catholic Church (affiliation with this church was considered proof of "Croatian identity") or a court certificate declaring that the person's last name was "Croatian".

The attitude of the Croatian authorities toward the citizenship status of other ethnicities was quite the opposite. Serbians who left the territory of Krajina after Croatian forces occupied it in 1995, for example, had difficulties getting their civil rights recognised. Despite the fact that they held Croatian citizenship, they could not obtain citizenship certificates (*domovnice)* and other documents, such as passports. These people were subsequently unable to exercise their other civil rights in Croatia, as they were hindered in this by the Croatian authorities. If they were also unable to acquire Serbian citizenship, they became *de facto* stateless.[711]

All permanent residents of the Republic of Croatia who did not acquire citizenship on the basis of the above-mentioned legal provisions became aliens and subject to the Law on the Movements and Residence of Aliens.[712] Article 79 of this law specified that the status of permanent resident alien was recognised under the condition of reciprocity for those Yugoslav citizens who had permanent residence in the Republic of Croatia on the day that the law came into force. All other Yugoslav citizens who had not obtained permanent resident status were considered aliens on "prolonged residence" which is equivalent to the status of an alien with a temporary residence permit.

711 Ragazzi, Štiks, EUDO Citizenship Observatory, Country Report: Croatia, 2010, pp. 1–8.

712 Official Gazette of the Republic of Croatia, No. 53/1991.

Comparing the regulation of citizenship in Slovenia and Croatia, we find that Croatian regulations were more restrictive, since the requirements for naturalisation were stricter (renouncement of other citizenships, five years of residence, etc.). However, Croatia adequately regulated the status of permanent, temporary, and actual residents who did not obtain Croatian citizenship. Article 79 of the Law on the Movements and Residence of Aliens is very similar to an amendment to Article 81 of the Slovenian Aliens Act proposed by Metka Mencin in the National Assembly before Slovenia became independent. According to this proposal, those citizens of the SFRY with permanent residence in Slovenia who did not obtain Slovenian citizenship would have been considered aliens with a permanent residence permit. The condition of reciprocity in the Croatian law was not problematic in application since reciprocity was presumed. Therefore, Croatian authorities did not verify whether Croatian citizens would be treated the same way in other countries, and Croatian permanent residents with Slovenian citizenship kept their status even though Slovenia deprived those of its permanent residents who had Croatian citizenship of their status.

Croatia not only acknowledged the continuity of the legal status of permanent residents, but also that of temporary and actual residents, as long as they were citizens of the SFRY. In comparison to the Slovenian regulations, which deprived all temporary and actual residents of their legal status, it shows a higher degree of inclusiveness and more respect for the human rights of the individual.

2.2 Bosnia and Herzegovina

Prior to the dissolution of Yugoslavia, citizenship in Bosnia-Herzegovina could be acquired similarly as in the other republics, primarily according to the *jus sanguinis* principle, and in certain cases also according to the *jus soli* principle and through naturalisation.[713]

Following the referendum on autonomy and independence, Bosnia and Herzegovina became an independent country in 1992, after Slovenia and Croatia had already declared independence. The Citizenship Act was passed on 6 October 1992, while armed conflict was occurring. According to this law, citizenship was issued *ex lege* i) by principle of legal continuity with citizenship in the Socialist Republic of Bosnia and Herzegovina and ii) by principle of registered residence in the territory of Bosnia-Herzegovina. Thus, citizenship of the new

---

713 Official Gazette of the People's Republic of Bosnia and Herzegovina, No. 5/1950, Official Gazette of the Socialist Republic of Bosnia and Herzegovina, No. 6/1965, and Official Gazette of the Socialist Republic of Bosnia and Herzegovina, No. 10/1977.

Republic of Bosnia and Herzegovina was automatically granted not only to all citizens of the Socialist Republic of Bosnia and Herzegovina but also to all registered residents. The first version of the law from 1992 contained a provision that individuals had to have had a registered residence for five consecutive years prior to 6 April 1992 in order to acquire citizenship. In 1993, this condition was abolished and registered residence on the specified date was considered sufficient. Certain groups of people were also permitted to acquire citizenship under far less stringent conditions. Some authors claim that the national interest was the reason for such liberal legislation. In the context of the war, a greater number of individuals who acquired citizenship meant a greater number of individuals who could be enlisted.

Simultaneously, the Republika Srpska, another entity within the country, passed its own law on citizenship. Its Law on Serbian Citizenship was based entirely on the principle of ethnocentrism. Similarly to the Law on Croatian Citizenship, the Law on Serbian Citizenship required the acceptance of Serbian culture and proficiency in the Serbian language and Cyrillic script.[714]

Bosnia and Herzegovina introduced the second most liberal citizenship policies in the former SFRY (when the Republic of Kosovo declared independence, its regulations were even more liberal). It respected the acquired rights of individuals. It is interesting that such a liberal system was introduced in exactly the country that, of all the former Yugoslav countries, did not design independence on the ethnocentric basis or with an aim to become a country of one ethnic group. At the same time, the international community was more present and involved in the preparation of legislation in Bosnia and Herzegovina (and later in Kosovo) than in the other countries. Even though this "zero option"[715] chosen by Bosnia and Herzegovina is unpopular among newly formed nation-states that express their sense of existential threat via restrictive and exclusionary policies, it is the best way to respect the rights of the individual.

714 Sarajlić, EUDO Citizenship Observatory, Country Report: Bosnia and Herzegovina, 2010, pp. 1–7.

715 A method of defining the body of citizens from zero, by including all those persons who are residing in the country and not only those who have already been regarded as citizens in the past or under the previous regime.

2.3 FYRO Macedonia

During the Yugoslav era, Macedonian citizenship was regulated similarly to other SFRY citizenships.[716] Macedonia declared independence on 8 September 1991, and the new Law on Citizenship was passed in 1992. Similarly as in Slovenia and Croatia, the authorities in Macedonia applied the continuity principle and automatically granted citizenship to the citizens of the Socialist Republic of Macedonia. SFRY citizens with a permanent residence in Macedonia faced extremely strict requirements for acquiring citizenship through extraordinary naturalisation. They had to demonstrate a constant means of subsistence, fifteen years of consecutive residence in the state, and the application had to be submitted within a year after the law came into force. The short deadline and the requirement of such a long duration of residence made the implementation of the law difficult; it forced many Albanians, Roma, and the members of other minorities to apply for citizenship through the regular naturalisation procedure. Although these people had been living in Macedonia for many years, they had no way to prove it. Moreover, they did not have sufficient information about the naturalisation procedure. Regular naturalisation procedures were even stricter, requiring proficiency in the language, and had an even higher fee. For this reason, the law was heavily criticised by the international community, and the minorities living in Macedonia.[717]

The situation was aggravated by the fact that the citizens of other republics with permanent, temporary or *de facto* residence in Macedonia who had not obtained Macedonian citizenship were deprived of their legal status. This happened to permanent residents when the deadlines for submitting applications for citizenship passed, and to temporary or *de facto* residents with the declaration of independence. The Law on the Movement and Residence of Aliens[718] passed in 1992 contains a provision that is identical to Article 81 of the Slovenian Aliens Act. This reflects the fact that Slovenian civil servants participated in drafting the Macedonian legislation and "exported" the worst possible policy measure. Article 86 of the Law on the Movement and Residence of Aliens specifies that, for the citizens of other republics of the former SFRY who did not apply for citizenship

716 Law on Citizenship of the Socialist Republic of Macedonia, Official Gazette of the Socialist Republic of Macedonia, No. 09/65, and Law on Citizenship of the Socialist Republic of Macedonia, Official Gazette of the Socialist Republic of Macedonia, No. 19/77.

717 Spaskovska, EUDO Citizenship Observatory, Country Report: Macedonia, 2010, pp. 1–8.

718 Official Gazette of the Republic of Macedonia, No. 36/1992.

or whose applications were denied, the provisions of the law would enter into force two months after the deadline for submitting an application had passed or after the final negative decision was delivered. SFRY passport validity was regulated exactly as in Slovenia (the passports were valid until expiry or two years after the law came into force). Legislative provisions concerning legal status of those who did not acquire Macedonian citizenship were just as discriminatory as in Slovenia, since permanent residence permits issued to aliens from third countries remained valid in accordance with the Law on the Movement and Residence of Aliens (Paragraph 3, Article 87).

As in Slovenia, "erased Macedonians" (who were in fact never called by that name) were deprived of their status and expected to reapply for legal status under the same conditions as aliens entering the country for the first time. As in Slovenia, the erased people of Macedonia found it difficult to define their status, since the Macedonian authorities required a valid passport, a means of subsistence and a reason such as employment, resident family members, etc. to issue a residence permit (Article 23 of the Law on the Movement and Residence of Aliens). The legislator in Macedonia also failed to consider this group's specific legal and actual situation and considered them equivalent to other aliens without a good reason. These policies caused the most harm to Albanians, Roma, Ashkali, and Egyptians. Their exact number is unknown; however, rough estimates show that it exceeds the number of people erased in Slovenia by a factor of ten. An additional problem in Macedonia was the fact that tens of thousands of people affected had never been registered (their births were not registered) and had not possessed any documents.

Although the situations were identical in the legal sense (less so in reality), they were addressed very differently. While the people who were erased in Slovenia primarily wanted to reclaim a status to which they were undoubtedly entitled – that of permanent resident – the people deprived of their legal status in Macedonia wanted to acquire citizenship. The authorities ignored the problem for many years before the parliament finally passed the amendments to the Law on Citizenship[719] in 2004. According to Article 14, those citizens of any other republic of the former SFRY who on 8 September 1991 had a registered permanent residence on the territory of the Republic of Macedonia and had effective ties to Macedonia were permitted to acquire the citizenship of Macedonia. The application had to be submitted within a two-year period after the law was enacted and

719 Law on Changes and Amendments of the Law on Citizenship of the Republic of Macedonia, Official Gazette of the Republic of Macedonia, No. 8/2004.

applicants had to prove their proficiency in the language and present a certificate of no criminal record against the safety and defence of Macedonia. Although a number of affected people were able to obtain legal status based on this law, as in the case of the Slovenian erasure, it was ultimately an insufficient attempt to address an ongoing problem.

2.4 Serbia

The citizenship issue was somewhat different in Serbia than in the other republics of former Yugoslavia. Despite the fact that, according to international law, Yugoslavia disintegrated and ceased to exist, and that all the states that emerged on its former territory were newly formed countries, Serbia considered itself the continuation of the SFRY for a period of time.

After all the other republics declared their independence, the SFRY renamed itself the Federative Republic of Yugoslavia (FRY). In 1992, it passed a new constitution that delineated the foundations of the FRY's citizenship. Like all previous constitutions, it posited that a special federal law would regulate the issue of citizenship. This new Law on Citizenship of the Federal Republic of Yugoslavia[720] was not passed until 1996. Citizenship in the FRY was based on the principle of continuity with citizenship in the SFRY. This was in accordance with the formal position of the Serbian authorities on the country's continuity with the SFRY. The law, however, contradicted itself, since other provisions stated that only those persons who held republic citizenship of Serbia or Montenegro on 27 April 1992, the date that the state was founded, or any of their children born after that date, could become *ex lege* citizens of the FRY (Article 46). The law also enabled individuals who had permanent residence on the territory of the republics of Serbia or Montenegro on 27 April 1992 and held the citizenship of any other SFRY republic to register as citizens of the FRY, on the condition that they did not have any other citizenship (Article 47). Applications had to be submitted within a year after the law went into force, or by 1 January 1998. A problem appeared in the application of the law. A large part of the population in Serbia did not have a registered permanent residence on the given day, as they were mostly refugees who had fled Croatia and Bosnia and Herzegovina after that date.[721] They were permitted to apply for citizenship of the FRY only if they did not hold any other citizenship or if they had renounced the citizenship of another successor state. This condition was not abolished until 2001, when an amendment to the

720 Official Gazette of Federal Republic of Yugoslavia, No. 33/1996.

721 Rava, EUDO Citizenship Observatory, Country Report: Serbia, 2010, p. 7.

citizenship law was passed.[722] The application of the law encountered some difficulties partly because the deadline to submit applications was relatively short and partly because of unclear administrative procedures.

In addition to the law regulating the acquisition of citizenship on the federal level, the Law on Citizenship of the Socialist Republic of Serbia[723] of 1979, which regulated the acquisition of republic citizenship in the Socialist Republic of Serbia, was still in force. The law had never been harmonised with the FRY law on citizenship, and therefore did not correspond to the actual situation in the post-SFRY period. This was particularly true of Kosovo, which was managed by the United Nations after the beginning of armed conflict in 1999.[724]

What was the legal status of the people who resided in the territory of Serbia and Montenegro after the new state as founded and did not hold citizenship of either of the two republics? A new law on citizenship was not passed until four years later. The answer is fairly simple. The SFRY's Law on the Movement and Residence of Aliens[725] of 1980 (with amendments) was in force in Serbia until 2008, when a new law on aliens was passed. It defined aliens as persons who did not hold citizenship of the SFRY (Paragraph 2 of Article 1), implying that that law did not apply to the citizens of the SFRY. Since the FRY considered itself the successor of the SFRY, everyone with a valid passport issued by the authorities of the SFRY enjoyed the same rights as before, including the freedom of movement across the country's borders, until the new citizenship law was passed. Difficulties arose only if a passport expired prior to that date, as extraordinary naturalisation first became possible in Serbia with the passage of the new law in 1996. Affected people were also able to acquire new identity cards, with the difference that they contained a code letter T indicating that they were not citizens of the FRY. These documents were issued by the Serbian authorities on the basis of various government decrees[726] to ensure that people would not lack valid documents; therefore the situation was considerably better than in Slovenia.

After the Federal Republic of Yugoslavia became the State Union of Serbia and Montenegro on the basis of the Constitutional Charter passed on 4 February

722 *Ibid.*, p. 10.

723 Official Gazette of the Socialist Republic of Serbia, No. 45/1979.

724 Serbian-Montenegrin Relations and the Question of Citizenship of FRY Citizens, Lawyers' Committee for Human Rights – YUCOM, Belgrade, November 2001.

725 Official Gazette of the Socialist Federal Republic of Yugoslavia, No. 56/80, 53/85, 30/89, 26/90, 53/91; Official Gazette of Federal Republic of Yugoslavia, No. 24/94 and 28/96.

726 Interview with Dejan Kladarin, UNHCR – Serbia and Montenegro, 9. 9. 2010.

2003, a new and liberal law, the Law on Citizenship of the Republic of Serbia[727] was passed in December 2004, replacing the Law on Citizenship of the Socialist Republic of Serbia and the 1996 Law on Citizenship of the Federal Republic of Yugoslavia. According to Article 51, citizenship of the Republic of Serbia was granted to those who held a republic citizenship of Serbia on the day that the Constitutional Charter was passed. Moreover, Article 52 of the new law allowed the citizens of other former SFRY republics or successor states who had resided in Serbia permanently for at least nine years to acquire citizenship by written request within a three-year deadline without having to renounce their previous citizenship. The regulation was important because it enabled refugees and all other persons who had migrated to Serbia in the 1990s to acquire citizenship.

After Montenegro declared independence, Article 52 of the Law on Citizenship of the Republic of Serbia was amended in 2007 to enable the citizens of Montenegro who were registered as permanent residents in Serbia on 3 June 2006 (the date on which the state was dissolved) to acquire Serbian citizenship within a five-year deadline. The aim of the amendment was to prevent Montenegro's newfound independence from causing some residents of Serbia to become stateless.[728] Serbia also enabled all persons of Serbian nationality, including emigrants and their descendants to acquire citizenship under favourable conditions (by written statement, with no obligation to renounce existing citizenships)[729] and as well as all persons who had lost Serbian citizenship.[730]

The legal regulation of citizenship in Serbia was therefore relatively favourable to all persons interested in obtaining it (However, for the non-Serbian residents of Kosovo, see below). This was due to specific circumstances such as the high number of refugees in Serbia, the preferential treatment of Serbians residing in Montenegro and persons of Serbian origin and citizens of former SFRY in general, which implied that citizenship was understood as means of ethnification.[731]

The problem of former SFRY citizens who had not acquired Serbian citizenship re-emerged when Montenegro declared independence. Serbia subsequently passed a new law on aliens in 2008.[732] Article 3 of that law defined aliens as persons without citizenship of the Republic of Serbia, which included all citizens of

727 Official Gazette of the Republic of Serbia, 135/2004.

728 Official Gazette of the Republic of Serbia, 90/2007.

729 Articles 18 and 23 of the Law on Citizenship of the Republic of Serbia.

730 *Ibid.*, Article 52.

731 Rava, EUDO Citizenship Observatory, Country Report: Serbia, 2010, pp. 11–12 and 22–23.

732 Official Gazette of the Republic of Serbia, No. 97/2008.

the former SFRY who had not acquired Serbian citizenship by the day when the law came into force. The law did not consider the special legal situation of aliens because it did not contain any specific regulations referring explicitly to that group of people. Due to the favourable conditions for acquiring citizenship according to the Law on Citizenship of the Republic of Serbia, the probability that interested persons would have failed to become citizens was very small. However, this could have had occurred, and a person in such a situation would have had to apply for citizenship through regular naturalisation according to the 2008 law.

Theoretically, these conditions did not eliminate the possibility that some individuals were deprived of their legal status. However, this did not apply to residents of Serbia with Montenegrin citizenship. The Agreement on transformation of the State Union of Serbia and Montenegro into a union of independent and internationally recognised states of Serbia and Montenegro of 18 March 2005 (also known as the Agreement on Principles, which also determined that the referendum of Montenegro would be the basis for independence) stated that the citizens of Montenegro and Serbia would have equal rights and obligations, apart from the right to vote, on the territory of both states.

2.5 Montenegro

Montenegro was the last of the five former SFRY republics to declare independence. Until 1999, citizenship in Montenegro was regulated in the same way as in Serbia, as it formed part of the FRY and the Law on Citizenship applied to its territory as well. The Citizenship Act of the Socialist Republic of Montenegro[733] was also still in force.

In 1999, Montenegro passed the Law on Montenegrin Citizenship.[734] This caused a conflict of legal norms, as that law provided that one could acquire Montenegrin citizenship without having to acquire federal citizenship of the FRY either beforehand or concurrently. The law implied that Montenegro was an independent state (illustrating the *creeping independence* phenomenon,[735] a slow way to gain state independence). Montenegrin citizenship acquired on the basis of the law was no longer tied to citizenship of FRY. The conditions for acquiring citizenship through naturalisation were strict. They included ten years of residence in the state, as the authorities aimed to prevent a great number of refugees from Croatia and Bosnia and Herzegovina who were assigned to live in

733 Official Gazette of the Socialist Republic of Montenegro, No. 26/75.

734 The law was passed on November 1, 1999.

735 Džankić, Lineages of Citizenship in Montenegro, 2010, p. 13.

Montenegro from acquiring citizenship and, consequently, the right to vote. The hidden fears behind these conditions were related to the country's planned independence. Most of the refugees were of Serbian ethnicity. Therefore, it was very likely that, if they won the right to vote, they would vote for the pro-Milošević party (and, after his extradition, for the parties that advocated for a common state with Serbia).[736]

When the Constitutional Charter was passed and came into force on 4 February 2003, the FRY became the State Union of Serbia and Montenegro (clarifying the link between citizenship and voting rights).[737] Then, after the referendum in 2006, Montenegro declared independence on 3 June 2006. Citizenship of independent Montenegro was regulated by the Law Implementing the Constitution of Montenegro. It provided that persons who on 3 June 2006 held the citizenship of both Montenegro and another state were permitted to retain both citizenships. Those who acquired the citizenship of another state after that date were forbidden to hold dual citizenship.[738] The Montenegrin Citizenship Act[739] was not passed until 14 February 2008, as a result of disagreements between pro-Serbian and pro-Montenegrin parties. It had a strict definition of citizenship as a legal bond between an individual and the state, and, in contrast to many other laws on citizenship in the region, not as an affiliation with a specific ethnic group.[740] The law defined a Montenegrin citizen as a person who acquired Montenegrin citizenship in accordance with previous regulations on citizenship and was in the registry of Montenegrin citizens in Montenegro. Further, it stated that Montenegrin citizens who held another citizenship on 3 June 2006 were permitted to retain it until the bilateral agreements with the country in question were signed. The law stated that the citizens of SFRY who had a registered permanent residence in Montenegro prior to 3 June 2006 were permitted to acquire Montenegrin citizenship through naturalisation under the following conditions: i) they held no other citizenship or submitted proof that they had renounced all other citizenships, ii) had a fixed residence, iii) had a stable source of income, iv) had

736 *Ibid.*

737 The importance the relationship between the right to vote and citizenship is best illustrated by the results of the 2006 referendum on Montenegro's independence. The EU quorum requirement for the referendum to be recognised was 55%, which was only surpassed by 2%. Džankić, EUDO Citizenship Observatory, Country Report: Montenegro, 2010, pp. 3–8.

738 *Ibid.*

739 Official Gazette of Montenegro, No. 13/08.

740 Džankić, Lineages of Citizenship in Montenegro, 2010, p. 6.

not been convicted of a sentence longer than a year or of a criminal offence, persecuted by official duty, v) did not represent a threat to national security and the defence of the state and vi) had paid their taxes. An application for citizenship had to be submitted within a period of one year following the date on which the law came into force. After the deadline, applicants were permitted to acquire citizenship through regular naturalisation only in case of statelessness and applications had to be submitted within a period of three years following the date on which the law came into force (Article 41).

The situation of the citizens of the SFRY or the FRY who had not acquired citizenship of Montenegro was regulated by the Aliens Act[741] passed in 2008. Paragraph 1, Article 54 stated that residents who had a registered permanent residence in Montenegro prior to 3 June 2006, had the right to reside permanently in the country without having to apply for a status of any kind; however, they were obliged to register. The content of this article is similar to Croatian regulations; the situation of permanent residents was regulated more favourably than in Slovenia or Macedonia. As for the citizens of SFRY who had a temporary or actual residence in Montenegro, only the legal status of citizens of Serbia was resolved on the basis of the Agreement on transformation of State Union of Serbia and Montenegro into the Union of independent and internationally acknowledged states of Serbia and Montenegro of 18 March 2005.

2.6 Kosovo

During the Yugoslav era, Kosovo was an autonomous territory of Serbia and the SFRY, and citizenship there was regulated the same way as in Serbia. Kosovo became an autonomous territory following constitutional changes in 1974, and acquired numerous competences of its own with their own constitution, but it did not have its own law on citizenship. Therefore, the citizens of Kosovo generally held the republic citizenship of Serbia and the federal citizenship of the SFRY, in accordance with the Law on Citizenship of the Socialist Republic of Serbia of 1979. However, the newly formed institutions in Kosovo were in charge of granting citizenship, of managing the registry of citizens on the territory of Kosovo, and of issuing Yugoslav passports (marked KA). Thus, even though the citizenship was formally Serbian and Yugoslav, it was actually specifically Kosovar in many ways. The situation changed in 1989, when Kosovo lost its status as an autonomous territory by force.

741 Official Gazette of Montenegro, No. 82/2008.

After the dissolution of Yugoslavia, Kosovo (as a part of Serbia) became part of the Federal Republic of Yugoslavia in 1992. Its territory continued to be governed by the same legislation as in Serbia. On the federal level, the citizenship law of the SFRY remained in force until 1996, and from 1997 on, the FRY's Law on Citizenship applied. On the republic level, the Law on Citizenship of the Socialist Republic of Serbia of 1979 remained in force.

However, these laws on citizenship did not reflect the situation on the ground. Between 1991 and 1998, most of the residents of Kosovo were *de facto* stateless. Albanians in Kosovo had already been deprived of their political and civil rights in 1989, when the Serbian authorities closed institutions, terminated employees, and shut schools and universities where classes were in Albanian. Acquiring a passport was conditional upon military service in the Serbian army, which at that time meant active service in conflicts in Bosnia and Herzegovina and in Croatia. Potential military recruits tried to avoid being drafted, which created a black market in counterfeit passports. Simultaneously, a parallel system of institutions, health services, and schools was forming in Kosovo, which functioned independently of Serbia. In the late 1990s, the situation escalated into armed conflict and humanitarian disaster; 850000 Kosovar Albanians were expelled from Kosovo, their records of ownership destroyed and their possessions confiscated. The conflict led to military intervention by NATO in the FRY in 1999. The United Nations Interim Administration Mission in Kosovo (UNMIK) was founded and started to form legislative, executive, and judicial institutions independently of Serbia. Consequently, the Serbian authorities lost their legal and actual control over Kosovo. According to international law, Kosovo remained part of Serbia and the Federal Republic of Yugoslavia. Thus, the residents of Kosovo who were born before 1999 continued to hold Yugoslav citizenship and were treated as such by third countries. However, residents born after 1999 could not be registered in the Yugoslav civil records, and they thus had no citizenship. UNMIK issued Regulation No. 2000/13 on the Central Civil Registry[742] in order to resolve this problem. According to Article 1.1 of the Regulation, all habitual residents of Kosovo were entered into the registry, namely i) persons born in Kosovo or who had at least one parent born in Kosovo, and ii) persons who were able to prove that they had resided in Kosovo for a continuous period of at least five years. Because most civil records from before 1999 had been destroyed together with residents' personal documents, the registration procedure was necessarily simple. The documents of various institutions, political, or religious communities were accepted

742 Regulation No. 2000/13 on the Central Civil Registry, UNMIK/REG/2000/13.

as well as oral or written statements. Furthermore, Regulation No. 2000/18 on Travel Documents[743] permitted every person in the registry to apply for a travel document. This was particularly specified in Article 1.2, which also noted that the document did not confer a nationality upon its holder, nor did it affect the holder's nationality in any way. In other words, a person with a UNMIK travel document could have held the passport of any country (including a Yugoslav passport, which some Albanians managed to acquire). In this way, UNMIK established a kind of proto-citizenship in Kosovo for the Albanians, as Serbs living in Kosovo had Yugoslav documents. However, this quasi-citizenship was not internationally recognised in the right and legal sense of the word, and most of the Kosovar Albanians were thus *de facto* stateless.

On 17 February 2008, Kosovo declared independence. The Kosovo assembly passed the Law on Citizenship of Kosovo on 20 February 2008.[744] In accordance with provisions 29.1 and 19.2, all pre-war residents of Kosovo who were citizens of the FRY and their lineal descendants acquired the citizenship of the Republic of Kosovo. Citizenship was therefore also granted to former residents who left Kosovo after 1999 and were not registered as habitual residents of Kosovo during the UNMIK administration. Citizenship was also granted *ex lege* to the habitual residents of Kosovo registered in the Civil Registry of the UNMIK. Article 155 of the Constitution of the Republic of Kosovo, which came into force on 15 June 2008, included both of these ways to acquire Kosovar citizenship. It thus granted citizenship to many Albanians who immigrated from Macedonia and Montenegro and were able to register in the Civil Registry of UNMIK using the simple registration process. This highly inclusive law, based on the zero-option and *jus soli* principles, was drafted with the cooperation of a number of international experts who had analysed many of the citizenship laws in the region. Their aim was to provide as many people as possible with the Kosovar citizenship, in contrast to other states, also taking into consideration the UNMIK solutions after the civil registry was established.[745]

2.7 Discussion

Among the successor states of the former Yugoslavia, Kosovo had the most liberal and inclusive citizenship legislation, because the key condition was habitual

743 Regulation No. 2000/18 on Travel Documents, UNMIK/REG/2000/18.

744 Official Gazette of the Republic of Kosovo, No. 26/2008.

745 Krasniqi, EUDO Citizenship Observatory, Country Report: Kosovo, 2010, p. 3 and following.

residence in the country on a particular date. Bosnia and Herzegovina had the second most inclusive regulations, which specified a registered residence on its territory on a particular date. All of the other states – Slovenia, Croatia, Serbia, Montenegro, and Macedonia – initially based their citizenship on continuity with citizenship in the equivalent republic of the former Yugoslavia. Their next step was to offer the possibility of naturalisation under various conditions. Serbia and Croatia had the most ethnicity-oriented citizenship policies, because they attempted to grant citizenship to as many people of the dominant ethnicity as possible. Macedonia had the strictest conditions for acquiring citizenship through extraordinary naturalisation; it required even permanent residents to demonstrate fifteen years of residence in the country. In this it was followed by Montenegro, which required a registered residence as well as many other conditions, and forbade dual citizenship. Slovenian regulations were middle-of-the-road with regard to the restrictiveness of the conditions (relatively short deadline for submitting applications, relatively small number of additional conditions for extraordinary naturalisation and no requirement to renounce other citizenships). The SFRY citizens who had a registered residence in a successor state but did not acquire citizenship or a legal status there were in the worst situation in Macedonia and Slovenia, where their legal status was initially not regulated at all. A similarly grave situation arose in Serbia after 2008, as it did not regulate the situation of permanent (or other) residents prior to 2008, except for the citizens of Montenegro. The situation of registered permanent residents who did not acquire citizenship was regulated in Croatia and in Montenegro. However, the situation of registered temporary residents and actual but non-registered residents was only regulated in Croatia, which thus had the most satisfactory transition legislation in this respect.

3. Newly Formed Eastern European Countries

3.1 Estonia

I am now turning to the Baltic states which not only gained their independence at about the same time as the successor states of the former Yugoslavia, but are also infamous – at least some of them – for their citizenship exclusion policies. The first country I looked at was Estonia. The Supreme Soviet of the Republic of Estonia passed the Citizenship Act[746] based on the pre-war Citizenship Law of 1938 on the same day that the erasure took effect in Slovenia, on 26 February

746 Official Gazette of Estonia, 1992, 7, 109.

1992. This law entitled everyone who held Estonian citizenship or whose parents held Estonian citizenship prior to 16 June 1940 (the day of the Soviet ultimatum, followed by the annexation of Estonia) to be Estonian citizens. All persons who came to Estonia after that date (one third of the population of Estonia, mostly Russian nationals) were allowed to apply for citizenship through the naturalisation procedure. Applicants had to meet the basic condition of having a registered permanent residence (*propiska*) on the territory of Estonia for at least two years prior to and at least one year after submitting their application. However, the two-year period could not start before 30 March 1990. The possibility of naturalisation was therefore *de facto* postponed and citizenships acquired through naturalisation could not be issued before 30 March 1993. Consequently, a large share of Estonia's residents did not have either active or passive voting rights when elections for the state assembly were held on 20 September 1992. In 1993, a special law (the Requirement for Applicants for Citizenship to Know Estonian Act[747]) introduced an additional condition of proficiency in the Estonian language, which made the naturalisation process even more restrictive.

On 19 January 1995, the new Citizenship Act[748] was passed, which tightened the requirements even further. It required residence in Estonia on a permanent residence permit for five years prior to and one year after submitting an application. It also required knowledge of the Estonian constitution and language. This law, as all of the previous laws, failed to acknowledge the rights of children whose parents were stateless until they acquired Estonian citizenship by the *jus soli* principle. This defect was first corrected in December 1998 by an amendment to the Citizenship Act, which granted the right of citizenship to children under the age of fifteen. Further amendments in June 2002 relaxed the criteria for naturalisation somewhat: certain groups of handicapped people received an exemption from examinations on the constitution and the language, and the language proficiency of persons who passed the Estonian language examinations in Russian-language schools was acknowledged.[749] The law also specified some exclusionary causes: members of the armed forces of foreign countries, reservists and army pensioners, and their spouses were not eligible for citizenship. Former soldiers were permitted to acquire citizenship only if they had been married for at least five years to a person who acquired Estonian citizenship through the *jus sanguinis* principle.

747 Official Gazette of Estonia, 1993, 11, 171.
748 Official Gazette of Estonia, I 1995, 12, 122.
749 Järve, Estonian citizenship: Between ethnic preferences and democratic obligations, in: Citizenship Policies in the New Europe, 2007, pp. 45–48.

The restrictive citizenship policies led to a high rate of statelessness in Estonia. In 1992, 32 per cent of residents had no defined citizenship. In 2000, 12.4 per cent of the population was still stateless. This rate was reduced to eight per cent by 2006, as many of the affected people died, emigrated, or acquired Russian citizenship.[750]

In Estonia, the conditions for acquiring citizenship on application were thus stricter than in Slovenia. Estonia did not establish an easier path to citizenship (e.g. extraordinary naturalisation) for permanent residents who had moved there as internal migrants when it was part of the Soviet Union. The difference was that Slovenia became part of the SFRY voluntarily, while Estonia was annexed to the Soviet Union by force. Estonian authorities thus argued that the Soviet Union was an occupying force. Russian-speaking residents who were deprived of the possibility of acquiring citizenship disagreed and demanded to be treated as individuals who had immigrated to the country as migrant workers and not as representatives of the occupying forces.[751] Both states had similar exclusionary clauses. The exclusionary clause in Estonia literally referred to soldiers or former soldiers and their spouses. In Slovenia, Paragraph 3, Article 40 of the Citizenship Act referred to people who posed a danger to the public order, security, or defence of the state, which was directed toward the same group of people (except for the spouses) – the former members of the Yugoslav Army.

The legal situation of the residents who did not acquire citizenship after Estonia gained independence remained unregulated, much as in Slovenia. Approximately 500000 persons were affected.[752] Their situation remained unresolved until 8 July 1993, when the Aliens Act was passed.[753] Paragraph 2, Article 20 permitted aliens who had a registered permanent residence (*propiska*) in Estonia on 1 July 1990, to acquire temporary resident permits and work permits according to the conditions of the law. The deadline to submit applications was 12 July 1994, but as up to 90 per cent of rightful claimants failed to apply for a permit by that date, this deadline was extended twice.[754] The law enabled most of the residents of Estonia who had not acquired Estonian citizenship to acquire permits for temporary and then permanent residence. However, many residents continued not to have legal status. Members of foreign armed forces, army retirees, their

---

750 Poleshchuk (ed.), Chance to Survive, 2009, pp. 12–13.

751 Järve, Estonian citizenship: Between ethnic preferences and democratic obligations, in: Citizenship Policies in the New Europe, 2007, pp. 45–48.

752 Poleshchuk, "Illegals" in Estonia: Final Solution?, 2001, p. 103.

753 Official Gazette of Estonia, I 1993, 44, 637; 1999, 50, 548; 2004, 58, 410.

754 Ruspini, Estonia, in: Regularization in Europe, 2009, p. 225.

spouses and their children were ineligible for temporary residence permits (An exception was made in 1994 which permitted members of the Russian military and their families to acquire temporary residence permits if they did not represent a danger to the national security of Estonia).[755] Persons who did not have a registered permanent residence in Estonia, former convicts, and immigrants to Estonia who arrived after 1991 were also ineligible for residence permits.[756] Many people who were unable to meet the legal requirements (a steady income, having resided in Estonia for a minimum of three of the past five years on a valid for temporary residence permit, a registered residence in Estonia) were denied a permanent residence permit.[757] The authorities estimated that approximately 35000 people did not have legal status in the early 1990s.

Former citizens of the Soviet Union also had problems with invalid personal documents until the mid-nineties. They were not granted the right to acquire passports for foreigners, to travel abroad or within Estonia until 1996.

All persons who lived in Estonia without legal status were given a possibility to resolve their status[758] in 1998 with the Obligation to Leave and Prohibition on Entry Act[759], which was similar to the Slovenian Legal Status Act passed a year later. People without legal status in Estonia had to meet the following conditions: to have migrated to Estonia prior to 1 July 1990; not to have left Estonia to reside in another state; and not to have caused any damage to the interests of Estonia by their presence (Article 9, Paragraph 1). The law enabled persons who received expulsion orders to obtain residence permits (outside the quota that was otherwise determined for aliens) within the period of one year. They were also permitted to submit their applications from within Estonia and not from abroad, as specified in the Aliens Act. If they did not apply for a permit and failed to resolve their legal status, they were subject to imprisonment and expulsion. When deciding on expulsion, the administrative court had to take into consideration the length of the alien's residence in Estonia, his/her personal, economical and other bonds with Estonia, the consequences of leaving Estonia for his/her family members, the circumstances of the issued order, the alien's age and health,

755 Poleshchuk (ed.), Chance to Survive, 2009, pp. 30, 35, 37.
756 Poleshchuk, "Illegals" in Estonia: Final Solution?, 2001, p. 103.
757 Poleshchuk (ed.), Chance to Survive, 2009, p. 35.
758 *Ibid.*, pp. 38–39.
759 Official Gazette of Estonia, I 1998, 98/99, 1575; Official Gazette of Estonia, I 2001, 68, 407.

etc. Affected people could demand court protection against a removal order and appeal an expulsion order issued by an administrative court.[760]

Most of the law's target population faced the difficulty of not having the legal basis to acquire a residence permit, as they did not have a spouse or relatives in Estonia. The people who the authorities were not able to expel, as there was nowhere to expel them to – they were stateless and held no valid documents – were held in deportation centres. Some of them were held there for several years.[761] In this sense, the situation was similar to the phenomenon of the erasure. The situation changed on 6 June 2001, when two orders were introduced: an order for legalisation and a removal order. For both, it was possible to demand court protection. The order for legalisation was issued to people who had family in Estonia, were of Estonian ethnicity or if they had immigrated to Estonia prior to 1 July 1990, had not left the country with the purpose of residing in another country, and their presence was not a danger to the interests of the state. People who had immigrated to Estonia after the specified date or who had immigrated to Estonia prior to that date but left the country for a certain period were still subject to expulsion and excluded from the possibility of legalising their status.[762]

The situation in Estonia was, therefore, very similar to the situation of erased people in Slovenia. In both countries, people were deprived of their legal status first through exclusionary citizenship policies (citizenship policies in Slovenia were far more inclusive than in Estonia) and second through a legal void in the legislation regarding alien status. In both countries, the same rules applied to former citizens of what had once, before independence, been the same state and to aliens from third countries. The difference was that, in Estonia, the Aliens Act was passed with a two-year delay, making it impossible to regulate one's status prior to 1993, while in Slovenia, some individuals were permitted to acquire temporary legal status soon after the erasure. Considering the data, the situation was no doubt considerably worse in Estonia than in Slovenia. Almost half a million people were deprived of their legal status right after Estonia became independent, and later possibilities for naturalisation were also much stricter than in Slovenia, where the first possibility of extraordinary naturalisation was followed by another in 2002.

---

760 *Ibid.* See also Poleshchuk, "Illegals" in Estonia: Final Solution?, 2001, p. 103.

761 Poleshchuk, "Illegals" in Estonia: Final Solution?, 2001, p. 103.

762 *Ibid.*, p. 104.

3.2 Latvia

Latvia's post-independence situation is widely known for officially introducing the term "non-citizens" to refer to persons without citizenship. How did this come to pass? Latvia declared independence on 4 May 1990. However, it actually became independent in August 1991, after the Moscow coup d'état. The Supreme Soviet of the Republic of Latvia passed a resolution on the Renewal of the Rights of Citizens of the Republic of Latvia and the Fundamental Provisions for Naturalisation on October 15, 1991, "reviving" the 1919 law on citizenship.

According to the resolution, Latvian citizenship was granted through the principle of continuity, as in Estonia, to persons who were citizens of Latvia on 17 June 1940 and their descendants if they lived in the state and were registered before 1 July 1992. Members of this group who did not reside in Latvia and held the citizenship of another country were only permitted to acquire the citizenship of Latvia if they submitted proof of having renounced that other citizenship. Citizenship was also granted to persons of unknown parentage who were born and resided in Latvia. The assumption behind these initial regulations was that only people who were citizens based on the 1919 law could establish a legitimate political system in Latvia and participate in the parliamentary elections in 1993.[763] The resolution excluded almost 35 per cent of the country's residents from automatically acquiring citizenship. Their only option was to apply for citizenship through naturalisation according to the 1919 law on citizenship. However, the conditions were so strict that no application for naturalisation was granted.[764]

The new Law on Citizenship,[765] which was passed on 22 July 1994 after heated discussion, established an extremely discriminatory quota system for different categories of residents, and made it possible to submit applications for citizenship through naturalisation under different criteria in certain time intervals.[766]

---

763 Krūma, Checks and Balances in Latvian Nationality Policies, in: Citizenship Policies in the New Europe, 2007, p. 69.

764 *Ibid.*, p. 65.

765 Official Gazette of Latvia, 1994, 93.

766 The first group was composed of people with citizenship on the day of the occupation, and their descendants, unless they held citizenship of another state on the day of declaration of independence; Latvians and Livonians who reside permanently in Latvia and do not hold another citizenship or renounced the citizenship of another country; women with permanent residence in Latvia who lost their citizenship according to the Citizenship Law of 1919 and their descendants unless after May 1990 they acquired citizenship of another country; naturalised persons; foundlings on the territory of Latvia whose parents are unknown; orphans living in orphanages or

After the international community put pressure on the government, it abolished these strict and arbitrarily determined quotas by amendments to the Citizenship Law starting in 1998. The amendments also enabled stateless or "non-citizen" children born in Latvia after 21 August 1991 to acquire citizenship. The naturalisation procedure was also made easier for some groups of people (people over 65 did not have to pass naturalisation examinations).[767]

According to the current Citizenship Law, the requirements for acquiring citizenship are to have had a registered residence in Latvia for at least five years since 4 May 1990, to have a legal source of income, to pass the naturalisation examination (requiring high proficiency in the language, knowledge of the constitution, the national anthem, and the history of Latvia), and an oath of loyalty.

The law also contains numerous exclusionary clauses. The following groups are not eligible to become Latvian citizens: people with a court order determining that they had acted against the independence of Latvia, promoted totalitarian ideas or encouraged racial hatred; officials of the state authorities of another state; employees of the armed forces or security services or police of another state; persons who chose to reside in Latvia after 17 June 1940 immediately after demobilisation from the armed forces of Russia on the starting day of their military service and had not resided permanently in Latvia; persons who were employed by the KGB or cooperated with it or with the security services of other states if that was established in a legal procedure; former convicts penalized for actions considered criminal in Latvia; and members of the Communist Party and certain other organisations hostile to Latvia.[768] The list of exclusionary clauses is

---

children's homes; persons who finished high school in Latvian, persons who had held citizenship of Lithuania or Estonia prior to 1940 and the spouses of Latvian citizens. Members of this group were not permitted to apply for citizenship until 1 February 1995. The second group permitted to apply for citizenship through naturalisation consisted of the people born in Latvia. People under 20 were permitted to submit a request from 1996 on, people under 25 from 1997 on, people under 30 from 1998 on, people 40 and under from 1999 on, and the rest from 2000 on. The third group consisted of immigrants who came to Latvia as minors; they were permitted to apply for citizenship from 2001 on; immigrants who came to Latvia before their thirtieth birthday from 2002 on and other immigrants from 2003 on. *Ibid.*, p. 64. See also Poleshchuk (ed.), Chance to Survive, 2009, p. 167.

767 Krūma, Checks and Balances in Latvian Nationality Policies, in: Citizenship Policies in the New Europe, 2007, p. 67.

768 Poleshchuk (ed.), Chance to Survive, 2009, p. 169.

lengthy[769] and similar in content to the exclusionary clauses of Estonia. In terms of its effects, it is also similar to Paragraph 3, Article 40 of the Citizenship Law of the Republic of Slovenia.

Due to all the aforementioned obstacles, many people in Latvia were deprived of their citizenship. In 1995, the number of non-citizens was 735000. There were still 432000 non-citizens in 2005, and the number has not decreased much since. Lately, interest in acquiring Latvian citizenship has grown slightly as a result of Latvia's membership in the European Union. The authorities expect that many non-citizens will be naturalised in the next few years. Nevertheless, the expectation is that approximately 130000 people will ultimately remain without citizenship.[770] The legal status of persons who did not acquire citizenship automatically after independence remained unclear until 1995. Only a few regulations were passed, which restricted their rights in comparison to that of citizens, which, *a contrario,* meant that their situation had not changed. In 1995, the Law on the Status of Former USSR Citizens Who Are Not Citizens of Latvia or Any Other State[771] was passed. It established the special status of "non-citizens". These persons had a registered residence (domicile) in Latvia on 1 July 1992, and did not possess citizenship of Latvia or any other country, except for a few retired army officers and their family members who had not acquired that status.[772] On the basis of the law, almost 15 per cent of Latvian residents were given the status of "non-citizens", who were mostly of Ukrainian, Belorussian, Russian, Lithuanian, and Jewish ethnicity.[773] The Latvian authorities claim and the Latvian Constitutional Court agrees that the "non-citizens" are neither citizens nor are they stateless according to the definition of international law, as they have a legal status recognised by the state of Latvia. The status of "non-citizen" is not revoked if they

769 The lengthy exclusionary list demonstrates how threatened ethnic Latvians felt in relation to the members of the former occupying forces, which represented one third of the population. In the Baltic States, it was considered a fact that the greater the share of inhabitants without automatic citizenship rights in a certain state was, the greater the resistance to participating in political life became. Järve, Estonian Citizenship: Between Ethnic Preferences and Democratic Obligations, in: Citizenship Policies in the New Europe, 2007, p. 45.

770 Krūma, Checks and Balances in Latvian Nationality Policies, in: Citizenship Policies in the New Europe, 2007, p. 67.

771 Official Gazette of Latvia, No. 63, April 25, 1995.

772 Poleshchuk (ed.), Chance to Survive, 2009, p. 173. See also Krūma, Checks and Balances in Latvian Nationality Policies, in: Citizenship Policies in the New Europe, 2007, p. 72.

773 Poleshchuk (ed.), Chance to Survive, 2009, pp. 148–149.

decide to move abroad. Their status can only be changed if they became citizens of another country.[774] However, non-governmental organisations took the opposite position and pointed out that "non-citizens" were *de facto* stateless.[775] What does it actually mean to be a "non-citizen"?

"Non-citizens" possess similar rights as citizens, such as the right to reside in Latvia without a visa or a residence permit. They are protected from expulsion as specified by Article 2 of the Law On the Status of Former USSR Citizens, unlike the citizens of third countries. When ratifying international conventions, Latvia generally declares that it treats citizens and "non-citizens" equally. They enjoy the consular protection of Latvia. However, they do not have passive voting rights in local and state elections, the right to become state officials, or to belong to certain professions. "Non-citizens" are also not EU citizens. However, they can acquire the status of long-term resident in accordance with the 2006 Law on the Status of a Long-term Resident of the European Community in the Republic of Latvia[776] (which was passed to comply with Directive 2003/109/EC concerning the status of third-country nationals who are long-term residents). "Non-citizens" are not permitted to found their own political parties according to the law on political parties.[777] However, they can join existing parties.[778]

"Non-citizens" also had long-term problems with the validity of their personal documents. Many did not acquire the new, internationally recognised passports for "non-citizens", and kept using their Soviet passports, which expired at the end of 1998. It was feared that "non-citizens" who were abroad at that time would not be permitted to return to Latvia, and passports' date of expiry was prolonged as a result.[779] The residents of Latvia who did not acquire the status of citizens or "non-citizens", or who lost their status of "non-citizens", were considered aliens in accordance with the Immigration Law.[780] According to the available data, their number was around 1600.[781]

---

774 *Ibid.*, p. 173.

775 Latvian Centre for Human Rights, Annual Report on Human Rights 1998, p. 13.

776 Official Gazette of Latvia, No. 107, 7 July 2006.

777 *Ibid.*

778 Krūma, Checks and Balances in Latvian Nationality Policies, in: Citizenship Policies in the New Europe, 2007, p. 73. *See also* Poleshchuk (ed.), Chance to Survive, 2009, pp. 178 and 229.

779 Latvian Centre for Human Rights, Annual Report on Human Rights 1998, pp. 13–14.

780 Official Gazette of Latvia, No. 169, 20 November 2002.

781 Poleshchuk (ed.), Chance to Survive, 2009, pp. 176 in 178.

Until 1998, around 6000 people were unable to acquire the new passports designed for "non-citizens". They included people whose temporary residence permits expired or their spouses, and people without valid personal documents. In 1998, the law on the status of "non-citizens" was amended and many of them were permitted to acquire "non-citizen" status, which slightly ameliorated their situation. Nonetheless, some groups were not able to become "non-citizens", e.g. people who left Latvia at a particular time after the country became independent, or people who acquired Russian citizenship after independence and then renounced it.[782] These people are not reported to have been expelled and were allowed to stay in the country, as the Latvian authorities were aware that expulsion would be against international legislation on human rights.[783] The Law on the Status of Stateless Persons in the Republic of Latvia was passed in 1999 to regulate the status of these persons. It specified that stateless people would acquire legal status.[784]

As in Estonia, the conditions of naturalisation in Latvia were very strict for people who did not acquire citizenship automatically. By comparison, the conditions were relatively favourable in Slovenia, although they also led to the exclusion of certain groups. Of the three countries, the possibility of naturalisation became available in Slovenia first, as soon as the country declared independence in 1991. Naturalisation became possible in Estonia in 1993 and in Latvia in 1995. Another obvious difference is whether citizenship was conditional on proficiency in the language. This was not a condition in Slovenia (although it was suggested in the legislative process). By contrast, Estonia and Latvia required a high level of language proficiency, which presented a great obstacle to acquiring citizenship.

All three states addressed the situation of former permanent residents who were not granted citizenship similarly. They were considered aliens, with Latvia even explicitly assigning them a specific "non-citizen" status. The situation in Slovenia and Estonia was similar; both applied the provisions of legislation intended for aliens migrating to the country to the former permanent residents. The pressure of the international community and negotiations to enter the EU forced Latvia, as well as Estonia and Slovenia to correct their mistakes regarding the legal status of these people, which were made during the process of gaining

782 Latvian Centre for Human Rights, Annual Report on Human Rights 1998, pp. 13–14.

783 Krūma, Checks and Balances in Latvian Nationality Policies, in: Citizenship Policies in the New Europe, 2007, p. 72.

784 Latvian Centre for Human Rights, Annual Report on Human Rights, 1999.

independence. All three countries were forced to pass legalisation (that is, regularisation) laws.

There is another similarity between the three countries. Estonia and Latvia's first citizenship laws were passed by the two Supreme Soviets, which were technically elected by the population. Whatever legitimacy they had as the governing body of a one-party system was therefore used to pass laws that were not in the interest of the majority of the population. The same is true of Slovenia in the sense that people who had a permanent residence registered on the territory of SRS were entitled to vote in the referendum. They mostly voted for independence and ensured its legitimacy; however, the laws meant to implement the independence process lacked legitimacy. The result was the same in all three states: certain people who were fully included in the cooperative process of managing public affairs were afterwards excluded.

In all three states – Estonia, Latvia, and Slovenia – the majority, as well as the minority, of the population were target groups of the politics of exclusion from citizenship and other forms of legal status. In all three states, the majority consisted of individuals whose ethnicity was different from the ethnicity whom the nation-state belonged. The minority consisted of members of the army or security services of the predecessor state, the Yugoslav People's Army in Slovenia (as was evident from the denied applications for citizenship and from generalisations that all erased people were former officers of the YPA), and the Soviet Army in Latvia and Estonia. It is true that the individuals who were ultimately deprived of their status or rights in Estonia and Latvia were often former soldiers of the Soviet Army and their families, or people who were believed to have acted against Latvian or Estonian independence. The armies went from being considered 'domestic' to 'foreign' armies, and consequently, occupying forces. Today these stateless persons do not have other options except to marry a Latvian or Estonian citizen, or move to Russia where former emigrants are still being accepted. However, many of them do not have any bond with Russia, or were born in the Baltic States and wish to remain on there. Estonia and Latvia never adopted a holistic strategy to address their legal and actual status,[785] like Slovenia and its 'erased' people. Based on the fact that two decades have passed since the Eastern Bloc became independent, some authors call for a reconsideration of

785 Lottmann, No Direction Home: Nationalism and Statelessness in the Baltics, Texas International Law Review, 43 (2008) 3, p. 509.

whether the systematic exclusion of military personnel from citizenship remains reasonable, as it is no longer possible to endanger the independence process.[786]

3.3 Lithuania

In contrast to Estonia and Latvia, Lithuania's approach to regulating citizenship was more liberal and inclusive. In Lithuania, the new Law on Citizenship[787] was passed in 1989, before independence and the dissolution of the Soviet Union in 1990. This may have been due to the fact that Soviet citizenship law left a part of citizenship competence to its republics. The Law on Citizenship defined two categories of citizens. Some people became citizens automatically through law (*ipso facto*), while others had to submit an application to acquire citizenship.

Citizenship was automatically granted to i) persons with citizenship or permanent residence in Lithuania prior to 15 July 1940, their children and grandchildren that were or remained permanent residents of Lithuania, and ii) persons with permanent residence in Lithuania, provided they were born in the state and were descendants of Lithuanians, and on the condition that they had no other citizenship. Persons permitted to apply for citizenship through the law had to have had their permanent residence in Lithuania for a minimum of two years before the law was passed. They also had to be employed or have other means of subsistence in Lithuania. Thus, people who came to Lithuania while it was still a Soviet republic were also permitted to acquire citizenship under favourable conditions. Applications could be submitted for two years after the day that the law came into force. The only additional condition for acquiring citizenship was an oath of loyalty to the Lithuanian constitution and legal order.

On the basis of this option, around 90 per cent of the permanent residents of Lithuania who were not ethnic Lithuanians acquired citizenship. Only one per cent of permanent residents chose not to acquire Lithuanian citizenship. The rest did not meet the specified conditions. Despite Lithuania's initially liberal approach to the question of citizenship, the situation slowly became more complicated after 1991. That year a new law on citizenship[788] was passed, with stricter conditions for acquiring citizenship. These included a language proficiency test and knowledge of the constitution. Permanent residents were also required to

786 *Ibid.*, p. 513.

787 Law on Citizenship of the Lithuanian Soviet Socialist Republic, 3 November 1989, No. XI-3329.

788 Republic of Lithuania Law on Amending Articles 1, 17 and 28 of the Law on Citizenship, 5 December 1991, No. I-2072, amended 2 July 1997, No. VIII-391.

actually reside in Lithuania, and were prohibited from having dual citizenship. The condition of permanent residence was not met by the members of armed forces and security services, as provided by the Resolution of the Supreme Soviet on procedure of execution of the Citizenship Law of the Republic of Lithuania,[789] except for certain groups of military personnel who were allowed to obtain citizenship. The principle of avoiding dual citizenship also made the conditions stricter. After the Law on Citizenship was amended, Lithuanian authorities required the citizenship holders (with some exceptions) to immigrate to Lithuania and renounce all other citizenships if they wished to keep their Lithuanian citizenship.[790]

It is evident that Lithuanian regulations for acquiring citizenship were more favourable than in Latvia and Estonia; they were closer to Slovenian regulations. While Latvia and Estonia tied permanent residents' acquisition of citizenship to restrictive terms (for example, the quota in Latvia, the language requirements in Estonia, and, in both countries, the fact residence in the country before the declaration of independence was not acknowledged for the purposes of naturalisation), Lithuania specified three initial requirements: two years of residence in Lithuania, a source of income, and a loyalty oath. The Slovenian regulation was somewhat less strict, as it required a registered permanent residence of six months (from 23 December 1990, to 25 June 1991) and actual residence in Slovenia. It did not, however, require either the source of income and the oath, nor the renouncement of other citizenships that Lithuania introduced later. However, the requirements for acquiring citizenship in Slovenia became stricter after the concept of a danger to public order, safety and state defence was introduced (the new Paragraph 3, Article 40 of the Citizenship Act of the Republic of Slovenia), while Lithuania never introduced such requirements. In contrast to the other two Baltic States, Lithuania permitted some former members of the military to acquire citizenship.

As in all newly formed states, the question of permanent residents who did not acquire Lithuanian citizenship (less than ten per cent according to the available data) arose in Lithuania as well. The Lithuanian authorities regulated their status with the Law on the Legal Status of Aliens in the Republic of Lithuania,[791] specifying in Paragraph 2, Article 6 that persons who were permanent residents

---

789 11 December 1991, No. I-2080.

790 Krūma, Lithuanian Nationality, in: Citizenship Policies in the New Europe, 2007, p. 90 and following.

791 Law on Legal Status of Foreigners in Republic of Lithuania, 4 September 1991, No. I-1750.

of Lithuania before the law went into force and had not acquired Lithuanian citizenship were considered aliens with permanent residence. Their legal status was therefore regulated at all times. Similar to Croatia, Lithuania regulated the situation of its permanent residents who had not acquired citizenship, and thus avoided having thousands of people without legal status on its territory after gaining independence. It also avoided mass statelessness, fulfilling its international and internal legal obligations to the people who would otherwise have been affected.

The reason for the relatively inclusive treatment of the people of non-Lithuanian nationality is supposed to be related to the fact that the number of immigrants (with no knowledge of the local language and local culture) in Lithuania was much lower than in Estonia and Latvia. The inhabitants of Lithuania, therefore, did not feel as "threatened" as the inhabitants of the other two Baltic States. That does not mean, however, that there are no anti-Russian tendencies in Lithuania. It does indicate that there were not many reasons to pursue restrictive policies.[792]

3.4 The Czech Republic and the Slovak Republic

It is interesting to compare the post-independence citizenship policies of the former Czechoslovak Republic and Yugoslavia, as the two countries had a similar federal regulatory structure and ethnic distribution. Like in Yugoslavia, every citizen of the Czechoslovak Republic had both federal citizenship and citizenship in either the Czech or the Slovak Republic.

In the autumn of 1992, when it became likely that Czechoslovakia would split into two countries, many citizens started thinking about their future citizenship in case the federal state was dissolved. They started to take advantage of the possibility of changing their citizenship afforded by the Federal Act on the Rules of Acquisition and Loss of Nationality[793] and the corresponding laws of the two republics.[794] These regulations enabled Czechoslovak citizens to change their republic citizenship easily, as in Yugoslavia. By the end of 1992, 65000 Slovak Republic citizens had switched to Czech citizenship, and many Czechs also

792 Lottmann, No Direction Home: Nationalism and Statelessness in the Baltics, Texas International Law Review 43 (2008) 3, pp. 505 and 509.

793 Federal Act No. 165/1968 Coll. on the Rules of Acquisition and Loss of Nationality.

794 Act No. 839/1969 Coll. of the Czech National Council on Acquisition and Loss of Citizenship of the Czech Socialist Republic, and Act No. 206/1968 Coll. of Slovak National Council on Acquisition and Loss of Citizenship of the Slovak Socialist Republic.

switched to Slovak citizenship. On the first day of 1993, the two new countries were officially founded.

The Czech and Slovak Republics both passed new citizenship acts.[795] Both laws had two steps for acquiring the citizenship of the newly founded countries. First, citizenship was automatically granted to all persons who held the citizenship of the given republic on 31 December 1992. When Czechoslovakian citizenship was terminated due to the dissolution of Czechoslovakia, the former republic citizenship transformed into full citizenship of a newly founded state. Second, both laws enabled all Czechoslovak citizens who did not automatically acquire the citizenship of their preferred state to acquire that citizenship under favourable conditions. Those persons who were automatically granted citizenship of Slovakia and wanted to obtain Czech citizenship had to demonstrate two years of registered residence in the Czech Republic and evidence that they had no criminal convictions.[796] The conditions of obtaining Slovakian citizenship were even more favourable: former citizens of Czechoslovakia had to submit a written form (including their place of birth and present residence) to the competent authorities in Slovakia by 31 December 1993, and prove that on 31 December 1992, they had held Czechoslovakian citizenship.[797]

Moreover, the residents of a successor state who did not acquire its citizenship did not become aliens. Paragraph 3, Article 1 of the Law on Aliens in the Federal Czech and Slovakian Republics[798] defined aliens as persons who are not citizens of the Czech and the Slovak federal republics. This federal law remained in force in both successor states after the dissolution of the federal state. Therefore, all persons who were able to prove that they were citizens of the Czech or the Slovak Republic or were assumed to be citizens, were not considered or treated as aliens in the newly independent Czech Republic and Slovakia. Their status was legally regulated, they were protected from expulsion, and they did not have to meet the requirements (passport, means of subsistence, residence, evidence of no criminal convictions) otherwise requested of aliens from third countries wishing to reside

---

795 Issue No. 40/1993 Collection of Acts and Collection of Laws of the Slovak Republic.

796 On this basis 240,000 former Czechoslovakian citizens acquired citizenship of the Czech Republic from 1 January 1993 to 30 June 1993.

797 Baršová, Czech Citizenship Legislation Between Past and Future, in: Citizenship Policies in the New Europe, 2007, p. 165 and following; Kusá, The Slovak Question and the Slovak Answer, in: Citizenship Policies in the New Europe, 2007, p. 193 and following.

798 Law on Foreigners of the Czecho-Slovakian Federal Republic, Collection of Acts No. 123/1992.

in the Czech Republic or Slovakia. In Slovakia, this federal law remained in force until 1995 when the new Law on Aliens of the Republic of Slovakia[799] was passed. In the Czech Republic, it remained in force until 1999; it was amended twice and finally replaced by an entirely new law.[800]

Despite the relatively favourable transitional regulation of the citizenship question, these processes did not occur without complications. While the legal situation of persons who did not reside in the successor state of which they were citizens was regulated, there were some difficulties regarding access to social rights, for example access to social aid or housing.[801] Without citizenship, affected people could lose their right to live in social housing, as housing policy gave citizens preferential treatment, much like in Slovenia. Somewhat later, difficulties also emerged in the field of employment when the Czech authorities started requiring work permits of Slovakian workers and vice versa. With the Law on Changes of Some Regulations on Employment of December 1993[802] the subjects of legislation, for example, were changed from Czechoslovak citizens to citizens of the Republic of Slovakia (e.g. Paragraph 2, Article 1). If workers wished to keep their jobs in 1994 and 1995, they had to apply for a work permit that the Labour Office had to issue within a period of thirty days. However, affected workers were not permitted to work during that time, and if there was a candidate with citizenship for their job, they could lose it.[803] Work permit requirements for former citizens of Czechoslovakia were later abolished, but the aforementioned obstacles were enough of an 'incentive' for many to emigrate. Nevertheless, the successor states reached numerous agreements in the years after the predecessor state was dissolved. These introduced the equal treatment of the citizens of the former Czechoslovakia with the citizens of the state in which the agreement was enforced (in the field of healthcare, education, social security etc.), at least partially neutralising the consequences of the dissolution of the state for the citizenship status of the individual.[804]

---

799 Law on Foreigners of the Republic of Slovakia, Collection of Acts No. 73/1995.

800 Law No. 190/1994 on Changes and Amendments to the Law No. 123/1992 on Foreigners in Czecho-Slovakian Federal Republic, and Law No. 150/1996 on Changes and Amendments to the Law No. 123/1992 on Foreigners in Czecho-Slovakian Federal Republic.

801 Interview with Darina Macková, 4 February 2011.

802 Law Amending Certain Rules on Employment, Collection of Acts No. 319/1993.

803 Interview with Darina Macková, 4 February 2011.

804 Macková, Some Legal Aspects of Dissolution of Former Czechoslovakia, in: Zbornik Pravnog Fakulteta u Zagrebu 53 (2003) 2.

Another problem was that both states presumed that persons who automatically acquired citizenship of one of the countries thereby renounced their former citizenship. As a result, it became difficult to assert certain rights, particularly when one successor state bound a certain right to citizenship and the other to permanent residence.[805] The two countries only amended their regulations on citizenship in 1997, when the Constitutional Court of the Czech Republic ruled that a Czech citizen who decided to also acquire Slovakian citizenship would not lose his/her Czech citizenship.[806] The former citizens of Czechoslovakia were exempted from the general prohibition of dual citizenship.[807] On the basis of legal changes in 1999, up to 6278 former Czechoslovakian citizens acquired Czech citizenship (followed by a few thousand more by 2003). These people were able to prove that they had continuously lived on the territory of the Czech Republic after Czechoslovakia was dissolved. Such a high number also demonstrates the necessity for legal changes.[808]

The third negative aspect of these citizenship policies was the disproportionate consequences they had on Roma people who were deprived of their legal status in the states that they lived in. Many of the affected people were born in Slovakia and migrated from Slovakia to the Czech Republic between 1945 and 1989. They thus became Slovakian citizens, in accordance with the general regulations, despite living in the Czech Republic. In addition to not residing in the state of which they automatically became citizens, many of these people did not have valid personal documents. They did not apply for citizenship in their state of residence as a result of not being informed. They discovered that their status was unresolved only when they were denied the rights that they attempted to exert.[809] In certain cases, their application was denied as a result of previous convictions.[810]

The consequences of the changes in legal status were reflected in the loss of employment, livelihood and social housing. The consequences were even more evident as a result of simultaneous economic transition and privatisation. Many

805 *Ibid.*

806 Constitutional Court of the Czech Republic, Ruling No. IV US 34/97, 5 May 1997.

807 Law No. 94/1999 Coll. Amending the Law No. 40/1993.

808 Baršová, Czech Citizenship Legislation Between Past and Future, in: Citizenship Policies in the New Europe, 2007, p. 168.

809 Macková, Some Legal Aspects of Dissolution of Former Czechoslovakia, in: Zbornik Pravnog Fakulteta u Zagrebu 53 (2003) p. 2.

810 Kusá, The Slovak Question and the Slovak Answer, in: Citizenship Policies in the New Europe, 2007, p. 198.

Slovakian Roma people worked in the Czech Republic, and after losing their citizenship, employment and residence, many were forced to return to Slovakia, since they held Slovakian citizenship. Often they had nowhere to go; improvised slums started spring up, particularly in Eastern Slovakia. Roma people who had been convicted of criminal offences were also expelled from the Czech Republic on the basis of expulsion orders issued by courts. This meant that they were banned for life from entering the Czech Republic, since no legal action could be taken against such an order and there was no possibility to terminate its effects. Expulsion orders were issued by courts without verification of the possible effects it would have on an expelled person's right of protection of the personal and family life. 663 citizens of Slovakia were thus expelled from the state between 1993 and mid-1996. Most of them were Roma and more than 90 per cent had an entry ban for life for actions that did not represent a grave threat to the public order.

The Law on Expulsion of Aliens was executed not only by the courts but also by the police, which did not need court orders. From 1993 to 1995 at least 869 Slovakian citizens with unresolved citizenship were expelled from the Czech Republic, and it is estimated that approximately 70 per cent of them were ethnically Roma. Human rights NGOs criticised the Czech and Slovak citizenship laws for their detrimental effect on the situation of Roma people.[811] Even though the Czech Republic and Slovakia had some of the best solutions in the field of regulating the legal status of residents post-succession, there were numerous difficulties. These were caused by a strict adherence to the principle of avoiding dual citizenship and a failure to recognise permanent or habitual residence as a basis for automatically acquiring citizenship in the case of succession. The regulations in the Czech Republic and in Slovakia were introduced in a manner that, similar to the successor states of the SFRY, prevented *de iure* statelessness in principle, but led to numerous equally important problems in practice. The regulations complied better with the constitutional and international obligations of the countries, since they reached numerous agreements granting all former Czechoslovakian citizens equal status independently of citizenship. This did not occur on the territory of former Yugoslavia, including in Slovenia. The Slovenian legislation, however, did not insist on a strict avoidance of dual citizenship, which meant that 171000 people were not forced to choose between two options in the process of acquiring citizenship through extraordinary naturalisation.

---

811 Struhárová, Disparate Impact: Removing Roma from the Czech Republic, 2004.

VII. Conclusion

> *The doorkeeper can see the man's come to his end, his hearing has faded, and so, so that he can be heard, he shouts to him: 'Nobody else could have got in this way, as this entrance was meant only for you. Now I'll go and close it'.*
>
> *Franz Kafka, The Trial*

I am approaching the end of my analysis of the erasure of a group of former SFRY citizens from the register of permanent residents with reference to constitutional law, international law, and the legislative and executive regulations. It is safe to claim that the erasure was a gross breach of human rights and constitutional principles unlike any other after Slovenia declared independence. In 2012, the events set in motion by the erasure culminated with the decision of the Grand Chamber of the ECHR. All that remains is to hope that this development will not lead to a loss of momentum and become a tool in the hands of populists, but encourage discussion about accountability and the measures that could correct the wrongdoings of the state. Indeed, certain encouraging signs inspire hope; public discussions have taken on a different character. Voices calling for reparations and action in accordance with the ECHR's decision have prevailed. Representatives of the political elite who still use the rhetoric of stigmatisation and oppose the solutions are now finding themselves increasingly alone in their opinions. A compensation mechanism, once unthinkable, has been established.

These changes are perhaps a consequence of the fact that increasingly large numbers of people recognise that the act of the erasure was a premeditated, purposeful, and informed action: the perpetrators of the erasure were warned of the consequences of their actions ahead of time. They turned a blind eye because their true goal was to achieve, not avoid, these consequences. The erasure was an unlawful act for which the authorities could have faced criminal prosecution had the statute of limitations not expired, as their actions show all the necessary indications of criminal abuse of power, abuse of office, or at least of misconduct at work. The erasure was part of a broader plan to remove as many people of non-Slovenian origin from the country as possible. This plan was apparent in the attempts to tighten the citizenship requirements for extraordinary naturalisation; the prevention of persons with temporary resident permits and persons actually living in Slovenia from obtaining citizenship; the unlawful blacklists; the attempted retrospective and retroactive amendments to Article 40 of the Citizenship Act which were intended to legitimise the blacklist; the arbitrary implementation of the Citizenship Act; the refusal to reinstate the legal status of persons who did not obtain Slovenian citizenship; the passage and implementation of unlawful internal guidelines; the organized stigmatisation of the erased persons; the denial of the erasure and the systemic campaign of lies about it; the obstruction and rejection of the implementation of the Constitutional Courts decisions; and in the passivity when it came to redressing the wrongdoings, which persists even today.

Depriving the members of an ethnic minority of their legal status was an act of racism that primarily affected the members of the lower working class; accordingly, it was also an act of class discrimination. It brought together the right and the left wing, with the former actively and aggressively opposing the redressal of wrongs using populist radicalism, and the latter, with only few exceptions, helping them by remaining passive. In this, they were supported by many members of academia, primarily legal experts, and also by the general public, which was deluded precisely by populist radicalism.

The erasure deprived people of "the right to have rights". Through a chain of conditions, it enabled the revocation of all the rights tied to legal status, which forms the basis of most rights in the world today. The revocation of legal status apparently gives the system legitimacy to revoke any of the individual's further rights and eventually even to remove the person – by forcing him/her into illegality, or removing him/her from the country physically. Apart from the most heinous crimes in international law such as torture, genocide, war crimes, and crimes against humanity, one can hardly think of a crime with more problematic and long-reaching consequences. Historically, the revocation of legal status was often the first step implemented by the state apparatus in order to remove undesirable segments of the population, often followed by harsher, more decisive actions. In this light, events like the erasure deserve special attention, as they are often used by states that do not dare make use of genocide or crimes against humanity.

The Slovenian Constitutional Court played a central role in uncovering the erasure and correcting the injustices. Its significance is apparent in the restrictions it set on direct democracy through referendums. The proposed referendums related to the erasure and the Constitutional Court's decisions raise doubts about the appropriateness of the current constitutional and legislative order, which barely restricts decision-making by referendum, even though that institution is clearly not an appropriate means of deciding issues which affect minorities and human rights abuses. Moreover, this form of decision-making is also inappropriate when decisions need to be made on complex questions which cannot be decided along the lines of "for" and "against", and which are too complex to readily allow voters to have an informed opinion. The history of the erasure clearly demonstrates a lack of awareness of the fact that decisions by referendum are equally subject to the Constitutional Court's assessment as the decisions of the legislature, that the Constitutional Court's decisions cannot be the subject of a referendum, and that such calls for referendums undermine the authority of the Constitutional Court (with authority being the sole source of the Court's power), which is the cornerstone of democracy.

To uphold and further develop constitutional democracy, and contemplate and overcome the elements of totalitarianism which are still present in the political and legal order, it is necessary for all segments of society (political and academic elites, the education system, civil society) to accept the facts of the erasure and encourage further regulations to be passed which could, at least partially, correct past wrongs. The regulations of the Legal Status Act that enabled erased persons to apply for the reinstatement of their legal status were inappropriate, as they included several requirements that could not possibly be met retroactively. Furthermore, the administrative procedure was lengthy and involved the payment of fees and the presentation of proof, all of which placed the burden on the victims. The Legal Status Act should therefore be understood as yet another attempt by the legislature to solve the issue of the erased persons, but not to also rectify the consequences of the erasure.

The situation requires a review and some changes. The Legal Status Act should be reopened, as some erased persons are still interested in having their status reinstated, but missed the deadline. The administrative procedure to issue permanent residence permits retrospectively needs to be simplified: applicants should only need to notify the authorities of their interest in obtaining a permit, and the only condition should be that the person was erased from the register of permanent residents. This would be consistent with the first point of the Constitutional Court's decision U-I-264/02, according to which the state is obliged to issue all erased persons with a residence permit valid from the day of the erasure onwards, irrespective of possible absences from the country or failure to meet other requirements. It should also be easier for erased persons to be reunited with their families, i.e. family members who were not erased; under current laws, erased persons who started a family after leaving Slovenia are not able to return to the country if their family members have no legal status. Hence, family members should be able to obtain permanent residence permits immediately after such a permit is granted to the person asserting the right to family unification.

When implementing the law, the Ministry of Internal Affairs should actively search for erased persons across the SFRY successor states and inform them of the new legal possibilities to regain their legal status. The low number of applications for permanent residence permits shows that the news about the Legal Status Act, passed in 2010, failed to reach the vast majority of eligible persons – in the first two years, only a few hundred of the altogether more than 13000 eligible persons applied to have their legal status reinstated. The low number could also be a sign that in the twenty years since the erasure, erased persons' interest in returning to Slovenia has waned, and they can no longer see a purpose in trying.

The most important step, which the European Court of Human Rights had also demanded, was to set up a compensation scheme, including the eligibility criteria for obtaining reparations. The current amount of compensation is merely symbolic, and hardly meets the damages actually incurred. It should be increased and made available to all erased persons irrespective of whether they regained legal status in Slovenia, as some of them are simply no longer interested in having their status reinstated.

Another necessary measure arises from the obligation to ensure the moral satisfaction of the victims of the erasure. This goes beyond issuing special declaratory decisions and should be implemented on the national level. This could take the form of an apology, passed as a resolution by the National Assembly and supported by all the key state actors. Unless this is done, the current state of affairs will continue indefinitely – erased persons will continue to be stigmatised and the state will continue to avoid taking responsibility for the erasure.

The main aim that this book seeks to achieve is to raise awareness on the international level about the fact that serious human rights violations which affect all areas of a person's life can also be perpetrated by states that are not willing to engage in, say, active persecution, blood-shed, torture, and similar. They can also occur with the use if administrative measures that seem to be based on law. Another, more specific aim of this book is to encourage Slovenian society to accept responsibility for the erasure. I am convinced that many citizens wish to understand the erasure and its consequences better, and to use their knowledge to compel the perpetrators of the erasure to take responsibility for it. Irrespective of whether these goals will be achieved, its purpose is also to explain that the erasure was a breach of human rights on a massive scale, and a specific, although recognisable, form of oppression exercised by the state.

Why would anyone wish to merely comprehend the erasure, one might ask? Let me respond in the words of Hannah Arendt:

> Comprehension does not mean denying the outrageous [...]. It means, rather, examining and bearing consciously the burden which our century has placed on us – neither denying its existence nor submitting meekly to its weight. Comprehension, in short, means the unpremeditated, attentive facing up to, and resisting of, reality – whatever it may be.[812]

Comprehending the erasure can help us understand the world around us and discern the mechanisms behind the breaches of human right. An attempt to comprehend is the first necessary step on the path to resisting non-thinking, which can absorb us and prevent us from understanding these patterns. In a legal environment full of norms which pressure us into non-thinking, the quest to comprehend is that much more important and the key to understanding that which is unjust within the law itself. It is the only way to resist injustice.

This is my understanding and my resistance.

812 Arendt, The Origins of Totalitarianism, 1973, p. viii.

VIII. Sources

Books, articles and reports

Accetto, Matej: Širše implikacije problema državljanstva – sorazmernost legitimnih interesov države in interesov posameznika, in: Dnevi javnega prava, Inštitut za javno upravo, Ljubljana 1999, pp. 591–606.

Agamben, Giorgio: Homo sacer. Suverena oblast in golo življenje, Koda, Ljubljana 2004.

Agamben, Giorgio: State of exception, University of Chicago, Chicago, London 2005.

Alexy, Robert: A Defence of Radbruch's Formula, in: David Dyzenhaus (ed.), Recrafting the Rule of Law: The Limits of Legal Order, Hart Publishing, Oxford, Portland, Oregon 1999.

Arendt, Hannah: Eichmann in Jerusalem. A Report on the Banality of Evil, Penguin Books, New York, London, Victoria, Toronto, Auckland, 1994.

Arendt, Hannah: The Origins of Totalitarianism, A Harvest Book, Hartcourt Brace & Company, San Diego, New York, London, Ljubljana 1973.

Bajt, Veronika: More Than Administratively Created "Foreigners": The Erased People and a Reflection of the Nationalist Construction of the Other in the Symbolic Idea about "Us", in: Neža Kogovšek and Brankica Petković (eds.), The Scars of the Erasure: A Contribution to the Critical Understanding of the Erasure of People from the Register of Permanent Residents of the Republic of Slovenia, Peace Institute, Ljubljana 2010, pp. 195–218.

Baršová, Andrea: Czech Citizenship Legislation Between Past and Future, in: Rainer Bauböck; Bernhard Perchinig; Wiebke Sievers (eds.), Citizenship Policies in the New Europe, Amsterdam University Press, Amsterdam 2007, pp. 163–194.

Bugarič, Bojan: "Preneseni", dejstva, interpelacija, in: Dnevnikov Objektiv, 28. 3. 2009.

Bugarič, Bojan: Ustavno sodstvo in (ali) parlamentarna demokracija: o doktrinah pravnega interesa in političnih vprašanj, Zbornik znanstvenih razprav, 55 (1995), pp. 43–66.

Čebulj, Janez: Posebnosti ustavne pritožbe s področja upravnega prava, in: Marijan Pavčnik and Arne Mavčič (eds.), Ustavno sodstvo, Cankarjeva založba, Ljubljana 2000, pp. 301–321.

Cerar, Miro: (Ne)političnost ustavnega sodstva, in: Marijan Pavčnik and Arne Mavčič (eds.), Ustavno sodstvo, Cankarjeva založba, Ljubljana 2000, pp. 349–389.

Cerar, Miro: Slovensko ustavno sodišče – med pravom in politiko, Dnevi javnega prava, Inštitut za javno upravo, Ljubljana 1998, pp. 113–130.

Cholewinski, Ryszard: Irregular migrants: Access to minimum social rights, Council of Europe Publishing, Strasbourg 2005.

Dedić, Jasminka: Konstrukcija kolektivnih identitet in genocid v nekdanji Jugoslaviji in Ruandi: primerjalna analiza, Doctoral Thesis, University of Ljubljana, Faculty of Social Science, Ljubljana 2008.

Dedić, Jasminka; Jalušič, Vlasta; Zorn, Jelka: The Erased: Organized Innocence and the Politics of Exclusion, Peace Institute, Ljubljana 2003.

Dyzenhaus, David (ed.): Recrafting the Rule of Law: The limits of legal order, Hart Publishing, Oxford, Portland (Oregon) 1999.

Dyzenhaus, David: Hard Cases in Wicked Legal Systems. Pathologies of Legality, Oxford University Press, New York 2010.

Džankić, Jelena: EUDO Citizenship Observatory, Country Report: Montenegro (2010), pp. 3–8, URL: http://eudo-citizenship.eu/docs/CountryReports/Montenegro.pdf (5 May 2011).

Džankić, Jelena: Lineages of citizenship in Montenegro, CITSEE Working Paper Series 14, University of Edinburgh, 2010.

Flander, Benjamin: Homines sacri – izbrisani kot konstitutivni element slovenske države, Pravna praksa 28 (2009) 14, p. 18.

Gallagher, Michael: Ireland: The referendum as a conservative device, in: Michael Gallagher; Pier Vincenzo Uleri (eds.), The Referendum Experience in Europe, Macmillan, Basingstoke 1996, pp. 94–115.

Gallagher, Michael; Uleri, Pier Vincenzo (ed.): The Referendum Experience in Europe, Macmillan, Basingstoke 1996.

Goldston, James A.: Holes in the Rights Framework: Racial Discrimination, Citizenship, and the Rights of Non-Citizens, Ethics and International Affairs 20 (2006) 3.

Gregorčič, Marta: Phantom Irresponsibility, or Fascism in Disguise, in: Journal for the Critique of Science 35 (2007) 228, pp. 115–132.

Hot, Meira: Reševanje vprašanja izbrisanih, Diploma Thesis, University of Ljubljana, Faculty of Law, 2004.

Igličar, Albin: Pravna kultura kot sestavina pravne države, in: Marijan Pavčnik (ed.), Pravna država, GV Založba, Ljubljana 2009, pp. 101–144.

Jalušič, Vlasta: Preface, in: Hannah Arendt, Vita Activa, Krtina, Ljubljana 1996.

Jalušič, Vlasta: Renouncing the Political Capacities: Organized Innocence and the Erasure of Citizenship Responsibility in Post-Yugoslav Nation-state Building, Journal for the Critique of Science, 35 (2007) 228, pp. 95–114.

Jalušič, Vlasta: Zlo nemišljenja. Arendtovske vaje v razumevanju posttotalitarne dobe in kolektivnih zločinov, Mirovni inštitut, Ljubljana 2010.

Jambrek, Peter: Ustavna demokracija, Državna založba Slovenije, Ljubljana 1992.

Järve, Priit: Estonian Citizenship: Between Ethnic Preferences and Democratic Obligations, in: Rainer Bauböck; Bernhard Perchinig; Wiebke Sievers (eds.), Citizenship Policies in the New Europe, Amsterdam University Press, Amsterdam 2007, pp. 43–62.

Jovanović, Svetolik Đ.: Državljanstvo socijalističke federativne republike Jugoslavije, Službeni list SFRJ, Beograd 1977.

Juhant, Jadranka: Upravnopravni vidikih statusnih zadev tujcev. Diploma Thesis, University of Ljubljana, Faculty of Law, 1996.

Kač, Miha; Krisch, Miha: Pregled predpisov o državljanstvu, Dnevi javnega prava, Inštitut za javno upravo, Ljubljana 1999, pp. 607–631.

Kaučič, Igor: Ustavna zasnova referenduma, Pravnik, 49 (1994) 1–3, pp. 17–30.

Kerševan, Erik: Upravnopravni vidik odškodninske odgovornosti države v primeru "izbrisanih", Pravna praksa 28 (2009) 19, p. 6.

Kerševan, Erik: Uradništvo med strokovnostjo in navodili: procesnopravni vidiki, Podjetje in delo 32 (2006) 6–7, pp. 1273–1281.

Kerševan, Erik: Vladavina prava in upravno pravo, in: Marijan Pavčnik (ed.), Pravna država, GV Založba, Ljubljana 2009, pp. 145–160.

Klein, Naomi: The Shock Doctrine. The Rise of Disaster Capitalism, Penguin Books, London 2007.

Kogovšek, Neža: The Erased People Yesterday, Today and Tomorrow. Erosion of Stereotypes and the Irreversible Road to Redressing Injustice, in: Neža Kogovšek and Brankica Petković (eds.), The Scars of the Erasure: A Contribution to the Critical Understanding of the Erasure of People from the Register of Permanent Residents of the Republic of Slovenia, Peace Institute, Ljubljana 2010, pp. 9–18.

Kogovšek, Neža: The Erasure as a Violation of Legally protected Human Rights, in: Neža Kogovšek and Brankica Petković (eds.), The Scars of the Erasure: A Contribution to the Critical Understanding of the Erasure of People from the Register of Permanent Residents of the Republic of Slovenia, Peace Institute, Ljubljana 2010.

Kogovšek, Neža: The Proposal of a Constitutional Law as the Negation of the Rule of Law, in: Journal for the Critique of Science, 35 (2007) 228, pp. 196–210.

Kogovšek, Neža; Petković, Brankica (eds.): The Scars of the Erasure: A Contribution to the Critical Understanding of the Erasure of People from the Register of Permanent Residents of the Republic of Slovenia, Peace Institute, Ljubljana 2010.

487Končina, Nada: Zakon o državljanstvu Republike Slovenije s komentarjem, Ministrstvo za notranje zadeve, Ljubljana 1993.

Kovač, Blaž: Izbrisanih ne izganjajo – ali pač?, in: Pravna praksa 27 (2008) 15, p. 23.

Kovač, Blaž; Kogovšek, Neža: Formalizem ali smrt, in: Pravna praksa 28 (2009) 20, pp. VI–VIII.

Kranjc, Janez: Ustavna pritožba kot institut varstva človekovih pravic, in: Marijan Pavčnik, Ada Polajnar-Pavčnik, Dragica Wedam Lukić (eds.), Temeljne pravice, Cankarjeva Založba, Ljubljana 1997.

Krasniqi, Gezim: EUDO Citizenship Observatory, Country Report: Kosovo (2010), URL: http://eudo-citizenship.eu/docs/CountryReports/Kosovo.pdf (5 May 2011).

Krivic, Matevž: "Nepismeno" proti odločbi ustavnega sodišča, Pravna praksa 30 (2003), p. 34.

Krivic, Matevž: Open letter in newspaper Večer, 15 January 2004.

Krivic, Matevž: Politični zločin, ne "administrativna napaka", Pravna praksa 26 (2007) 9, p. 21.

Krivic, Matevž: Pravno nepismeni politiki proti izbrisanim, Mladina 49 (2003).

Krivic, Matevž: Slabo prikrito in po vsebini zgrešeno izpodkopavanje odločbe Ustavnega sodišča, Pravna praksa 28 (2009) 20, pp. II–III.

Krivic, Matevž: Ustavno sodišče: pristojnosti in postopek, in: Marijan Pavčnik; Arne Mavčič (eds.), Ustavno sodstvo, Cankarjeva založba, Ljubljana 2000, pp. 47–211.

Krivic, Matevž: V sistemu deljene oblasti ni najvišjega organa, non-published paper for Dnevi javnega prava, 2011.

Krūma, Kristīne: Checks and Balances in Latvian Nationality Policies: National Agendas and International Frameworks, in: Rainer Bauböck; Bernhard Perchinig; Wiebke Sievers (eds.), Citizenship Policies in the New Europe, Amsterdam University Press, Amsterdam 2007, pp. 63–88.

Krūma, Kristīne: Lithuanian Nationality: Trump Card to Independence and Its Current Challenges, in: Rainer Bauböck; Bernhard Perchinig; Wiebke Sievers (eds.), Citizenship Policies in the New Europe, Amsterdam University Press, Amsterdam 2007, pp. 89–109.

Kurnik, Andrej: The Erased Go to Heaven, in: Journal for the Critique of Science 35 (2007) 228, pp. 133–144.

Kusá, Dagmar: The Slovak Question and the Slovak Answer: Citizenship During the Quest for National Self-Determination and After, in: Rainer Bauböck; Bernhard Perchinig; Wiebke Sievers (eds.), Citizenship Policies in the New Europe, Amsterdam University Press, Amsterdam 2007, pp. 185–212.

Kutoš, Samo: Pregled sodne prakse Vrhovnega sodišča RS v zvezi s 40. členom Zakona o državljanstvu (državljani drugih republik SFRJ), Dnevi javnega prava, Inštitut za javno upravo, Ljubljana 1999, pp. 633–646.

Lazarova Trajkovska, Mirjana: Pilot Judgments Procedure before the European Court of Human Rights, Doctoral Thesis, Mentor dr. Ciril Ribičič, University of Ljubljana, Faculty of Law, 2012.

Lipovec Čebron, Uršula: Erased Rights, Invisible Diseases: An Analysis of the Health Consequences of the Erasure, in: Neža Kogovšek; Brankica Petković (eds.), The Scars of the Erasure: A Contribution to the Critical Understanding of the Erasure of People from the Register of Permanent Residents of the Republic of Slovenia, Peace Institute, Ljubljana 2010, pp. 151–190.

Lipovec Čebron, Uršula: The Metastasis of the Erasure, in: Journal for the Critique of Science 35 (2007) 228, pp. 71–88.

Lottmann, Annelies: No Direction Home: Nationalism and Statelessness in the Baltics, Texas International Law Review 43 (2008) 3, pp. 503–519.

Lumbar, Metka: Vabila, Okno uprave, 28 March 2003, URL: <http://izbrisani.siol.net/intervju-9.rtf> (5 May 2011).

Macková, Darina: Some Legal Aspects of Dissolution of Former Czechoslovakia, Zbornik Pravnog Fakulteta u Zagrebu 53 (2003) 2, pp. 375–391.

Medved, Felicita: From Civic to Ethnic Community? The Evolution of Slovenian Citizenship, in: Rainer Bauböck; Bernhard Perchinig; Wiebke Sievers (eds.), Citizenship Policies in the New Europe, Amsterdam University Press, Amsterdam 2007, pp. 213–242.

Medvešček, Ivanka: Pravni položaj prebivalcev Slovenije po razpadu skupne države, Master Thesis, Faculty for State and European Studies, Kranj 2005.

Mekina, Borut: A Monument to the Erased, in: Journal for the Critique of Science 35 (2007) 228, pp. 44–51.

Mekina, Igor: The Erasure of the Erasure, in Journal for the Critique of Science 35 (2007) 228, pp. 174–189.

Mesojedec Pervinšek, Alenka: Predpisi o državljanih in tujcih z uvodnimi pojasnili, Uradni list Republike Slovenije, Ljubljana 1997.

Mesojedec Pervinšek, Alenka: Učinek mednarodnega prava v notranjem pravu Republike Slovenije na področju državljanstva, in: Dnevi javnega prava, Inštitut za javno upravo, Ljubljana 1999, pp. 647–661.

Morel, Laurence: France: Towards a Less Controversial Use of the Referendum, in: Michael Gallagher; Pier Vincenzo Uleri (eds.), The Referendum Experience in Europe, Macmillan, Basingstoke 1996, pp. 79–91.

Ogradi, Maja: Izbrisani državljani SFRJ, Diploma Thesis, University of Ljubljana, Faculty of Law, 2003.

Pavčnik, Marijan: Narava pravne države in njene prvine, in: Marijan Pavčnik (ed.), Pravna država, GV Založba, Ljubljana 2009, pp. 29–56.

Pavčnik, Marijan: Pravni in ustavni temelji prava, in: Marijan Pavčnik; Arne Mavčič (eds.), Ustavno sodstvo, Cankarjeva založba, Ljubljana 2000, pp. 391–431.

Pavčnik, Marijan: Razumevanje (temeljnih) človekovih pravic, in: Marijan Pavčnik, Ada Polajnar-Pavčnik, Dragica Wedam Lukić (eds.), Temeljne pravice, Cankarjeva založba, Ljubljana 1997, pp. 84–116.

Pavčnik, Marijan: Teorija prava. Prispevek k razumevanju prava, Cankarjeva založba, Ljubljana 1997.

Pečarič, Mirko: Uradništvo med formalnim in neformalnim vplivom na politiko in državljane, Uradni list RS, Ljubljana 2008.

Pistotnik, Sara: The Erasure as a Testing Ground for European Migration Policies, or Pardon Me, but Your Regulations Have Erased My Status, in: Neža Kogovšek and Brankica Petković (eds.), The Scars of the Erasure: A Contribution to the Critical Understanding of the Erasure of People from the Register of Permanent Residents of the Republic of Slovenia, Peace Institute, Ljubljana 2010, pp. 53–78.

Podgorecki, Adam: Preface, in: Adam Podgorecki; Vittorio Olgiati (eds.), Totalitarian and Post-Totalitarian Law, Aldershot, Dartmouth 1996.

Podgorecki, Adam: Totalitarian Law: Concepts and Issues, in: Adam Podgorecki; Vittorio Olgiati (eds.), Totalitarian and Post-Totalitarian Law, Aldershot, Dartmouth 1996, pp. 3–37.

Poleshchuk, Vadim (ed.): Chance to Survive. Minority Rights in Estonia and Latvia, Foundation for Historical Outlook, Moscow, Paris, Talinn 2009.

Poleshchuk, Vadim: "Illegals" in Estonia: Final Solution?, Presentation at the international conference The Baltic Sea as an Escape Route, 16–18 November 2001.

Polič, Vasilij: Kdo "tukaj dejansko živi", Pravna praksa 12 (1993) 22, pp. 16–17.

Ragazzi, Francesco; Štiks, Igor: EUDO Citizenship Observatory, Country Report: Croatia, 2010, URL: <http://eudo-citizenship.eu/docs/CountryReports/Croatia.pdf> (5 May 2011).

Rava, Nenad: EUDO Citizenship Observatory, Country Report: Serbia (2010), p. 7, URL: http://eudo-citizenship.eu/docs/CountryReports/Serbia.pdf (5 May 2011).

Ribičič, Ciril: Človekove pravice in ustavna demokracija, Študentska založba, Second Edition, Ljubljana 2010.

Ribičič, Ciril: Evropsko pravo človekovih pravic, Pravna fakulteta, Ljubljana 2007.

Ribičič, Ciril: Nevarno ustavno sodišče?, Mladina, 24 (2011).

Rosenberg, Gerald N.: The Hollow Hope. Can Courts Bring About Social Change?, University of Chicago, Chicago, London 1991.

Ruspini, Paolo: Estonia, in: Martin Balwin-Edwards; Albert Kraler (eds.), Regularization in Europe, Amsterdam University Press, Amsterdam 2009, pp. 223–228.

Sadurski, Wojciech: Rights before Courts. A Study of Constitutional Courts in Postcommunist States of Central and Eastern Europe, Springer, Dordrecht 2008.

Sarajlić, Eldar: EUDO Citizenship Observatory, Country Report: Bosnia and Herzegovina, 2010, URL: <http://eudo-citizenship.eu/docs/CountryReports/Bosnia%20and%20 Herzegovina.pdf> (5 May 2011).

Savanović, Gvozden: Geografska interpretacija izbrisa prebivalstva iz registra stalnih prebivalcev, Diploma Thesis, Faculty of Arts, University of Ljubljana, 2007.

Shiblak, Abbas: Stateless Palestinians, Forced Migration Review 26 (2006).

Šinkovec, Janez: Samoomejevanje ustavnih sodišč, Dnevi javnega prava, Inštitut za javno upravo, Ljubljana 1998, pp. 173–184.

Smith, Anthony D.: Nationalism: Theory, Ideology, History, Wiley-Blackwell, Cambridge 2001.

Spaskovska, Ljubica: EUDO Citizenship Observatory, Country Report: Macedonia (2010), pp. 1–8, URL: <http://eudo-citizenship.eu/docs/CountryReports/Macedonia.pdf> (5 May 2011).

Stariha, Gorazd: "Z nobenim delom se ne pečajo, le z lažnivo beračijo!", Zgodovina za vse 14 (2007) 1, pp. 37–76.

Struhárová, Beata: Disparate impact: Removing Roma from the Czech Republic, European Roma Rights Centre, 2004, URL: <http://www.errc.org/cikk.php?cikk=549> (1 February 2011).

Šturm, Lovro (ed.): Komentar Ustave Republike Slovenije, Faculty for State and European Studies, Kranj 2010.

Šturm, Lovro: Vloga ustavnega sodstva v sistemu delitve oblasti in oblike za ustavnosodno presojo aktov zakonodajne oblasti, Dnevi javnega prava, Inštitut za javno upravo, Ljubljana 1998, pp. 185–233.

Teršek, Andraž: Legitimnost kot prvina političnih in pravnih konceptov sodobne ustavne demokracije, Doctoral Thesis, Mentor prof. dr. Ciril Ribičič, University of Ljubljana, Faculty of Law, 2008.

Teršek, Andraž: Ustavnopravna strnjenka problema izbrisanih, Pravna praksa 27 (2008) 49–50, p. 26.

Testen, Franc: Tehnike ustavnosodnega odločanja, in: Marijan Pavčnik; Arne Mavčič (eds.), Ustavno sodstvo, Cankarjeva založba, Ljubljana 2000, pp. 231–273.

The story of an erased person "I missed Slovenia, I was born there", in: Neža Kogovšek and Brankica Petković (eds.), The Scars of the Erasure: A Contribution to the Critical Understanding of the Erasure of People from the Register of Permanent Residents of the Republic of Slovenia, Peace Institute, Ljubljana 2010, pp. 191–194.

The story of an erased person "I was lucky", in: Neža Kogovšek and Brankica Petković (eds.), The Scars of the Erasure: A Contribution to the Critical Understanding of the Erasure of People from the Register of Permanent Residents of the Republic of Slovenia, Peace Institute, Ljubljana 2010, pp. 145–150.

The story of an erased person "You cannot fight the system alone", in: Neža Kogovšek and Brankica Petković (eds.), The Scars of the Erasure: A Contribution to the Critical Understanding of the Erasure of People from the Register of Permanent Residents of the Republic of Slovenia, Peace Institute, Ljubljana 2010, pp. 47–52.

Toš, Niko (ed.): Vrednote na prehodu III. Slovensko javno mnenje 1999–2004. Dokumenti SJM, FDV IDV, CJMMK, 2004.

Trechsel, Alexander H.; Kriesi, Hanspeter: Switzerland: The Referendum and Initiative as a Centrepiece of the Political System, in: Michael Gallagher; Pier Vincenzo Uleri (eds.), The Referendum Experience in Europe, Macmillan, Basingstoke 1996, pp. 185–208.

Tršinar, Irena: Izbrisani, Okno uprave, 28 March 2003, URL: <http://izbrisani.siol.net/intervju-9.rtf> (5 May 2011).

Tršinar, Irena: Centralni register prebivalstva, Uradni list RS, Ljubljana 1999.

Türk, Danilo: Temelji mednarodnega prava, GV založba, Ljubljana 2007.

Vuksanović, Igor: Protipravnost kot eden od elementov odškodninske odgovornosti do izbrisanih, Pravna praksa 28 (2009) 20, pp. IV–VI.

Williams, Raymond: Base and Superstructure in Marxist Cultural Theory, New Left Review, I/82, November-December 1973, URL: <https://newleftreview.org/I/82> (15 March 2016).

Zdravković, Lana: The Struggle Against the Denial of Citizenship as a Paradigm of Emancipatory Politics, in: Neža Kogovšek and Brankica Petković (eds.), The Scars of the Erasure: A Contribution to the Critical Understanding of the Erasure of People from the Register of Permanent Residents of the Republic of Slovenia, Peace Institute, Ljubljana 2010, pp. 257–277.

Zorn, Jelka: "We, the Ethno-citizens of Ethno-democracy" – The Formation of Slovene Citizenship, Journal for the Critique of Science 35 (2007) 228, pp. 52–70.

Zorn, Jelka: Registered as Workers, Erased as non-Slovenes: The Transition Period from the Perspective of the Erased People, in: Neža Kogovšek and Brankica Petković (eds.), The Scars of the Erasure: A Contribution to the Critical Understanding of the Erasure of People from the Register of Permanent Residents of the Republic of Slovenia, Peace Institute, Ljubljana 2010, pp. 19–46.

Conventions, laws and bylaws

International and European law

Convention on the Reduction of Statelessness, New York, 30 August, 1961, entered into force 13 December 1975. United Nations, Treaty Series, vol. 989, 175.

Convention on the Rights of the Child, adopted on 20 November, 1989, entry into force 2 September 1990.

Council Directive 2003/109/EC of 25 November 2003 Concerning the Status of Third-Country Nationals Who Are Long-Term Residents, OJ L 16, 23 January 2004, p. 44.

Draft Articles on Nationality of Natural Persons in Relation to the Succession of States, UN International Law Commission, Annex to General Assembly Resolution 55/153, 2001.

European Convention on Nationality, done in Strasbourg under the auspices of the Council of Europe on 6 November 1997, entry into force 1 March 2000.

International Convention on the Elimination of All Forms of Racial Discrimination, adopted on 21 December 1965, entry into force 4 January 1969.

International Covenant on Civil and Political Rights, adopted on 16 December 1966, entry into force 23 March 1976, GA res. 2200A (XXI), 21 UN GAOR Supp. (No. 16) at 52, UN Doc. A/6316 (1966); 999 UNTS 171; 6 ILM 368 (1967).

The Hague Convention on Certain Questions relating to the Conflict of Nationality Laws, done on 12 April 1930 under the auspices of the League of Nations, entered into force 1 July 1937.

Universal Declaration of Human Rights, G.A. res. 217A (III), U.N. Doc A/810 at 71 (1948).

Vienna Convention on Succession of States in respect of Treaties, Vienna, 23 August, 1978, entered into force 6 November 1996. United Nations, Treaty Series, vol. 1946, 3.

National law

Czech Republic, Law No. 150/1996 on Changes and Amendments to the Law No. 123/1992 on Foreigners in Czecho-Slovakian Federal Republic.

Czech Republic, Law No. 190/1994 on Changes and Amendments to the Law No. 123/1992 on Foreigners in Czecho-Slovakian Federal Republic.

Czech Socialist Republic, Act No. 839/1969 Coll. of the Czech National Council on Acquisition and Loss of Citizenship of the Czech Socialist Republic.

Czechoslovakia, Federal Act No. 165/1968 Coll. on the Rules of Acquisition and Loss of Nationality, Czechoslovakia.

Czecho-Slovakian Federal Republic, Law on Foreigners of the Czecho-Slovakian Federal Republic, Collection of Acts No. 123/1992.

Democratic Federal Yugoslavia, Zakon o volilnih imenikih (*Law on Voters Registers*), Official Gazette of the Democratic Federal Yugoslavia, No. 59/1945.

Federal People's Republic of Yugoslavia, Odredba o spremembah in dopolnitvah odredbe o prijavah stalnega in začasnega prebivališča, Official Gazette of Federal People's Republic of Yugoslavia, No. 62/1952.

Federal People's Republic of Yugoslavia, Pravilnik o prijavljanju stalnega in začasnega prebivališča (*Rule Book on Permanent and Temporary Residence Registration*), Official Gazette of Federal People's Republic of Yugoslavia, No. 9/59.

Federal People's Republic of Yugoslavia, Pravilnik za izvajanje zakona o državljanstvu FLRJ (*Rule Book on the Implementation of the Law on Citizenship of FPRY*), Official Gazette of Federal People's Republic of Yugoslavia, No. 98/1946.

Federal People's Republic of Yugoslavia, Uredba o prijavljanju prebivališča (*Decree on Residence Registration*), Official Gazette of Federal People's Republic of Yugoslavia, No. 56/1948 in 39/1950.

Federal People's Republic of Yugoslavia, Zakon o državljanstvu Demokratične federativne Jugoslavije, Official Gazette of Democratic Federal Yugoslavia,

No. 64/1945; amended Official Gazette of Federal People's Republic of Yugoslavia, No. 54/1946, 90/1946, 104/1947, 88/1948, 105/1948.

Federal People's Republic of Yugoslavia, Zakon o odvzemu državljanstva oficirjem in podoficirjem bivše jugoslovanske vojske, ki se nočejo vrniti v domovino, pripadnikom vojaških formacij, ki so služili okupatorju in pobegnili v inozemstvo ter osebam, ki so pobegnile v inozemstvo po osvoboditvi (*Law on the Revocation of Citizenship for Army Officers and Sub-officers of the Former Yugoslav Army who Refused to Return to the Country, the Members of Military Units that Served the Occupying Forces and Fled Abroad, and Persons who Fled Abroad after the Liberation*), Official Gazette of the Federal People's Republic of Yugoslavia, No. 64/1945, 86/1946 and 22/1968.

Federal People's Republic of Yugoslavia, Zakon o splošnem upravnem postopku (*General Administrative Procedure Act*), Official Gazette of the Federal People's Republic of Yugoslavia, No. 52/1956, Official Gazette of the Socialist Federal Republic of Yugoslavia, No. 10/1965, 18/1965, 4/1977, 11/1978, and Official Gazette of the Republic of Slovenia, No. 4/1992.

Federal People's Republic of Yugoslavia, Zakon o spremembah zakona o državljanstvu Demokratične federativne Jugoslavije (*Act Amending the Citizenship Act of Democratic Federal Yugoslavia*), Official Gazette of the Federal People's Republic of Yugoslavia, No. 105/1948.

Federal People's Republic of Yugoslavia, Zakon o veljavi ustave, zakonov in drugih zveznih pravnih predpisov na ozemlju, na katero se je z mednarodnim sporazumom razširila civilna uprava Federativne ljudske republike Jugoslavije (*Law on the Validity of the Constitution, Laws and Other Federal Legal Rules in the Territory Which under International Agreements Came under the Civil Administration of the Federal People's Republic of Yugoslavia*), Official Gazette of the Federal People's Republic of Yugoslavia, No. 45/1954.

Federal Republic of Yugoslavia, Law on Citizenship of the Federal Republic of Yugoslavia, Official Gazette of Federal Republic of Yugoslavia, No. 33/1996.

Kingdom SCS, Uredba o pridobitvi in izgubi državljanstva Kraljevine SHS z opcijo in prošnjo (*Decree on the acquisition and loss of citizenship of the Kingdom of SCS through an application*), Official Gazette of regional administration for Slovenia, Kingdom SCS, No. 147/1920 in 122/1921.

Kingdom SCS, Zakon o državljanstvu (*Law on Citizenship*), Official Gazette of Kingdom SCS, No. 254/1928.

Kosovo, Regulation No. 2000/13 on the Central Civil Registry, UNMIK/REG/2000/13.

Kosovo, Regulation No. 2000/18 on Travel Documents, UNMIK/REG/2000/18.

Law on the Status of a Long-term Resident of the European Community in the Republic of Latvia, Official Gazette of Latvia, No. 107, 7 July 2006.

Lithuanian Soviet Socialist Republic, Law on Citizenship of the Lithuanian Soviet Socialist Republic, 3 November 1989, No. XI-3329.

People's Republic of Croatia, Law on Citizenship of the People's Republic of Croatia, Official Gazette of the People's Republic of Croatia, No. 23/1950, and Law on the Citizenship of the Socialist Republic of Croatia, Official Gazette of the Socialist Republic of Croatia, No. 32/1977.

People's Republic of Slovenia, Navodilo za vodstvo razvida državljanov Ljudske Republike Slovenije, Official Gazette of the People's Republic of Slovenia, No. 42/1947.

People's Republic of Slovenia, Odredba o razširitvi obveznosti prijave stalnega prebivališča oziroma prijave spremembe stanovanja in z navodilom o prijavljanju prebivališča državljanov FLRJ v Ljudski republiki Sloveniji, Official Gazette of People's Republic of Slovenia, No. 22/1950.

People's Republic of Slovenia, Uredba o ustanovitvi in vodenju registra stalnega prebivalstva (*Regulation on the Establishment and Keeping of the Register of Permanent Residents*), Official Gazette of People's Republic of Slovenia, No. 9/1953 in 49/1957.

People's Republic of Slovenia, Zakon o državljanstvu Ljudske republike Slovenije (*Law on the Citizenship of the People's Republic of Slovenia*), Official Gazette of People's Republic of Slovenia, No. 20/1950.

People's Republic of Bosnia and Herzegovina, Law on Citizenship of the People's Republic of Bosnia and Herzegovina, Official Gazette of the People's Republic of Bosnia and Herzegovina, No. 5/1950.

Republic of Croatia, Law on Croatian Citizenship, Official Gazette of the Republic of Croatia, No. 53/1991.

Republic of Croatia, Law on the Movement and Residence of Aliens, Official Gazette of the Republic of Croatia, No. 53/1991.

Republic of Estonia, Aliens Act, Official Gazette of Estonia, I 1993, 44, 637; 1999, 50, 548; 2004, 58, 410.

Republic of Estonia, Citizenship Act, Official Gazette of Estonia, 1992, 7, 109.

Republic of Estonia, Citizenship Act, Official Gazette of Estonia, I 1995, 12, 122.

Republic of Estonia, Obligation to Leave and Prohibition on Entry Act, Official Gazette of Estonia, I 1998, 98/99, 1575, Official Gazette of Estonia I 2001, 68, 407.

Republic of Estonia, Requirement for Applicants for Citizenship to Know Estonian Act, Official Gazette of Estonia, 1993, 11, 171.

Republic of Kosovo, Law on Citizenship of Kosovo, Official Gazette of the Republic of Kosovo, No. 26/2008.

Republic of Latvia, Immigration Law, Official Gazette of Latvia, No. 169, 20 November 2002.

Republic of Latvia, Law on Citizenship, Official Gazette of Latvia, 1994, 93.

Republic of Latvia, Law on the Status of Former USSR Citizens Who Are Not Citizens of Latvia or Any Other State, Official Gazette of Latvia, No. 63, 25 April 1995.

Republic of Lithuania, Citizenship Law of the Republic of Lithuania, 11 December 1991, No. I-2080.

Republic of Lithuania, Law on Amending Articles 1, 17 and 28 of the Law on Citizenship, 5 December 1991, No. I-2072, amended 2 July 1997, No. VIII-391.

Republic of Lithuania, Law on Legal Status of Foreigners in Republic of Lithuania, 4 September 1991, No. I-1750.

Republic of Macedonia, Law on Changes and Amendments of the Law on Citizenship of the Republic of Macedonia, Official Gazette of the Republic of Macedonia, No. 8/2004.

Republic of Macedonia, Law on the Movement and Residence of Aliens, Official Gazette of the Republic of Macedonia, No. 36/1992.

Republic of Macedonia, Law on the Movement and Residence of Foreigners, Official Gazette of the Republic of Macedonia, No. 36/1992.

Republic of Montenegro, Aliens Act, Official Gazette of Montenegro, 82/2008.

Republic of Montenegro, Law on Montenegrin Citizenship, Official Gazette of Montenegro, 9 November 1999.

Republic of Montenegro, Montenegrin Citizenship Act, Official Gazette of Montenegro, No. 13/2008.

Republic of Serbia, Aliens Act, Official Gazette of the Republic of Serbia, No. 97/2008.

Republic of Serbia, Aliens Act, Official Gazette of the Republic of Serbia, No. 97/2008.

Republic of Serbia, Amendments to the Law on Citizenship of the Republic of Serbia, Official Gazette of the RS Republic of Serbia, No. 90/2007.

Republic of Serbia, Law on Citizenship of the Republic of Serbia, Official Gazette of the Republic of Serbia, No. 135/2004.

Republic of Slovenia, Dispatch of the Uniformed Police Directorate, part of the General Police Directorate (State Border and Foreigners Section) sent to all Police Directorates in the RS, No. M0001755, dated 19 March 2002.

Republic of Slovenia, Draft Law Amending the Law on Citizenship of the Republic of Slovenia of 21 October 1991.

Republic of Slovenia, Executive Council of the Assembly of the Republic of Slovenia, Decision No. 22610, dated 27 June 1991.

Republic of Slovenia, Executive Council of the National Assembly of the Republic of Slovenia, Decision No. 20701/ 914/ 68 dated 13 January 1992.

Republic of Slovenia, Government of the Republic of Slovenia, Decision No. 260-01/91-2/5-8 dated 3 September 1992.

Republic of Slovenia, Letter by the Ministry of the Interior to all local administrations, No. 0302-16/01-209-Sl./99 dated 24 September 1999.

Republic of Slovenia, Letter from the Ministry of the Interior to the Government of the Republic of Slovenia entitled "Open issues related to the implementation of he Aliens Act", No. 0016/1-S-010/3-91 dated 4 June 1992.

Republic of Slovenia, Letter of the Ministry of the Interior to all local administration bodies entitled Začetek veljavnosti določb Zakona o tujcih – 81. člen, No. 0012/8-252-206 dated 15 September 1995.

Republic of Slovenia, Pravilnik o obrazcu za prijavo oziroma odjavo stalnega prebivališča, o obrazcu osebnega kartona in kartona gospodinjstev ter o načinu in vzdrževanju registra stalnega prebivalstva (*Rules on Permanent Residence Registration/Cancellation Form, Personal and Household Records and the Manner and Maintenance of the Register of Permanent Residents*), Official Gazette of the Republic of Slovenia, No. 27/92.

Republic of Slovenia, Predlog Zakona o izvršitvi 8. točke odločbe Ustavnega sodišča RS št. U-I-246/02-28 (*Draft Act on the Implementation of Point 8 of the Constitutional Court Ruling No. U-I-246/02-28*), 4 September 2003.

Republic of Slovenia, Stanovanjski zakon (*Housing Act*), Official Gazette of the Republic of Slovenia, No. 18-I/1991.

Republic of Slovenia, Temeljna ustavna listina o samostojnosti in neodvisnosti Republike Slovenije (*Basic Constitutional Charter on the Independence and Sovereignty of the Republic of Slovenia*), Official Gazette of the Republic of Slovenia, No. 1/91-I.

Republic of Slovenia, The In-House Instruction of the Ministry of the Interior to All Local Administration Bodies entitled *Izvajanje Zakona o tujcih in Zakona o potnih listinah državljanov Republike Slovenije* (The Implementation of the Aliens Act and the Passports of Citizens of the Republic of Slovenia Act), No. 0016/8-S-010/14-91 dated 26 June 1991.

Republic of Slovenia, The In-House Instruction of the Ministry of the Interior to All Local Administration Bodies Entitled *Izvajanje Zakona o tujcih in Zakona o potnih listinah državljanov Republike Slovenije – spremembe stališč izdanih pod št. 0016/8-S-010/4-91 z dne 26. junija 1991* (The Implementation of the Aliens Act and the Passports of Citizens of the Republic of Slovenia Act – changes to the instructions No. 0016/8-S-010/4-91 dated 26 June 1991), No. 0016/8-S-010/4-91 dated 30 July 1991.

Republic of Slovenia, The In-House Instruction of the Ministry of the Interior to All Local Administration Bodies Entitled *Zakon o tujcih – zaključki s posvetovanja z dne 23/11-1992* (The Aliens Act – conclusions of the consultation meeting on 23/1-1992), No. 0016/9-S-26/3-92 dated 5 February 1992.

Republic of Slovenia, The In-House Instruction of the Ministry of the Interior to All Local Administration Bodies Entitled *Problematika tujcev, zaposlenih v gradbenih podjetjih – stališče* (The issue of aliens employed by construction companies – a stance), No. 0016/4-1255-8 dated 18 February 1992.

Republic of Slovenia, The In-House Instruction of the Ministry of the Interior to All Local Administration Bodies Entitled *Izvajanje Zakona o tujcih – navodilo* (The Implementation of the Aliens Act – An Instruction), No. 0016/4-1496-8 dated 27 February 1992.

Republic of Slovenia, The In-House Instruction of the Ministry of the Interior to All Local Administration Bodies Entitled *Zaključki s posvetovanja, ki je bilo dne 28/5-1992 za referente, ki delajo na področju registra stalnega prebivalstva* (The conclusions of the consulting session held on May 28, 1992 for employees working with registers of permanent residents), No. 0016/2-S1.-92 dated 15 June 1992.

Republic of Slovenia, Uredba o merilih za ugotavljanje izpolnjevanja določenih pogojev za pridobitev državljanstva Republike Slovenije z naturalizacijo (*Regulation on the Criteria for Establishing the Fulfilment of Certain Requirements for Obtaining Citizenship of the Republic of Slovenia through Naturalization*), Official Gazette of the Republic of Slovenia, No. 47/1994.

Republic of Slovenia, Zakon o dopolnitvi zakona o državljanstvu Republike Slovenije (*Act Amending Citizenship of the Republic of Slovenia Act*), Official Gazette of the Republic of Slovenia, No. 30/1991-I.

Republic of Slovenia, Zakon o evidenci nastanitve občanov in o registru prebivalstva (*Law on the Record of Residences of Members of Public and the Population Register*), Official Gazette of Socialist Republic of Slovenia, No. 6/1983; Official Gazette of the Republic of Slovenia, No. 26/1990, 11/1991-1, 4/1992.

Republic of Slovenia, Zakon o lastninskem preoblikovanju podjetij (*Ownership Transformation of Companies Act*), Official Gazette of the Republic of Slovenia, No. 55/1992.

Republic of Slovenia, Zakon o obligacijskih razmerjih (*Obligations Act*), Official Gazette of the Republic of Slovenia, No. 29/1978 as amended.

Republic of Slovenia, Zakon o plebiscitu o samostojnosti in neodvisnosti Republike Slovenije (*Plebiscite on the Sovereignty and Independence of the Republic of Slovenia Act*), Official Gazette of the Republic of Slovenia, No. 44/1990.

Republic of Slovenia, Zakon o poklicnem in strokovnem izobraževanju (*Vocational Education Act*), Official Gazette of the Republic of Slovenia, No. 12/1996.

Republic of Slovenia, Zakon o spremembah in dopolnitvah Zakona o državljanstvu Republike Slovenije – ZDRS-Č (*Act Amending the Act on Citizenship of the Republic of Slovenia*), Official Gazette of the Republic of Slovenia, No. 96/2002.

Republic of Slovenia, Zakon o spremembah in dopolnitvah zakona o državljanstvu Republike Slovenije (*Act Amending the Act on Citizenship of the Republic of Slovenia*), Official Gazette of the Republic of Slovenia, No. 13/1994.

Republic of Slovenia, Zakon o spremembah in dopolnitvah zakona o državljanstvu Republike Slovenije (*Act Amending the Act on Citizenship of the Republic of Slovenia*), Official Gazette of the Republic of Slovenia, No. 96/2002.

Republic of Slovenia, Zakon o spremembah in dopolnitvah zakona o varnosti cestnega prometa (*Amendments to the Road Traffic Safety Act*), Official Gazette of the Republic of Slovenia, No. 1/1991.

Republic of Slovenia, Zakon o spremembah zakona o tujcih (*Act Amending the Aliens Act*), Official Gazette of the Republic of Slovenia, No. 44/1997.

Republic of Slovenia, Zakon o tujcih (*Aliens Act*), Official Gazette of the Republic of Slovenia, No. 1/91-I.

Republic of Slovenia, Zakon o urejanju statusa državljanov drugih držav naslednic SFRJ v Republiki Sloveniji (*Act Regulating the Legal Status of Citizens of Former Yugoslavia Living in the Republic of Slovenia*), Official Gazette of the Republic of Slovenia, No. 61/1999.

Republic of Slovenia, Zakon o zaposlovanju in delu tujcev (*Employment and Work of Aliens Act*), Official Gazette of the Republic of Slovenia, No. 66/2000.

Republic of Slovenia, Zakon o zaposlovanju tujcev (*Employment of Aliens Act*), Official Gazette of the Republic of Slovenia, No. 33/1992.

Slovak Republic, Citizenship Act, Collection of Acts and Collection of Laws of the Slovak Republic, Issue No. 40/1993.

Slovak Republic, Law Amending Certain Rules on Employment, Collection of Acts No. 319/1993.

Slovak Republic, Law on Foreigners of the Republic of Slovakia, Collection of Acts No. 73/1995.

Slovak Socialist Republic, Act No. 206/1968 Coll. of Slovak National Council on Acquisition and Loss of Citizenship of the Slovak Socialist Republic.

Slovenian National Liberation Council, Uredba Ministrstva za notranje zadeve o prijavni in odjavni dolžnosti prebivalstva (*Decree on the Obligation of Registering and Cancelling Residence*), Official Gazette SNOS, No. 46/1945.

Socialist Federal Republic of Yugoslavia, Agreement on the distribution of register numbers for the unique personal ID of the population, Official Gazette of Socialist Federal Republic of Yugoslavia, No. 13/1978.

Socialist Federal Republic of Yugoslavia, Law on the Movement and Residence of Aliens, Official Gazette of Socialist Federal Republic of Yugoslavia, No. 56/80, 53/85, 30/89, 26/90, 53/91; Official Gazette of Socialist Republic of Yugoslavia, No. 24/94 and 28/96.

Socialist Federal Republic of Yugoslavia, Law on the Movement and Residence of Foreigners, Official Gazette of the Socialist Federal Republic of Yugoslavia, No. 56/1980, 53/1985, 30/1989 and 26/1990.

Socialist Federal Republic of Yugoslavia, Law on Yugoslav Citizenship, Official Gazette of the Socialist Federal Republic of Yugoslavia, No. 38/1964.

Socialist Federal Republic of Yugoslavia, Temeljni zakon o evidenci stalnega in začasnega prebivališča občanov (*Fundamental Law on Keeping the Record of Permanent and Temporary Residence of Members of the Public*), Official Gazette of Socialist Federal Republic of Yugoslavia, No. 9/1965.

Socialist Federal Republic of Yugoslavia, Ustava Socialistične federativne republike Jugoslavije (*Constitution of the Socialist Federal Republic of Yugoslavia*), Official Gazette of Socialist Federal Republic of Yugoslavia, No. 9/1974.

Socialist Federal Republic of Yugoslavia, Zakon o državljanstvu SFRJ (*Law on Citizenship of the SFRY*), Official Gazette of Socialist Federal Republic of Yugoslavia, No. 58/1976.

Socialist Federal Republic of Yugoslavia, Zakon o potnih listinah državljanov SFRJ (Law on the Passports of SFRY Citizens), Official Gazette of the Socialist Federal Republic of Yugoslavia, No. 30/79 and 53/85.

Socialist Federal Republic of Yugoslavia, Zakon o splošnem upravnem postopku (*General Administrative Procedure Act*), Official Gazette of the Socialist Federal Republic of Yugoslavia, No. 47/86.

Socialist Federal Republic of Yugoslavia, Zakon o uvedbi matične številke občanov (*Law on the Introduction of the Personal Identification Number*), Official Gazette of the Socialist Federal Republic of Yugoslavia, No. 58/1976.

Socialist Republic of Bosnia and Herzegovina, Law on Citizenship of the Socialist Republic of Bosnia and Herzegovina, Official Gazette of the Socialist Republic of Bosnia and Herzegovina, No. 6/1965.

Socialist Republic of Bosnia and Herzegovina, Law on Citizenship of the Socialist Republic of Bosnia and Herzegovina, Official Gazette of the Socialist Republic of Bosnia and Herzegovina, No. 10/1977.

Socialist Republic of Macedonia, Law on Citizenship of the Socialist Republic of Macedonia, Official Gazette of the Socialist Republic of Macedonia, No. 09/65.

Socialist Republic of Macedonia, Law on Citizenship of the Socialist Republic of Macedonia, Official Gazette of the Socialist Republic of Macedonia, No. 19/77.

Socialist Republic of Montenegro, Law on Citizenship of the Socialist Republic of Montenegro, Official Gazette of the Socialist Republic of Montenegro, No. 26/75.

Socialist Republic of Serbia, Law on Citizenship of the Socialist Republic of Serbia, Official Gazette of the Socialist Republic of Serbia, No. 45/1979.

Socialist Republic of Slovenia, Izjava o dobrih namenih (*Statement of Good Intentions*), Official Gazette RS, No. 44/1990.

Socialist Republic of Slovenia, Pravilnik za izvajanje zakona o enotni matični številki občanov (*Rule Book on Implementation of the Law on Unique Personal Number*), Official Gazette of Socialist Republic of Slovenia, No. 7/1980.

Socialist Republic of Slovenia, Ustava Socialistične republike Slovenije (Constitution of the Socialist Republic of Slovenia), Official Gazette of Socialist Republic of Slovenia, No. 6-44/1974.

Socialist Republic of Slovenia, Ustavni amandmaji IX do XC k Ustavi Socialistične Republike Slovenije (*Constitutional amendments IX to XC to the 1974 Constitution of the Socialist Republic of Slovenia*), Official Gazette of Socialist Republic of Slovenia, No. 32/1989.

Socialist Republic of Slovenia, Zakon o državljanstvu Socialistične republike Slovenije (*Law on the Citizenship of the Socialist Republic of Slovenia*), Official Gazette of Socialist Republic of Slovenia, No. 11/1965.

Socialist Republic of Slovenia, Zakon o državljanstvu Socialistične republike Slovenije (*Law on the Citizenship of the Socialist Republic of Slovenia*), Official Gazette of Socialist Republic of Slovenia, No. 23/1976.

Socialist Republic of Slovenia, Zakon o enotni matični številki občanov (*Law on the Unique Personal Number of Members of the Public*), Official Gazette of Socialist Republic of Slovenia, No. 1/1980.

Socialist Republic of Slovenia, Zakon o evidenci nastanitve občanov in o registru prebivalstva (*Law on the Record of Residences of Members of Public and the Population Register*), Official Gazette of Socialist Republic of Slovenia, No. 4/1974.

Socialist Republic of Slovenia, Zakon o registru stalnega prebivalstva in o razvidu začasnega prebivališča (*Law on the Register of Permanent and Temporary Residence*), Official Gazette of the Socialist Republic of Slovenia, No. 36/1965.

Socialist Republic of Slovenia, Zakon o stanovanjskih razmerjih (*Law on Housing Relations*), Official Gazette of the Socialist Republic of Slovenia, No. 35/1982.

Socialist Republic of Slovenia, Zakon o uvedbi centralnega registra stalnega prebivalstva v SR Sloveniji (*Law on the Introduction of the Central Register of Permanent Residents in SR Slovenia*), Official Gazette of the Socialist Republic of Slovenia, No. 40/1970.

Socialist Republic of Slovenia, Zakon o volitvah v skupščine (*Law on the Elections to the National Assemblies*), Official Gazette of the Socialist Republic of Slovenia, No. 42/1989.

Case law

ECHR

ECHR (GC), *Broniowski v. Poland*, Application No. 31443/96, 22 June 2004.

ECHR, *D.H. and Others v. The Czech Republic*, Application No. 57325/00, 13 November 2007.

ECHR, *Kurić and Others v. Slovenia*, Application No. 26828/06, 13 June 2010.

ECHR, *Lukenda v. Slovenia*, Application No. 23032/02, 6 October 2005.

ECHR, *Shevanova v. Latvia*, Application No. 58822/00, 7 December 2007.

Dissenting opinion of Judge Boštjan M. Zupančič in the case ECHR, *Ždanoka v. Latvia*, Application No. 58278/00, 16 March 2006.

Constitutional Courts

Concurring opinion of Judge Boštjan M. Zupančič to Constitutional Court of the Republic of Slovenia Ruling No. U-I-266/95, 20 November 1995.

Constitutional Court of the Czech Republic, Ruling No. IV US 34/97, 5 May 1997.

Constitutional Court of the Republic of Slovenia, Decision No. U-I-284/94, 24 June 1998.

Constitutional Court of the Republic of Slovenia, Ruling No. U-I-114/95, 7 December 1995.

Constitutional Court of the Republic of Slovenia, Ruling No. U-I-123/92, 18 November 1993.

Constitutional Court of the Republic of Slovenia, Ruling No. U-I-147/92, 6 May 1993.

Constitutional Court of the Republic of Slovenia, Ruling No. U-I-200/97, 13 February 1998.

Constitutional Court of the Republic of Slovenia, Ruling No. U-I-23/93, 20 March 1997.

Constitutional Court of the Republic of Slovenia, Ruling No. U-I-246/02, 3 April 2003.

Constitutional Court of the Republic of Slovenia, Ruling No. U-I-259/01, 20 November 2003.

Constitutional Court of the Republic of Slovenia, Ruling No. U-I-266/95, 20 November 1995.

Constitutional Court of the Republic of Slovenia, Ruling No. U-I-284/94, 4 February 1999.

Constitutional Court of the Republic of Slovenia, Ruling No. U-I-295/99-13, 18 May 2000.

Constitutional Court of the Republic of Slovenia, Ruling No. U-I-47/94, 19 January 1995.

Constitutional Court of the Republic of Slovenia, Ruling No. U-I-86/94, 14 November 1996.

Constitutional Court of the Republic of Slovenia, Ruling No. U-I-89/99, 10 June 1999.

Constitutional Court of the Republic of Slovenia, Ruling No. U-II-1/04, 26 February 2004.

Constitutional Court of the Republic of Slovenia, Ruling No. U-II-1/10-19, 10 June 2010.

Constitutional Court of the Republic of Slovenia, Ruling No. U-II-3/03-15, 22 December 2003.

Constitutional Court of the Republic of Slovenia, Ruling No. U-II-3/04, 20 April 2004.

Constitutional Court of the Republic of Slovenia, Ruling No. Up-211/04-21, 2 March 2006.

Constitutional Court of the Republic of Slovenia, Ruling No. Up-77/94, 16 September 1997.

Dissenting opinion of Judge Jadranka Sovdat to Constitutional Court Ruling No. U-II-1/10-19, 10 June 2010.

Dissenting opinion of Judge Jan Zobec to the Constitutional Court Ruling No. U-II-1/10-19, 10 June 2010.

Other Courts of the Republic of Slovenia

Higher Court Celje, Judgment No. Cp 386/2009, 8 October 2009.

Higher Court Koper, Judgment No. I Cp 739/2005, 19 September 2006.

Higher Court Ljubljana, Judgment No. I Cp 1128/2010, 9 June 2010.

Higher Court Ljubljana, Judgment No. II Cp 1291/2008, 15 October 2008.

Higher Court Ljubljana, Judgment No. II Cp 1589/2009, 23 September 2009.

Higher Court Ljubljana, Judgment No. II Cp 3978/2009, 10 March 2010.

Higher Court Ljubljana, Judgment No. II Cp 4262/2009, 4 March 2010.

Higher Court Ljubljana, Judgment No. II Cp 4277/2009, 24 February 2010.

Higher Court Ljubljana, Judgment No. II Cp 4395/2009, 3 March 2010.

Higher Court Ljubljana, Judgment No. II Cp 725/2008, 10 September 2008.

Higher Court Maribor, Judgment No. I Cp 2556/2007, 3 December 2008.

Higher Court Maribor, Judgment No. I Cp 428/2008, 7 May 2008.

Supreme Court of the Republic of Slovenia, Decision No. II Ips 397/94, 7 February 1996.

Supreme Court of the Republic of Slovenia, Ruling No. I Up 1162/2002, 9 March 2005.

Supreme Court of the Republic of Slovenia, Ruling No. I Up 12/2004, 14 January 2004.

Supreme Court of the Republic of Slovenia, Ruling No. I Up 278/99, 17 October 2001.

Supreme Court of the Republic of Slovenia, Ruling No. I Up 486/99, 15 May 2002.

Supreme Court of the Republic of Slovenia, Ruling No. I Up 501/99, 10 October 2002.

Supreme Court of the Republic of Slovenia, Ruling No. I Up 562/99, 17 October 2002.

Supreme Court of the Republic of Slovenia, Ruling No. II Ips 315/2010, 21 October 2009.

Supreme Court of the Republic of Slovenia, Ruling No. U 1003/93-12, 17 November 1994.

Supreme Court of the Republic of Slovenia, Ruling No. U 1083/92, 24 June 1993.

Supreme Court of the Republic of Slovenia, Ruling No. U 1086/95-5, 11 June 1997.

Supreme Court of the Republic of Slovenia, Ruling No. U 1092/92-4, 29 April 1993.

Supreme Court of the Republic of Slovenia, Ruling No. U 1186/92-7, 26 August 1993.

Supreme Court of the Republic of Slovenia, Ruling No. U 1342/96, 20 January 1999.

Supreme Court of the Republic of Slovenia, Ruling No. U 1489/93-4, 14 September 1994.

Supreme Court of the Republic of Slovenia, Ruling No. U 1577/94-7, 28 August 1997.

Supreme Court of the Republic of Slovenia, Ruling No. U 1686/94-4, 19 November 1997.

Supreme Court of the Republic of Slovenia, Ruling No. U 1837/94-7, 3 April 1997.

Supreme Court of the Republic of Slovenia, Ruling No. U 204/94, 17 November 1994.

Supreme Court of the Republic of Slovenia, Ruling No. U 230/92, 23 October 1993.

Supreme Court of the Republic of Slovenia, Ruling No. U 241/92, 7 January 1993.

Supreme Court of the Republic of Slovenia, Ruling No. U 25/1993, 28 October 1993.

Supreme Court of the Republic of Slovenia, Ruling No. U 2824/2005, 6 October 2006.

Supreme Court of the Republic of Slovenia, Ruling No. U 287/1992, 14 January 1993.

Supreme Court of the Republic of Slovenia, Ruling No. U 296/1992, 1 April 1993.

Supreme Court of the Republic of Slovenia, Ruling No. U 317/94-4, 1 February 1996.

Supreme Court of the Republic of Slovenia, Ruling No. U 325/93-6, 14 September 1994.

Supreme Court of the Republic of Slovenia, Ruling No. U 426/93, 29 June 1994.

Supreme Court of the Republic of Slovenia, Ruling No. U 473/92, 6 May 1993.

Supreme Court of the Republic of Slovenia, Ruling No. U 562/93, 15 June 1994.

Supreme Court of the Republic of Slovenia, Ruling No. U 632/92, 23 September 1993.

Supreme Court of the Republic of Slovenia, Ruling No. U 634/95-7, 26 February 1997.

Supreme Court of the Republic of Slovenia, Ruling No. U 679/93, 16 June 1994.

Supreme Court of the Republic of Slovenia, Ruling No. U 680/95-8, 6 February 1997.

Supreme Court of the Republic of Slovenia, Ruling No. U 688/92, 30 June 1993.
Supreme Court of the Republic of Slovenia, Ruling No. U 753/92, 29 April 1993.
Supreme Court of the Republic of Slovenia, Ruling No. U 774/94-6, 14 February 1996.
Supreme Court of the Republic of Slovenia, Ruling No. U 777/92-6, 21 June 1993.
Supreme Court of the Republic of Slovenia, Ruling No. U 778/92-6, 16 September 1993.
Supreme Court of the Republic of Slovenia, Ruling No. U 781/93, 7 September 1994.
Supreme Court of the Republic of Slovenia, Ruling No. U 805/1993, 15 September 1994.
Supreme Court of the Republic of Slovenia, Ruling No. U 823/93-5, 13 April 1994.
Supreme Court of the Republic of Slovenia, Ruling No. U 832/92, 11 February 1993.
Supreme Court of the Republic of Slovenia, Ruling No. U 891/92, 10 June 1993.
Supreme Court of the Republic of Slovenia, Ruling No. X Ips 451/2004, 4 October 2007.

Other Sources

Amendment of the ZLSD parliament group dated 6 July 1999, No. 213-04/99-28/3, EPA 749-II.
Annual reports on work of the Constitutional Court of the Republic of Slovenia, URL: <www.ue-rs.si/o-sodiscu/letna-porocila/> (15 January 2011).
CESCR, Concluding observations on Slovenia No. E/C.12/SVN/CO/1, of 25 November 2005.
CIA, Human Resource Exploitation Training Manual, 1983.
Complaint No. 26828/06 to ECHR in the Case *Kurić and Others v. Slovenia.*
ECHR, The Pilot Judgment Procedure, Information note issued by the Registrar, URL: <http://www.echr.coe.int/NR/rdonlyres/DF4E8456-77B3-4E67-8944-B908143A7E2C/0/Information_Note_on_the_PJP_for_Website.pdf> (11 February 2011).
Equal Rights Trust, Legal Working Paper: The Protection of Stateless Persons in Detention under International Law, 2009.
Human Rights Ombudsman of the Republic of Slovenia, Problematika izbrisanih v letnih poročilih varuha (*Problem of Erased People in Annual Reports of the Ombudsman*), Posebno poročilo, 2004, pp. 25–27.

Interview with Ciril Ribičič, 25 July 2011.

Interview with Darina Macková, 4 February 2011.

Interview with Dejan Kladarin, UNHCR – Serbia and Montenegro, 9 September 2010.

Interview with Lev Kreft, 14 July 2011.

Latvian Centre for Human Rights, Annual Report on Human Rights, 1998.

Latvian Centre for Human Rights, Annual Report on Human Rights, 1999.

Letter from the Ministry of the Interior to the Government of the Republic of Slovenia entitled "Open issues related to the implementation of the Aliens Act", No. 0016/1-S-010/3-91 dated 4 June 1992.

Ministry of the Interior. Issuing of the additional decisions on the ground of point 8 of the Constitutional Court's decision No. U-I-246/02 dated 3 April 2003.

Od plebiscita do samostojnosti (*From Plebiscite to Sovereignty*), URL: <http://www.slovenija2001.gov.si/pot/ kronologija> (10 September 2010).

Public letter of nineteen petitioners, 18 April 2003.

Regular report of the European Commission on the progress of Slovenia in entering the EU, 1998.

Regular reports of the European Commission on the progress of Slovenia in entering the EU, between 1998 and 2002, URL: <http://www.svrez.gov.si/si/zakonodaja_in_dokumenti/eu_dokumenti/redna_porocila_evropske_komisije_o_napredku_slovenije_pri_vkljucevanju_v_evropsko_unijo/> (20 January 2010).

Serbian-Montenegrin Relations and the Question of Citizenship of FRY Citizens, Lawyers' Committee for Human Rights – YUCOM, Belgrade, November 2001.

"Slovenija ne more več čakati, nabralo se je preveč slabega", statement of Jože Pučnik, published in Delo daily, 17 December 1990, p. 2, URL: <http://www.mladina.si/152489/pucnikova-odgovornost/> (18 March 2016).

The response of the Government of the Republic of Slovenia concerning the acceptability and the grounds of the appeal against the lawsuit in the case *Makuc and others v. Slovenia* (now *Kurić and others v. Slovenia*), dated 26 October 2007.

Transcription of the 30th sitting of the National Assembly of the Republic of Slovenia, 29 October 2003.

Appendix I: Extract from the Grand Chamber Judgment in *Kurić and Others v. Slovenia* Case

European Court of Human Rights
Application No. 26828/06
26 June 2012

II. ALLEGED VIOLATION OF ARTICLE 8 OF THE CONVENTION

314. The applicants claimed that they had been arbitrarily deprived of the possibility of preserving their status as permanent residents in Slovenia. They invoked Article 8 of the Convention, which reads as follows:

"1. Everyone has the right to respect for his private and family life, his home and his correspondence.
2. There shall be no interference by a public authority with the exercise of this right except such as is in accordance with the law and is necessary in a democratic society in the interests of national security, public safety or the economic well-being of the country, for the prevention of disorder or crime, for the protection of health or morals, or for the protection of the rights and freedoms of others."

A. Arguments of the parties

1. The applicants

315. The applicants alleged that they had not been in a position to submit a formal request for citizenship within the short period set out in the domestic legislation. As a result, on 26 February 1992 their names had been unlawfully "erased" from the Register. The applicants Mr Kurić, Mr Dabetić and initially also Mr Ademi were also unable to acquire citizenship of any other successor State of the SFRY and had become, *de facto*, stateless persons. Subsequently, the applicants had not been in a position to successfully apply for permanent residence in Slovenia until the entry into force of the amended Legal Status Act in 2010.

316. Before the Chamber, the applicants submitted that the provisions of the Aliens Act were neither accessible nor foreseeable in effect. With respect to accessibility, the authorities had failed to provide adequate and detailed information to all persons concerned. As to foreseeability, the Aliens Act did not expressly apply to the "erased" since it was designed to regulate the status of illegal aliens.

In addition, the applicants regarded the Slovenian authorities' overall conduct as arbitrary. The interference complained of was not proportionate to the aim allegedly pursued, namely the control of the entry and residence of aliens, since the applicants had had permanent residence in Slovenia at the time of its independence.

317. The applicants essentially agreed with the Chamber's findings and urged that the Government's passive attitude be stigmatised in stronger terms. They stated that they had not been properly informed about the consequences of not having successfully applied for Slovenian citizenship; public announcements and newspaper articles were not enough. The "erasure" had been carried out arbitrarily, without any legal basis and in secret, and had concerned 25,671 persons.

318. It was only in 1999, after the decision of the Constitutional Court, that the "erased" had begun to discover what had really happened. In the subsequent years, the Constitutional Court's decisions had been systematically and deliberately disregarded by the Government and Parliament. The new framework legislation – the amended Legal Status Act – had been passed eleven years after the first leading decision on the unlawfulness of the "erasure" and seven years after the second leading ruling. Contrary to the Government, the applicants submitted that no genuine change had taken place in the policy of the Slovenian authorities since that Act had been passed.

319. The "erased" were not only denied access to Slovenian citizenship but were also bereft of any legal status conferring "the right to have rights". This was a serious encroachment on human dignity. The "erasure" irremediably affected their private or family life or both under Article 8 of the Convention, which also protected the right to establish details of a person's identity as an individual human being (the applicants cited, *inter alia*, *Christine Goodwin v. the United Kingdom* [GC], no. 28957/95, § 90, ECHR 2002-VI, and *Mikulić v. Croatia*, no. 53176/99, § 53, ECHR 2002-I). From being citizens in full possession of their rights, they had become illegal aliens overnight; some of them had also become stateless, and had lived for twenty years in a most precarious situation and been seriously hindered in the full enjoyment of their basic human rights. The difficulties the "erased" had to surmount were illustrated by the applicants' personal histories.

320. The Government had continued to minimise the unlawfulness and arbitrariness of the "erasure". The weakness of the Government's argument that the presence of the "erased" was tolerated was brought out by the fact that many had been forcibly deported from Slovenia, including five of the present applicants.

321. The Government had also minimised the consequences ensuing from the Constitutional Court's decisions of 1999 and 2003. The prior legislative

framework or its implementation or both by the competent administrative authorities were clearly inadequate. Most of the applicants had obtained their residence permits very recently, under the amended Legal Status Act. In spite of that, their situation had not yet been settled in the absence of any financial redress.

322. As to the amended Legal Status Act, only thirty permits had been granted so far. According to the official data, approximately 13,000 of the "erased" were therefore still waiting for the situation to be settled. It was therefore clear that the effects of the Court's judgment would extend well beyond the specific situations of each applicant since the judgment would concern the entire category of the "erased".

323. As to the Government's criticism of the Chamber's findings concerning statelessness, the Chamber had in any event not ruled that the "erasure" as such had caused statelessness or that the violations of the applicants' rights had originated from their statelessness, but had recorded an undisputable objective fact. The applicants believed that the Chamber should have gone further in assessing the real impact the "erasure" had had on citizenship rights, taking into account the relevant substantive and procedural rules of international law concerning the avoidance of statelessness. The "erasure" had created a factual situation in which it was much more difficult, and sometimes impossible, for the applicants to regularise their citizenship in accordance with the relevant legislation either in Slovenia or in the other former republics of the SFRY.

324. The Government's assumption that every former SFRY citizen should have kept his or her previous republic citizenship was not entirely correct. There were many reported cases showing the opposite, such as that of Mr Dabetić (see paragraph 97 above). Mr Ademi had only recently, in August 2010, been issued with a Macedonian passport (see paragraph 172 above). The Government had failed to give any consideration at all to situations where a person had not had the citizenship of a republic. This occurred in particular where the person concerned was born in Slovenia to parents with the citizenship of another republic or with no republic citizenship at all. Since 1968, the practice had been to enter one's citizenship in the registers kept in Slovenia, but the relevant data were in practice often not reported to the republic of origin in spite of the existing legislation. At the time of the dissolution of the SFRY, the Government had been under an obligation to give all persons living in Slovenia a choice between obtaining Slovenian citizenship and a residence permit.

2. The Government

325. Before the Chamber, the Government submitted that the events in 1991 had involved the historic creation of a new State and that it had therefore been

necessary, on the one hand, to establish rapidly a corpus of citizens in view of parliamentary elections and, on the other hand, to regulate the status of aliens, including that of citizens of the other former republics of the SFRY with permanent residence in Slovenia. This pivotal time for the establishment of a new State called for the quick adoption of decisions owing to the pressing social need. Under both the Statement of Good Intentions and the independence legislation (see paragraphs 21–22 and 24–25 above), the Republic of Slovenia had allowed citizens of the other former republics of the SFRY with permanent residence on its territory to acquire Slovenian citizenship by naturalisation under exceptionally favourable conditions. Those who had not taken advantage of this had become aliens and should have regularised their status. In the sphere of immigration, the State was entitled not only to regulate the stay and residence of aliens but also to take dissuasive measures, such as deportation. It had therefore been necessary to enact the appropriate legislation, which was accessible to the applicants and foreseeable in effect, in order to ensure public safety. Such legislation was necessary in a democratic society and proportionate to the aims pursued.

326. Before the Grand Chamber, the Government acknowledged that the "erasure" had been illegal and had led to an unconstitutional situation. They had fully complied in recent years with the Constitutional Court's decisions in order to redress the consequences of the "erasure": on 24 July 2010 the amended Legal Status Act had entered into force, and in 2009, after the change in government, the Ministry had resumed issuing *ex tunc* permanent residence permits. Moreover, various media had been used to provide information to the "erased" (for example, a brochure, the Internet and a free phone line). The Chamber judgment had failed to attach sufficient weight to these activities.

327. In 1991 the applicants had already been sufficiently informed, via publication in the official gazette and the press, about the possibility of regularising their status and the need to acquire a permanent or a temporary residence permit if they wished to continue residing in Slovenia under the general provisions of the Aliens Act (section 16). Between 1992 and 1997 a total of 4,893 such permits had been issued and the relevant conditions had been interpreted favourably. Approximately 12,500 permanent residence permits had been granted under both the Legal Status Act and the amended Legal Status Act (see paragraphs 67, 76 and 80 above).

328. In addition, although Article 8 of the Convention could not be construed as guaranteeing, as such, the right to a particular type of residence permit, and although the choice as to the most appropriate means of achieving respect for the rights enshrined in the Convention was a matter for the domestic authorities

alone (the Government cited *Sisojeva and Others*, cited above, § 91), the Republic of Slovenia had decided to grant the "erased" permanent retroactive residence permits, as the most favourable legal status for aliens. This exceeded the minimum required by the Convention.

329. The Government challenged in particular the statements contained in the Chamber judgment concerning the issue of statelessness. They stressed that the "erasure" had resulted only in the cessation of registered permanent residence and had had no impact on the individual's citizenship. Therefore, the Chamber's findings on this issue had been legally and substantively inaccurate.

330. They drew attention to the concept of "dual citizenship": in principle, all SFRY citizens had had citizenship of one of the republics. Since the SFRY system had not permitted statelessness, the break-up of the SFRY should not have created it.

3. The third parties

331. Open Society Justice Initiative stated that a process by which individuals were left at risk of being arbitrarily denied citizenship and becoming stateless had such a profound impact upon the victims as to interfere with Article 8 of the Convention. According to UNHCR data, at the end of 2009, 4,090 former SFRY citizens who had been "erased" in 1992 and were now stateless were living in Slovenia. According to a European Union study, only five stateless persons had been naturalised in Slovenia after 2002.

332. Under customary international law there was a positive obligation to avoid statelessness and to ameliorate the condition of those who were left stateless, especially in cases of State succession. Stateless persons were marginalised and particularly vulnerable. Open Society Justice Initiative relied on the provisions of the European Convention on Nationality, which placed a distinct emphasis on the importance of habitual residence in nationality rules, the notion of a "genuine and effective link" and the State's obligation to facilitate the acquisition of nationality by stateless persons habitually resident on the territory, and in particular children.

333. Moreover, the Council of Europe Convention on the Avoidance of Statelessness in relation to State Succession had entered into force on 1 August 2010. The explanatory report stated that the avoidance of statelessness formed a part of customary international law binding on Slovenia, even though the latter had not ratified this treaty.

334. Serious issues of statelessness had occurred in the context of the successor States of the SFRY. Among the group of the "erased" in Slovenia, a significant number remained stateless. The fact that the SFRY successor States had chosen

to grant nationality on the basis of the list of names in their registers on republic citizenship had a number of consequences: some former SFRY citizens did not possess or could not prove their republic citizenship for different reasons (destruction of documents or registers or both in the context of an armed conflict, impossibility of obtaining confirmation of one's republic citizenship at the place of birth, and so on). UNHCR had had substantial information and legal-aid programmes in place for a number of years in five of the successor States. The situation had disproportionately affected vulnerable groups, particularly minority groups from other former republics and Roma people.

335. The Government's efforts to regularise the status of the "erased" by issuing residence permits *ex proprio motu* and by implementing the amended Legal Status Act were welcomed. However, UNHCR remained concerned that the reforms would not allow all those affected by the "erasure" to receive a permanent residence permit and citizenship because of the onerous requirements imposed. The other third-party interveners basically agreed with the submissions of Open Society Justice Initiative.

B. The Chamber judgment

336. The Chamber observed that before 1991 the applicants had had their lawful permanent residence on Slovenian territory under the SFRY legislation applicable at the material time for several years, and most of them for decades, and had had a stronger residence status than long-term migrants. They had all spent a substantial part of their lives in Slovenia and had developed there the network of personal, social, cultural, linguistic and economic relations that made up the private life of every human being; most of them had also formed families in Slovenia or maintained ties with their families living there.

337. The Chamber concluded that the applicants had therefore had a private or family life or both in Slovenia at the material time within the meaning of Article 8 § 1 of the Convention. Furthermore, the repercussions of the "erasure" and the prolonged refusal of the Slovenian authorities to comprehensively regulate the applicants' situation constituted an interference with the exercise of their rights under Article 8 of the Convention, in particular in cases of statelessness (see paragraphs 348–361 of the Chamber judgment).

338. As to whether that interference was "in accordance with the law" under paragraph 2 of Article 8, the Chamber held that the "erasure" had been found to be unlawful by the Constitutional Court and saw no reason to depart from that court's decisions. The Chamber therefore found a violation of Article 8, also in the light of relevant international-law standards aimed at the avoidance of

statelessness, especially in situations of State succession (see paragraphs 362–376 of the Chamber judgment).

C. The Grand Chamber's assessment

1. Whether Article 8 applied to the applicants' complaints

339. The Grand Chamber observes at the outset that the Government did not contest before it that the "erasure" and its repercussions had had an adverse effect on the applicants and amounted to an interference with their "private or family life" or both within the meaning of Article 8 § 1 of the Convention (see *Slivenko v. Latvia* [GC], no. 48321/99, § 96, ECHR 2003-X). Having regard to both parties' arguments, the Grand Chamber sees no reason to depart from the Chamber's findings that, although the "erasure" had been carried out before 28 June 1994, when the Convention entered into force in respect of Slovenia, the applicants had a private or family life or both in Slovenia within the meaning of Article 8 § 1 of the Convention at the material time, and that the "erasure" interfered with their Article 8 rights and continues to do so (see paragraph 337 above).

340. It remains to be examined whether that interference was compatible with the second paragraph of Article 8 of the Convention, that is, whether it was "in accordance with the law", pursued one or more of the legitimate aims listed in that paragraph and was "necessary in a democratic society".

2. Justification of the interference

(a) Was the interference "in accordance with the law"?

341. According to the Court's established case-law, the expression "in accordance with the law" requires that the impugned measure should have some basis in domestic law, and it also refers to the quality of the law in question, requiring that it should be accessible to the person concerned and foreseeable as to its effects (see *Amann v. Switzerland* [GC], no. 27798/95, § 50, ECHR 2000-II, and *Slivenko*, cited above, § 100).

342. The Court observes that the "erasure" of the applicants' names from the Register, together with the names of more than 25,000 other former SFRY citizens, occurred as a result of the joint effect of two sections of the independence legislation enacted on 25 June 1991: section 40 of the Citizenship Act and section 81 of the Aliens Act (see paragraphs 25 and 27 above). Those ex-SFRY citizens with the citizenship of one of the other republics and permanent residence in Slovenia who failed to submit requests for Slovenian citizenship by 25 December 1991, or whose requests had been rejected, fell under the second subsection of section 81 of the Aliens Act. On 26 February 1992, when the latter provision became directly applicable, the applicants became aliens.

343. The Court considers that section 40 of the Citizenship Act and section 81 of the Aliens Act were legal instruments which were accessible to any interested persons. The applicants could therefore foresee that by failing to apply for Slovenian nationality, they would be treated as aliens. However, in the Court's opinion, they could not reasonably have expected, in the absence of any clause to that effect, that their status as aliens would entail the unlawfulness of their residence on Slovenian territory and would lead to such an extreme measure as the "erasure". In this connection, it is to be recalled that the "erasure" was carried out automatically and without prior notification. Nor were the applicants given the opportunity to challenge it before the competent domestic authorities or to give explanations as to the reasons for their failure to apply for Slovenian citizenship. The absence of any notification or personal information could have led them to believe that their status as residents had remained unchanged and that they could continue residing and working in Slovenia as they had done for several years. Indeed, it was only incidentally that they learned about the "erasure" (see paragraphs 89, 111, 126, 137, 162 and 177 above). Serious doubts may therefore arise as to the foreseeability of the measure complained of.

344. Moreover, the Court cannot but attach significant weight to the fact that in its leading decision of 4 February 1999, the Constitutional Court held that the transfer of the names of the "erased" from the Register of Permanent Residents to the Register of Aliens without a Residence Permit had no domestic legal basis; neither the Aliens Act nor the Inhabitants' Evidence of Residence and Population Registry Act provided for such *ex lege* deregistration and transfer (see paragraphs 41 and 214 above). Furthermore, the Constitutional Court found that no legal provision regulated the transition of the legal status of the "erased" to the status of aliens living in Slovenia; sections 13 and 16 of the Aliens Act (see paragraph 207 above) were designed for aliens entering Slovenia and were therefore not applicable to the applicants (see paragraphs 41–42, 44–45 and 214 above). There was therefore a legal vacuum in the legislation at the time since for those ex-SFRY citizens holding the citizenship of one of the other republics who fell within the scope of the second subsection of section 81 of the Aliens Act, no procedure was put in place to request permanent residence permits. Under section 13 of the Aliens Act, they could only apply for a temporary residence permit, as if they were aliens entering Slovenia with a valid visa who wished to remain longer on Slovenian territory.

345. In addition, it is evident from the administrative circulars addressed by the Ministry of the Interior to the administrative units, in particular those dated 27 February and 15 June 1992 relating to the implementation of the Aliens Act,

the interpretation of section 81 and the keeping of records (see paragraphs 28, 30 and 35 above), that the Slovenian authorities were aware at the material time of the negative consequences of the "erasure", which was carried out in secret. By definition, these administrative circulars were not accessible to the applicants.

346. The Court therefore finds that, until 8 July 1999, when the Legal Status Act was passed, the impugned Slovenian legislation and administrative practice which resulted in the "erasure" lacked the requisite standards of foreseeability and accessibility, as developed in the Court's case-law.

347. It is true that following the Constitutional Court's decision of 4 February 1999, on 8 July 1999 the Legal Status Act was passed in order to regularise the situation of the "erased" (see paragraphs 49–50 above). However, the Constitutional Court held on 3 April 2003 that certain provisions of the Legal Status Act were unconstitutional, in particular since they failed to grant the "erased" retroactive permanent residence permits and to regulate the situation of those who had been deported (see paragraphs 58–60 and 215 above). Finally, it took more than seven years, until 24 July 2010, for the latter decision of the Constitutional Court ordering general measures to be complied with, when the amended Legal Status Act was enacted (see paragraph 76 above).

348. It follows that, at least until 2010, the domestic legal system failed to regulate clearly the consequences of the "erasure" and the residence status of those who had been subjected to it. Therefore, not only were the applicants not in a position to foresee the measure complained of, but they were also unable to envisage its repercussions on their private or family life or both.

349. This is sufficient for the Court to come to the conclusion that the interference with the applicants' Article 8 rights was not "in accordance with the law" and that this provision has been violated.

350. However, in the particular circumstances of the present case, and given the widespread repercussions of the "erasure", the Court considers it necessary to examine also whether, quite apart from its lack of sufficient legal basis, this measure pursued a legitimate aim and was proportionate to it.

(b) Did the interference pursue a legitimate aim?

351. The Government submitted that at the time when the new State was being created, the independence legislation had pursued the legitimate aim of protecting national security. Moreover, the right for the State to control the entry and residence of aliens within its territory presupposed that it could take dissuasive measures, such as deportation, against persons infringing immigration laws (see paragraph 325 above).

352. The Court considers that the aim of the independence legislation and the measures taken in respect of the applicants cannot be dissociated from the wider context of the dissolution of the SFRY, the achievement of Slovenia's independence in 1991 and the establishment of an effective political democracy, which entailed the formation of a "corpus of Slovenian citizens" with a view to the parliamentary elections. The interference complained of (the "erasure") has to be seen within this general framework.

353. The Court therefore considers that with the enactment of the independence legislation, which contained an option for all citizens of the other former republics of the SFRY resident in Slovenia to acquire Slovenian citizenship within a short period of time only, the Slovenian authorities sought to create a "corpus of Slovenian citizens" and thus to protect the interests of the country's national security (see, *mutatis mutandis*, *Slivenko*, cited above, §§ 110–111), a legitimate aim within the meaning of Article 8 § 2 of the Convention.

(c) Was the interference "necessary in a democratic society"?

354. This independence legislation, however, had adverse consequences for those former SFRY citizens who had not applied for Slovenian citizenship within the prescribed time-limit of six months and who consequently became aliens unlawfully residing on Slovenian territory because their names were "erased" from the Register of Permanent Residents. The Court will assess the compatibility of this measure with the applicants' right to respect for their private or family life or both. It reiterates that a measure interfering with rights guaranteed by Article 8 § 1 of the Convention can be regarded as being "necessary in a democratic society" if it has been taken in order to respond to a pressing social need and if the means employed are proportionate to the aims pursued. The Court's task consists in ascertaining whether the impugned measures struck a fair balance between the relevant interests, namely the individual's rights protected by the Convention on the one hand and the community's interests on the other (see *Slivenko*, cited above, § 113).

355. According to the Court's case-law, the Convention does not guarantee the right of an alien to enter or to reside in a particular country and Contracting States have the right, as a matter of well-established international law and subject to their treaty obligations, including the Convention, to control the entry, residence and expulsion of aliens (see, among many other authorities, *Chahal v. the United Kingdom*, 15 November 1996, § 73, *Reports* 1996-V; *El Boujaïdi v. France*, 26 September 1997, § 39, *Reports* 1997-VI; *Baghli v. France*, no. 34374/97, § 45, ECHR 1999-VIII; *Boultif v. Switzerland*, no. 54273/00, § 39, ECHR 2001-IX; *Üner v. the Netherlands* [GC], no. 46410/99, § 54, ECHR 2006-XII; and *Slivenko*,

cited above, § 115). However, measures restricting the right to reside in a country may, in certain cases, entail a violation of Article 8 of the Convention if they create disproportionate repercussions on the private or family life, or both, of the individuals concerned (see *Boultif*, cited above, § 55; *Slivenko*, cited above, § 128; *Radovanovic v. Austria*, no. 42703/98, §§ 36-37, 22 April 2004; and *Maslov v. Austria* [GC], no. 1638/03, § 100, ECHR 2008).

356. In the present case, the applicants, who, prior to Slovenia's declaration of independence, had been lawfully residing in Slovenia for several years, had, as former SFRY citizens, enjoyed a wide range of social and political rights. Owing to the "erasure", they experienced a number of adverse consequences, such as the destruction of identity documents, loss of job opportunities, loss of health insurance, the impossibility of renewing identity documents or driving licences, and difficulties in regulating pension rights. Indeed, the legal vacuum in the independence legislation (see paragraph 344 above) deprived the applicants of their legal status, which had previously given them access to a wide range of rights.

357. Allegedly, the "erasure" was a consequence of their failure to seek to obtain Slovenian citizenship. However, the Court points out that an alien lawfully residing in a country may wish to continue living in that country without necessarily acquiring its citizenship. As shown by the difficulties faced by the applicants, for many years, in obtaining a valid residence permit, the Slovenian legislature failed to enact provisions aimed at permitting former SFRY citizens holding the citizenship of one of the other republics to regularise their residence status if they had chosen not to become Slovenian citizens or had failed to do so. Such provisions would not have undermined the legitimate aims of controlling the residence of aliens or creating a corpus of Slovenian citizens, or both.

358. In this connection, the Court reiterates that, while the essential object of Article 8 is to protect the individual against arbitrary action by the public authorities, it does not merely compel the State to abstain from such interference: in addition to this negative undertaking, there may be positive obligations inherent in effective "respect" for private or family life or both, in particular in the case of long-term migrants such as the applicants (see, *mutatis mutandis*, *Gül v. Switzerland*, 19 February 1996, § 38, *Reports* 1996-I; *Ahmut v. the Netherlands*, 28 November 1996, § 67, *Reports* 1996-VI; and *Mehemi v. France (no. 2)*, no. 53470/99, § 45, ECHR 2003-IV).

359. The Court is of the opinion that, in the particular circumstances of the present case, the regularisation of the residence status of former SFRY citizens was a necessary step which the State should have taken in order to ensure that failure to obtain Slovenian citizenship would not disproportionately affect the

Article 8 rights of the "erased". The absence of such regulation and the prolonged impossibility of obtaining valid residence permits have upset the fair balance which should have been struck between the legitimate aim of the protection of national security and effective respect for the applicants' right to private or family life or both.

(d) Conclusion

360. The Court considers that, despite the efforts made after the Constitutional Court's decisions of 1999 and 2003, as well as recently with the enactment of the amended Legal Status Act, the Slovenian authorities have failed to remedy comprehensively and with the requisite promptness the blanket nature of the "erasure" and its grave consequences for the applicants.

361. For the reasons set out above, the measures complained of were neither "prescribed by law" nor "necessary in a democratic society" to achieve the legitimate aim of the protection of national security.

362. Accordingly, there has been a violation of Article 8 of the Convention.

III. ALLEGED VIOLATION OF ARTICLE 13 TAKEN IN CONJUNCTION WITH ARTICLE 8 OF THE CONVENTION

363. The applicants maintained that they had no effective remedy at their disposal in respect of their grievances under Article 8 of the Convention.

They invoked Article 13 of the Convention, which reads as follows:

"Everyone whose rights and freedoms as set forth in [the] Convention are violated shall have an effective remedy before a national authority notwithstanding that the violation has been committed by persons acting in an official capacity."

A. Arguments of the parties

1. The applicants

364. Relying on the Court's judgment in the case of *M.S.S. v. Belgium and Greece* ([GC], no. 30696/09, § 291, ECHR 2011), and on the arguments set out in paragraphs 279–280 above, the applicants alleged that none of the remedies at their disposal at the material time had proved to be capable of addressing the substance of their complaints under Article 8 of the Convention and of awarding them appropriate relief.

365. In spite of the Constitutional Court's leading decisions, the Government were not even willing to issue *ex tunc* residence permits to those who were already in possession of *ex nunc* permits, let alone to adopt a comprehensive legal solution to the problem arising from the "erasure" over a considerable number of years.

2. The Government

366. The Government maintained that the legal remedies at the applicants' disposal – the administrative proceedings, the individual constitutional complaint and the action for damages – had been both accessible and effective, in compliance with Article 13 of the Convention.

3. The third parties

367. The third parties maintained that as a result of the State's prolonged failure to enforce the Constitutional Court's decision of 3 April 2003, which was legally binding, the applicants' right to an effective remedy had been violated, owing to a lack of political will.

B. The Chamber judgment

368. The Chamber found a violation of Article 13 in conjunction with Article 8 of the Convention on account of the non-compliance with the leading decisions of the Constitutional Court and held that the Government had failed to establish that the remedies available to the applicants were effective (see paragraphs 383–386 of the Chamber judgment).

C. The Grand Chamber's assessment

369. As the Court has held on many occasions, Article 13 of the Convention guarantees the availability at national level of a remedy to enforce the substance of the Convention rights and freedoms in whatever form they may happen to be secured in the domestic legal order. The effect of Article 13 is thus to require the provision of a domestic remedy to deal with the substance of an "arguable complaint" under the Convention and to grant appropriate relief (see *Kudła v. Poland* [GC], no. 30210/96, § 157, ECHR 2000-XI).

370. The Court has already found that the applicants' "erasure" amounted to a violation of Article 8 of the Convention (see paragraph 362 above). The applicants' complaints in that regard are therefore "arguable" for the purposes of Article 13.

371. The Court refers to its finding that the Government failed to establish that the remedies available to the applicants were "adequate" and "effective" in order to redress, at the material time, the alleged violation of Article 8 of the Convention (see paragraphs 295–313 above).

372. Accordingly, there has been a violation of Article 13 in conjunction with Article 8 of the Convention.

IV. ALLEGED VIOLATION OF ARTICLE 14 TAKEN IN CONJUNCTION WITH ARTICLE 8 OF THE CONVENTION

373. The applicants claimed that in enjoying their rights under Article 8 of the Convention, they had been discriminated against on the ground of their national origin, when compared to other foreign citizens (the so-called "real" aliens) who continued to live in Slovenia on the basis of temporary or permanent residence permits.

374. They invoked Article 14 of the Convention, which reads as follows:

"The enjoyment of the rights and freedoms set forth in [the] Convention shall be secured without discrimination on any ground such as sex, race, colour, language, religion, political or other opinion, national or social origin, association with a national minority, property, birth or other status."

A. Arguments of the parties

1. The applicants

375. The applicants argued that they had been treated less favourably than "real" aliens who had lived in Slovenia since before independence and whose permanent residence permits remained valid under section 82 of the Aliens Act.

376. In the applicants' view, the issue of discriminatory treatment of the "erased" was one of the main features of the present case, and the Grand Chamber should examine the merits of their complaint under Article 14 (they cited *Chassagnou and Others v. France* [GC], nos. 25088/94, 28331/95 and 28443/95, § 89, ECHR 1999-III, and *Nachova and Others v. Bulgaria* [GC], nos. 43577/98 and 43579/98, §§ 160–168, ECHR 2005-VII). They underlined that the Constitutional Court itself had confirmed the existence of discrimination. If the continuous right to residence of "real" aliens was recognised by the Aliens Act, the same should apply all the more to the "erased".

377. Lastly, the applicants contested the respondent Government's allegations (see paragraph 379 below) that positive discrimination had been carried out in respect of them since they had not been subjected to deportation; five of the applicants had in fact been deported.

2. The Government

378. The Government stated that at the time of its independence, the Republic of Slovenia had allowed citizens of the other former republics of the SFRY with permanent residence in Slovenia to acquire Slovenian citizenship under exceptionally favourable conditions. In addition, the 1991 Constitutional Law guaranteed them equal treatment to Slovenian citizens until their acquisition of Slovenian citizenship or the expiry of the time-limits set by the Aliens Act

(see paragraph 202 above). However, bearing in mind the necessity of forming a corpus of Slovenian citizens – especially with a view to the 1992 parliamentary elections – this equality in treatment could not last indefinitely. Therefore, it was up to the permanent residents without Slovenian citizenship to seize the opportunity to acquire citizenship of the independent Slovenia; this was not granted automatically.

379. The applicants' position was therefore linked to the fact that they, as aliens, had not acquired permanent residence permits. They had been treated like all other aliens without a residence permit. As to the SFRY legislation and the provisions of the Aliens Act, the applicants and the "real" aliens had never been in a comparable situation. Moreover, the applicants had benefited from positive discrimination, since they had in principle not been deported from Slovenia.

3. The third parties

380. Apart from the Serbian Government, the other third parties' submissions before the Chamber focused primarily on the issue of discrimination, which had been recognised as being of fundamental importance in the Court's case-law.

381. The third-party interveners stated that the "erased" had been subject to discrimination, both direct and indirect, on the ground of national origin or ethnicity or both (citing *D.H. and Others v. the Czech Republic*, cited above, § 175). The Aliens Act contained stricter provisions for the "erased" than for other aliens. Because the Slovenian population was ethnically homogeneous as compared to other former SFRY republics, the "erasure" disproportionately affected non-ethnic Slovenes, ex-SFRY minorities, and Roma, thereby also discriminating among residents on ethnic grounds. There was no objective justification for what had resulted in decades of legal limbo experienced by the "erased". Lastly, other Council of Europe bodies had interpreted the right to non-discrimination as requiring positive action on the part of member States.

B. The Chamber judgment

382. The Chamber considered that, in view of its finding of a violation of Article 8 of the Convention, it was not necessary to rule on the applicants' complaint under Article 14 (see paragraph 400 of the Chamber judgment).

C. The Grand Chamber's assessment

383. Having regard to the importance of the discrimination issue in the present case, the Grand Chamber considers, unlike the Chamber, that the applicants' complaint under Article 14 of the Convention should be examined.

1. Applicability of Article 14 of the Convention

384. As the Court has consistently held, Article 14 complements the other substantive provisions of the Convention and its Protocols. It has no independent existence since it has effect solely in relation to "the enjoyment of the rights and freedoms" safeguarded by those provisions. Although the application of Article 14 does not presuppose a breach of those provisions – and to this extent it is autonomous – there can be no room for its application unless the facts in issue fall within the ambit of one or more of the latter (see, among many other authorities, *Van Raalte v. the Netherlands*, 21 February 1997, § 33, *Reports* 1997-I; *Petrovic v. Austria*, 27 March 1998, § 22, *Reports* 1998-II; and *Zarb Adami v. Malta*, no. 17209/02, § 42, ECHR 2006-VIII).

385. In the present case, the Court has found that the measures complained of constituted an unlawful interference with the applicants' "private or family life" or both within the meaning of Article 8 § 1 of the Convention (see paragraph 339 above). Article 8 thus being applicable to the facts of the case, Article 14 is applicable too.

2. Compliance with Article 14 of the Convention taken in conjunction with Article 8

(a) General principles

386. According to the Court's well-established case-law, discrimination means treating differently, without an objective and reasonable justification, persons in relevantly similar situations (see *Willis v. the United Kingdom*, no. 36042/97, § 48, ECHR 2002-IV). A difference in treatment has no objective and reasonable justification if it does not pursue a "legitimate aim" or if there is not a "reasonable relationship of proportionality" between the means employed and the aim sought to be realised. Where the difference in treatment is based on race, colour or ethnic origin, the notion of objective and reasonable justification must be interpreted as strictly as possible (see, among many other authorities, *Oršuš and Others v. Croatia* [GC], no. 15766/03, § 156, ECHR 2010).

387. The Contracting States enjoy a certain margin of appreciation in assessing whether and to what extent differences in otherwise similar situations justify a difference in treatment (see *Gaygusuz v. Austria*, 16 September 1996, § 42, *Reports* 1996-IV). The scope of the margin of appreciation will vary according to the circumstances, the subject matter and its background (see *Rasmussen v. Denmark*, 28 November 1984, § 40, Series A no. 87, and *Inze v. Austria*, 28 October 1987, § 41, Series A no. 126), but the final decision as to observance of the Convention's requirements rests with the Court. Since the Convention is first and foremost a system for the protection of human rights, the Court must, however,

have regard to the changing conditions in Contracting States and respond, for example, to any emerging consensus as to the standards to be achieved (see *Ünal Tekeli v. Turkey*, no. 29865/96, § 54, ECHR 2004-X, and, *mutatis mutandis*, *Stafford v. the United Kingdom* [GC], no. 46295/99, § 68, ECHR 2002-IV).

388. That being said, Article 14 does not prohibit Contracting Parties from treating groups differently in order to correct "factual inequalities" between them. Indeed, in certain circumstances a failure to attempt to correct inequality through different treatment may, without an objective and reasonable justification, give rise to a breach of that Article (see *Thlimmenos v. Greece* [GC], no. 34369/97, § 44, ECHR 2000-IV, and *Sejdić and Finci v. Bosnia and Herzegovina* [GC], nos. 27996/06 and 34836/06, § 44, ECHR 2009). The Court has also accepted that a general policy or measure that has disproportionately prejudicial effects on a particular group may be considered discriminatory notwithstanding that it is not specifically aimed at that group, and that discrimination potentially contrary to the Convention may result from a *de facto* situation (see *D.H. and Others v. the Czech Republic*, cited above, § 175, and the authorities cited therein).

389. Lastly, as to the burden of proof in relation to Article 14 of the Convention, the Court has held that once the applicant has shown a difference in treatment, it is for the Government to show that it was justified (ibid., § 177).

(b) Whether there has been a difference in treatment between persons in similar situations

390. Turning to the instant case, the Court observes that the status of citizens of States other than the former SFRY republics who had lived in Slovenia before its independence (the so-called "real" aliens) was regulated by section 82 of the Aliens Act, which provided that their permanent residence permits remained valid (see paragraph 207 above). However, the Aliens Act failed to regulate the status of the citizens of other SFRY republics who were residing in Slovenia. As underlined above (see paragraph 344 above), this legal vacuum resulted in the "erasure" of the latter and the unlawfulness of their stay on the Slovenian territory.

391. It could be argued that before the independence of Slovenia there was a difference between these two groups, since one was composed of aliens, whereas the other was composed of citizens of the former federal State of which Slovenia was a constituent part. However, in the Court's opinion, after the declaration of independence and the coming into existence of the new State, their situation became at least comparable. The two groups were both composed of aliens holding citizenship of a State other than Slovenia or stateless people. As an effect of the "erasure", members of only one of the groups could keep their residence permits.

392. Therefore, there has been a difference in treatment between two groups – "real" aliens and citizens of former SFRY Republics other than Slovenia – which were in a similar situation in respect of residence-related matters.

(c) Whether there is objective and reasonable justification

393. The Court does not see how the necessity, referred to by the Government, of forming a corpus of Slovenian citizens with a view to the parliamentary elections of 1992 (see paragraph 378 above) could have required differential treatment in granting foreigners the possibility of residing in Slovenia, as a residence permit did not confer the right to vote on the holder. It is true that only the "erased", and not "real" aliens, were given the possibility of acquiring Slovenian nationality on favourable conditions. However, the Court has already underlined that, as such, a failure to apply for citizenship cannot be considered a reasonable ground for depriving a group of aliens of their residence permits (see paragraph 357 above).

394. Under these circumstances, the Court considers that the differential treatment complained of was based on the national origin of the persons concerned – as former SFRY citizens were treated differently from other foreigners – and that it did not pursue a legitimate aim and therefore lacked an objective and reasonable justification (see, *mutatis mutandis*, *Sejdić and Finci*, cited above, §§ 45–50). Moreover, the situation of the former SFRY citizens, including the applicants, was significantly altered after the declaration of independence when compared with that of "real" aliens. Before 1991, former SFRY citizens were, in matters connected to residence, in a privileged position in comparison with "real" aliens. At the relevant time, citizenship of the federal State could have been looked at as an objective ground for such preferential treatment. However, as a consequence of the independence legislation, former SFRY citizens suddenly found themselves in a situation of unlawfulness which has been found to breach Article 8 (see paragraphs 361–362 above) and in a disadvantaged position *vis-à-vis* "real" aliens, as only the permanent residence permits of the latter remained valid, even in the absence of an application for Slovenian nationality (see paragraph 390 above). In the Court's view, the legislation at stake thus placed a disproportionate and excessive burden on former SFRY citizens.

395. The above conclusion is also confirmed by the decision of 4 February 1999 in which the Constitutional Court held that the "erased" were in a less favourable legal position than "real" aliens who had been living in Slovenia before independence and whose special permanent residence permits remained valid under section 82 of the Aliens Act (see paragraph 42 above).

396. Having regard to the foregoing, the Court finds that there has been a violation of Article 14 taken in conjunction with Article 8 of the Convention.

V. ARTICLE 46 OF THE CONVENTION

397. Article 46 of the Convention provides, in so far as relevant:

"1. The High Contracting Parties undertake to abide by the final judgment of the Court in any case to which they are parties.

2. The final judgment of the Court shall be transmitted to the Committee of Ministers, which shall supervise its execution.

..."

398. Under this provision, the applicants requested the Court to indicate general measures aimed at redressing the situation of the "erased".

A. Arguments of the parties

1. The applicants

399. The applicants submitted that, at this stage and in the absence of any settled practice, the enactment and implementation of the amended Legal Status Act could not be regarded as general measures capable of removing the systemic violation of the rights of the "erased".

400. The amended Legal Status Act was *prima facie* an insufficient legal remedy, the decision of 3 April 2003 being applied in the most minimal and restrictive way, preserving the main features and requirements of the previous legislation. The condition of "actually residing in Slovenia" had been changed in order to include some exceptions. However, not all the cases of the "erased" fell under any of the exceptions mentioned. The procedure was cumbersome and costly and the burden of proof was incumbent on the "erased". In the event of prolonged absence from Slovenia, they had to show that they had tried to return during the first ten years, which was extremely difficult to prove. It was therefore not surprising that according to the latest statistics as of June 2011, out of 127 applications submitted (from a total of 13,000 eligible persons), only thirty had been successful while sixty had been dismissed. The heavy rate of rejected applications showed that the legislation had serious shortcomings.

401. As to the individual measures, the issuing of permanent residence permits did not constitute sufficient redress for the violations found. The serious non-pecuniary and pecuniary damage suffered required further remedial action, namely the adoption of individual measures of reparation. This had also been stressed in the 2010 concluding observations of the Committee on the Elimination of Racial Discrimination. The Council of Europe's Commissioner for Human Rights had also stated that other measures were necessary in order to redress the violations suffered by the "erased", for instance in relation to family reunion. He had stressed that the new legislation did not provide for any specific mechanism for affording fair compensation for the many years of unregulated

status. The concluding observations of the Committee against Torture had also urged the respondent Government to facilitate the full integration of the "erased", including those belonging to Roma communities. Furthermore, the three above-mentioned international bodies had underlined the shortcomings of the amended Legal Status Act.

2. The Government

402. The Government maintained that the enactment and implementation of the amended Legal Status Act had constituted an appropriate, comprehensive and general measure for ensuring the right to private or family life, or both, of the "erased". With this, the Constitutional Court's decision of 2003 had been fully implemented.

403. In their view, the Chamber had failed to attach sufficient weight to the fact that the amended Legal Status Act was about to enter into force. The Republic of Slovenia had therefore already taken appropriate steps before the delivery of the Chamber judgment. Moreover, various media had been used to provide information to the "erased" (a brochure, the Internet, a free phone line, and so on). This was also the main reason why referral to the Grand Chamber had been requested.

404. Furthermore, on 25 November 2011 an intergovernmental commission had been set up in order to deal with the problem of the "erased". The implementation of the Act was also regularly monitored by the authorities. Sixty-four permanent residence permits and 111 supplementary permits had been issued under the amended Legal Status Act. Altogether, 12,500 of the "erased" had regularised their status.

B. The Chamber judgment

405. The Chamber held that the violation found on account of the failure by the Slovenian legislative and administrative authorities to comply with the Constitutional Court's decisions clearly indicated the appropriate general and individual measures to be adopted in the Slovenian domestic legal order: enactment of appropriate legislation and regulation of the situation of the individual applicants by issuing retroactive permanent residence permits (see paragraphs 401–407 of the Chamber judgment).

C. The Court's assessment

406. By Article 46 of the Convention the High Contracting Parties undertake to abide by the final judgments of the Court in any case to which they are parties, execution being supervised by the Committee of Ministers. It follows, *inter alia*,

that a judgment in which the Court finds a breach imposes on the respondent State a legal obligation not just to pay those concerned the sums awarded by way of just satisfaction under Article 41, but also to choose the general or, if appropriate, individual measures or both to be adopted. As the Court's judgments are essentially declaratory, the respondent State remains free, subject to the supervision of the Committee of Ministers, to choose the means by which it will discharge its legal obligation under Article 46 of the Convention, provided that such means are compatible with the conclusions set out in the Court's judgment (see *Scozzari and Giunta v. Italy* [GC], nos. 39221/98 and 41963/98, § 249, ECHR 2000-VIII; *Sejdovic*, cited above, § 119; and *Aleksanyan v. Russia*, no. 46468/06, § 238, 22 December 2008).

407. However, in exceptional cases, with a view to helping the respondent State to fulfil its obligations under Article 46, the Court will seek to indicate the type of measure that might be taken in order to put an end to a situation it has found to exist (see, for example, *Broniowski*, cited above, § 194).

408. In the present case, the Court has found violations of the applicants' rights guaranteed by Articles 8, 13 and 14, which essentially originated in the prolonged failure of the Slovenian authorities, in spite of the Constitutional Court's leading judgments, to regularise the applicants' residence status following their "erasure" and to provide them with adequate redress.

409. The "erasure" concerned an entire category of former SFRY citizens with permanent residence in Slovenia who had the citizenship of one of the other former SFRY republics at the time of Slovenia's declaration of independence. It has therefore affected and still affects a large number of persons.

410. However, it should be borne in mind that various legislative reforms, notably the amended Legal Status Act (see paragraphs 76–79 and 211 above), have been implemented after the delivery of the Chamber judgment. This new law enables the "erased" to take steps to regularise their residence in Slovenia. It is also worth noting that the six applicants in respect of whom the Court has found a breach of the Convention have been provided with permanent residence permits (see paragraphs 95, 123, 133, 158, 173 and 194 above) and that the Government have set up an intergovernmental commission in order to monitor the implementation of the amended Legal Status Act and to tackle the problem of the "erased" (see paragraph 404 above).

411. It is true that the amended Legal Status Act has been in place since 24 July 2010 and that some international monitoring bodies have underlined certain of its shortcomings (see paragraphs 223 and 227–228 above). However, the Court considers that it would be premature at this stage, in the absence of

any settled domestic practice, to examine whether the reforms outlined above and the various steps taken by the Government have achieved the result of satisfactorily regulating the residence status of the "erased" (see, *mutatis mutandis*, *Sejdovic*, cited above, §§ 119 and 123).

412. At the same time, the Court has found that the applicants were not awarded proper financial redress for the years during which they were in a position of vulnerability and legal insecurity and that, as matters currently stand, the possibility of obtaining compensation at the domestic level in civil proceedings or before the State Attorney's Office is still remote (see paragraph 268 above). Therefore, the Court finds that the facts of the case disclose the existence, within the Slovenian legal order, of a shortcoming as a consequence of which the whole category of the "erased" are still denied compensation for the infringement of their fundamental rights.

413. The Court considers that the present case is suitable for the adoption of a pilot-judgment procedure within the meaning of Rule 61 of the Rules of Court, given that one of the fundamental implications of this procedure is that the Court's assessment of the situation complained of in a "pilot" case necessarily extends beyond the sole interests of the individual applicants and requires it to examine that case also from the perspective of the general measures that need to be taken in the interest of other potentially affected persons (see *Broniowski v. Poland* (friendly settlement) [GC], no. 31443/96, § 36, ECHR 2005-IX, and *Hutten-Czapska v. Poland* (friendly settlement) [GC], no. 35014/97, § 33, 28 April 2008). In this connection, the Court observes that, further to the pilot judgment in the case of *Lukenda v. Slovenia* (no. 23032/02, §§ 89–98, ECHR 2005-X), concerning the excessive length of judicial proceedings and the malfunctioning of the domestic legal system in this respect, the Government adopted a number of measures, including the setting up of a special financial mechanism. This has enabled the Court to dispose of a high number of pending cases.

414. Although only a few similar applications lodged by "erased" persons are currently pending before the Court, in the context of systemic, structural or similar violations the potential inflow of future cases is also an important consideration in terms of preventing the accumulation of such repetitive cases on the Court's docket. As regards the consultation of the parties to the proceedings on this matter, as provided for by Rule 61 § 2 (a), the Court would point out that this provision entered into force on 1 April 2011, well after this case was brought before the Grand Chamber, thus preventing it from being applied in the present case.

415. The Court therefore decides to indicate, in accordance with Rule 61 § 3, that the respondent Government should, within one year, set up an *ad hoc* domestic compensation scheme (see, *mutatis mutandis*, *Hutten-Czapska*, cited above, § 239, and *Xenides-Arestis v. Turkey* (merits), no. 46347/99, § 40, 22 December 2005). Pursuant to Rule 61 § 6 (a), the examination of all similar applications will be adjourned pending the adoption of the remedial measures at issue.

VI. ARTICLE 41 OF THE CONVENTION

416. Article 41 of the Convention provides:

"If the Court finds that there has been a violation of the Convention or the Protocols thereto, and if the internal law of the High Contracting Party concerned allows only partial reparation to be made, the Court shall, if necessary, afford just satisfaction to the injured party."

417. The applicants claimed awards for pecuniary and non-pecuniary damage, as well as the reimbursement of the costs and expenses incurred before the Court. The Government disputed their claims.

A. Arguments of the parties

1. The applicants

418. The applicants contended that the Government's position that they should first file their compensation claims before the domestic courts or the State Attorney's Office had no merit (they cited *Barberà, Messegué and Jabardo v. Spain* (Article 50), 13 June 1994, § 17, Series A no. 285-C). The admissibility of claims for just satisfaction was not subordinate to the prior exercise of domestic legal remedies. This was particularly true where, as in the present case, the remedies in question were manifestly incapable of offering the injured parties a speedy and simple opportunity to obtain pecuniary reparation.

419. Before the Grand Chamber, the applicants updated their just satisfaction claims. Each applicant with no income requested an amount corresponding to the social and housing allowances which he or she could have received if the "erasure" had not taken place.

The applicants submitted the following claims in respect of pecuniary damage:

- Mr Kurić: EUR 37,929.85;
- Ms Mezga: EUR 58,104.03;
- Mr Ristanović: EUR 15,698.07;
- Mr Berisha: EUR 104,174.25;
- Mr Sadik: EUR 41,374.95;
- Mr Minić: EUR 40,047.24.

420. Furthermore, in respect of non-pecuniary damage, the applicants stated that the "erasure" had had extremely serious consequences for them and had caused dramatic and wide-ranging upheaval in their lives: unregulated status, loss of employment, living conditions unworthy of a human being, and serious health problems for many of them. In short, they had sustained different forms of suffering recognised by the Court's case-law: pain and feelings of deep instability and insecurity about the future, which they had endured for an extremely long period, anxiety deriving from the danger of deportation, and a deep sensation of anxiety and sadness because of xenophobic attitudes and because of the absence of effective remedies. They contended that the non-pecuniary damage should be calculated from February 1999, the date of the Constitutional Court's first decision, and claimed the following amounts:

- Mr Kurić: EUR 147,822;
- Ms Mezga: EUR 151,986;
- Mr Ristanović: EUR 151,986;
- Mr Berisha: EUR 146,781;
- Mr Sadik: EUR 154,068;
- Mr Minić: EUR 154,068.

421. Lastly, the applicants claimed EUR 49,975.82, plus VAT and additional taxes (EUR 62,369.82), for the costs and expenses incurred before the Court. They underlined that given the exceptional circumstances of the case and their extremely poor living conditions, their representatives had agreed to waive their fees should the Court reject their complaints. Therefore, no payment had been made so far by the applicants, and no relevant supporting documents could be produced.

2. The Government

422. The Government stated that none of the applicants had claimed compensation before the domestic courts. Only Mr Berisha and Mr Minić had filed a partial claim for damages with the State Attorney's Office, which had been rejected.

B. The Chamber judgment

423. The Chamber considered that the question of the application of Article 41 of the Convention was not ready for decision and accordingly decided to reserve it as a whole (see paragraphs 422–423 of the Chamber judgment and point 7 of its operative provisions).

C. The Grand Chamber's assessment

1. Pecuniary damage

424. In the circumstances of the present case, the Court considers that the question of compensation for pecuniary damage is not ready for decision. That question must accordingly be reserved and the subsequent procedure fixed, having due regard to any agreement which might be reached between the Government and the applicants and in the light of such individual or general measures as may be taken by the Government in the execution of the present judgment (Rule 61 § 7 and Rule 75 § 1 of the Rules of Court).

2. Non-pecuniary damage

425. Having regard to the nature of the violations found in the instant case and the suffering endured by the applicants, the Court is prepared to uphold their claims in part and to award, on an equitable basis, EUR 20,000 to each successful applicant (Mr Kurić, Ms Mezga, Mr Ristanović, Mr Berisha, Mr Ademi and Mr Minić) in respect of non-pecuniary damage.

3. Costs and expenses

426. According to the Court's case-law, an applicant is entitled to reimbursement of his costs and expenses only in so far as it has been shown that these have been actually and necessarily incurred and were reasonable as to quantum (see, for example, *Iatridis v. Greece* (just satisfaction) [GC], no. 31107/96, § 54, ECHR 2000-XI).

427. The Court notes that the case involved perusing a certain amount of factual and documentary evidence and required a fair degree of research and preparation. Although the Court does not doubt that the fees claimed were actually incurred, it considers the amount claimed for the costs and expenses relating to the proceedings before it excessive. Having regard to the fact that the legal issues raised by the application were similar for all the applicants, the Court decides to award them the overall sum of EUR 30,000.

4. Default interest

428. The Court considers it appropriate that the default interest rate should be based on the marginal lending rate of the European Central Bank, to which should be added three percentage points.

FOR THESE REASONS, THE COURT

1. *Holds,* by fifteen votes to two, that it does not have jurisdiction to examine the complaints raised by Mr Petreš and Mr Jovanović;
2. *Dismisses,* unanimously, the Government's objections that the application is incompatible *ratione materiae* and *ratione temporis* with the provisions of the Convention and was lodged out of time;
3. *Holds,* unanimously, that Mr Kurić, Ms Mezga, Mr Ristanović, Mr Berisha, Mr Ademi and Mr Minić may claim to be "victims", for the purposes of Article 34 of the Convention, of the alleged violations of their Convention rights;
4. *Upholds,* by nine votes to eight, the Government's preliminary objection of non-exhaustion of domestic remedies in respect of Mr Dabetić and Mrs Ristanović;
5. *Dismisses,* unanimously, the Government's preliminary objection of non-exhaustion of domestic remedies in respect of the remaining applicants (Mr Kurić, Ms Mezga, Mr Ristanović, Mr Berisha, Mr Ademi and Mr Minić);
6. *Holds,* unanimously, that there has been a violation of Article 8 of the Convention;
7. *Holds,* unanimously, that there has been a violation of Article 13 in conjunction with Article 8 of the Convention;
8. *Holds,* unanimously, that there has been a violation of Article 14 in conjunction with Article 8 of the Convention;
9. *Holds,* unanimously, that the respondent Government should, within one year of the delivery of the present judgment, set up an *ad hoc* domestic compensation scheme (see paragraph 415 above);
10. *Holds,* unanimously, that, as far as any pecuniary damage resulting from the violations found in the present case is concerned, the question of the application of Article 41 is not ready for decision and accordingly,
    (a) *reserves* the said question in this respect;
    (b) *invites* the Government and the applicants to submit, within three months, their written observations on the matter and, in particular, to notify the Court of any agreement that they may reach;
    (c) *reserves* the further procedure and *delegates* to the President of the Court the power to fix the same if need be.
11. *Holds,* unanimously,
    (a) that the respondent State is to pay, within three months, the following amounts:

(i) EUR 20,000 (twenty thousand euros) each to Mr Kurić, Ms Mezga, Mr Ristanović, Mr Berisha, Mr Ademi and Mr Minić in respect of non-pecuniary damage, plus any tax that may be chargeable on these sums;

(ii) EUR 30,000 (thirty thousand euros) to the applicants jointly, plus any tax that may be chargeable to the applicants, in respect of costs and expenses;

(b) that from the expiry of the above-mentioned three months until settlement simple interest shall be payable on the above amounts at a rate equal to the marginal lending rate of the European Central Bank during the default period plus three percentage points;

12. *Dismisses,* unanimously, the remainder of the applicants' claims under Article 41 in respect of non-pecuniary damage and costs and expenses.

Done in English and in French, and delivered at a public hearing in the Human Rights Building, Strasbourg, on 26 June 2012.

Vincent Berger	Nicolas Bratza
Jurisconsult	President"

Index

D

E

www.ingramcontent.com/pod-product-compliance
Ingram Content Group UK Ltd.
Pitfield, Milton Keynes, MK11 3LW, UK
UKHW021843100926
8556IPUK00019B/1018

9 783631 671689